Corporate Finance and Portfolio Management

**LEVEL I
2007**

CFA® PROGRAM CURRICULUM · VOLUME 4

PEARSON

Custom Publishing

Printed in the United States of America

10 9 8 7 6 5 4 3 2

ISBN 0-536-17197-1

2005160772

BK/JS

Please visit our web site at *www.pearsoncustom.com*

PEARSON CUSTOM PUBLISHING
75 Arlington Street, Suite 300, Boston, MA 02116
A Pearson Education Company

CONTENTS

4⅝ 4¹¹/₁₆ ⅜
5½ 5½ — ⅜
5½ 21³/₁₆ — ¹/₁₆
20⅝ 21³/₁₆ — ¹/₁₆
17⅜ 18⅛ + ⅞
18½ 6½ — ½
6½ 6½ — ½
7¼ 31/32 — ⅛
15/16
9/16 9/16
7¹⁵/₁₆ 7¹³/₁₆ 7¹⁵/₁₆
25⅝ 2¹¹/₃₂ 2½ +
2¾ 2¼ 2¼
12¹/₁₆ 11⅜ 11¼ +
33¾ 33 33¹/₁₆ —
25⅝ 24⁹/₁₆ 25⅜ +
12 11⅝ 11⅞ +
16 10½ 10½ 10½ —
78 15⅞ 15¹³/₁₆ 15⅞ —
9¹/₁₆ 8¼ 8⅛
430 11¼ 10⅛

HOW TO USE THE CFA PROGRAM CURRICULUM

Congratulations on your decision to enter the Chartered Financial Analyst (CFA®) Program. This exciting and rewarding program of study reflects your desire to become a serious investment professional. You are embarking on a program noted for its requirement of ethics and breadth of knowledge, skills, and abilities.

The credential you seek is respected around the world as a mark of accomplishment and dedication, and each level of the program represents a distinct achievement in professional development. Successful completion of the program is rewarded with membership in a prestigious global community of investment professionals. CFA charterholders are dedicated to life-long learning and maintaining currency with the ever-changing dynamics of a challenging profession.

Curriculum Development

The CFA Program curriculum is grounded in the practice of the investment profession. CFA Institute regularly conducts a practice analysis survey of investment professionals around the world to determine the knowledge, skills, and abilities that are relevant to the profession. The survey results define the Candidate Body of Knowledge (CBOK™), an inventory of knowledge and responsibilities expected of the investment management professional at the level of a new CFA charterholder. The survey also determines how much emphasis each of the major topic areas receives on the CFA examinations.

A committee made up of practicing charterholders, in conjunction with CFA Institute staff, designs the CFA Program curriculum to deliver the CBOK to candidates. The examinations, also written by practicing charterholders, are designed for you to demonstrate mastery of the CBOK as set forth in the CFA Program curriculum. As you structure your personal study program, you should emphasize mastery of the CBOK and the practical application of that knowledge. For more information on the practice analysis, CBOK, and development of the CFA Program curriculum, please visit www.cfainstitute.org/course.

Organization

The 2007 Level I CFA Program curriculum is organized into 10 topic areas. Each topic area begins with a topic level learning outcome that summarizes the broad objective of the material to follow and indicates the depth of knowledge expected. Each topic area is then divided into one or more study sessions, each devoted to a sub-topic (or group of sub-topics) within that topic area. The 2007 Level I curriculum is organized into 18 study sessions. Each study session begins with a purpose statement defining the content structure and objective of that session. Finally, each study session is further divided into reading assignments. *The outline on the inside front cover of each volume should further illustrate this important hierarchy.*

The reading assignments are the basis for all examination questions. The readings are selected or developed specifically to teach candidates the CBOK. Readings are drawn from textbook chapters, professional journal articles, research analyst reports, CFA Program-commissioned content, and cases. Many readings include problems and solutions as well as appendices to help you learn.

Reading-specific Learning Outcome Statements (LOS) are listed in the study session opener page as well as prior to each reading. Reading-specific LOS indicate what you should be able to accomplish after studying the reading. It is important, however, not to interpret LOS narrowly by focusing on a few key sentences in a reading. Readings, particularly CFA Program-commissioned readings, provide context for the learning outcome and enable you to apply a principle or concept in a variety of scenarios. Thus, you should use the LOS to guide and focus your study, as each examination question is based explicitly on one or more LOS. We encourage you to thoroughly review how to properly use LOS and the list and descriptions of commonly used LOS command words at www.cfainstitute.org/toolkit. The command words signal the depth of learning you are expected to achieve from the reading.

Features for 2007

 ▶ **Required vs. Optional segments** - Several reading assignments use only a portion of the original source textbook chapter or journal article. In order to allow you to read the assignment within its full context, however, we have reprinted the entire chapter or article in the curriculum. When an optional segment begins, you will see an icon. A vertical solid bar in the outside margin will continue until the optional segment ends, symbolized by another icon. Unless the material is specifically noted as optional, you should assume it is required. Keep in mind that the optional material is provided strictly for your convenience and will not be tested. *You should rely on the required segments and the reading-specific LOS in preparing for the examination.*

▶ **Problems/Solutions** - When appropriate, we have developed and assigned problems after readings to demonstrate practical application and reinforce understanding of the concepts presented. The solutions to the problems are provided in an appendix at the back of each volume. Candidates should consider all problems and solutions required material as your ability to solve these problems will prepare you for exam questions.

▶ **Margins** - We have inserted wide margins throughout each volume to allow for easier note taking.

 ▶ **Two-color format** - To enrich the visual appeal and clarity of the exhibits, tables, and required vs. optional treatments, we have printed the curriculum in two-color format.

 ▶ **Six- volume structure** - To improve the portability of the curriculum, we have spread the material over six volumes versus the four we had last year.

 ▶ **Glossary and Index** - For your convenience, we have printed a comprehensive glossary and index in each volume. Throughout the curriculum, a **bolded blue** word in a reading denotes a glossary term.

Designing your personal study program:

Create a schedule - An orderly, systematic approach to preparation is critical to successful completion of the examination. You should dedicate a consistent block of time every week to reading and studying. Complete all reading assignments and the associated problems and solutions in each study session. Review the LOS both before and after you study each reading to ensure that you have mastered the applicable content and can complete the action(s) specified. Upon completion of each study session, review the session's purpose statement and confirm that you thoroughly understand the subject matter. When you complete a topic area, review the topic level learning outcome and verify that you have mastered the objectives.

CFA Institute estimates that you will need to devote a minimum of 10-15 hours per week for 18 weeks to study the assigned readings. Allow a minimum of one week for each study session spread over several days, with completion scheduled for at least 30-45 days prior to the examination. This schedule will allow you to spend the final four to six weeks before the examination reviewing the assigned material and taking multiple on-line sample examinations. At CFA Institute, we believe that candidates need to commit to a *minimum* of 250 hours reading and reviewing the curriculum and taking online sample exams to master the material. This recommendation, however, may substantially underestimate the hours needed for appropriate exam preparation depending on individual circumstances and academic background.

You will undoubtedly adjust your study time to conform to your own strengths and weaknesses and academic background, and you will probably spend more time on some study sessions than on others. You should allow ample time for both in-depth study of all topic areas and additional concentration on those topic areas for which you feel least prepared.

Preliminary Readings - The reading assignments in Economics and Financial Statement Analysis assume candidates already have a basic mastery of the concepts typically presented in introductory university-level economics and accounting courses. Information on suggested readings to improve your knowledge of these topics precedes these study sessions.

Candidate Preparation Toolkit - We have created the online toolkit to provide a single comprehensive location for resources and guidance for candidate preparation. In addition to in-depth information on study program planning, the CFA Program curriculum, and the online sample exams, the toolkit also contains curriculum errata, printable study session outlines, sample exam questions, and more. We encourage you to use the toolkit as your central preparation resource during your tenure as a candidate. Visit the toolkit at www.cfainstitute.org/toolkit.

Online Sample Exams - After completing your study of the assigned curriculum, use the CFA Institute online sample exams to measure your knowledge of the topics and improve your exam-taking skills. After each question, you will receive immediate feedback noting the correct response and indicating the assigned curriculum for further study. The sample exams are designed by the same people who create the actual CFA exams, and reflect the question formats, topics, and level of difficulty of the actual CFA examinations, in a timed environment. Aggregate data indicate that the CFA examination pass rate was higher among candidates who took one or more online sample examinations than for candidates who did not take the online sample exams. For more information on the online sample exams, please visit www.cfainstitute.org/toolkit.

Review Programs - After you enroll in the CFA Program, you may receive numerous solicitations for preparatory courses and review materials. Although preparatory courses and notes may be helpful to some candidates, you should view these resources as *supplements to the assigned CFA Program curriculum*. The CFA exams reference *only* the 2007 CFA Institute assigned curriculum; no preparatory course or review course materials are consulted or referenced.

Furthermore, CFA Institute does not endorse, promote, review, or warrant the accuracy of the products or services offered by preparatory organizations. CFA Institute does not verify or endorse the pass rates or other claims made by these organizations.

Feedback

At CFA Institute, we are committed to delivering a comprehensive and rigorous curriculum for the development of competent, ethically grounded investment professionals. We rely on candidate and member feedback as we work to incorporate content, design, and packaging improvements. You can be assured that we will continue to listen to your suggestions. Please send any comments or feedback to curriculum@cfainstitute.org. Ongoing improvements in the curriculum will help you prepare for success on the upcoming examinations, and for a lifetime of learning as a serious investment professional.

CORPORATE FINANCE

STUDY SESSION

Study Session 11   Corporate Finance

TOPIC LEVEL LEARNING OUTCOME

The candidate should be able to demonstrate a working knowledge of capital budgeting concepts and analysis, capital structure issues, and dividend policy considerations. Candidates should understand how corporate finance concepts, such as cash flow, liquidity, leverage, cost of capital, and dividends, are used in the valuation process, and be familiar with corporate governance issues and risks affecting companies.

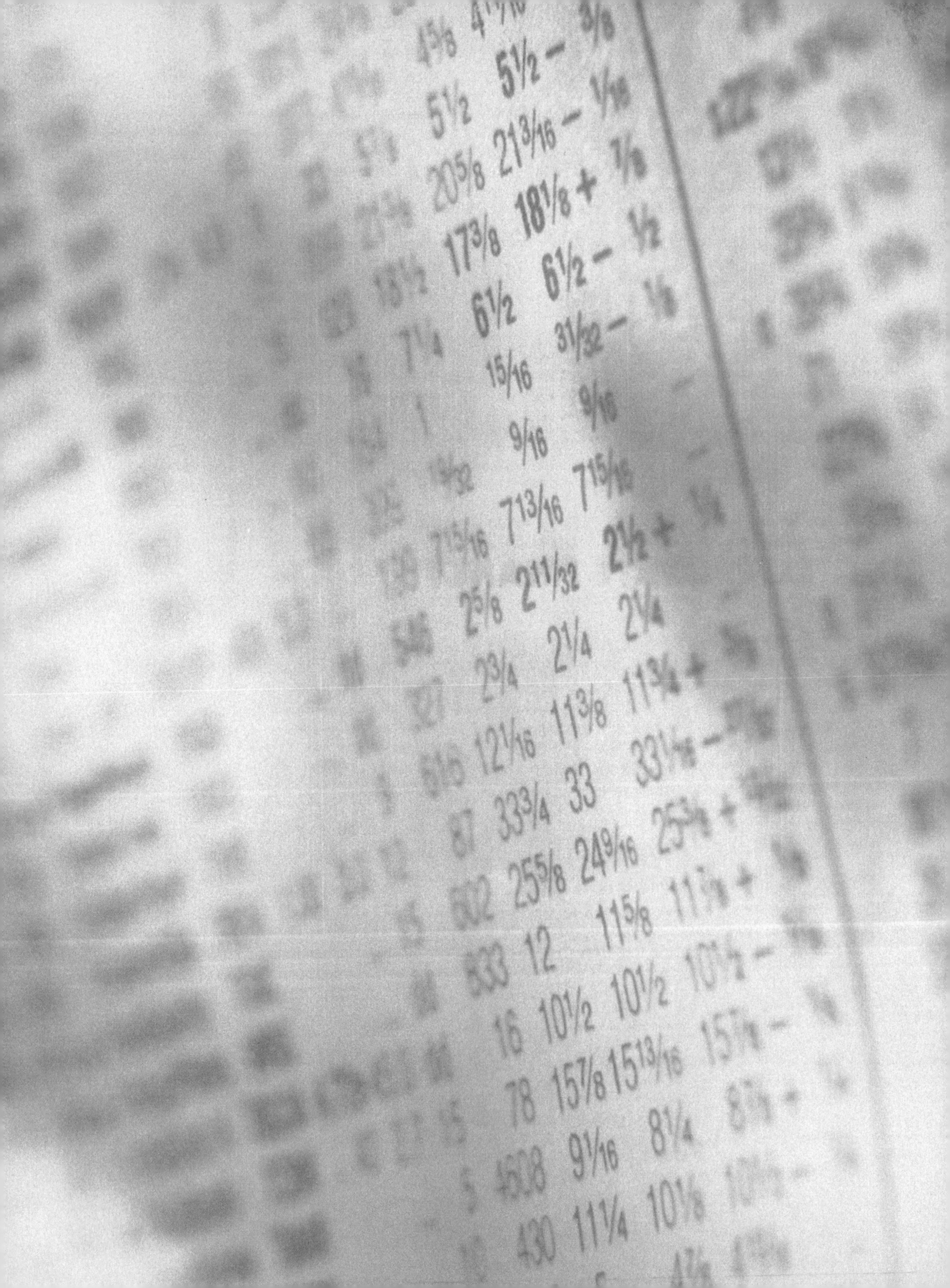

STUDY SESSION 11
CORPORATE FINANCE

READING ASSIGNMENTS

Reading 47   Capital Budgeting
Reading 48   Cost of Capital
Reading 49   Capital Structure and Leverage
Reading 50   Dividends and Dividend Policy
Reading 51   The Corporate Governance of Listed Companies: A Manual
                 for Investors

This study session covers the principles of those financial decisions that corporations typically have to make. The first group of decisions (capital budgeting) addresses the asset side of the balance sheet: What projects should the corporation accept for investment, and what projects should it reject? The decisions in the second group (capital structure, leverage, and dividend policy) are financing decisions. For example, can management increase the value of the corporation either by consciously targeting a specific debt/equity ratio or by choosing an optimal balance between paying cash dividends and issuing new stock?

Certain governance practices expose the firm to a heightened risk of ethical lapses within its management. Although these practices may not be inherently unethical, they create the potential for conflicts of interest to develop between shareholders and managers.

LEARNING OUTCOMES

Reading 47: Capital Budgeting
The candidate should be able to:

a. define the capital budgeting process, explain the administrative steps of the process, and categorize the capital projects which can be evaluated;

b. summarize and explain the principles of capital budgeting, including the choice of the proper cash flows and the identification of the proper discount rate;

c. explain how the following project interactions affect the evaluation of a capital project: (1) independent versus mutually exclusive projects, (2) project sequencing, and (3) unlimited funds versus capital rationing;

d. calculate and interpret the results produced from each of the following methods when evaluating a single capital project: net present value (NPV), internal rate of return (IRR), payback period, discounted payback period, average accounting rate of return (AAR), and profitability index (PI);

e. explain the NPV profile, compare and contrast the NPV and IRR methods when evaluating more than one capital project, and describe the multiple IRR and no-IRR problems that can arise when calculating an IRR;

f. describe the relative popularity of the various capital budgeting methods and explain the importance of the NPV in estimating the value of a stock price.

Reading 48: Cost of Capital

The candidate should be able to:

a. determine and interpret the weighted average cost of capital (WACC) of a company, and explain the adjustments to it that an analyst should make in developing a cost of capital for a specific project;

b. describe the role of taxes in the cost of capital from the different capital sources;

c. describe alternative methods of calculating the weights used in the weighted average cost of capital, including the use of the company's target capital structure;

d. explain the analyst's concern with the marginal cost of capital in evaluating investment projects, and explain the use of the marginal cost of capital and the investment opportunity schedule in determining the optimal capital budget for a company;

e. explain the marginal cost of capital's role in determining the net present value of a project;

f. calculate and analyze the cost of fixed rate debt capital using the yield-to-maturity approach and the debt-rating approach;

g. calculate the cost of noncallable, nonconvertible preferred stock;

h. calculate and analyze the cost of equity capital using the capital asset pricing model approach, the dividend discount approach, and the bond yield plus risk premium approach.

Reading 49: Capital Structure and Leverage

The candidate should be able to:

a. define and explain leverage, business risk, sales risk, operating risk, and financial risk;

b. calculate and interpret the degree of operating leverage, the degree of financial leverage, and the degree of total leverage;

c. characterize the operating leverage, financial leverage, and total leverage of a company given a description of it;

d. calculate the breakeven quantity of sales and determine the company's net income at various sales levels;

  e. describe the effect of financial leverage on a company's net income and return on equity;

  f. compare and contrast the risks of creditors and owners.

Reading 50: Dividends and Dividend Policy
The candidate should be able to:

  a. review cash dividends, stock dividends, stocks splits, and reverse stock splits and calculate and discuss their impact on a shareholder;

  b. compare the impact on shareholder wealth of a share repurchase and a cash dividend of equal amount;

  c. calculate the earnings per share effect of a share repurchase when the repurchase is made with borrowed funds and the company's after-tax cost of debt is greater (less) than its earnings yield;

  d. calculate the book value effect of a share repurchase when the market value of a share is greater (less) than book value per share;

  e. compare and contrast share repurchase methods;

  f. review dividend payment chronology including declaration, holder-of-record, ex-dividend, and payment dates and indicate when the share price will most likely reflect the dividend;

  g. summarize the factors affecting dividend payout policy;

  h. calculate the effective tax rate on a dollar of corporate earnings distributed as a dividend using the double-taxation, split-rate, and tax imputation systems;

  i. discuss the types of information that dividend initiations, increases, decreases, and omissions may convey, and cross-country differences in the signalling content of dividends.

Reading 51: The Corporate Governance of Listed Companies: A Manual for Investors
The candidate should be able to:

  a. define corporate governance;

  b. discuss and critique characteristics and practices related to board and committee independence, experience, compensation, external consultants and frequency of elections and determine whether they are supportive of shareowner protection;

  c. define board independence and explain the importance of independent board members in corporate governance;

  d. identify factors that indicate a board and its members possess the experience required to govern the company for the benefit of its shareowners;

  e. explain the provisions that should be included in a strong corporate code of ethics and the implications of a weak code of ethics with regard to related-party transactions and personal use of company assets;

  f. state the key areas of responsibility for which board committees are typically created and explain the criteria for assessing whether each committee is able to adequately represent shareowner interests;

  g. evaluate, from a shareowner's perspective, company policies related to voting rules, shareowner sponsored proposals, common stock classes and takeover defenses.

45/8 411/16   3/8
51/2   51/2 — 3/8
51/2 213/16 — 1/4
205/8 213/16   7/8
173/8 181/8 +
181/2   61/2 — 1/2
61/2   61/2 — 1/8
71/4 31/32
15/16   9/16
9/16
19/32
715/16 713/16 715/16
25/8 211/32   21/2 +
23/4   21/4   21/4
121/16 113/8   111/4 +
87 333/4   33   331/4 —
602 255/8 249/16 253/8 +
833   12   115/8   117/8 +
16 101/2 101/2 107/8 —
78 157/8 1513/16 157/8 —
4608 91/16   81/4   87/8
430 111/4 101/8

CAPITAL BUDGETING

by John D. Stowe and Jacques R. Gagné

LEARNING OUTCOMES

The candidate should be able to:

a. define the capital budgeting process, explain the administrative steps of the process, and categorize the capital projects which can be evaluated;

b. summarize and explain the principles of capital budgeting, including the choice of the proper cash flows and the identification of the proper discount rate;

c. explain how the following project interactions affect the evaluation of a capital project: (1) independent versus mutually exclusive projects, (2) project sequencing, and (3) unlimited funds versus capital rationing;

d. calculate and interpret the results produced from each of the following methods when evaluating a single capital project: net present value (NPV), internal rate of return (IRR), payback period, discounted payback period, average accounting rate of return (AAR), and profitability index (PI);

e. explain the NPV profile, compare and contrast the NPV and IRR methods when evaluating more than one capital project, and describe the multiple IRR and no-IRR problems that can arise when calculating an IRR;

f. describe the relative popularity of the various capital budgeting methods and explain the importance of the NPV in estimating the value of a stock price.

INTRODUCTION 1

Capital budgeting is the process that companies use for decision making on capital projects—those projects with a life of a year or more. This is a fundamental area of knowledge for financial analysts for many reasons.

▶ First, capital budgeting is very important for corporations. Capital projects, which make up the long-term asset portion of the balance sheet, can be so large that sound capital budgeting decisions ultimately decide the future of many corporations. Capital decisions cannot be reversed at a low cost, so mistakes are very costly. Indeed, the real capital investments of a company describe a company better than its working capital or capital structures, which are intangible and tend to be similar for many corporations.

▶ Second, the principles of capital budgeting have been adapted for many other corporate decisions, such as investments in working capital, leasing, mergers and acquisitions, and bond refunding.

▶ Third, the valuation principles used in capital budgeting are similar to the valuation principles used in security analysis and portfolio management. Many of the methods used by security analysts and portfolio managers are based on capital budgeting methods. Conversely, there have been innovations in security analysis and portfolio management that have also been adapted to capital budgeting.

▶ Finally, although analysts have a vantage point outside the company, their interest in valuation coincides with the capital budgeting focus of maximizing shareholder value. Because capital budgeting information is not ordinarily available outside the company, the analyst may attempt to estimate the process, within reason, at least for companies that are not too complex. Further, analysts may be able to appraise the quality of the company's capital budgeting process; for example, on the basis of whether the company has an accounting focus or an economic focus.

This reading is organized as follows: Section 2 presents the steps in a typical capital budgeting process. After introducing the basic principles of capital budgeting in Section 3, in Section 4 we discuss the criteria by which a decision to invest in a project may be made. Section 5 presents a crucial element of the capital budgeting process: organizing the cash flow information that is the raw material of the analysis. Section 6 looks further at cash flow analysis. Section 7 demonstrates methods to extend the basic investment criteria to address economic alternatives and risk. Finally, Section 8 compares other income measures and valuation models that analysts use to the basic capital budgeting model.

2   THE CAPITAL BUDGETING PROCESS

The specific capital budgeting procedures that a manager uses depend on the manager's level in the organization, the size and complexity of the project being evaluated, and the size of the organization. The typical steps in the capital budgeting process are as follows:

▶ Step One, Generating Ideas—Investment ideas can come from anywhere, from the top or the bottom of the organization, from any department or functional area, or from outside the company. Generating good investment ideas to consider is the most important step in the process.

▶ Step Two, Analyzing Individual Proposals—This step involves gathering the information to forecast cash flows for each project and then evaluating the project's profitability.

▶ Step Three, Planning the Capital Budget—The company must organize the profitable proposals into a coordinated whole that fits within the company's overall strategies, and it also must consider the projects' timing. Some projects that look good when considered in isolation may be undesirable strategically. Because of financial and real resource issues, scheduling and prioritizing projects is important.

▶ Step Four, Monitoring and Post-auditing—In a post-audit, actual results are compared to planned or predicted results, and any differences must be explained. For example, how do the revenues, expenses, and cash flows realized from an investment compare to the predictions? Post-auditing capital projects is important for several reasons. First, it helps monitor the forecasts and analysis that underlie the capital budgeting process. Systematic errors, such as overly optimistic forecasts, become apparent. Second, it helps improve business operations. If sales or costs are out of line, it will focus attention on bringing performance closer to expectations if at all possible. Finally, monitoring and post-auditing recent capital investments will produce concrete ideas for future investments. Managers can decide to invest more heavily in profitable areas and scale down or cancel investments in areas that are disappointing.

Planning for capital investments can be very complex, often involving many persons inside and outside of the company. Information about marketing, science, engineering, regulation, taxation, finance, production, and behavioral issues must be systematically gathered and evaluated. The authority to make capital decisions depends on the size and complexity of the project. Lower-level managers may have discretion to make decisions that involve less than a given amount of money, or that do not exceed a given capital budget. Larger and more complex decisions are reserved for top management, and some are so significant that the company's board of directors ultimately has the decision-making authority.

Like everything else, capital budgeting is a cost–benefit exercise. At the margin, the benefits from the improved decision making should exceed the costs of the capital budgeting efforts.

Companies often put capital budgeting projects into some rough categories for analysis. One such classification would be as follows:

1. Replacement projects. These are among the easier capital budgeting decisions. If a piece of equipment breaks down or wears out, whether to replace it may not require careful analysis. If the expenditure is modest and if not investing has significant implications for production, operations, or sales, it would be a waste of resources to overanalyze the decision. Just make the replacement. Other replacement decisions involve replacing existing equipment with newer, more efficient equipment, or perhaps choosing one type of equipment over another. These replacement decisions are often amenable to very detailed analysis, and you might have a lot of confidence in the final decision.

2. Expansion projects. Instead of merely maintaining a company's existing business activities, expansion projects increase the size of the business. These expansion decisions may involve more uncertainties than replacement decisions, and these decisions will be more carefully considered.

3. New products and services. These investments expose the company to even more uncertainties than expansion projects. These decisions are more complex and will involve more people in the decision-making process.

4. Regulatory, safety, and environmental projects. These projects are frequently required by a governmental agency, an insurance company, or

some other external party. They may generate no revenue and might not be undertaken by a company maximizing its own private interests. Often, the company will accept the required investment and continue to operate. Occasionally, however, the cost of the regulatory/safety/environmental project is sufficiently high that the company would do better to cease operating altogether or to shut down any part of the business that is related to the project.

5. Other. The projects above are all susceptible to capital budgeting analysis, and they can be accepted or rejected using the net present value (NPV) or some other criterion. Some projects escape such analysis. These are either pet projects of someone in the company (such as the CEO buying a new aircraft) or so risky that they are difficult to analyze by the usual methods (such as some research and development decisions).

3   BASIC PRINCIPLES OF CAPITAL BUDGETING

Capital budgeting has a rich history and sometimes employs some pretty sophisticated procedures. Fortunately, capital budgeting relies on just a few basic principles. Capital budgeting usually uses the following assumptions:

1. Decisions are based on cash flows. The decisions are not based on accounting concepts, such as net income. Furthermore, intangible costs and benefits are often ignored because, if they are real, they should result in cash flows at some other time.

2. Timing of cash flows is crucial. Analysts make an extraordinary effort to detail precisely when cash flows occur.

3. Cash flows are based on opportunity costs. What are the incremental cash flows that occur with an investment compared to what they would have been without the investment?

4. Cash flows are analyzed on an after-tax basis. Taxes must be fully reflected in all capital budgeting decisions.

5. Financing costs are ignored. This may seem unrealistic, but it is not. Most of the time, analysts want to know the after-tax operating cash flows that result from a capital investment. Then, these after-tax cash flows and the investment outlays are discounted at the "required rate of return" to find the net present value (NPV). Financing costs are reflected in the required rate of return. If we included financing costs in the cash flows and in the discount rate, we would be double-counting the financing costs. So even though a project may be financed with some combination of debt and equity, we ignore these costs, focusing on the operating cash flows and capturing the costs of debt (and other capital) in the discount rate.

Capital budgeting cash flows are not accounting net income. Accounting net income is reduced by noncash charges such as accounting depreciation. Furthermore, to reflect the cost of debt financing, interest expenses are also subtracted from accounting net income. (No subtraction is made for the cost of equity financing in arriving at accounting net income.) Accounting net income also differs from economic income, which is the cash inflow plus the change in the market value of the company. Economic income does not subtract the cost of debt financing, and it is based on the changes in the market value of the company, not changes in its book value (accounting depreciation). We will further consider cash flows, accounting income, economic income, and other income measures at the end of this reading.

In assumption 5 above, we referred to the rate used in discounting the cash flows as the "required rate of return." The required rate of return is the discount rate that investors should require given the riskiness of the project. This discount rate is frequently called the "opportunity cost of funds" or the "cost of capital." If the company can invest elsewhere and earn a return of r, or if the company can repay its sources of capital and save a cost of r, then r is the company's opportunity cost of funds. If the company cannot earn more than its opportunity cost of funds on an investment, it should not undertake that investment. Unless an investment earns more than the cost of funds from its suppliers of capital, the investment should not be undertaken. The cost-of-capital concept is discussed more extensively elsewhere. Regardless of what it is called, an economically sound discount rate is essential for making capital budgeting decisions.

Although the principles of capital budgeting are simple, they are easily confused in practice, leading to unfortunate decisions. Some important capital budgeting concepts that managers find very useful are given below.

▶ A **sunk cost** is one that has already been incurred. You cannot change a sunk cost. Today's decisions, on the other hand, should be based on current and future cash flows and should not be affected by prior, or sunk, costs.

▶ An **opportunity cost** is what a resource is worth in its next-best use. For example, if a company uses some idle property, what should it record as the investment outlay: the purchase price several years ago, the current market value, or nothing? If you replace an old machine with a new one, what is the opportunity cost? If you invest $10 million, what is the opportunity cost? The answers to these three questions are, respectively: the current market value, the cash flows the old machine would generate, and $10 million (which you could invest elsewhere).

▶ An **incremental cash flow** is the cash flow that is realized because of a decision: the cash flow *with* a decision minus the cash flow *without* that decision. If opportunity costs are correctly assessed, the incremental cash flows provide a sound basis for capital budgeting.

▶ An **externality** is the effect of an investment on other things besides the investment itself. Frequently, an investment affects the cash flows of other parts of the company, and these externalities can be positive or negative. If possible, these should be part of the investment decision. Sometimes externalities occur outside of the company. An investment might benefit (or harm) other companies or society at large, and yet the company is not compensated for these benefits (or charged for the costs). **Cannibalization** is one externality. Cannibalization occurs when an investment takes customers and sales away from another part of the company.

▶ **Conventional versus nonconventional cash flows**—A conventional cash flow pattern is one with an initial outflow followed by a series of inflows. In a nonconventional cash flow pattern, the initial outflow is not followed by inflows only, but the cash flows can flip from positive to negative again (or even change signs several times). An investment that involved outlays (negative cash flows) for the first couple of years that were then followed by positive cash flows would be considered to have a conventional pattern. If cash flows change signs once, the pattern is conventional. If cash flows change signs two or more times, the pattern is nonconventional.

Several types of project interactions make the incremental cash flow analysis challenging. The following are some of these interactions:

▶ **Independent versus mutually exclusive projects**—Independent projects are projects whose cash flows are independent of each other. Mutually exclusive projects compete directly with each other. For example, if Projects A and B are mutually exclusive, you can choose A or B, but you cannot choose both. Sometimes there are several mutually exclusive projects, and you can choose only one from the group.

▶ **Project sequencing**—Many projects are sequenced through time, so that investing in a project creates the option to invest in future projects. For example, you might invest in a project today and then in one year invest in a second project if the financial results of the first project or new economic conditions are favorable. If the results of the first project or new economic conditions are not favorable, you do not invest in the second project.

▶ **Unlimited funds versus capital rationing**—An unlimited funds environment assumes that the company can raise the funds it wants for all profitable projects simply by paying the required rate of return. Capital rationing exists when the company has a fixed amount of funds to invest. If the company has more profitable projects than it has funds for, it must allocate the funds to achieve the maximum shareholder value subject to the funding constraints.

4   INVESTMENT DECISION CRITERIA

Analysts use several important criteria to evaluate capital investments. The two most comprehensive measures of whether a project is profitable or unprofitable are the net present value (NPV) and internal rate of return (IRR). In addition to these, we present four other criteria that are frequently used: the payback period, discounted payback period, average accounting rate of return (AAR), and profitability index (PI). An analyst must fully understand the economic logic behind each of these investment decision criteria as well as its strengths and limitations in practice.

4.1 Net Present Value

For a project with one investment outlay, made initially, the net present value (NPV) is the present value of the future after-tax cash flows minus the investment outlay, or

$$\text{NPV} = \sum_{t=1}^{n} \frac{\text{CF}_t}{(1 + r)^t} - \text{Outlay} \tag{47-1}$$

where

CF_t = after-tax cash flow at time t

r = required rate of return for the investment

Outlay = investment cash flow at time zero

To illustrate the net present value criterion, we will take a look at a simple example. Assume that Gerhardt Corporation is considering an investment of €50 million in a capital project that will return after-tax cash flows of €16 million per year for the next four years plus another €20 million in year five. The required rate of return is 10 percent.

For the Gerhardt example, the NPV would be

$$NPV = \frac{16}{1.10^1} + \frac{16}{1.10^2} + \frac{16}{1.10^3} + \frac{16}{1.10^4} + \frac{20}{1.10^5} - 50$$
$$NPV = 14.545 + 13.223 + 12.021 + 10.928 + 12.418 - 50$$
$$NPV = 63.136 - 50 = €13.136 \text{ million.}[1]$$

The investment has a total value, or present value of future cash flows, of €63.136 million. Since this investment can be acquired at a cost of €50 million, the investing company is giving up €50 million of its wealth in exchange for an investment worth €63.136 million. The investor's wealth increases by a net of €13.136 million.

Because the NPV is the amount by which the investor's wealth increases as a result of the investment, the decision rule for the NPV is as follows:

Invest if   NPV > 0
Do not invest if   NPV < 0

Positive NPV investments are wealth-increasing, while negative NPV investments are wealth-decreasing.

Many investments have cash flow patterns in which outflows may occur not only at time zero, but also at future dates. It is useful to consider the NPV to be the present value of all cash flows:

$$NPV = CF_0 + \frac{CF_1}{(1+r)^1} + \frac{CF_2}{(1+r)^2} + \ldots + \frac{CF_n}{(1+r)^n}, \text{ or}$$

$$NPV = \sum_{t=0}^{n} \frac{CF_t}{(1+r)^t}$$

(47-2)

In Equation 47-2, the investment outlay, CF_0, is simply a negative cash flow. Future cash flows can also be negative.

4.2 Internal Rate of Return

The internal rate of return (IRR) is one of the most frequently used concepts in capital budgeting and in security analysis. The IRR definition is one that all analysts know by heart. For a project with one investment outlay, made initially, the IRR is the discount rate that makes the present value of the future after-tax cash flows equal that investment outlay. Written out in equation form, the IRR solves this equation:

$$\sum_{t=1}^{n} \frac{CF_t}{(1+IRR)^t} = \text{Outlay}$$

where IRR is the internal rate of return. The left-hand side of this equation is the present value of the project's future cash flows, which, discounted at the IRR, equals the investment outlay. This equation will also be seen rearranged as

$$\sum_{t=1}^{n} \frac{CF_t}{(1+IRR)^t} - \text{Outlay} = 0$$

(47-3)

---

[1] Occasionally, you will notice some rounding errors in our examples. In this case, the present values of the cash flows, as rounded, add up to 63.135. Without rounding, they add up to 63.13627, or 63.136. We will usually report the more accurate result, the one that you would get from your calculator or computer without rounding intermediate results.

In this form, Equation 47-3 looks like the NPV equation, Equation 47-1, except that the discount rate is the IRR instead of r (the required rate of return). Discounted at the IRR, the NPV is equal to zero.

In the Gerhardt Corporation example, we want to find a discount rate that makes the total present value of all cash flows, the NPV, equal zero. In equation form, the IRR is the discount rate that solves this equation:

$$-50 + \frac{16}{(1 + \text{IRR})^1} + \frac{16}{(1 + \text{IRR})^2} + \frac{16}{(1 + \text{IRR})^3} + \frac{16}{(1 + \text{IRR})^4} + \frac{20}{(1 + \text{IRR})^5} = 0$$

Algebraically, this equation would be very difficult to solve. We normally resort to trial and error, systematically choosing various discount rates until we find one, the IRR, that satisfies the equation. We previously discounted these cash flows at 10 percent and found the NPV to be €13.136 million. Since the NPV is positive, the IRR is probably greater than 10 percent. If we use 20 percent as the discount rate, the NPV is −€0.543 million, so 20 percent is a little high. One might try several other discount rates until the NPV is equal to zero; this approach is illustrated in Table 47-1:

TABLE 47-1   Trial and Error Process for Finding IRR

Discount Rate	NPV
10%	13.136
20%	−0.543
19%	0.598
19.5%	0.022
19.51%	0.011
19.52%	0.000

The IRR is 19.52 percent. Financial calculators and spreadsheet software have routines that calculate the IRR for us, so we do not have to go through this trial and error procedure ourselves. The IRR, computed more precisely, is 19.5197 percent.

The decision rule for the IRR is to invest if the IRR exceeds the required rate of return for a project:

Invest if	IRR > r
Do not invest if	IRR < r

In the Gerhardt example, since the IRR of 19.52 percent exceeds the project's required rate of return of 10 percent, Gerhardt should invest.

Many investments have cash flow patterns in which the outlays occur at time zero and at future dates. Thus, it is common to define the IRR as the discount rate that makes the present values of all cash flows sum to zero:

$$\sum_{t=0}^{n} \frac{CF_t}{(1 + \text{IRR})^t} = 0 \tag{47-4}$$

Equation 47-4 is a more general version of Equation 47-3.

4.3 Payback Period

The payback period is the number of years required to recover the original investment in a project. The payback is based on cash flows. For example, if you invest $10 million in a project, how long will it be until you recover the full original investment? Table 47-2 below illustrates the calculation of the payback period by following an investment's cash flows and cumulative cash flows.

TABLE 47-2   Payback Period Example

Year	0	1	2	3	4	5
Cash flow	−10,000	2,500	2,500	3,000	3,000	3,000
Cumulative cash flow	−10,000	−7,500	−5,000	−2,000	1,000	4,000

In the first year, the company recovers 2,500 of the original investment, with 7,500 still unrecovered. You can see that the company recoups its original investment between Year 3 and Year 4. After three years, 2,000 is still unrecovered. Since the Year 4 cash flow is 3,000, it would take 2/3 of the Year 4 cash flow to bring the cumulative cash flow to zero. So, the payback period is 3 years plus 2/3 of the Year 4 cash flow, or 3.67 years.

The drawbacks of the payback period are transparent. Since the cash flows are not discounted at the project's required rate of return, the payback period ignores the time value of money and the risk of the project. Additionally, the payback period ignores cash flows after the payback period is reached. In the table above, for example, the Year 5 cash flow is completely ignored in the payback computation!

Example 47-1 below is designed to illustrate some of the implications of these drawbacks of the payback period.

Example 47-1

Drawbacks of the Payback Period

The cash flows, payback periods, and NPVs for Projects A through F are given in Table 47-3. For all of the projects, the required rate of return is 10 percent.

TABLE 47-3   Examples of Drawbacks of the Payback Period

Year	Cash Flows					
	Project A	Project B	Project C	Project D	Project E	Project F
0	−1,000	−1,000	−1,000	−1,000	−1,000	−1,000
1	1,000	100	400	500	400	500
2		200	300	500	400	500
3		300	200	500	400	10,000
4		400	100		400	
5		500	500		400	

(Table continued on next page …)

TABLE 47-3   Examples of Drawbacks of the Payback Period (continued)

| | Cash Flows | | | | | |
Year	Project A	Project B	Project C	Project D	Project E	Project F
Payback period	1.0	4.0	4.0	2.0	2.5	2.0
NPV	−90.91	65.26	140.60	243.43	516.31	7,380.92

Comment on why the payback period provides misleading information about the following:

1. Project A
2. Project B versus Project C
3. Project D versus Project E
4. Project D versus Project F

▶ **Solution 1.** Project A does indeed pay itself back in one year. However, this result is misleading because the investment is unprofitable, with a negative NPV.

▶ **Solution 2.** Although Projects B and C have the same payback period and the same cash flow after the payback period, the payback period does not detect the fact that Project C's cash flows within the payback period occur earlier and result in a higher NPV.

▶ **Solution 3.** Projects D and E illustrate a common situation. The project with the shorter payback period is the less profitable project. Project E has a longer payback and higher NPV.

▶ **Solution 4.** Projects D and F illustrate an important flaw of the payback period—that the payback period ignores cash flows after the payback period is reached. In this case, Project F has a much larger cash flow in Year 3, but the payback period does not recognize its value.

The payback period has many drawbacks—it is a measure of payback and not a measure of profitability. By itself, the payback period would be a dangerous criterion for evaluating capital projects. Its simplicity, however, is an advantage. The payback period is very easy to calculate and to explain. The payback period may also be used as an indicator of project liquidity. A project with a two-year payback may be more liquid than another project with a longer payback.

Because it is not economically sound, the payback period has no decision rule like that of the NPV or IRR. If the payback period is being used (perhaps as a measure of liquidity), analysts should also use an NPV or IRR to ensure that their decisions also reflect the profitability of the projects being considered.

4.4 Discounted Payback Period

The discounted payback period is the number of years it takes for the cumulative discounted cash flows from a project to equal the original investment. The discounted payback period partially addresses the weaknesses of the payback period. Table 47-4 gives an example of calculating the payback period and dis-

TABLE 47-4 Payback Period and Discounted Payback Period						
Year	0	1	2	3	4	5
Cash flow (CF)	−5,000	1,500.00	1,500.00	1,500.00	1,500.00	1,500.00
Cumulative CF	−5,000	−3,500.00	−2,000.00	−500.00	1,000.00	2,500.00
Discounted CF	−5,000	1,363.64	1,239.67	1,126.97	1,024.52	931.38
Cumulative discounted CF	−5,000	−3,636.36	−2,396.69	−1,269.72	−245.20	686.18

counted payback period. The example assumes a discount rate of 10 percent. The payback period is 3 years plus $500/1500 = 1/3$ of the fourth year's cash flow, or 3.33 years. The discounted payback period is between four and five years. The discounted payback period is 4 years plus $245.20/931.38 = 0.26$ of the fifth year's discounted cash flow, or 4.26 years.

The discounted payback period relies on discounted cash flows, much as the NPV criterion does. If a project has a negative NPV, it will usually not have a discounted payback period since it never recovers the initial investment.

The discounted payback does account for the time value of money and risk within the discounted payback period, but it ignores cash flows after the discounted payback period is reached. This drawback has two consequences. First, the discounted payback period is not a good measure of profitability (like the NPV or IRR) because it ignores these cash flows. Second, another idiosyncrasy of the discounted payback period comes from the possibility of negative cash flows after the discounted payback period is reached. It is possible for a project to have a negative NPV but to have a positive cumulative discounted cash flow in the middle of its life and, thus, a reasonable discounted payback period. The NPV and IRR, which consider all of a project's cash flows, do not suffer from this problem.

4.5 Average Accounting Rate of Return

The average accounting rate of return (AAR) can be defined as

$$AAR = \frac{\text{Average net income}}{\text{Average book value}}$$

To understand this measure of return, we will use a numerical example.

Assume a company invests $200,000 in a project that is depreciated straight-line over a five-year life to a zero salvage value. Sales revenues and cash operating expenses for each year are as shown in Table 47-5. The table also shows the annual income taxes (at a 40 percent tax rate) and the net income.

For the five-year period, the average net income is $18,000. The initial book value is $200,000, declining by $40,000 per year until the final book value is $0. The average book value for this asset is ($200,000 − $0) / 2 = $100,000. The average accounting rate of return is

$$AAR = \frac{\text{Average net income}}{\text{Average book value}} = \frac{18,000}{100,000} = 18\%$$

The advantages of the AAR are that it is easy to understand and easy to calculate. The AAR has some important disadvantages, however. Unlike the other capital

TABLE 47-5	Net Income for Calculating an Average Accounting Rate of Return				
	Year 1	**Year 2**	**Year 3**	**Year 4**	**Year 5**
Sales	$100,000	$150,000	$240,000	$130,000	$80,000
Cash expenses	50,000	70,000	120,000	60,000	50,000
Depreciation	40,000	40,000	40,000	40,000	40,000
Earnings before taxes	10,000	40,000	80,000	30,000	−10,000
Taxes (at 40 percent)	4,000	16,000	32,000	12,000	−4,000*
Net income	6,000	24,000	48,000	18,000	−6,000

* Negative taxes occur in Year 5 because the earnings before taxes of −$10,000 can be deducted against earnings on other projects, thus reducing the tax bill by $4,000.

budgeting criteria discussed here, the AAR is based on accounting numbers and not based on cash flows. This is an important conceptual and practical limitation. The AAR also does not account for the time value of money, and there is no conceptually sound cutoff for the AAR that distinguishes between profitable and unprofitable investments. The AAR is frequently calculated in different ways, so the analyst should verify the formula behind any AAR numbers that are supplied by someone else. Analysts should know the AAR and its potential limitations in practice, but they should rely on more economically sound methods like the NPV and IRR.

4.6 Profitability Index

The profitability index (PI) is the present value of a project's future cash flows divided by the initial investment. It can be expressed as

$$\text{PI} = \frac{\text{PV of future cash flows}}{\text{Initial investment}} = 1 + \frac{\text{NPV}}{\text{Initial investment}} \qquad \textbf{(47-5)}$$

You can see that the PI is closely related to the NPV. The PI is the *ratio* of the PV of future cash flows to the initial investment, while an NPV is the *difference* between the PV of future cash flows and the initial investment. Whenever the NPV is positive, the PI will be greater than 1.0, and conversely, whenever the NPV is negative, the PI will be less than 1.0. The investment decision rule for the PI is as follows:

Invest if	PI > 1.0
Do not invest if	PI < 1.0

Because the PV of future cash flows equals the initial investment plus the NPV, the PI can also be expressed as 1.0 plus the ratio of the NPV to the initial investment, as shown in Equation 47-5 above. Example 47-2 illustrates the PI calculation.

Example of a PI Calculation

The Gerhardt Corporation investment (discussed earlier) had an outlay of €50 million, a present value of future cash flows of €63.136 million, and an NPV of €13.136 million. The profitability index is

$$PI = \frac{PV \text{ of future cash flows}}{\text{Initial investment}} = \frac{63.136}{50.000} = 1.26$$

The PI can also be calculated as

$$PI = 1 + \frac{NPV}{\text{Initial investment}} = 1 + \frac{13.136}{50.000} = 1.26$$

Because the PI > 1.0, this is a profitable investment.

The PI indicates the value you are receiving in exchange for one unit of currency invested. Although the PI is used less frequently than the NPV and IRR, it is sometimes used as a guide in capital rationing, which we will discuss later. The PI is usually called the profitability index in corporations, but it is commonly referred to as a "benefit-cost ratio" in governmental and not-for-profit organizations.

4.7 NPV Profile

The NPV profile shows a project's NPV graphed as a function of various discount rates. Typically, the NPV is graphed vertically (on the *y*-axis) and the discount rates are graphed horizontally (on the *x*-axis). The NPV profile for the Gerhardt capital budgeting project is shown in Example 47-3.

NPV Profile

For the Gerhardt example, we have already calculated several NPVs for different discount rates. At 10 percent the NPV is €13.136 million; at 20 percent the NPV is −€0.543 million; and at 19.52 percent (the IRR), the NPV is zero. What is the NPV if the discount rate is 0 percent? The NPV discounted at 0 percent is €34 million, which is simply the sum of all of the undiscounted cash flows. Table 47-6 and Figure 47-1 show the NPV profile for the Gerhardt example for discount rates between 0 percent and 30 percent.

TABLE 47-6   Gerhardt NPV Profile

Discount Rate	NPV € millions
0%	34.000
5.00%	22.406
10.00%	13.136
15.00%	5.623
19.52%	0.000
20.00%	−0.543
25.00%	−5.661
30.00%	−9.954

FIGURE 47-1   Gerhardt NPV Profile

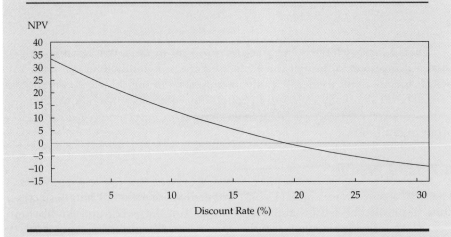

Three interesting points on this NPV profile are where the profile goes through the vertical axis (the NPV when the discount rate is zero), where the profile goes through the horizontal axis (where the discount rate is the IRR), and the NPV for the required rate of return (NPV is €13.136 million when the discount rate is the 10 percent required rate of return).

The NPV profile in Figure 47-1 is very well-behaved. The NPV declines at a decreasing rate as the discount rate increases. The profile is convex from the origin (convex from below). You will shortly see some examples in which the NPV profile is more complicated.

4.8 Ranking Conflicts between NPV and IRR

For a single conventional project, the NPV and IRR will agree on whether to invest or to not invest. For independent, conventional projects, no conflict exists between the decision rules for the NPV and IRR. However, in the case of two mutually exclusive projects, the two criteria will sometimes disagree. For example, Project A might have a larger NPV than Project B, but Project B has a higher IRR than Project A. In this case, should you invest in Project A or in Project B?

Differing cash flow patterns can cause two projects to rank differently with the NPV and IRR. For example, suppose Project A has shorter-term payoffs than Project B. This situation is presented in Example 47-4.

Example 47-4

Ranking Conflict due to Differing Cash Flow Patterns

Projects A and B have similar outlays but different patterns of future cash flows. Project A realizes most of its cash payoffs earlier than Project B. The cash flows as well as the NPV and IRR for the two projects are shown in Table 47-7. For both projects, the required rate of return is 10 percent.

TABLE 47-7   Cash Flows, NPV, and IRR for Two Projects with Different Cash Flow Patterns

	Cash Flows						
Year	0	1	2	3	4	NPV	IRR
Project A	−200	80	80	80	80	53.59	21.86%
Project B	−200	0	0	0	400	73.21	18.92%

If the two projects were not mutually exclusive, you would invest in both because they are both profitable. However, you can choose either A (which has the higher IRR) or B (which has the higher NPV).

Table 47-8 and Figure 47-2 show the NPVs for Project A and Project B for various discount rates between 0 percent and 30 percent.

TABLE 47-8   NPV Profiles for Two Projects with Different Cash Flow Patterns

Discount Rate	NPV for Project A	NPV for Project B
0%	120.00	200.00
5.00%	83.68	129.08
10.00%	53.59	73.21
15.00%	28.40	28.70
15.09%	27.98	27.98
18.92%	11.41	0.00
20.00%	7.10	−7.10
21.86%	0.00	−18.62
25.00%	−11.07	−36.16
30.00%	−26.70	−59.95

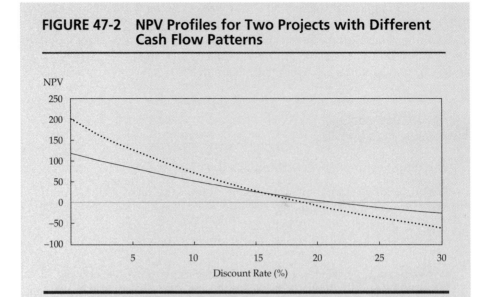

FIGURE 47-2   NPV Profiles for Two Projects with Different Cash Flow Patterns

Note that Project B has the higher NPV for discount rates between 0 percent and 15.09 percent. Project A has the higher NPV for discount rates exceeding 15.09 percent. The crossover point of 15.09 percent in Figure 47-2 corresponds to the discount rate at which both projects have the same NPV (of 27.98). Project B has the higher NPV below the crossover point, and Project A has the higher NPV above it.

Whenever the NPV and IRR rank two mutually exclusive projects differently, as they do in the example above, you should choose the project based on the NPV. Project B, with the higher NPV, is the better project because of the reinvestment assumption. Mathematically, whenever you discount a cash flow at a particular discount rate, you are implicitly assuming that you can reinvest a cash flow at that same discount rate.[2] In the NPV calculation, you use a discount rate of 10 percent for both projects. In the IRR calculation, you use a discount rate equal to the IRR of 21.86 percent for Project A and 18.92 percent for Project B.

Can you reinvest the cash inflows from the projects at 10 percent, or 21.86 percent, or 18.92 percent? When you assume the required rate of return is 10 percent, you are assuming an opportunity cost of 10 percent—you are assuming that you can either find other projects that pay a 10 percent return or pay back your sources of capital that cost you 10 percent. The fact that you earned 21.86 percent in Project A or 18.92 percent in Project B does not mean that you can reinvest future cash flows at those rates. (In fact, if you can reinvest future cash flows at 21.86 percent or 18.92 percent, these should have been used as your required rate of return instead of 10 percent.) Because the NPV criterion uses the most realistic discount rate—the opportunity cost of funds—the NPV criterion should be used for evaluating mutually exclusive projects.

---

[2] For example, assume that you are receiving $100 in one year discounted at 10 percent. The present value is $100/1.10 = $90.91. Instead of receiving the $100 in one year, invest it for one additional year at 10 percent, and it grows to $110. What is the present value of $110 received in two years discounted at 10 percent? It is the same $90.91. Because both future cash flows are worth the same, you are implicitly assuming that reinvesting the earlier cash flow at the discount rate of 10 percent has no effect on its value.

Another circumstance that frequently causes mutually exclusive projects to be ranked differently by NPV and IRR criteria is project scale—the sizes of the projects. Would you rather have a small project with a higher rate of return or a large project with a lower rate of return? Sometimes, the larger, low rate of return project has the better NPV. This case is developed in Example 47-5.

Example 47-5

Ranking Conflicts due to Differing Project Scale

Project A has a much smaller outlay than Project B, although they have similar future cash flow patterns. The cash flows as well as the NPVs and IRRs for the two projects are shown in Table 47-9. For both projects, the required rate of return is 10 percent.

TABLE 47-9   Cash Flows, NPV, and IRR for Two Projects of Differing Scale

| | Cash Flows | | | | | | |
Year	0	1	2	3	4	NPV	IRR
Project A	−100	50	50	50	50	58.49	34.90%
Project B	−400	170	170	170	170	138.88	25.21%

If they were not mutually exclusive, you would invest in both projects because they are both profitable. However, you can choose either Project A (which has the higher IRR) or Project B (which has the higher NPV).

Table 47-10 and Figure 47-3 show the NPVs for Project A and Project B for various discount rates between 0 percent and 30 percent.

TABLE 47-10   NPV Profiles for Two Projects of Differing Scale

Discount Rate	NPV for Project A	NPV for Project B
0%	100.00	280.00
5.00%	77.30	202.81
10.00%	58.49	138.88
15.00%	42.75	85.35
20.00%	29.44	40.08
21.86%	25.00	25.00
25.00%	18.08	1.47
25.21%	17.65	0.00
30.00%	8.31	−31.74
34.90%	0.00	−60.00
35.00%	−0.15	−60.52

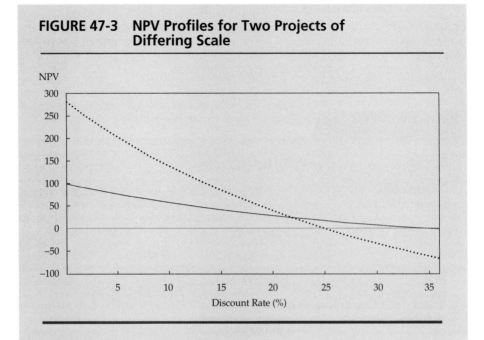

FIGURE 47-3   NPV Profiles for Two Projects of Differing Scale

Note that Project B has the higher NPV for discount rates between 0 percent and 21.86 percent. Project A has the higher NPV for discount rates exceeding 21.86 percent. The crossover point of 21.86 percent in Figure 47-3 corresponds to the discount rate at which both projects have the same NPV (of 25.00). Below the crossover point, Project B has the higher NPV, and above it, Project A has the higher NPV. When cash flows are discounted at the 10 percent required rate of return, the choice is clear—Project B, the larger project, which has the superior NPV.

The good news is that the NPV and IRR criteria will usually indicate the same investment decision for a given project. They will usually both recommend acceptance or rejection of the project. When the choice is between two mutually exclusive projects and the NPV and IRR rank the two projects differently, the NPV criterion is strongly preferred. There are good reasons for this preference. The NPV shows the amount of gain, or wealth increase, as a currency amount. The reinvestment assumption of the NPV is the more economically realistic. The IRR does give you a rate of return, but the IRR could be for a small investment or for only a short period of time. As a practical matter, once a corporation has the data to calculate the NPV, it is fairly trivial to go ahead and calculate the IRR and other capital budgeting criteria. However, the most appropriate and theoretically sound criterion is the NPV.

4.9 The Multiple IRR Problem and the No IRR Problem

A problem that can arise with the IRR criterion is the "multiple IRR problem." We can illustrate this problem with the following nonconventional cash flow pattern:[3]

Time	0	1	2
Cash Flow	−1,000	5,000	−6,000

---

[3] This example is adapted from Hirschleifer (1958).

The IRR for these cash flows satisfies this equation:

$$-1,000 + \frac{5,000}{(1 + \text{IRR})^1} + \frac{-6,000}{(1 + \text{IRR})^2} = 0$$

It turns out that there are two values of IRR that satisfy the equation: IRR = 1 = 100% and IRR = 2 = 200%. To further understand this problem, consider the NPV profile for this investment, which is shown in Table 47-11 and Figure 47-4.

TABLE 47-11   NPV Profile for a Multiple IRR Example

Discount Rate	NPV
0%	−2,000.00
25%	−840.00
50%	−333.33
75%	−102.04
100%	0.00
125%	37.04
140%	41.67
150%	40.00
175%	24.79
200%	0.00
225%	−29.59
250%	−61.22
300%	−125.00
350%	−185.19
400%	−240.00
500%	−333.33
1,000%	−595.04
2,000%	−775.51
3,000%	−844.95
4,000%	−881.62
10,000%	−951.08
1,000,000%	−999.50

FIGURE 47-4   NPV Profile for a Multiple IRR Example

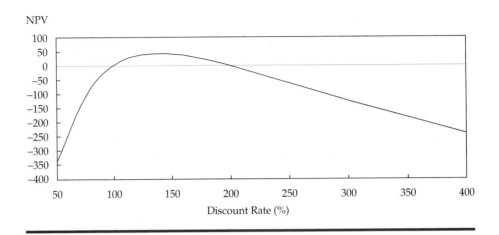

As you can see in the NPV profile, the NPV is equal to zero at IRR = 100% and IRR = 200%. The NPV is negative for discount rates below 100 percent, positive between 100 percent and 200 percent, and then negative above 200 percent. The NPV reaches its highest value when the discount rate is 140 percent.

It is also possible to have an investment project with no IRR. The "no-IRR problem" occurs with this cash flow pattern:[4]

Time	0	1	2
Cash Flow	100	−300	250

The IRR for these cash flows satisfies this equation:

$$100 + \frac{-300}{(1 + \text{IRR})^1} + \frac{250}{(1 + \text{IRR})^2} = 0$$

For these cash flows, no discount rate exists that results in a zero NPV. Does that mean this project is a bad investment? In this case, the project is actually a good investment. As Table 47-12 and Figure 47-5 show, the NPV is positive for all discount rates. The lowest NPV, of 10, occurs for a discount rate of 66.67 percent, and the NPV is always greater than zero. Consequently, no IRR exists.

For conventional projects that have outlays followed by inflows—negative cash flows followed by positive cash flows—the multiple IRR problem cannot occur. However, for nonconventional projects, as in the example above, the multiple IRR problem can occur. The IRR equation is essentially an nth degree polynomial. An nth degree polynomial can have up to n solutions, although it will have no more real solutions than the number of cash flow sign changes. For example, a project with two sign changes could have zero, one, or two IRRs. Having two sign changes does not mean that you *will* have multiple IRRs; it just means that you *might*. Fortunately, most capital budgeting projects have only one IRR. Analysts should always be aware of the unusual cash flow patterns that can generate the multiple IRR problem.

---

[4] This example is also adapted from Hirschleifer.

TABLE 47-12 NPV Profile for a Project with No IRR	
Discount Rate	**NPV**
0%	50.00
25%	20.00
50%	11.11
66.67%	10.00
75%	10.20
100%	12.50
125%	16.05
150%	20.00
175%	23.97
200%	27.78
225%	31.36
250%	34.69
275%	37.78
300%	40.63
325%	43.25
350%	45.68
375%	47.92
400%	50.00

FIGURE 47-5   NPV Profile for a Project with No IRR

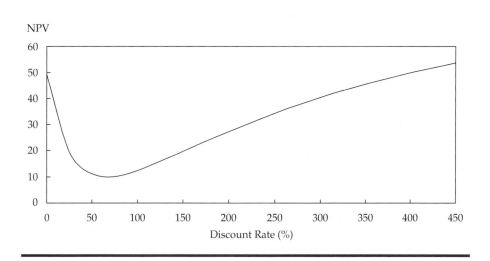

4.10 Popularity and Usage of the Capital Budgeting Methods

Analysts need to know the basic logic of the various capital budgeting criteria as well as the practicalities involved in using them in real corporations. Before delving into the many issues involved in applying these models, we would like to present some feedback on their popularity.

The usefulness of any analytical tool always depends on the specific application. Corporations generally find these capital budgeting criteria useful. Two recent surveys by Graham and Harvey (2001) and Brounen, De Jong, and Koedijk (2004) report on the frequency of their use by U.S. and European corporations. Table 47-13 gives the mean responses of executives in five countries to the question "How frequently does your company use the following techniques when deciding which projects or acquisitions to pursue?"

TABLE 47-13	Mean Responses about Frequency of Use of Capital Budgeting Techniques				
	U.S.	U.K.	Netherlands	Germany	France
Internal rate of return*	3.09	2.31	2.36	2.15	2.27
Net present value*	3.08	2.32	2.76	2.26	1.86
Payback period*	2.53	2.77	2.53	2.29	2.46
Hurdle rate	2.13	1.35	1.98	1.61	0.73
Sensitivity analysis	2.31	2.21	1.84	1.65	0.79
Earnings multiple approach	1.89	1.81	1.61	1.25	1.70
Discounted payback period*	1.56	1.49	1.25	1.59	0.87
Real options approach	1.47	1.65	1.49	2.24	2.20
Accounting rate of return*	1.34	1.79	1.40	1.63	1.11
Value at risk	0.95	0.85	0.51	1.45	1.68
Adjusted present value	0.85	0.78	0.78	0.71	1.11
Profitability index*	0.85	1.00	0.78	1.04	1.64

Respondents used a scale ranging from 0 (never) to 4 (always).
* These techniques were described in this section of the reading. You will encounter the others elsewhere.

Although financial textbooks preach the superiority of the NPV and IRR techniques, it is clear that several other methods are heavily used.[5] In the four European countries, the payback period is used as often as, or even slightly more often than, the NPV and IRR. In these two studies, larger companies tended to prefer the NPV and IRR over the payback period. The fact that the U.S. companies were larger, on average, partially explains the greater U.S. preference for the NPV and IRR. Other factors influence the choice of capital budgeting techniques. Private corporations used the payback period more frequently than did

---

[5] Analysts often refer to the NPV and IRR as "discounted cash flow techniques" because they accurately account for the timing of all cash flows when they are discounted.

public corporations. Companies managed by an MBA had a stronger preference for the discounted cash flow techniques. Of course, any survey research also has some limitations. In this case, the persons in these large corporations responding to the surveys may not have been aware of all of the applications of these techniques.

These capital budgeting techniques are essential tools for corporate managers. Capital budgeting is also relevant to external analysts. Because a corporation's investing decisions ultimately determine the value of its financial obligations, the corporation's investing processes are vital. The NPV criterion is the criterion most directly related to stock prices. If a corporation invests in positive NPV projects, these should add to the wealth of its shareholders. Example 47-6 illustrates this scenario.

Example 47-6

NPVs and Stock Prices

Freitag Corporation is investing €600 million in distribution facilities. The present value of the future after-tax cash flows is estimated to be €850 million. Freitag has 200 million outstanding shares with a current market price of €32.00 per share. This investment is new information, and it is independent of other expectations about the company. What should be the effect of the project on the value of the company and the stock price?

▶ **Solution.** The NPV of the project is €850 million − €600 million = €250 million. The total market value of the company prior to the investment is €32.00 × 200 million shares = €6,400 million. The value of the company should increase by €250 million to €6,650 million. The price per share should increase by the NPV per share, or €250 million / 200 million shares = €1.25 per share. The share price should increase from €32.00 to €33.25.

The effect of a capital budgeting project's positive or negative NPV on share price is more complicated than Example 47-6 above, in which the value of the stock increased by the project's NPV. The value of a company is the value of its existing investments plus the net present values of all of its future investments. If an analyst learns of an investment, the impact of that investment on the stock price will depend on whether the investment's profitability is more or less than expected. For example, an analyst could learn of a positive NPV project, but if the project's profitability is less than expectations, this stock might drop in price on the news. Alternatively, news of a particular capital project might be considered as a signal about other capital projects underway or in the future. A project that by itself might add, say, €0.25 to the value of the stock might signal the existence of other profitable projects. News of this project might increase the stock price by far more than €0.25.

The integrity of a corporation's capital budgeting processes is important to analysts. Management's capital budgeting processes can demonstrate two things about the quality of management: the degree to which management embraces the goal of shareholder wealth maximization, and its effectiveness in pursuing that goal. Both of these factors are important to shareholders.

CASH FLOW PROJECTIONS

In Section 4, we presented the basic capital budgeting models that managers use to accept or reject capital budgeting proposals. In that section, we assumed the cash flows were given, and we used them as inputs to the analysis. In Section 5, we detail how these cash flows are found for an "expansion" project. An expansion project is an independent investment that does not affect the cash flows for the rest of the company. In Section 6, we will deal with a "replacement" project, in which the cash flow analysis is more complicated. A replacement project must deal with the differences between the cash flows that occur with the new investment and the cash flows that would have occurred for the investment being replaced.

5.1 Table Format with Cash Flows Collected by Year

The cash flows for a conventional expansion project can be grouped into (1) the investment outlays, (2) after-tax operating cash flows over the project's life, and (3) terminal year after-tax non-operating cash flows. Table 47-14 gives an example of the cash flows for a capital project where all of the cash flows are collected by year.

TABLE 47-14   Capital Budgeting Cash Flows Example (Cash Flows Collected by Year)

Year	0	1	2	3	4	5
Investment outlays:						
Fixed capital	−200,000					
Net working capital	−30,000					
Total	−230,000					
Annual after-tax operating cash flows:						
Sales		220,000	220,000	220,000	220,000	220,000
Cash operating expenses		90,000	90,000	90,000	90,000	90,000
Depreciation		35,000	35,000	35,000	35,000	35,000
Operating income before taxes		95,000	95,000	95,000	95,000	95,000
Taxes on operating income		38,000	38,000	38,000	38,000	38,000
Operating income after taxes		57,000	57,000	57,000	57,000	57,000
Add back: Depreciation		35,000	35,000	35,000	35,000	35,000
After-tax operating cash flow		92,000	92,000	92,000	92,000	92,000
Terminal year after-tax non-operating cash flows:						
After-tax salvage value						40,000
Return of net working capital						30,000
Total						70,000
Total after-tax cash flow	−230,000	92,000	92,000	92,000	92,000	162,000

(Table continued on next page …)

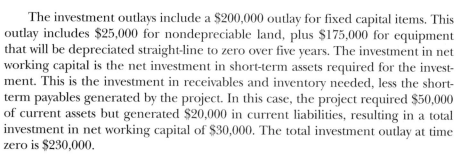

TABLE 47-14	Capital Budgeting Cash Flows Example (Cash Flows Collected by Year)(continued)					
Year	0	1	2	3	4	5
Net present value at 10 percent required rate of return	162,217					
Internal rate of return	32.70%					

The investment outlays include a $200,000 outlay for fixed capital items. This outlay includes $25,000 for nondepreciable land, plus $175,000 for equipment that will be depreciated straight-line to zero over five years. The investment in net working capital is the net investment in short-term assets required for the investment. This is the investment in receivables and inventory needed, less the short-term payables generated by the project. In this case, the project required $50,000 of current assets but generated $20,000 in current liabilities, resulting in a total investment in net working capital of $30,000. The total investment outlay at time zero is $230,000.

Each year, sales will be $220,000 and cash operating expenses will be $90,000. Annual depreciation for the $175,000 depreciable equipment is $35,000 (one-fifth of the cost). The result is an operating income before taxes of $95,000. Income taxes at a 40 percent rate are $0.40 \times \$95,000 = \$38,000$. This leaves operating income after taxes of $57,000. Adding back the depreciation charge of $35,000 gives the annual after-tax operating cash flow of $92,000.[6]

At the end of year five, the company will sell off the fixed capital assets. In this case, the fixed capital assets (including the land) are sold for $50,000, which represents a gain of $25,000 over the remaining book value of $25,000. The gain of $25,000 is taxed at 40 percent, resulting in a tax of $10,000. This leaves $40,000 for the fixed capital assets after taxes. Additionally, the net working capital investment of $30,000 is recovered, as the short-term assets (such as inventory and receivables) and short-term liabilities (such as payables) are no longer needed for the project. Total terminal year non-operating cash flows are then $70,000.

The investment project has a required rate of return of 10 percent. Discounting the future cash flows at 10 percent and subtracting the investment outlay gives an NPV of $162,217. The internal rate of return is 32.70 percent. Because the investment has a positive NPV, this project should be accepted. The IRR investment decision criterion would also recommend accepting the project because the IRR is greater than the required rate of return.

5.2 Table Format with Cash Flows Collected by Type

In the layout in Table 47-14, we essentially collected the cash flows in the columns, by *year*, and then found the NPV by summing the present values of the annual cash flows (at the bottom of each column). There is another way of organizing the same information. We could also find the NPV by finding the present values of the cash flows in Table 47-14 by rows, which are the *types* of cash flows. This approach is shown in Table 47-15.

---

[6] Examining the operating cash flows in Table 47-14, we have a $220,000 inflow from sales, a $90,000 outflow for cash operating expenses, and a $38,000 outflow for taxes. This is an after-tax cash flow of $92,000.

TABLE 47-15   Capital Budgeting Cash Flows Example (Cash Flows Collected by Type)

Time	Type of Cash Flow	Before-tax Cash Flow	After-tax Cash Flow	PV at 10%
0	Fixed capital	−200,000	−200,000	−200,000
0	Net working capital	−30,000	−30,000	−30,000
1–5	Sales minus cash expenses	220,000 − 90,000 = 130,000	130,000(1 − 0.40) = 78,000	295,681
1–5	Depreciation tax savings	None	0.40(35,000) = 14,000	53,071
5	After-tax salvage value	50,000	50,000 − 0.40(50,000 − 25,000) = 40,000	24,837
5	Return of net working capital	30,000	30,000	18,628
			NPV=	162,217

As Table 47-15 shows, the outlays in fixed capital and in net working capital at time zero total \$230,000. For Years 1 though 5, the company realizes an after-tax cash flow for sales minus cash expenses of \$78,000, which has a present value of \$295,681. The depreciation charge results in a tax savings of \$14,000 per year, which has a present value of \$53,071. The present values of the after-tax salvage and of the return of net working capital are also shown in the table. The present value of all cash flows is an NPV of \$162,217. Obviously, collecting the after-tax cash flows by year, as in Table 47-14, or by type, as in Table 47-15, results in the same NPV.

5.3 Equation Format for Organizing Cash Flows

The capital budgeting cash flows in the example project above were laid out in one of two alternative tabular formats. Analysts may wish to take even another approach. Instead of producing a table, you can also look at the cash flows using equations such a s the following:

(1) Initial outlay:
For a new investment
$$Outlay = FCInv + NWCInv$$

where

$FCInv$ = Investment in new fixed capital
$NWCInv$ = Investment in net working capital

The above equation can be generalized for a replacement project (covered in Section 6.2), in which existing fixed capital is sold and provides some of the funding for the new fixed capital purchased. The outlay is then

$$Outlay = FCInv + NWCInv − Sal_0 + T(Sal_0 − B_0) \qquad \textbf{(47-6)}$$

where
Sal_0 = Cash proceeds (salvage value) from sale of old fixed capital
T = Tax rate
B_0 = Book value of old fixed capital

(2) Annual after-tax operating cash flow:

$$CF = (S - C - D)(1 - T) + D, \text{ or} \qquad \textbf{(47-7)}$$

$$CF = (S - C)(1 - T) + TD \qquad \textbf{(47-8)}$$

where
 S = sales
 C = cash operating expenses
 D = depreciation charge

(3) Terminal year after-tax non-operating cash flow:

$$TNOCF = Sal_T + NWCInv - T(Sal_T - B_T) \qquad \textbf{(47-9)}$$

where
 Sal_T = Cash proceeds (salvage value) from sale of fixed capital on
      termination date
 B_T = Book value of fixed capital on termination date

The outlay in the example is found with Equation 47-6:

$$Outlay = 200,000 + 30,000 - 0 + 0 = \$230,000$$

For a replacement project, the old fixed capital would be sold for cash (Sal_0) and then there would be taxes paid on the gain (if $Sal_0 - B_0$ were positive) or a tax saving (if $Sal_0 - B_0$ were negative). In this example, Sal_0 and $T(Sal_0 - B_0)$ are zero because no existing fixed capital is sold at time zero.

Using Equation 47-7, we find that the annual after-tax operating cash flow is

$$
\begin{aligned}
CF &= (S - C - D)(1 - T) + D \\
&= (220,000 - 90,000 - 35,000)(1 - 0.40) + 35,000 = 95,000\,(0.60) \\
&\quad + 35,000 \\
&= 57,000 + 35,000 = \$92,000
\end{aligned}
$$

Equation 47-7 is the project's net income plus depreciation. An identical cash flow results if we use Equation 47-8:

$$
\begin{aligned}
CF &= (S - C)(1 - T) + TD \\
&= (220,000 - 90,000)(1 - 0.40) + 0.40(35,000) \\
&= 130,000(0.60) + 0.40(35,000) = 78,000 + 14,000 = \$92,000
\end{aligned}
$$

Equation 47-8 is the after-tax sales and cash expenses plus the depreciation tax savings. The analyst can use either equation.

Equation 47-9 provides the terminal year non-operating cash flow:

$$
\begin{aligned}
TNOCF &= Sal_T + NWCInv - T(Sal_T - B_T) \\
&= 50,000 + 30,000 - 0.40(50,000 - 25,000) \\
&= 50,000 + 30,000 - 10,000 = \$70,000
\end{aligned}
$$

The old fixed capital (including land) is sold for $50,000, but $10,000 of taxes must be paid on the gain. Including the $30,000 return of net working capital gives a terminal year non-operating cash flow of $70,000.

The NPV of the project is the present value of the cash flows—an outlay of $230,000 at time zero, an annuity of $92,000 for five years, plus a single payment of $70,000 in five years:

$$NPV = -230,000 + \sum_{t=1}^{5} \frac{92,000}{(1.10)^t} + \frac{70,000}{(1.10)^5}$$

$$= -230,000 + 348,752 + 43,465 = \$162,217$$

We obtain an identical NPV of $162,217 whether we use a tabular format collecting cash flows by year, a tabular format collecting cash flows by type, or an equation format using Equations 47-6 through 47-9. The analyst usually has some flexibility in choosing how to solve a problem. Furthermore, the analysis that an analyst receives from someone else could be in varying formats. The analyst must interpret this information correctly regardless of format. An analyst may need to present information in alternative formats, depending on what the client or user of the information wishes to see. All that is important is that the cash flows are complete (with no cash flows omitted and none double-counted), that their timing is recognized, and that the discounting is done correctly.

MORE ON CASH FLOW PROJECTIONS

Cash flow analysis can become fairly complicated. Section 6 extends the analysis of the previous section to include more details on depreciation methods, replacement projects (as opposed to simple expansion projects), the use of spreadsheets, and the effects of inflation.

6.1 Straight-Line and Accelerated Depreciation Methods

Before going on to more complicated investment decisions, we should mention the variety of depreciation methods that are in use. The example in Section 5.1 assumed straight-line depreciation down to a zero salvage value. Most accounting texts give a good description of the straight-line method, the sum-of-years digits method, the double-declining balance method (and the 150 percent declining balance method), and the units-of-production and service hours method.[7]

Many countries specify the depreciation methods that are acceptable for tax purposes in their jurisdictions. For example, in the U.S., corporations use the MACRS (modified accelerated cost recovery system) for tax purposes. Under MACRS, real property (real estate) is usually depreciated straight-line over a 27.5- or 39-year life, and other capital assets are usually grouped into MACRS asset classes and subject to a special depreciation schedule in each class. These MACRS classes and the depreciation rates for each class are shown in Table 47-16.

For the first four MACRS classes (3-year, 5-year, 7-year, and 10-year), the depreciation is double-declining-balance with a switch to straight-line when optimal and with a half-year convention. For the last two classes (15-year and 20-year), the depreciation is 150 percent-declining-balance with a switch to straight-line when optimal and with a half-year convention. Take 5-year property in Table 47-16 as an example. With double-declining-balance, the depreciation each year is $2/5 = 40\%$ of the beginning-of-year book value. However, with a half-year convention, the asset is assumed to be in service for only six months during the first year, and only one half of the depreciation is allowed the first year. After the first year, the depreciation rate is 40 percent of the beginning balance until Year 4, when straight-line depreciation would be at least as large, so we switch to straight-line. In Year 6, we have one-half of a year of the straight-line depreciation remaining because we assumed the asset was placed in service half-way through the first year.

Accelerated depreciation generally improves the NPV of a capital project compared to straight-line depreciation. For an example of this effect, we will assume the same capital project as in Table 47-14, except that the depreciation is

[7] White, Sondhi, and Fried (2003) is a good example. Consult their chapter 8, "Analysis of Long-Lived Assets: Part II—Analysis of Depreciation and Impairment" for review and examples.

TABLE 47-16 Depreciation Rates under U.S. MACRS

Year	Recovery Period Class					
	3-year	**5-year**	**7-year**	**10-year**	**15-year**	**20-year**
1	33.33%	20.00%	14.29%	10.00%	5.00%	3.75%
2	44.45	32.00	24.49	18.00	9.50	7.22
3	14.81	19.20	17.49	14.40	8.55	6.68
4	7.41	11.52	12.49	11.52	7.70	6.18
5		11.52	8.93	9.22	6.93	5.71
6		5.76	8.93	7.37	6.23	5.28
7			8.93	6.55	5.90	4.89
8			4.45	6.55	5.90	4.52
9				6.55	5.90	4.46
10				6.55	5.90	4.46
11				3.29	5.90	4.46
12					5.90	4.46
13					5.90	4.46
14					5.90	4.46
15					5.90	4.46
16					2.99	4.46
17						4.46
18						4.46
19						4.46
20						4.46
21						2.25

MACRS 3-year property. When using straight-line, the depreciation was 20 percent per year ($35,000). The depreciation percentages for MACRS 3-year property are given in Table 47-16. The first-year depreciation is $0.3333 \times 175,000 = \$58,327.50$, second year depreciation is $0.4445 \times 175,000 = \$77,787.50$, third year depreciation is $0.1481 \times 175,000 = \$25,917.50$, fourth year depreciation is $0.0741 \times 175,000 = \$12,967.50$, and fifth year depreciation is zero. The impact on the NPV and IRR of the project is shown in Table 47-17.

TABLE 47-17 Capital Budgeting Example with MACRS

Year	0	1	2	3	4	5
Investment outlays:						
Fixed capital	−200,000					
Net working capital	−30,000					
Total	−230,000					

(Table continued on next page …)

Year	0	1	2	3	4	5
TABLE 47-17 Capital Budgeting Example with MACRS (continued)						
Annual after-tax operating cash flows:						
Sales		220,000	220,000	220,000	220,000	220,000
Cash operating expenses		90,000	90,000	90,000	90,000	90,000
Depreciation		58,328	77,788	25,918	12,968	0
Operating income before taxes		71,673	52,213	104,083	117,033	130,000
Taxes on operating income (40%)		28,669	20,885	41,633	46,813	52,000
Operating income after taxes		43,004	31,328	62,450	70,220	78,000
Add back: Depreciation		58,328	77,788	25,918	12,968	0
After-tax operating cash flow		101,331	109,115	88,367	83,187	78,000
Terminal year after-tax non-operating cash flows:						
After-tax salvage value						40,000
Return of net working capital						30,000
Total						70,000
Total after-tax cash flows	−230,000	101,331	109,115	88,367	83,187	148,000
Net present value at 10% required rate of return	$167,403					
Internal rate of return	34.74%					

As the table shows, the depreciation charges still sum to $175,000 (except for $2 of rounding), but they are larger in Years 1 and 2 and smaller in Years 3, 4, and 5. Although this method reduces operating income after taxes in Years 1 and 2 (and increases it in Years 3, 4, and 5), it reduces tax outflows in Years 1 and 2 and increases them later. Consequently, the after-tax operating cash flows (which were $92,000 per year) increase in early years and decrease in later years. This increases the NPV from $162,217 to $167,403, a difference of $5,186. The IRR also increases from 32.70 percent to 34.74 percent.[8]

The impact of accelerated depreciation can be seen without going through the complete analysis in Table 47-17. We previously showed in Table 47-15 that the present value of the depreciation tax savings (which was an annuity of 0.40 × $35,000 = $14,000 a year for five years) was $53,071. The present value of the tax savings from accelerated depreciation is shown in Table 47-18.

By using the accelerated depreciation schedule, we increase the present value of the tax savings from $53,071 (from Table 47-15) to $58,257, an increase of $5,186. The tax deferral associated with the accelerated depreciation (compared to straight-line) adds $5,186 to the NPV of the project.

---

[8] This example assumes that the investment occurs on the first day of the tax year. If the outlay occurs later in the tax year, the depreciation tax savings for the tax years are unchanged, which means that the cash savings occur sooner, increasing their present values. The result is a higher NPV and IRR.

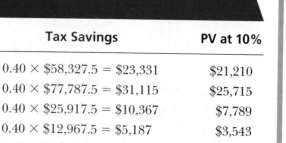

Year	Depreciation	Tax Savings	PV at 10%
1	$58,327.50	$0.40 \times \$58,327.5 = \$23,331$	$21,210
2	$77,787.50	$0.40 \times \$77,787.5 = \$31,115$	$25,715
3	$25,917.50	$0.40 \times \$25,917.5 = \$10,367$	$7,789
4	$12,967.50	$0.40 \times \$12,967.5 = \$5,187$	$3,543
5	$ 0	$0.40 \times \$0 = \$0$	$0
Total present value			$58,257

There are a myriad of tax and depreciation schedules that apply to investment projects around the world. These tax and depreciation schedules are also subject to change from year to year. To accurately assess the profitability of a particular capital project, it is vital to identify and apply the schedules that are relevant to the capital budgeting decision at hand.

6.2 Cash Flows for a Replacement Project

In Section 5.1, we evaluated the cash flows for an expansion project, basing our after-tax cash flows on the outlays, annual operating cash flows after tax, and salvage value for the project by itself. In many cases, however, investing in a project will be more complicated. Investing could affect many of the company's cash flows. In principle, the cash flows relevant to an investing decision are the incremental cash flows: the cash flows the company realizes *with* the investment compared to the cash flows the company would realize *without* the investment. For example, suppose we are investing in a new project with an outlay of $100,000 and we sell off existing assets that the project replaces for $30,000. The incremental outlay is $70,000.

A very common investment decision is a replacement decision, in which you replace old equipment with new equipment. This decision requires very careful analysis of the cash flows. The skills required to detail the replacement decision cash flows are also useful for other decisions in which an investment affects other cash flows in the company. We use the term "replacement" loosely, primarily to indicate that the cash flow analysis is more complicated than it was for the simpler expansion decision.

Assume we are considering the replacement of old equipment with new equipment that has more capacity and is less costly to operate. The characteristics of the old and new equipment are given on the next page. If the new equipment replaces the old equipment, an additional investment of $80,000 in net working capital will be required. The tax rate is 30 percent, and the required rate of return is 8 percent.

The cash flows can be found by carefully constructing tables like Table 47-14 or by using Equations 47-6 through 47-9. The initial outlay is the investment in

Old Equipment		New Equipment	
Current book value	$400,000		
Current market value	$600,000	Acquisition cost	$1,000,000
Remaining life	10 years	Life	10 years
Annual sales	$300,000	Annual sales	$450,000
Cash operating expenses	$120,000	Cash operating expenses	$150,000
Annual depreciation	$40,000	Annual depreciation	$100,000
Accounting salvage value	$0	Accounting salvage value	$0
Expected salvage value	$100,000	Expected salvage value	$200,000

the new equipment plus the additional investment in net working capital less the after-tax proceeds from selling the old equipment:

$$\text{Outlay} = \text{FCInv} + \text{NWCInv} - \text{Sal}_0 + T(\text{Sal}_0 - B_0)$$
$$\text{Outlay} = 1,000,000 + 80,000 - 600,000$$
$$+ 0.3(600,000 - 400,000) = \$540,000$$

In this case, the outlay of $540,000 is $1,080,000 for new equipment and net working capital minus the after-tax proceeds of $540,000 the company receives from selling the old equipment. The incremental operating cash flows are

$$\begin{aligned} CF &= [S - C - D](1 - T) + D \\ &= \big[(450,000 - 300,000) - (150,000 - 120,000) \\ &\quad - (100,000 - 40,000)\big](1 - 0.30) + (100,000 - 40,000) \\ &= (150,000 - 30,000 - 60,000)(1 - 0.30) + 60,000 = \$102,000 \end{aligned}$$

The incremental sales are $150,000, incremental cash operating expenses are $30,000, and incremental depreciation is $60,000. The incremental after-tax operating cash flow is $102,000 per year.

At the project termination, the new equipment is expected to be sold for $200,000, which constitutes an incremental cash flow of $100,000 over the $100,000 expected salvage price of the old equipment. Since the accounting salvage values for both the new and old equipment were zero, this gain is taxable at 30 percent. The company also recaptures its investment in net working capital. The terminal year after-tax non-operating cash flow is

$$\begin{aligned} \text{TNOCF} &= \text{Sal}_T + \text{NWCInv} - T(\text{Sal}_T - B_T) \\ &= (200,000 - 100,000) + 80,000 - 0.30 \\ &\quad \big[(200,000 - 100,000) - (0 - 0)\big] \\ &= \$150,000 \end{aligned}$$

Once the cash flows are identified, the NPV and IRR are readily found. The NPV, found by discounting the cash flows at the 8 percent required rate of return, is

$$\text{NPV} = -540,000 + \sum_{t=1}^{10} \frac{102,000}{1.08^t} + \frac{150,000}{1.08^{10}} = \$213,907$$

The IRR, found with a financial calculator, is 15.40 percent. Because the NPV is positive, this equipment replacement decision is attractive. The fact that the IRR exceeds the 8 percent required rate of return leads to the same conclusion.

The key to estimating the incremental cash flows for the replacement is to compare the cash flows that occur with the new investment to the cash flows that would have occurred without the new investment. The analyst is comparing the cash flows with a particular course of action to the cash flows with an alternative course of action.

6.3 Spreadsheet Modeling

Although the examples in this book can be readily solved with a financial calculator, capital budgeting is usually done with the assistance of personal computers and spreadsheets such as Microsoft Excel®. Spreadsheets are heavily used for several reasons. Spreadsheets provide a very effective way of building even complex models. Built-in spreadsheet functions (such as those for finding rates of return) are easy to use. The model's assumptions can be changed and solved easily. Models can be shared with other analysts, and they also help in presenting the results of the analysis. The example below shows how a spreadsheet can be used to solve a capital budgeting problem.

Example 47-7

Capital Budgeting with a Spreadsheet

Lawton Enterprises is evaluating a project with the following characteristics:

- ▶ Fixed capital investment is $2,000,000.
- ▶ The project has an expected six-year life.
- ▶ The initial investment in net working capital is $200,000. At the end of each year, net working capital must be increased so that the cumulative investment in net working capital is one-sixth of the next year's projected sales.
- ▶ The fixed capital is depreciated 30 percent in Year 1, 35 percent in Year 2, 20 percent in Year 3, 10 percent in Year 4, 5 percent in Year 5, and 0 percent in Year 6.
- ▶ Sales are $1,200,000 in Year 1. They grow at a 25 percent annual rate for the next two years, and then grow at a 10 percent annual rate for the last three years.
- ▶ Fixed cash operating expenses are $150,000 for Years 1–3 and $130,000 for Years 4–6.
- ▶ Variable cash operating expenses are 40 percent of sales in Year 1, 39 percent of sales in Year 2, and 38 percent in Years 3–6.
- ▶ Lawton's marginal tax rate is 30 percent.
- ▶ Lawton will sell its fixed capital investments for $150,000 when the project terminates and recapture its cumulative investment in net working capital. Income taxes will be paid on any gains.
- ▶ The project's required rate of return is 12 percent.
- ▶ If taxable income on the project is negative in any year, the loss will offset gains elsewhere in the corporation, resulting in a tax savings.

1. Determine whether this is a profitable investment using the NPV and IRR.

2. If the tax rate increases to 40 percent and the required rate of return increases to 14 percent, is the project still profitable?

▶ **Solution to 1.**

TABLE 47-19	Cash Flows for Lawton Investment (rounded to nearest $1,000)

Year	0	1	2	3	4	5	6
Fixed capital investment	−2,000						
NWC investments	−200	−50	−63	−31	−34	−38	
Sales		1,200	1,500	1,875	2,063	2,269	2,496
Fixed cash expenses		150	150	150	130	130	130
Variable cash expenses		480	585	713	784	862	948
Depreciation		600	700	400	200	100	0
Operating income before taxes		−30	65	613	949	1177	1417
Taxes on operating income		−9	20	184	285	353	425
Operating income after taxes		−21	45	429	664	824	992
Add back: Depreciation		600	700	400	200	100	0
After-tax operating cash flow		579	745	829	864	924	992
Salvage value							150
Taxes on salvage value							−45
Return of NWC							416
Total after-tax cash flows	−2,200	529	682	798	830	886	1,513
NPV (at r = 12 percent)	1,181						
IRR	26.60%						

Because the NPV of $1,181,000 is positive, the project is profitable for Lawton to undertake. The IRR investment decision rule also indicates that the project is profitable because the IRR of 26.60 percent exceeds the 12 percent required rate of return.

▶ **Solution to 2.** The tax rate and required return can be changed in the spreadsheet model. When these changes are made, the NPV becomes $736,000 and the IRR becomes 24.02 percent. (The revised spreadsheet is not printed here.) Although profitability is lower, the higher tax rate and required rate of return do not change the investment decision.

6.4 Effects of Inflation on Capital Budgeting Analysis

Inflation affects capital budgeting analysis in several ways. The first decision the analyst must make is whether to do the analysis in "normal" terms or in "real" terms. Nominal cash flows include the effects of inflation, while real cash flows are adjusted downward to remove the effects of inflation. It is perfectly acceptable to do the analysis in either nominal or real terms, and sound decisions can be made either way. However, inflation creates some issues regardless of the approach.

The cash flows and discount rate used should both be nominal or both be real. In other words, nominal cash flows should be discounted at a nominal discount rate, and real cash flows should be discounted at a real rate. The real rate, just like real cash flows, has had the effect of inflation taken out. In general, the relationship between real and nominal rates is

$$(1 + \text{Nominal rate}) = (1 + \text{Real rate})(1 + \text{Inflation rate})$$

Inflation reduces the value of depreciation tax savings (unless the tax system adjusts depreciation for inflation). The effect of expected inflation is captured in the discounted cash flow analysis. If inflation is higher than expected, the profitability of the investment is correspondingly lower than expected. Inflation essentially shifts wealth from the taxpayer to the government. Higher-than-expected inflation increases the corporation's real taxes because it reduces the value of the depreciation tax shelter. Conversely, lower-than-expected inflation reduces real taxes (the depreciation tax shelters are more valuable than expected).

Inflation also reduces the value of fixed payments to bondholders. When bonds are originally issued, bondholders pay a price for the bonds reflecting their inflationary expectations. If inflation is higher than expected, the real payments to bondholders are lower than expected. Higher-than-expected inflation shifts wealth from bondholders to the issuing corporations. Conversely, if inflation is lower than expected, the real interest expenses of the corporation increase, shifting wealth from the issuing corporation to its bondholders.

Finally, inflation does not affect all revenues and costs uniformly. The company's after-tax cash flows will be better or worse than expected depending on how particular sales outputs or cost inputs are affected. Furthermore, contracting with customers, suppliers, employees, and sources of capital can be complicated as inflation rises.

The capital budgeting model accommodates the effects of inflation, although inflation complicates the capital budgeting process (and the operations of a business, in general).

PROJECT ANALYSIS AND EVALUATION   7

Assessing the opportunity costs and analyzing the risks of capital investments becomes more complex and sophisticated as you examine real cases. The first project interaction we examine in this section is that of comparing mutually exclusive projects with unequal lives. We will briefly describe other project interactions, but will not examine them in detail. We also examine the process of capital budgeting under capital rationing.

Up to this point, we have largely ignored the issue of accounting for risk. We will introduce risk analysis in two ways. The first is accounting for risk on a stand-alone basis. The second is accounting for risk on a systematic basis.

7.1 Mutually Exclusive Projects with Unequal Lives

We have previously looked at mutually exclusive projects and decided that the best project is the one with the greatest NPV. However, if the mutually exclusive projects have differing lives and the projects will be replaced (or replicated) repeatedly when they wear out, the analysis is more complicated. The analysis of a one-shot (one time only) investment differs from that of an investment chain (in which the asset is replaced regularly in the future).

For example, assume we have two projects with unequal lives of two and three years, with the following after-tax cash flows:

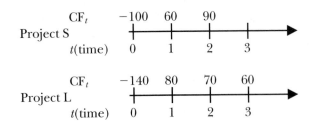

Both projects have a 10 percent required rate of return. The NPV of Project S is $28.93 and the NPV of Project L is $35.66. Given that the two projects are mutually exclusive, Project L, with the greater NPV, should be chosen.

However, let us now assume that these are not one-shot investments, but investments in assets that the company will need to replace when they wear out. Project S would be replaced every two years and Project L every three years. This situation is often referred to as a replacement chain. In this type of problem, you should examine the entire chain and not just the first link in the chain. If the projects are part of a replacement chain, examining the cash flows for only the initial investment for Projects S and L is improper because Project L provides cash flows during Year 3, when Project S provides none.

There are two logically equivalent ways of comparing mutually exclusive projects in a replacement chain. They are the "least common multiple of lives" approach and the "equivalent annual annuity" approach.

7.1.1 Least Common Multiple of Lives Approach

For the least common multiple of lives approach, the analyst extends the time horizon of analysis so that the lives of both projects will divide exactly into the horizon. For Projects S and L, the least common multiple of 2 and 3 is 6: The two-year project would be replicated three times over the six-year horizon and the three-year project would be replicated two times over the six-year horizon.[9] The cash flows for replicating Projects S and L over a six-year horizon are shown below.

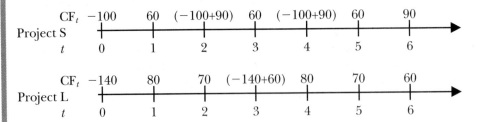

Discounting the cash flows for the six-year horizon results in an NPV for Project S of $72.59 and an NPV for Project L of $62.45. Apparently, investing in Project S and replicating the investment over time has a greater NPV than choosing Project L and replicating it. This decision is the reverse of the one we made when looking solely at the NPVs of the initial investments!

Because the NPV of a single investment represents the present values of its cash flows, you can also visualize the NPV of a replacement chain as the present

---

[9] The least common multiple of lives is not necessarily the product of the two lives, as in the case of Projects S and L. For example, if two projects have lives of 8 and 10 years, the least common multiple of lives is 40 years, not 80. Both 8 and 10 are exactly divisible into 40.

value of the NPVs of each investment (or link) in the chain. For Projects S and L, the NPVs of each investment are shown on the timelines below:

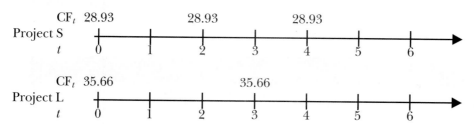

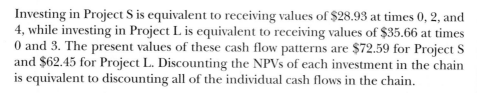

Investing in Project S is equivalent to receiving values of \$28.93 at times 0, 2, and 4, while investing in Project L is equivalent to receiving values of \$35.66 at times 0 and 3. The present values of these cash flow patterns are \$72.59 for Project S and \$62.45 for Project L. Discounting the NPVs of each investment in the chain is equivalent to discounting all of the individual cash flows in the chain.

7.1.2 Equivalent Annual Annuity Approach

The other method for properly evaluating a replacement chain is called the equivalent annual annuity (EAA) approach. The name for this approach is very descriptive. For an investment project with an outlay and variable cash flows in the future, the project NPV summarizes the equivalent value at time zero. For this same project, the EAA is the annuity payment (series of equal annual payments over the project's life) that is equivalent in value to the NPV.

Analysts can use a simple two-step procedure to find the EAA. The first step is to find the present value of all of the cash flows for an investment—the investment's NPV. The second step is to calculate an annuity payment that has a value equivalent to the NPV. For Project S above, we already calculated the NPV of the project over its two-year life to be \$28.93. The second step is to find an annuity payment for the two-year life that is equivalent. For a two-year life and a 10 percent discount rate, a payment of \$16.66 is the equivalent annuity.

The EAA for Project L is found by annuitizing its \$35.66 NPV over three years, so the EAA for Project L is \$14.34.

The decision rule for the EAA approach is to choose the investment chain that has the highest EAA, which in this case is Project S.

Given these two approaches to comparing replacement chains, which one should the analyst use? As a practical matter, the two approaches are logically equivalent and will result in the same decision.[10] Consequently, the analyst can choose one approach over the other based on personal preference. Or, if the audience for the analyst's work prefers to see the analysis using one approach, the analyst can simply produce the analysis in that format.

7.2 Capital Rationing

Capital rationing is the case in which the company's capital budget has a size constraint. For example, the capital budget is a fixed money amount. A fixed capital budget can place the company in several interesting situations. To illustrate these,

---

[10] For Projects S and L, the NPVs of a replacement chain over the least common multiple of lives (six years) were \$72.59 for Project S and \$62.45 for Project L. If we discount the EAA for Project S (\$16.66) and the EAA for Project L (\$14.34) for six years (treating each as a six-year annuity), we have the same NPVs. Hence, the least common multiple of lives and EAA approaches are consistent with each other.

we will assume that the company has a fixed $1,000 capital budget and has the opportunity to invest in four projects. The projects are of variable profitability.

In the first situation, the budget is adequate to invest in all profitable projects. Consider the four projects in Table 47-20:

TABLE 47-20 First Capital Rationing Example

	Investment Outlay	NPV	PI	IRR
Project 1	600	220	1.37	15%
Project 2	200	70	1.35	16%
Project 3	200	−60	0.70	10%
Project 4	400	−100	0.75	8%

In this case, the company has two positive-NPV projects, Projects 1 and 2, which involve a total outlay of $800. Their total NPV is $290. The company should choose these projects, and it will have $200 in its capital budget left over. These excess funds can be used elsewhere in the company (moved to someone else's budget, used to pay dividends or repurchase shares, or used to pay down debt). If a manager is afraid to return the excess funds and chooses to invest in Project 3, the manager will consume the whole capital budget but reduce the total NPV to $230, essentially destroying $60 of wealth for the company.

A second case exists in which the company has more profitable projects than it can choose, but it is able to invest in the most profitable ones available. Continuing with the $1,000 capital budget, this second case is illustrated in Table 47-21:

TABLE 47-21 Second Capital Rationing Example

	Investment Outlay	NPV	PI	IRR
Project 5	600	300	1.50	16%
Project 6	200	80	1.40	18%
Project 7	200	60	1.30	12%
Project 8	200	40	1.20	14%

When the analyst has a fixed budget, the PI is especially useful because it shows the profitability of each investment per currency unit invested. If we rank these projects by their PIs, Projects 5, 6, and 7 are the best projects and we are able to select them. This selection results in a total NPV of $440. The IRRs, shown in the last column, are not a reliable guide to choosing projects under capital rationing because a high-IRR project may have a low NPV. Wealth maximization is best guided by the NPV criterion.

A third case exists in which the company has more profitable projects than it can choose, but it is not able to invest in the most profitable ones available.

Assume the company cannot invest in fractional projects: It must take all or none of each project it chooses. Continuing with the $1,000 capital budget, this case is illustrated in Table 47-22:

TABLE 47-22 Third Capital Rationing Example				
	Investment Outlay	NPV	PI	IRR
Project 9	600	300	1.50	15%
Project 10	600	270	1.45	16%
Project 11	200	80	1.40	12%
Project 12	400	100	1.25	11%

In this example, an unlimited budget of $1,800 would generate a total NPV of $750. However, when the budget constraint is imposed, the highest NPV results from choosing Projects 9 and 12. The company is forced to choose its best project and its fourth-best project, as indicated by their relative PIs. Any other combination of projects either violates the budget or has a lower total NPV.

Capital rationing has the potential to misallocate resources. Capital markets are supposed to allocate funds to their highest and best uses, with the opportunity cost of funds (used as the discount rate for NPVs or the hurdle rate for IRRs) guiding this allocation process. Capital rationing violates market efficiency if society's resources are not allocated where they will generate the best returns. Companies that use capital rationing may be doing either "hard" or "soft" capital rationing. Under hard capital rationing, the budget is fixed and the managers cannot go beyond it. Under soft capital rationing, managers may be allowed to over-spend their budgets if they argue effectively that the additional funds will be deployed profitably.

In the case of hard rationing, choosing the optimal projects that fit within the budget and maximize the NPV of the company can be computationally intensive. Sometimes, managers use estimates and trial and error to find the optimal set of projects. The PI can be used as a guide in this trial and error process. Other times, the number of possibilities is so daunting that mathematical programming algorithms are used.

7.3 Risk Analysis of Capital Investments— Stand-Alone Methods

So far, we have evaluated projects by calculating a single NPV to decide whether a project is profitable. We took a single value, or point estimate, of each input into the model and combined the values to calculate the NPV.

Risk is usually measured as a dispersion of outcomes. In the case of stand-alone risk, we typically measure the riskiness of a project by the dispersion of its NPVs or the dispersion of its IRRs. Sensitivity analysis, scenario analysis, and simulation analysis are very popular stand-alone risk analysis methods. These risk measures depend on the variation of the project's cash flows.

To illustrate the stand-alone risk tools, we will use the following "base case" capital project:

Unit price	$5.00
Annual unit sales	40,000
Variable cost per unit	$1.50
Investment in fixed capital	$300,000
Investment in working capital	$50,000
Project life	6 years
Depreciation (straight-line)	$50,000
Expected salvage value	$60,000
Tax rate	40 percent
Required rate of return	12 percent

The outlay, from Equation 47-6, is $300,000 plus $50,000, or $350,000. The annual after-tax operating cash flow, from Equation 47-7, is

$$\begin{aligned} CF &= (S - C - D)(1 - T) + D \\ &= [(5 \times 40{,}000) - (1.50 \times 40{,}000) - (50{,}000)](1 - 0.40) + 50{,}000 \\ &= \$104{,}000 \end{aligned}$$

The terminal year after-tax non-operating cash flow, from Equation 47-9, is

$$\begin{aligned} TNOCF &= Sal_6 + NWCInv - T(Sal_6 - B_6) \\ &= 60{,}000 + 50{,}000 - 0.40(60{,}000 - 0) = \$86{,}000 \end{aligned}$$

The project NPV is

$$NPV = -350{,}000 + \sum_{t=1}^{6} \frac{104{,}000}{1.12^t} + \frac{86{,}000}{1.12^6} = -350{,}000 + 471{,}157 = \$121{,}157$$

7.3.1 Sensitivity Analysis

Sensitivity analysis calculates the effect on the NPV of changes in one input variable at a time. The base case above has several input variables. If we wish to do a sensitivity analysis of several of them, we must specify the changes in each that we wish to evaluate. Suppose we want to consider the following:

	Base Value	Low Value	High Value
Unit price	$5.00	$4.50	$5.50
Annual unit sales	40,000	35,000	45,000
Variable cost per unit	$1.50	$1.40	$1.60
Expected salvage value	$60,000	$30,000	$80,000
Tax rate	40%	38%	42%
Required rate of return	12%	10%	14%

We have changed each of six input variables. Table 47-23 shows the NPV calculated for the base case. Then the NPV is recalculated by changing one variable from its base case value to its high or low value.

TABLE 47-23 Sensitivity of Project NPV to Changes in a Variable				
	Project NPV			
Variable	**Base Case**	**With Low Estimate**	**With High Estimate**	**Range of Estimates**
Unit price	$121,157	$71,820	$170,494	$98,674
Annual unit sales	$121,157	$77,987	$164,326	$86,339
Cost per unit	$121,157	$131,024	$111,289	$19,735
Salvage value	$121,157	$112,037	$127,236	$15,199
Tax rate	$121,157	$129,165	$113,148	$16,017
Required return	$121,157	$151,492	$93,602	$57,890

As Table 47-23 shows, the project's NPV is most sensitive to changes in the unit price variable. The project's NPV is least sensitive to changes in the salvage value. Roughly speaking, the project's NPV is most sensitive to changes in unit price and in unit sales. It is least affected by changes in cost per unit, salvage value, and the tax rate. Changes in the required rate of return also have a substantial effect, but not as much as changes in price or unit sales.

In a sensitivity analysis, the manager can choose which variables to change and by how much. Many companies have access to software that can be instructed to change a particular variable by a certain amount—for example, to increase or decrease unit price, unit sales, and cost per unit by 10 percent. The software then produces the changes in NPV for each of these changes. Sensitivity analysis can be used to establish which variables are most influential on the success or failure of a project.

7.3.2 Scenario Analysis

Sensitivity analysis calculates the effect on the NPV of changes in one variable at a time. In contrast, scenario analysis creates scenarios that consist of changes in several of the input variables and calculates the NPV for each scenario. Although corporations could do a large number of scenarios, in practice they usually do only three. They can be labeled variously, but we will present an example with "pessimistic," "most likely," and "optimistic" scenarios. Continuing with the basic example from the section above, the values of the input variables for the three scenarios are given in the table below.

TABLE 47-24 Input Variables and NPV for Scenario Analysis			
	Scenario		
Variable	**Pessimistic**	**Most Likely**	**Optimistic**
Unit price	$4.50	$5.00	$5.50
Annual unit sales	35,000	40,000	45,000

(Table continued on next page …)

TABLE 47-24   Input Variables and NPV for Scenario Analysis (continued)

	Scenario		
Variable	Pessimistic	Most Likely	Optimistic
Variable cost per unit	$1.60	$1.50	$1.40
Investment in fixed capital	$320,000	$300,000	$280,000
Investment in working capital	$50,000	$50,000	$50,000
Project life	6 years	6 years	6 years
Depreciation (straight-line)	$53,333	$50,000	$46,667
Salvage value	$40,000	$60,000	$80,000
Tax rate	40%	40%	40%
Required rate of return	13%	12%	11%
NPV	−$5,725	$121,157	$269,685
IRR	12.49%	22.60%	34.24%

The most likely scenario is the same as the base case we used above for sensitivity analysis, and the NPV for the most likely scenario is $121,157. To form the pessimistic and optimistic scenarios, managers change several of the assumptions for each scenario. For the pessimistic scenario, several of the input variables are changed to reflect higher costs, lower revenues, and a higher required rate of return. As the table shows, the result is a negative NPV for the pessimistic scenario and an IRR that is less than the pessimistic scenario's 13 percent required rate of return. For the optimistic scenario, the more favorable revenues, costs, and required rate of return result in very good NPV and IRR.

For this example, the scenario analysis reveals the possibility of an unprofitable investment, with a negative NPV and with an IRR less than the cost of capital. The range for the NPV is fairly large compared to the size of the initial investment, which indicates that the investment is fairly risky. This example included three scenarios for which management wants to know the profitability of the investment for each set of assumptions. Other scenarios can be investigated if management chooses to do so.

7.3.3 Simulation (Monte Carlo) Analysis

Simulation analysis is a procedure for estimating a probability distribution of outcomes, such as for the NPV or IRR for a capital investment project. Instead of assuming a single value (a point estimate) for the input variables in a capital budgeting spreadsheet, the analyst can assume several variables to be stochastic, following their own probability distributions. By simulating the results hundreds or thousands of times, the analyst can build a good estimate of the distributions for the NPV or IRR. Because of the volume of computations, analysts and corporate managers rel heavily on their personal computers and specialized simulation software such as @RISK.[11] Example 47-8 presents a simple simulation analysis.

---

[11] @RISK is a popular and powerful risk analysis tool sold by Palisade Corporation. @RISK is an add-in for Microsoft Excel that allows simulation techniques to be incorporated into spreadsheet models.

Example 47-8

Capital Budgeting Simulation

Gouhua Zhang has made the following assumptions for a capital budgeting project:

▶ Fixed capital investment is 20,000; no investment in net working capital is required.

▶ The project has an expected five-year life.

▶ The fixed capital is depreciated straight-line to zero over a five-year life. The salvage value is normally distributed with an expected value of 2,000 and a standard deviation of 500.

▶ Unit sales in Year 1 are normally distributed with a mean of 2,000 and a standard deviation of 200.

▶ Unit sales growth after Year 1 is normally distributed with a mean of 6 percent and standard deviation of 4 percent. Assume the same sales growth rate for Years 2–5.

▶ The sales price is 5.00 per unit, normally distributed with a standard deviation of 0.25 per unit. The same price holds for all five years.

▶ Cash operating expenses as a percentage of total revenue are normally distributed with a mean and standard deviation of 30 percent and 3 percent, respectively.

▶ The discount rate is 12 percent and the tax rate is 40 percent.

1. What are the NPV and IRR using the expected values of all input variables?

2. Perform a simulation analysis and provide probability distributions for the NPV and IRR.

▶ **Solution to 1.**

TABLE 47-25   Expected Cash Flows for Simulation Example

Time	0	1	2	3	4	5
Fixed capital	−20,000					
After-tax salvage value						1,200
Price		5.00	5.00	5.00	5.00	5.00
Output		2,000	2,120	2,247	2,382	2,525
Revenue		10,000	10,600	11,236	11,910	12,625
Cash operating expenses		3,000	3,180	3,371	3,573	3,787
Depreciation		4,000	4,000	4,000	4,000	4,000
Operating income before taxes		3,000	3,420	3,865	4,337	4,837
Taxes on operating income		1,200	1,368	1,546	1,735	1,935

(Table continued on next page …)

TABLE 47-25	Expected Cash Flows for Simulation Example (continued)					
Time	0	1	2	3	4	5
Operating income after taxes		1,800	2,052	2,319	2,602	2,902
Depreciation		4,000	4,000	4,000	4,000	4,000
Total after-tax cash flow	−20,000	5,800	6,052	6,319	6,602	8,102
NPV (at $r = 12$ percent)	3,294					
IRR	18.11%					

Based on the point estimates for each variable (the mean values for each), which are shown in Table 47-25 above, Zhang should find the NPV to be 3,294 and the IRR to be 18.11 percent.

▶ **Solution to 2.** Zhang performs a simulation using @RISK with 10,000 iterations. For each iteration, values for the five stochastic variables (price, output, output growth rate, cash expense percentage, and salvage value) are selected from their assumed distributions and the NPV and IRR are calculated. After the 10,000 iterations, the resulting information about the probability distributions for the NPV and IRR is shown in Figure 47-6 and Table 47-26.

FIGURE 47-6   Probability Distributions for NPV and IRR

A. Distribution for NPV

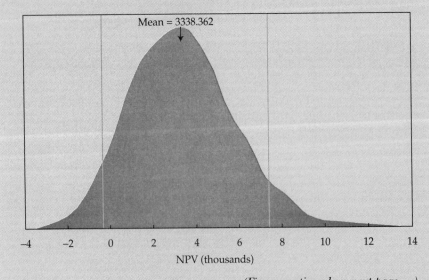

NPV (thousands)

(Figure continued on next page ...)

FIGURE 47-6 (continued)

B. Distribution for IRR

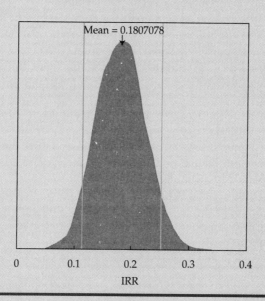

As the figure shows, the distributions for the NPV and IRR are somewhat normal looking. The means and standard deviations for each are given in Table 47-26. Both distributions have a slight positive skewness, which means the distributions are skewed to the right. The two kurtosis values are fairly close to 3.0, which means

TABLE 47-26 Summary Statistics for NPV and IRR

Statistic	NPV	IRR
Mean	3,338	18.07%
Standard deviation	2,364	4.18%
Skewness	0.2909	0.1130
Kurtosis	3.146	2.996
Median	3,236	18.01%
90% confidence interval	−3,779 to 7,413	11.38% to 25.13%

Correlations between Input Variables and NPV and IRR

Input Variable	NPV	IRR
Output	0.71	0.72
Output growth rate	0.49	0.47
Price	0.34	0.34
Cash expense proportion	−0.28	−0.29
Salvage value	0.06	0.05

OPTIONAL SEGMENT

that the distributions are not peaked or fat-tailed compared to the standard normal distribution. The median is the value at which 50 percent of the 10,000 outcomes fall on either side. The 90 percent confidence intervals show that 90 percent of the observations fall between $-3,779$ and $7,413$ for the NPV and between 11.38 percent and 25.13 percent for the IRR. Although not shown in the table, 7.04 percent of the observations had a negative NPV and an IRR less than the 12 percent discount rate.

The means of the NPV and IRR from the simulation (in Table 47-26) are fairly close to their values calculated using point estimates for all of the input variables (in Table 47-25). This is not always the case, but it is here. The additional information from a simulation is the dispersions of the NPV and IRR. Given his assumptions and model, the simulation results show Zhang the distributions of NPV and IRR outcomes that should be expected. Managers and analysts often prefer to know these total distributions rather than just their mean values.

The correlations in Table 47-26 can be interpreted as sensitivity measures. Changes in the "output" variable have the highest correlation with NPV and IRR outcomes. The salvage value has the lowest (absolute value) correlation.

This capital budgeting simulation example was not very complex, with only five stochastic variables. The example's five input variables were assumed to be normally distributed—in reality, many other distributions can be employed. Finally, the randomly chosen values for each variable were assumed to be independent. They can be selected jointly instead of independently. Simulation techniques have proved to be a boon for addressing capital budgeting problems.

Sensitivity analysis, scenario analysis, and simulation analysis are well-developed stand-alone risk analysis methods. These risk measures depend on the variation of the project's cash flows. Market risk measures, presented in the next section, depend not only on the variation of a project's cash flows, but also on how those cash flows covary with (or correlate with) market returns.

7.4 Risk Analysis of Capital Investments— Market Risk Methods

When using market risk methods, the discount rate to be used in evaluating a capital project is the rate of return required on the project by a diversified investor. The discount rate should thus be a risk-adjusted discount rate, which includes a premium to compensate investors for risk.[12] This risk premium should reflect factors that are priced or valued in the marketplace. The two equilibrium models for estimating this risk premium are the capital asset pricing model (CAPM) and **arbitrage pricing theory (APT)**. We will discuss the CAPM as a way of finding risk-adjusted discount rates, although you should be aware that other methods can be used.

In the CAPM, total risk can be broken into two components: systematic risk and unsystematic risk. Systematic risk is the portion of risk that is related to the market and that cannot be diversified away. **Unsystematic risk** is non-market risk,

---

[12] Our approach to capital budgeting is to discount expected cash flows at a risk-adjusted cost of capital. An alternative approach, which is also conceptually sound, is the "certainty-equivalent method." In this method, certainty-equivalent cash flows (expected cash flows that are reduced to certainty equivalents) are valued by discounting them at a risk-free discount rate. The use of risk-adjusted discount rates is more intuitive and much more popular.

risk that is idiosyncratic and that can be diversified away. Diversified investors can demand a risk premium for taking systematic risk, but not unsystematic risk.[13] Hence, the stand-alone risk measures—total risk measured by the dispersion of the NPV or the IRR—are inappropriate when the corporation is diversified, or, as is more likely, when the corporation's investors are themselves diversified.

In the capital asset pricing model, a project's or asset's "beta," or β, is generally used as a measure of systematic risk. **The security market line (SML)** expresses the asset's required rate of return as a function of β:

$$r_i = R_F + \beta_i[E(R_M) - R_F] \qquad \textbf{(47-10)}$$

where

r_i = required return for project or asset i
R_F = risk-free rate of return
β_i = beta of project or asset i
$[E(R_M) - R_F]$ = **market risk premium**, the difference between the expected market return and the risk-free rate of return

The project's required rate of return is equal to the risk-free rate plus a risk premium, where the risk premium is the product of the project beta and the market risk premium.

Here, the required rate of return (sometimes called a hurdle rate) is specific to the risk of the project. There is no one hurdle rate appropriate for all projects.

The security market line (SML) is graphed in Figure 47-7. This line indicates the required rate of return for a project, given its beta. The required rate of return can be used in two ways:

▶ The SML is used to find the required rate of return. The required rate of return is then used to find the NPV. Positive NPV projects are accepted and negative NPV projects are rejected.

FIGURE 47-7   SML for Capital Budgeting Projects

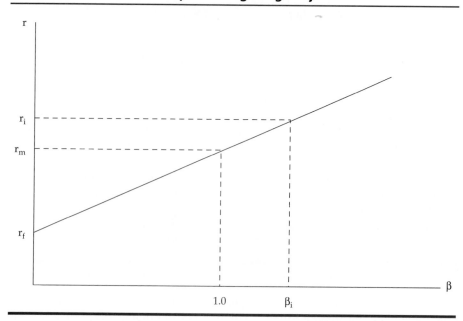

---

[13] The capital asset pricing model uses this intuition to show how risky assets should be priced relative to the market. While the CAPM assigns a single market risk premium for each security, the APT develops a set of risk premia. The CAPM and APT are developed in detail elsewhere in the CFA curriculum.

▶ The SML is used to find the required rate of return. The project's IRR is compared to the required rate of return. If the IRR is greater than the required return, the project is accepted (this point would plot above the SML in Figure 47-7). If the IRR is less than the required rate of return (below the SML), the project is rejected.

Example 47-9 illustrates how the capital asset pricing model and the security market line are used as part of the capital budgeting process.

Example 47-9

Using the SML to Find the Project Required Rate of Return

Premont Systems is evaluating a capital project with the following characteristics:

▶ The initial outlay is €150,000.

▶ Annual after-tax operating cash flows are €28,000.

▶ After-tax salvage value at project termination is €20,000.

▶ Project life is 10 years.

▶ The project beta is 1.20.

▶ The risk-free rate is 4.2 percent and the expected market return is 9.4 percent.

1. Compute the project NPV. Should the project be accepted?

2. Compute the project IRR. Should the project be accepted?

▶ **Solution to 1.** The project required rate of return is

$$r_i = R_F + \beta_i[E(R_M) - R_F] = 4.2\% + 1.20(9.4\% - 4.2\%)$$
$$= 4.2\% + 6.24\% = 10.44\%$$

The cash flows discounted at 10.44 percent give an NPV of

$$NPV = -150,000 + \sum_{t=1}^{10} \frac{28,000}{1.1044^t} + \frac{20,000}{1.1044^{10}} = €26,252$$

The project should be accepted because it has a positive NPV.

▶ **Solution to 2.** The IRR, found with a financial calculator, is 14.24 percent. The required rate of return, established with the SML as in the solution to Question 1 above, is 10.44 percent. Since the IRR exceeds the required rate of return, the project should be accepted. For a beta of 1.20, the IRR of 14.24 percent would plot above the SML.

Using project betas to establish required rates of return for capital projects is especially important when a project's risk differs from that of the company. The cost of capital for a company is estimated for the company as a whole—it is based on the average riskiness of the company's assets as well as its financial structure. The required rates of return of debt and equity are used to estimate the weighted (overall) average cost of capital (WACC) for the company. When a project under consideration is more risky or less risky than the company, the WACC should not be used as the project required rate of return.

For example, assume that the risk-free rate of return is 3 percent, the market return is 8 percent, and the company beta is 0.9. Assume also that the company is considering three projects: Project A with a 0.5 beta, Project B with a 0.9 beta, and Project C with a 1.1 beta. The required rates of return for the company and for each project are as follows:

Company: $3\% + 0.9(8\% - 3\%) = 7.5\%$
Project A: $3\% + 0.5(8\% - 3\%) = 5.5\%$
Project B: $3\% + 0.9(8\% - 3\%) = 7.5\%$
Project C: $3\% + 1.1(8\% - 3\%) = 8.5\%$

If management uses the company WACC as the required return for all projects, this rate is too high for Project A, making it less likely that Project A would be accepted. Project B has the same risk as the company, so it would be evaluated fairly. Using the WACC for Project C makes the error of using a discount rate that is too low, which would make it more likely that this high-risk project would be accepted. Whenever possible, it is desirable to use project-specific required rates of return instead of the company's overall required rate of return.

Market returns are readily available for publicly traded companies. The stock betas of these companies can then be calculated, and this calculation assists in estimating the companies' betas and WACC. Unfortunately, however, the returns for specific capital projects are not directly observable, and we have to use proxies for their betas. Frequently, we can employ the pure-play method, in which the analyst identifies other publicly traded stocks in the same business as the project being considered. The betas for the stocks of these companies are used to estimate a project beta. In the pure-play method, these proxy companies need to be relatively focused in the same line of business as the project. When the pure-play method is not possible, other methods, such as estimating accounting betas or cross-sectional regression analysis, are used.

7.5 Real Options

Real options are capital budgeting options that allow managers to make decisions in the future that alter the value of capital budgeting investment decisions made today. Instead of making all capital budgeting decisions now, at time zero, managers can wait and make additional decisions at future dates when these future decisions are contingent upon future economic events or information. These sequential decisions, in which future decisions depend on the decisions made today as well as on future economic events, are very realistic capital budgeting applications.

Real options are like financial options—they just deal with real assets instead of financial assets. A simple financial option could be a call option on a share of stock. Suppose the stock is selling for $50, the exercise (strike) price is $50, and the option expires in one year. If the stock goes up to $60, you exercise the option and have a gain of $10 in one year. If the stock goes down to $40, you do not exercise, and you have no gain. However, no gain is better than the $10 loss you would have had if you had purchased the stock at the beginning of the year. Real options, like financial options, entail the right to make a decision, but not the obligation. The corporation should exercise a real option only if it is value-enhancing.

Just as financial options are contingent on an underlying asset, real options are contingent on future events. The flexibility that real options give to managers can greatly enhance the NPV of the company's capital investments. The following are several types of these real options:

Timing Options   Instead of investing now, the company can delay investing. Delaying an investment and basing the decision on hopefully improved information that you might have in, say, a year could help improve the NPV of the projects selected.

Sizing Options   If after investing, the company can abandon the project when the financial results are disappointing, it has an **abandonment option**. At some future date, if the cash flow from abandoning a project exceeds the present value of the cash flows from continuing the project, managers should exercise the abandonment option. Conversely, if the company can make additional investments when future financial results are strong, the company has a **growth option** or an **expansion option**.

Flexibility Options   Once an investment is made, other operational flexibilities may be available besides abandonment or expansion. For example, suppose demand exceeds capacity. Management may be able to exercise a **price-setting option**. By increasing prices, the company could benefit from the excess demand, which it cannot do by increasing production. There are also **production-flexibility** options. Even though it is expensive, the company can profit from working overtime or from adding additional shifts. The company can also work with customers and suppliers for their mutual benefit whenever a demand–supply mismatch occurs. This type of option also includes the possibility of using different inputs or producing different outputs.

Fundamental Options   In cases like those above, there are options embedded in a project that can raise its value. In other cases, the whole investment is essentially an option. The payoffs from the investment are contingent on an underlying asset, just like most financial options. For example, the value of an oil well or refinery investment is contingent upon the price of oil. The value of a gold mine is contingent upon the price of gold. If oil prices are low, you may not drill a well. If oil prices are high, you go ahead and drill. Many R&D (research and development) projects also look like options.

There are several approaches to evaluating capital budgeting projects with real options. One of the difficulties with real options is that the analysis can be very complicated. Although some of the problems are simple and can be readily solved, many of them are so complex that they are expensive to evaluate or you may not have much confidence in the analysis. Four common sense approaches to real options analysis are presented below.

1. Use DCF analysis without considering options. If the NPV is positive without considering real options, and the project has real options that would simply add more value, it is unnecessary to evaluate the options. Just go ahead and make the investment.

2. Consider the Project NPV = NPV(based on DCF alone) − Cost of options + Value of options. Go ahead and calculate the NPV based on expected cash flows. Then simply add the value associated with real options. For example, if a project has a negative NPV based on DCF alone of $50 million, will the options add at least that much to its value?

3. Use decision trees. Although they are not as conceptually sound as option pricing models, decision trees can capture the essence of many sequential decision making problems.

4. Use option pricing models. Except for simple options, the technical requirements for solving these models may require you to hire special consultants or "quants." Some large companies have their own specialists.

The analyst is confronted with (1) a variety of real options that investment projects may possess and (2) a decision about how to reasonably value these options. Example 47-10 deals with production flexibility; in this case, an additional investment outlay gives the company an option to use alternative fuel sources.

Example 47-10

Production-Flexibility Option

Sackley AquaFarms estimated the NPV of the expected cash flows from a new processing plant to be −$0.40 million. Sackley is evaluating an incremental investment of $0.30 million that would give management the flexibility to switch between coal, natural gas, and oil as an energy source. The original plant relied only on coal. The option to switch to cheaper sources of energy when they are available has an estimated value of $1.20 million. What is the value of the new processing plant including this real option to use alternative energy sources?

▶ **Solution.** The NPV, including the real option, should be

$$\text{Project NPV} = \text{NPV(based on DCF alone)} - \text{Cost of options} + \text{Value of options}$$
$$\text{Project NPV} = -0.40 \text{ million} - 0.30 \text{ million} + 1.20 \text{ million} = \$0.50 \text{ million}.$$

Without the flexibility offered by the real option, the plant is unprofitable. The real option to adapt to cheaper energy sources adds enough to the value of this investment to give it a positive NPV.

Two of the most valuable options are to abandon or expand a project at some point after the original investment. Example 47-11 illustrates the abandonment option.

Example 47-11

Abandonment Option

Nyberg Systems is considering a capital project with the following characteristics:

▶ The initial outlay is €200,000.

▶ Project life is four years.

▶ Annual after-tax operating cash flows have a 50 percent probability of being €40,000 for the four years and a 50 percent probability of being €80,000.

▶ Salvage value at project termination is zero.

▶ The required rate of return is 10 percent.

▶ In one year, after realizing the first-year cash flow, the company has the option to abandon the project and receive the salvage value of €150,000.

1. Compute the project NPV assuming no abandonment.

2. What is the optimal abandonment strategy? Compute the project NPV using that strategy.

▶ **Solution to 1.** The expected annual after-tax operating cash flow is $0.50(40,000) + 0.50(80,000) = €60,000$. The cash flows discounted at 10 percent give an NPV of

$$NPV = -200,000 + \sum_{t=1}^{4} \frac{60,000}{1.10^t} = -€9,808$$

The project should be rejected because it has a negative NPV.

▶ **Solution to 2.** The optimal abandonment strategy would be to abandon the project in one year if the subsequent cash flows are worth less than the abandonment value. If at the end of the first year the low cash flow occurs, you can abandon for €150,000 and give up €40,000 for the following three years. The €40,000 annual cash flow, discounted for three years at 10 percent, has a present value of only €99,474, so you should abandon. Three years of the higher €80,000 cash flow has a present value of €198,948, so you should not abandon. After the first year, abandon if the low cash flow occurs, and do not abandon if the high cash flow occurs.

If the high cash flow occurs and you do not abandon, the NPV is

$$NPV = -200,000 + \sum_{t=1}^{4} \frac{80,000}{1.10^t} = €53,589$$

If you abandon when the low cash flow occurs, you receive the first year cash flow and the abandonment value and then no further cash flows. In that case, the NPV is

$$NPV = -200,000 + \frac{40,000 + 150,000}{1.10} = -€27,273$$

The expected NPV is then

$$NPV = 0.50(53,589) + 0.50(-27,273) = €13,158$$

Optimal abandonment raises the NPV by $13,158 - (-€9,808) = €22,966$.

A fundamental real option could be a gold mine or an oil well. Example 47-12 looks at the possibility of purchasing the rights to a gold mining property.

A critical assumption of many applications of traditional capital budgeting tools is that the investment decision is made now, with no flexibility considered in future decisions. A more reasonable approach is to assume that the corporation is

Example 47-12

Erichmann Gold Mine

The Erichmann family has offered a five-year option on one of its small gold mining properties for $10 million. The current price of gold is $400 per ounce. The mine holds an estimated 500,000 ounces that could be mined at an average cost of $450 per ounce. The maximum production rate is 200,000 ounces per year. How would you assess the Erichmann family's offer?

▶ **Solution.** A binomial option model can be built for the underlying price of gold. These binomial models are very common in assessing the value of financial options such as puts and calls on stocks, callable bonds, or mortgages with prepayment options. Whenever the price path for gold is above $450 per ounce, it might be attractive to commence mining. Of course, you would cease mining whenever the price is lower. With additional information about the volatility of gold prices and the risk-free interest rate, an expert could build this binomial model and value the real option. Comparing the value of this real option to its $10 million cost would enable you to make an investment decision.

making sequential decisions, some now and some in the future. A combination of optimal current and future decisions is what will maximize company value. Real options analysis tries to incorporate rational future decisions into the assessment of current investment decision making. This future flexibility, exercised intelligently, enhances the value of capital investments. Some real options can be valued with readily available option pricing models, such as the binomial model or the Black–Scholes–Merton option pricing model.[14] Unfortunately, many real options are very complex and hard to value, which poses a challenge as the analyst tries to lay out the economic contingencies of an investment and assess their values. A real option, with the future flexibility it provides, can be an important piece of the value of many projects.

7.6 Common Capital Budgeting Pitfalls

Although the principles of capital budgeting may be easy to learn, applying the principles to real world investment opportunities can be challenging. Some of the common mistakes that managers make are listed in Table 47-27.

TABLE 47-27   Common Capital Budgeting Pitfalls

Not incorporating economic responses into the investment analysis

Misusing capital budgeting templates

Pet projects

Basing investment decisions on EPS, net income, or return on equity

(Table continued on next page ...)

---

[14] Chapter 4 of Chance (2003) gives an excellent overview of option pricing models.

TABLE 47-27   Common Capital Budgeting Pitfalls (continued)

Using IRR to make investment decisions

Bad accounting for cash flows

Overhead costs

Not using the appropriate risk-adjusted discount rate

Spending all of the investment budget just because it is available

Failure to consider investment alternatives

Handling sunk costs and opportunity costs incorrectly

Economic responses. Economic responses to an investment often affect its profitability, and these responses have to be correctly anticipated. For example, in response to a successful investment, competitors can enter and reduce the investment's profitability. Similarly, vendors, suppliers, and employees may want to gain from a profitable enterprise. Companies that make highly profitable investments often find that a competitive marketplace eventually causes profitability to revert to normal levels.

Template errors. Because hundreds or even thousands of projects need to be analyzed over time, corporations have standardized capital budgeting templates for managers to use in evaluating projects. This situation creates risks in that the template model may not match the project, or employees may input inappropriate information.

Pet projects. Pet projects are projects that influential managers want the corporation to invest in. Ideally, pet projects will receive the normal scrutiny that other investments receive and will be selected on the strength of their own merits. Often, unfortunately, pet projects are selected without undergoing normal capital budgeting analysis. Or the pet project receives the analysis, but overly optimistic projections are used to inflate the project's profitability.

EPS, net income, or ROE. Managers sometimes have incentives to boost EPS, net income, or ROE. Many investments, even those with strong NPVs, do not boost these accounting numbers in the short run and may even reduce them. Paying attention to short-run accounting numbers can result in choosing projects that are not in the long-run economic interests of the business.

Basing decisions on the IRR. The NPV criterion is economically sound. The IRR criterion is also sound for independent projects (with conventional cash flow patterns). If projects are mutually exclusive or competitive with each other, investing in projects based on the IRR will tend to result in choosing smaller, short-term projects with high IRRs at the expense of larger, longer-term, high NPV projects. Basing decisions on paybacks or accounting rates of return is even more dangerous. These measures can be economically unsound.

Bad accounting for cash flows. In analyzing a complicated project, it is easy to omit relevant cash flows, double count cash flows, and mishandle taxes.

Overhead costs. In large companies, the cost of a project must include the overhead it generates for such things as management time, information technology support, financial systems, and other support. Although these items are hard to estimate, over- or underestimating these overhead costs can lead to poor investment decisions.

Discount rate errors. The required rate of return for a project should be based on its risk. If a project is being financed with debt (or with equity), you should still use the project's required rate of return and not the cost of debt (or the cost of equity). Similarly, a high-risk project should not be discounted at the company's overall cost of capital, but at the project's required rate of return. Discount rate errors have a huge impact on the computed NPVs of long-lived projects.

Overspending and underspending the capital budget. Politically, many managers will spend all of their budget and argue that their budget is too small. In a well-run company, managers will return excess funds whenever their profitable projects cost less than their budget, and managers will make a sound case for extra funds if their budget is too small.

Failure to consider investment alternatives. Generating good investment ideas is the most basic step in the capital budgeting process, and many good alternatives are never even considered.

Sunk costs and opportunity costs. Ignoring sunk costs is difficult for managers to do. Furthermore, not identifying the economic alternatives (real and financial) that are the opportunity costs is probably the biggest failure in much analysis. Only costs that change with the decision are relevant.

OTHER INCOME MEASURES AND VALUATION MODELS

8

Capital budgeting was one of the first widespread applications of discounted cash flow analysis. In the basic capital budgeting model, the analyst values an investment by discounting future after-tax cash flows at the rate of return required by investors. Subtracting the initial investment results in the project's NPV. The future cash flows consist of after-tax operating cash flows plus returns of investment (such as salvage value and sale of working capital).

Analysts will employ and encounter other concepts of income and other valuation approaches besides this basic capital budgeting model. Because some of these other approaches are economically sound and widely employed, we will briefly describe some of them here. By considering these approaches, you can see the distinguishing features of each approach and that they should result in consistent valuations (if they are used correctly).

To facilitate the comparison of income measures and valuation models, we will employ as an example a simple company (the Granite Corporation) that invests in one project. The company goes out of business when that project expires. After evaluating that project with the NPV and IRR capital budgeting models, we will examine that same project using the following alternative methods:

▶ Economic income and accounting income
▶ Economic profit valuation
▶ Residual income valuation
▶ Claims valuation

Our purpose is to show how the various income measures and valuation methods are related to each other.

Table 47-28 Basic Capital Budgeting Example for Granite Corporation						
Year	0	1	2	3	4	5
Fixed capital investment	−150,000					
Sales		150,000	200,000	250,000	200,000	150,000
Variable cash expenses		75,000	100,000	125,000	100,000	75,000
Fixed cash expenses		20,000	20,000	20,000	20,000	20,000
Depreciation		30,000	30,000	30,000	30,000	30,000
Operating income before taxes		25,000	50,000	75,000	50,000	25,000
Taxes at 40 percent		10,000	20,000	30,000	20,000	10,000
Operating income after taxes		15,000	30,000	45,000	30,000	15,000
After-tax operating cash flow		45,000	60,000	75,000	60,000	45,000
Salvage value						10,000
Taxes on salvage value						4,000
After-tax salvage value						6,000
Total after-tax cash flow	−150,000	45,000	60,000	75,000	60,000	51,000
NPV (at r = 10 percent)	69,492					
IRR	26.27%					

8.1 The Basic Capital Budgeting Model

The basic capital budgeting model (presented earlier) identifies the after-tax operating cash flows from an investment as well as non-operating cash flows (such as the initial investment or future recovery of invested capital or net working capital). Then, these cash flows are discounted at the required rate of return for the asset to establish the NPV.

The base-case capital budgeting project is the following. The company is going to invest $150,000 and generate sales for the next five years as shown in Table 47-28. Variable cash operating expenses will be 50 percent of sales each year, and fixed cash operating expenses are $20,000. Depreciation is straight-line to zero, $30,000 per year with a zero book value at the end of five years. The income tax rate is 40 percent. Salvage value is $10,000, which is taxable at 40 percent, leaving an after-tax salvage value of $6,000 at the end of five years. The required rate of return is 10 percent.

The present value of the after-tax cash flows for Years 1–5 is $219,492. Subtracting the investment of $150,000 results in the NPV of $69,492. The IRR for the investment is 26.27 percent.

8.2 Economic and Accounting Income

Economic income and accounting income differ from the after-tax operating cash flows used in the basic capital budgeting model.

Economic income is the profit realized from an investment. For a given year, economic income is the investment's after-tax cash flow plus the change in the market value:

$$\text{Economic income} = \text{Cash flow} + \text{Change in market value}$$
$$\text{Economic income} = \text{Cash flow} + (\text{Ending market value} - \text{Beginning market value})$$

or

$$\text{Economic income} = \text{Cash flow} - (\text{Beginning market value} - \text{Ending market value})$$
$$\text{Economic income} = \text{Cash flow} - \text{Economic depreciation}^{15}$$

(47-11)

For the Granite Corporation, the cash flows are already calculated in Table 47-28. The beginning market value at time zero is the present value of the future after-tax cash flows at the 10 percent required rate of return, or $219,492. The market value at any future date is the present value of subsequent cash flows discounted back to that date. For the Granite Corporation, the cash flows, changes in market value, and economic incomes are shown in Table 47-29.

In Year 1, the beginning value is $219,492 and the ending value is $196,441, so the change in value is −$23,051. The economic income is the cash flow plus the change in value, or $45,000 + (−$23,051) = $21,949. The economic income for Years 2–5 is found similarly. The economic rate of return is the year's economic income divided by its beginning market value. Notice that the economic rate of return is precisely 10 percent each year, which was the required rate of return on the project.

Accounting income for this company will differ from the economic income for two reasons. First, the accounting depreciation is based on the original cost of the investment (not the market value of the investment). Consequently, the accounting depreciation schedule does not follow the declines in the market value of an asset. Besides being based on accounting depreciation instead of economic depreciation, accounting net income is the after-tax income remaining after paying interest expenses on the company's debt obligations. In contrast, interest expenses are ignored when computing the economic income for an asset or the after-tax operating cash flows in the basic capital budgeting model. As explained in Section 3, the effects of financing costs are captured in the

TABLE 47-29   Economic Income for Granite Corporation

Year	1	2	3	4	5
Beginning market value	219,492	196,441	156,086	96,694	46,364
Ending market value	196,441	156,086	96,694	46,364	0
Change in market value	−23,051	−40,356	−59,391	−50,331	−46,364
After-tax cash flow	45,000	60,000	75,000	60,000	51,000
Economic income	21,949	19,644	15,609	9,669	4,636
Economic rate of return	10%	10%	10%	10%	10%

---

[15] These equations are conceptually identical because economic depreciation is the negative of the change in market value. For example, assume the cash flow is 10, the beginning market value is 30, and the ending market value is 25. Cash flow + Change in market value = Cash flow + (Ending market value − Beginning market value) = 10 + (25 − 30) = 5. Or, Cash flow − Economic depreciation = Cash flow − (Beginning market value − Ending market value) = 10 − (30 − 25) = 5.

discount rate, not in the cash flows. In the capital budgeting model, if we included interest expenses in the cash flows, we would be double counting them.

To illustrate these differences, we will assume that the company borrows an amount equal to one-half of the value of the company, which is 50 percent of $219,492, or $109,746, and that it pays 8 1/3 percent interest each year on the beginning balance. With a 40 percent tax rate, the after-tax interest cost is 8 1/3% $(1 − 0.40) = 5.0\%$. Because the Granite Corporation has a five-year life, it does not need to borrow or retain earnings for the future, and all cash flows will be distributed to bondholders and stockholders. Granite will maintain a 50 percent debt/value ratio on the company's debt, so bondholders will receive 8 1/3 percent interest on their beginning bond balance and the debt will also be amortized (paid down) whenever the value of the company goes down. Furthermore, after all operating costs, interest expenses, and taxes are paid, stockholders will receive all remaining cash flows each year as a cash dividend or share repurchase.[16]

The financial statements for the Granite Corporation are shown in Table 47-30.

TABLE 47-30   Condensed Financial Statements for Granite Corporation

Year	0	1	2	3	4	5
Balance Sheets:						
Assets	150,000	120,000	90,000	60,000	30,000	0
Liabilities	109,746	98,221	78,043	48,347	23,182	0
Net worth	40,254	21,779	11,957	11,653	6,818	0
Income Statements:						
Sales		150,000	200,000	250,000	200,000	150,000
Variable cash expenses		75,000	100,000	125,000	100,000	75,000
Fixed cash expenses		20,000	20,000	20,000	20,000	20,000
Depreciation		30,000	30,000	30,000	30,000	30,000
EBIT		25,000	50,000	75,000	50,000	25,000
Interest expense		9,146	8,185	6,504	4,029	1,932
EBT		15,854	41,815	68,496	45,971	23,068
Taxes at 40 percent		6,342	16,726	27,399	18,388	9,227
Net income before salvage		9,513	25,089	41,098	27,583	13,841
After-tax salvage value						6,000
Net income		9,513	25,089	41,098	27,583	19,841
Statements of Cash Flows:						
Operating cash flows:						
Net income		9,513	25,089	41,098	27,583	19,841
Depreciation		30,000	30,000	30,000	30,000	30,000
Total		39,513	55,089	71,098	57,583	49,841
Financing cash flows:						
Debt repayment		−11,525	−20,178	−29,696	−25,165	−23,182
Dividends/repurchases		−27,987	−34,911	−41,402	−32,417	−26,659
Total		−39,513	−55,089	−71,098	−57,583	−49,841
Investing cash flows		0	0	0	0	0
Total cash flows		0	0	0	0	0

---

[16] The assumptions may be unrealistic, but this is a very simple corporation.

The income statement for financial reporting purposes differs from that used in the capital budgeting model because the interest on debt obligations is now taken out as an expense before arriving at net income. The book value of the company's assets is based on the original accounting cost minus accumulated accounting depreciation. Note that the liabilities and net worth are also declining in the balance sheet. The liabilities decline each year, reflecting the amounts that were paid annually to reduce the principal of the loan. Notice, also, that the net worth is declining. Normally, the net worth of a company increases because beginning equity is increased by net retentions—the excess of net income over dividends paid. In this case, the company is shrinking and going out of business in five years, so the distributions to shareholders (which can be either cash dividends or share repurchases) exceed net income and net worth declines. The amounts that are paid each year to reduce debt and for dividends/share repurchases are shown in the financing section of the statement of cash flows.

Accounting measures of performance also can differ from economic measures of performance. Table 47-31 repeats the economic income and accounting income from Tables 47-29 and 47-30. The table also shows the economic rate of return each year and two popular accounting measures of performance: the return on equity (ROE = net income divided by beginning equity) and return on assets (ROA = EBIT divided by beginning assets).

TABLE 47-31	Economic Income, Accounting Income, and Rates of Return for Granite Corporation				
Year	**1**	**2**	**3**	**4**	**5**
Economic income	21,949	19,644	15,609	9,669	4,636
Accounting income	9,513	25,089	41,098	27,583	19,841
Economic rate of return	10.00%	10.00%	10.00%	10.00%	10.00%
Return on equity (ROE)	23.63%	115.20%	343.71%	236.70%	291.00%
Return on assets (ROA)	16.67%	41.67%	83.33%	83.33%	83.33%

As Table 47-31 illustrates, economic and accounting incomes differ substantially. Over the five years, economic income is much less than accounting income, and the patterns certainly differ. In addition, the accounting rates of return, the ROE and ROA, for this admittedly unusual company are quite different from the economic rate of return.

8.3 Economic Profit, Residual Income, and Claims Valuation

Although the capital budgeting model is widely employed, analysts have used other procedures to divide up the cash flows from a company or project and then value them using discounted cash flow methods. We present three of these alternative models here: the economic profit model, the residual income model, and the claims valuation model. Used correctly, they are all consistent with the basic capital budgeting model and with each other.

8.3.1 *Economic Profit*

The first alternative method for measuring income and valuing assets is based on economic profit (EP).[17] Economic profit has been used in asset valuation as well as in performance measurement and management compensation. Its calculation is loosely as follows:

$$EP = NOPAT - \$WACC \qquad\qquad (47\text{-}12)$$

where

$$
\begin{aligned}
EP &= \text{Economic profit}\\
NOPAT &= \text{Net operating profit after tax} = EBIT(1 - \text{Tax rate})\\
EBIT &= \text{Operating income before taxes, or Earnings before interest and}\\
&\quad\ \text{taxes}\\
\$WACC &= \text{Dollar cost of capital} = WACC \times \text{Capital}\\
WACC &= \text{Weighted average (or overall) cost of capital}\\
\text{Capital} &= \text{Investment}
\end{aligned}
$$

EP is a periodic measure of profit above and beyond the dollar cost of the capital invested in the project. The dollar cost of capital is the dollar return that the company must make on the project in order to pay the debt holders and the equity holders their respective required rates of return.[18]

For the Granite Corporation, for the first year, we have the following:

$$
\begin{aligned}
NOPAT &= EBIT(1 - \text{Tax rate}) = 25{,}000(1 - 0.40) = \$15{,}000\\
\$WACC &= WACC \times \text{Capital} = 10\% \times 150{,}000 = \$15{,}000\\
EP &= NOPAT - \$WACC = 15{,}000 - 15{,}000 = \$0
\end{aligned}
$$

Table 47-32 shows the EP for all five years for the Granite Corporation.

EP is readily applied to valuation of an asset or a security. The NPV found by discounted cash flow analysis in the basic capital budgeting model will be

TABLE 47-32   EP for Granite Corporation

Year	1	2	3	4	5**
Capital*	150,000	120,000	90,000	60,000	30,000
NOPAT	15,000	30,000	45,000	30,000	21,000
$WACC	15,000	12,000	9,000	6,000	3,000
EP	0	18,000	36,000	24,000	12,000

*Depreciation is $30,000 per year.

**The $6,000 after-tax gain from salvage is included in NOPAT in Year 5.

---

[17] Economic Value Added® or EVA, trademarked by the consulting firm Stern Stewart & Company, is a well known commercial application of the economic profit approach. See Stewart (1991) and Peterson and Peterson (1996) for complete discussion.

[18] In Reading 48 on cost of capital, we will explain the relationship between the required rate of return on the project or WACC (here 10 percent), the rate of return required by debtholders (here 8 1/3 percent), and the rate of return required by equityholders (here 15 percent).

equal to the present value of future EP discounted at the weighted average cost of capital.

$$NPV = \sum_{t=1}^{\infty} \frac{EP_t}{(1 + WACC)^t}$$

(47-13)

This NPV is also called the **market value added (MVA)**.[19] So we have

$$NPV = MVA = \sum_{t=1}^{\infty} \frac{EP_t}{(1 + WACC)^t}$$

(47-14)

Discounting the five years of EP for the Granite Corporation at the 10 percent WACC gives an NPV (and MVA) of \$69,492. The total value of the company (of the asset) is the original investment of \$150,000 plus the NPV of \$69,492, or \$219,492. The valuation using EP is the same as that found with the basic capital budgeting model.

8.3.2 Residual Income

Another method for estimating income and valuing an asset is the residual income method.[20] This method focuses on the returns to equity, where

Residual income = Net income − Equity charge,

or

$$RI_t = NI_t - r_e B_{t-1}$$

(47-15)

where

RI_t = Residual income during period t

NI_t = Net income during period t

$r_e B_{t-1}$ = Equity charge for period t, which is the required rate of return on equity, r_e, times the beginning-of-period book value of equity, B_{t-1}

For the first year for the Granite Corporation, the net income is \$9,513. The beginning book value of equity is \$40,254 (from the balance sheet in Table 47-30), and the required rate of return on equity is 15 percent. Consequently, the residual income for Year 1 is:

$$RI_t = NI_t - r_e B_{t-1} = 9,513 - 0.15(40,254) = 9,513 - 6,038 = \$3,475$$

The residual income for all five years for Granite is shown in Table 47-33.

TABLE 47-33   Residual Income for Granite Corporation

Year	1	2	3	4	5*
NI_t	9,513	25,089	41,098	27,583	19,841
$r_e B_{t-1}$	6,038	3,267	1,794	1,748	1,023
RI_t	3,475	21,822	39,304	25,835	18,818

* The \$6,000 after-tax gain from salvage is included in NI in Year 5.

[19] Peterson and Peterson define MVA as the market value of the company minus the capital invested, which is an NPV.

[20] See Chapter 5 in Stowe, Robinson, Pinto, and McLeavey (2002) and Edwards and Bell (1961) for treatments of residual income analysis.

Residual income, like EP, can also be applied to valuation of an asset or security. The NPV of an investment is the present value of future residual income discounted at the required rate of return on equity.

$$\text{NPV} = \sum_{t=1}^{\infty} \frac{\text{RI}_t}{(1 + r_e)^t} \qquad \textbf{(47-16)}$$

Discounting the residual income for the Granite Corporation at the 15 percent required rate of return on equity gives an NPV of $69,492. The total value of the company (of the asset) is the present value of the residual income, the original equity investment, plus the original debt investment:

PV of residual income	$69,492
Equity investment	40,254
Debt investment	109,746
Total value	$219,492

The value of the company is the original book value of its debt and equity plus the present value of the residual income (which is the project's NPV). Again, this is the same value we found with the basic capital budgeting model and with the EP model.

8.3.3 Claims Valuation

To value a company, the EP valuation approach essentially adds the present value of EP to the original investment. The residual income approach adds the present value of residual income to the original debt and equity investments in the company. Since the EP approach is from the perspective of all suppliers of capital, EP is discounted at the overall WACC. The residual income approach takes the perspective of equity investors, so residual income is discounted at the cost of equity.

The third and final alternative valuation approach that we present is to divide the operating cash flows between securityholder classes (in this example, debt and equity), and then value the debt and equity cash flows separately.

Balance Sheet

Assets	Liabilities
	Equity

The basic capital budgeting approach is to value the asset, which is on the left-hand side of the balance sheet above. The claims valuation approach values the liabilities and equity, the claims against the assets, which are on the right-hand side of the balance sheet. The value of the claims should equal the value of the assets.

For the Granite Corporation, the cash flows to debtholders are the interest payments and principal payments. These are valued by discounting them at the cost of debt, which is 8 1/3 percent. The cash flows to stockholders are the dividends and share repurchases, which are valued by discounting them at

TABLE 47-34	Payments to Bondholders and Stockholders of Granite Corporation				
Year	1	2	3	4	5
Interest payments	9,146	8,185	6,504	4,029	1,932
Principal payments	11,525	20,178	29,696	25,165	23,182
Total debt payments	20,671	28,363	36,199	29,194	25,114
Equity distributions	27,987	34,911	41,402	32,417	26,659

the 15 percent cost of equity. Table 47-34 lists the future cash flows for debt and equity. The present value of the total debt payments, discounted at the cost of debt, is $109,746. The value of the equity distributions, discounted at the cost of equity, is $109,746. The total value of the company is the combined value of debt and equity, which is $219,492.

In our example, the basic capital budgeting model, the economic profit model, the residual income model, and the claims valuation model all result in the same valuation of the company. In the real world, analysts must deal with many accounting complications. Some of these complications may include pension liability adjustments, valuations of marketable securities held, exchange rate gains and losses, and adjustments for leases, inventories, goodwill, deferred taxes, etc. In theory, all of the valuation models are equivalent. In practice, even with due diligence and care, analysts may prefer one approach over others and disagree about valuations.

There are other approaches to valuation that analysts use and run across. Two common ones are the free cash flow to the firm and free cash flow to equity approaches.[21] The free cash flow to the firm approach is fundamentally the same as the basic capital budgeting approach. The free cash flow to equity approach is related to the claims valuation approach. In corporate finance, corporate managers usually value an asset by valuing its total after-tax cash flows. Security analysts typically value equity by valuing the cash flows to stockholders. Real estate investors often evaluate real estate investments by valuing the cash flows to the equity investor after payments to creditors, which is like the claims valuation approach.

---

[21] The free cash flow to the firm and free cash flow to equity approaches are developed in Chapter 3 of Stowe, Robinson, Pinto, and McLeavey (2002).

ENDS

SUMMARY

Capital budgeting is the process that companies use for decision making on capital projects—those projects with a life of a year or more. This reading developed the principles behind the basic capital budgeting model, the cash flows that go into the model, and several extensions of the basic model.

- ▶ Capital budgeting undergirds the most critical investments for many corporations—their investments in long-term assets. The principles of capital budgeting have been applied to other corporate investing and financing decisions and to security analysis and portfolio management.
- ▶ The typical steps in the capital budgeting process are: (1) generating ideas, (2) analyzing individual proposals, (3) planning the capital budget, and (4) monitoring and post-auditing.
- ▶ Projects susceptible to capital budgeting process can be categorized as: (1) replacement, (2) expansion, (3) new products and services, and (4) regulatory, safety and environmental.
- ▶ Capital budgeting decisions are based on incremental after-tax cash flows discounted at the opportunity cost of funds. Financing costs are ignored because both the cost of debt and the cost of other capital are captured in the discount rate.
- ▶ The net present value (NPV) is the present value of all after-tax cash flows, or

$$NPV = \sum_{t=0}^{n} \frac{CF_t}{(1 + r)^t}$$

where the investment outlays are negative cash flows included in the CF_ts and where r is the required rate of return for the investment.

- ▶ The IRR is the discount rate that makes the present value of all future cash flows sum to zero. This equation can be solved for the IRR:

$$\sum_{t=0}^{n} \frac{CF_t}{(1 + IRR)^t} = 0$$

- ▶ The payback period is the number of years required to recover the original investment in a project. The payback is based on cash flows.
- ▶ The discounted payback period is the number of years it takes for the cumulative discounted cash flows from a project to equal the original investment.
- ▶ The average accounting rate of return (AAR) can be defined as follows:

$$AAR = \frac{\text{Average net income}}{\text{Average book value}}$$

- ▶ The profitability index (PI) is the present value of a project's future cash flows divided by the initial investment:

$$PI = \frac{\text{PV of future cash flows}}{\text{Initial investment}} = 1 + \frac{NPV}{\text{Initial investment}}$$

▶ The capital budgeting decision rules are to invest if the NPV > 0, if the IRR > r, or if the PI > 1.0 There are no decision rules for the payback period, discounted payback period, and AAR because they are not always sound measures.

▶ The NPV profile is a graph that shows a project's NPV graphed as a function of various discount rates.

▶ For mutually exclusive projects that are ranked differently by the NPV and IRR, it is economically sound to choose the project with the higher NPV.

▶ The "multiple IRR problem" and the "no IRR problem" can arise for a project with nonconventional cash flows—cash flows that change signs more than once during the project's life.

▶ The fact that projects with positive NPVs theoretically increase the value of the company and the value of its stock could explain the popularity of NPV as an evaluation method.

▶ Analysts often organize the cash flows for capital budgeting in tables, summing all of the cash flows occurring at each point in time. These totals are then used to find an NPV or IRR. Alternatively, tables collecting cash flows by type can be used. Equations for the capital budgeting cash flows are as follows:

> Initial outlay:
> $$\text{Outlay} = \text{FCInv} + \text{NWCInv} - \text{Sal}_0 + T(\text{Sal}_0 - B_0)$$
> Annual after-tax operating cash flow:
> $$CF = (S - C - D)(1 - T) + D, \text{ or}$$
> $$CF = (S - C)(1 - D) + TD$$
> Terminal year after-tax non-operating cash flow:
> $$\text{TNOCF} = \text{Sal}_T + \text{NWCInv} - T(\text{Sal}_T - B_T)$$

▶ Depreciation schedules affect taxable income, taxes paid, and after-tax cash flows, and therefore capital budgeting valuations.

▶ Spreadsheets are heavily used for capital budgeting valuation.

▶ When inflation exists, the analyst should perform capital budgeting analysis in "nominal" terms if cash flows are nominal and in "real" terms if cash flows are real.

▶ Inflation reduces the value of depreciation tax savings (unless the tax system adjusts depreciation for inflation). Inflation reduces the value of fixed payments to bondholders. Inflation usually does not affect all revenues and costs uniformly. Contracting with customers, suppliers, employees, and sources of capital can be complicated as inflation rises.

▶ Two ways of comparing mutually exclusive projects in a replacement chain are the "least common multiple of lives" approach and the "equivalent annual annuity" approach.

▶ For the least common multiple of lives approach, the analyst extends the time horizon of analysis so that the lives of both projects will divide exactly into the horizon. The projects are replicated over this horizon, and the NPV for the total cash flows over the least common multiple of lives is used to evaluate the investments.

▶ The equivalent annual annuity is the annuity payment (series of equal annual payments over the project's life) that is equivalent in value to the project's actual cash flows. Analysts find the present value of all of the cash flows for an investment (the NPV) and then calculate an annuity payment that has a value equivalent to the NPV.

▶ With capital rationing, the company's capital budget has a size constraint. Under "hard" capital rationing, the budget is fixed. In the case of hard rationing, managers use trial and error and sometimes mathematical programming to find the optimal set of projects. In that situation, it is best to use the NPV or PI valuation methods.

▶ Sensitivity analysis calculates the effect on the NPV of changes in one input variable at a time.

▶ Scenario analysis creates scenarios that consist of changes in several of the input variables and calculates the NPV for each scenario.

▶ Simulation (Monte Carlo) analysis is used to estimate probability distributions for the NPV or IRR of a capital project. Simulations randomly select values for stochastic input variables and then repeatedly calculate the project NPV and IRR to find their distributions.

▶ Risk-adjusted discount rates based on market risk measures should be used as the required rate of return for projects when the investors are diversified. The capital asset pricing model (CAPM) and arbitrage pricing theory (APT) are common approaches for finding market-based risk-adjusted rates.

▶ In the CAPM, a project's or asset's beta, or β, is used as a measure of systematic risk. The security market line (SML) estimates the asset's required rate of return as $r_i = R_F + \beta_i [E(R_M) - R_F]$.

▶ Project-specific betas should be used instead of company betas whenever the risk of the project differs from that of the company.

▶ Real options can be classified as (1) timing options; (2) sizing options, which can be abandonment options or growth (expansion) options; (3) flexibility options, which can be price-setting options or production-flexibility options; and (4) fundamental options. Simple options can be evaluated with decision trees; for more complex options, the analyst should use option pricing models.

▶ Economic income is the investment's after-tax cash flow plus the change in the market value. Accounting income is revenues minus expenses. Accounting depreciation, based on the original cost of the investment, is the decrease in the book (accounting) value, while economic depreciation is the decrease in the market value of the investment. Accounting net income is net of the after-tax interest expenses on the company's debt obligations. In computing economic income, financing costs are ignored.

▶ Economic profit is

$$EP = NOPAT - \$WACC$$

where NOPAT = Net operating profit after tax = EBIT$(1 - $ Tax rate$)$ and $WACC = Dollar cost of capital = WACC × Capital. When applied to the valuation of an asset or security, the NPV of an investment (and its market value added) is the present value of future EP discounted at the weighted average cost of capital.

$$NPV = MVA = \sum_{t=1}^{\infty} \frac{EP_t}{(1 + WACC)^t}$$

The total value of the company (of the asset) is the original investment plus the NPV.

▶ Residual income = Net income = Equity charge, or $RI_t = NI_t - r_e B_{t-1}$ where RI_t = Residual income during period t, NI_t = Net income during period t, r_e = the cost of equity, and B_{t-1} = the beginning-of-period book value of equity. The NPV of an investment is the present value of future residual income discounted at the required rate of return on equity:

$$NPV = \sum_{t=1}^{\infty} \frac{RI_t}{(1 + r_e)^t}$$

The total value of the company (of the asset) is the NPV plus the original equity investment plus the original debt investment.

▶ The claims valuation approach values an asset by valuing the claims against the asset. For example, an asset financed with debt and equity has a value equal to the value of the debt plus the value of the equity.

PROBLEMS FOR READING 47

1. Given the following cash flows for a capital project, calculate the NPV and IRR. The required rate of return is 8 percent.

Year	0	1	2	3	4	5
Cash flow	−50,000	15,000	15,000	20,000	10,000	5,000

	NPV	IRR
A.	$1,905	10.9%
B.	$1,905	26.0%
C.	$3,379	10.9%
D.	$3,379	26.0%

2. Given the following cash flows for a capital project, calculate its payback period and discounted payback period. The required rate of return is 8 percent. The discounted payback period is

Year	0	1	2	3	4	5
Cash flow	−50,000	15,000	15,000	20,000	10,000	5,000

A. 0.16 years longer than the payback period.

B. 0.80 years longer than the payback period.

C. 1.01 years longer than the payback period.

D. 1.85 years longer than the payback period.

3. An investment of $100 generates after-tax cash flows of $40 in Year 1, $80 in Year 2, and $120 in Year 3. The required rate of return is 20 percent. The net present value is *closest* to

A. $42.22

B. $58.33

C. $68.52

D. $98.95

4. An investment of $150,000 is expected to generate an after-tax cash flow of $100,000 in one year and another $120,000 in two years. The cost of capital is 10 percent. What is the internal rate of return?

A. 28.19 percent

B. 28.39 percent

C. 28.59 percent

D. 28.79 percent

5. Kim Corporation is considering an investment of 750 million won with expected after-tax cash inflows of 175 million won per year for seven years. The required rate of return is 10 percent. What is the project's

	NPV?	IRR?
A.	102 million won	14.0%
B.	102 million won	23.3%
C.	193 million won	14.0%
D.	193 million won	23.3%

6. Kim Corporation is considering an investment of 750 million won with expected after-tax cash inflows of 175 million won per year for seven years. The required rate of return is 10 percent. Expressed in years, what is the project's

	payback period?	discounted payback period?
A.	4.3	5.4
B.	4.3	5.9
C.	4.8	5.4
D.	4.8	5.9

7. An investment of $20,000 will create a perpetual after-tax cash flow of $2,000. The required rate of return is 8 percent. What is the investment's profitability index?

   A. 1.00

   B. 1.08

   C. 1.16

   D. 1.25

8. Hermann Corporation is considering an investment of €375 million with expected after-tax cash inflows of €115 million per year for seven years and an additional after-tax salvage value of €50 million in Year seven. The required rate of return is 10 percent. What is the investment's PI?

   A. 1.19

   B. 1.33

   C. 1.56

   D. 1.75

9. Erin Chou is reviewing a profitable investment project that has a conventional cash flow pattern. If the cash flows for the project, initial outlay, and future after-tax cash flows all double, Chou would predict that the IRR would

   A. increase and the NPV would increase.

   B. increase and the NPV would stay the same.

   C. stay the same and the NPV would increase.

   D. stay the same and the NPV would stay the same.

10. Shirley Shea has evaluated an investment proposal and found that its payback period is one year, it has a negative NPV, and it has a positive IRR. Is this combination of results possible?

   A. Yes.

   B. No, because a project with a positive IRR has a positive NPV.

   C. No, because a project with a negative NPV has a negative payback period.

   D. No, because a project with such a rapid payback period has a positive NPV.

11. An investment has an outlay of 100 and after-tax cash flows of 40 annually for four years. A project enhancement increases the outlay by 15 and the annual after-tax cash flows by 5. As a result, the vertical intercept of the NPV profile of the enhanced project shifts

    A. up and the horizontal intercept shifts left.

    B. up and the horizontal intercept shifts right.

    C. down and the horizontal intercept shifts left.

    D. down and the horizontal intercept shifts right.

12. Projects 1 and 2 have similar outlays, although the patterns of future cash flows are different. The cash flows as well as the NPV and IRR for the two projects are shown below. For both projects, the required rate of return is 10 percent.

			Cash Flows				
Year	**0**	**1**	**2**	**3**	**4**	**NPV**	**IRR**
Project 1	−50	20	20	20	20	13.40	21.86%
Project 2	−50	0	0	0	100	18.30	18.92%

The two projects are mutually exclusive. What is the appropriate investment decision?

A. Invest in Project 1 because it has the higher IRR.

B. Invest in Project 2 because it has the higher NPV.

C. Invest half in each project.

D. Invest in both projects.

13. Consider the two projects below. The cash flows as well as the NPV and IRR for the two projects are given. For both projects, the required rate of return is 10 percent.

			Cash Flows				
Year	**0**	**1**	**2**	**3**	**4**	**NPV**	**IRR**
Project 1	−100	36	36	36	36	14.12	16.37%
Project 2	−100	0	0	0	175	19.53	15.02%

What discount rate would result in the same NPV for both projects?

A. A rate between 0.00 percent and 10.00 percent.

B. A rate between 10.00 percent and 15.02 percent.

C. A rate between 15.02 percent and 16.37 percent.

D. A rate above 16.37 percent.

14. Wilson Flannery is concerned that this project has multiple IRRs.

Year	0	1	2	3
Cash flow	−50	100	0	−50

How many discount rates produce a zero NPV for this project?

A. One, a discount rate of 0 percent.

B. Two, discount rates of 0 percent and 32 percent.

C. Two, discount rates of 0 percent and 62 percent.

D. Two, discount rates of 0 percent and 92 percent.

$4\frac{5}{8}$ $4\frac{11}{16}$ $3\frac{7}{8}$

$5\frac{1}{2}$ $5\frac{1}{2}$ — $3\frac{7}{8}$

$5\frac{1}{2}$ $5\frac{1}{2}$ — $\frac{1}{16}$

$20\frac{5}{8}$ $21\frac{3}{16}$ — $\frac{7}{8}$

$17\frac{3}{8}$ $18\frac{1}{8}$ + $\frac{7}{8}$

$15\frac{1}{2}$ $6\frac{1}{2}$ $6\frac{1}{2}$ — $\frac{1}{2}$

$7\frac{1}{4}$ $6\frac{1}{2}$ $31\frac{1}{32}$ — $\frac{1}{8}$

$\frac{15}{16}$

$9\frac{5}{8}$

$9\frac{9}{16}$

$1\frac{1}{32}$ $7\frac{13}{16}$ $7\frac{15}{16}$

$7\frac{11}{16}$

$2\frac{5}{8}$ $2\frac{11}{32}$ $2\frac{1}{2}$ +

$2\frac{3}{4}$ $2\frac{1}{4}$ $2\frac{1}{4}$

$12\frac{1}{16}$ $11\frac{3}{8}$ $11\frac{3}{4}$ +

$33\frac{3}{4}$ 33 $33\frac{1}{16}$ —

$25\frac{5}{8}$ $24\frac{9}{16}$ $25\frac{3}{8}$ +

12 $11\frac{5}{8}$ $11\frac{7}{8}$ +

16 $10\frac{1}{2}$ $10\frac{1}{2}$ $10\frac{1}{2}$ —

78 $15\frac{7}{8}$ $15\frac{13}{16}$ $15\frac{1}{4}$ —

$9\frac{1}{16}$ $8\frac{1}{4}$ $8\frac{7}{8}$ +

$11\frac{1}{4}$ $10\frac{1}{8}$

COST OF CAPITAL

by Yves Courtois, Gene C. Lai, and Pamela P. Peterson

LEARNING OUTCOMES

The candidate should be able to:

a. determine and interpret the weighted average cost of capital (WACC) of a company, and explain the adjustments to it that an analyst should make in developing a cost of capital for a specific project;

b. describe the role of taxes in the cost of capital from the different capital sources;

c. describe alternative methods of calculating the weights used in the weighted average cost of capital, including the use of the company's target capital structure;

d. explain the analyst's concern with the marginal cost of capital in evaluating investment projects, and explain the use of the marginal cost of capital and the investment opportunity schedule in determining the optimal capital budget for a company;

e. explain the marginal cost of capital's role in determining the net present value of a project;

f. calculate and analyze the cost of fixed rate debt capital using the yield-to-maturity approach and the debt-rating approach;

g. calculate the cost of noncallable, nonconvertible preferred stock;

h. calculate and analyze the cost of equity capital using the capital asset pricing model approach, the dividend discount approach, and the bond yield plus risk premium approach.

INTRODUCTION 1

A company grows by making investments that are expected to increase revenues and profits. The company acquires the capital or funds necessary to make such investments by borrowing or using funds from owners. By applying this capital to investments with long-term benefits, the company is producing value today. But, how much value? The answer depends not only on the investments' expected future cash flows but also on the cost of the funds. Borrowing is not costless. Neither is using owners' funds.

The cost of this capital is an important ingredient in both investment decision making by the company's management and the valuation of the company by investors. If a company invests in projects that produce a return in excess of the cost of capital, the company has created value; in contrast, if the company invests in projects whose returns are less than the cost of capital, the company has actually destroyed value. Therefore, the estimation of the cost of capital is a central issue in corporate financial management. For the analyst seeking to evaluate a company's investment program and its competitive position, an accurate estimate of a company's cost of capital is important as well.

Cost of capital estimation is a challenging task. As we have already implied, the cost of capital is not observable but, rather, must be estimated. Arriving at a cost of capital estimate requires a host of assumptions and estimates. Another challenge is that the cost of capital that is appropriately applied to a specific investment depends on the characteristics of that investment: The riskier the investment's cash flows, the greater its cost of capital. In reality, a company must estimate project-specific costs of capital. What is often done, however, is to estimate the cost of capital for the company as a whole and then adjust this overall corporate cost of capital upward or downward to reflect the risk of the contemplated project relative to the company's average project.

This reading is organized as follows: In the next section, we introduce the cost of capital and its basic computation. Section 3 presents a selection of methods for estimating the costs of the various sources of capital, and Section 4 discusses issues an analyst faces in using the cost of capital.

2   COST OF CAPITAL

The **cost of capital** is the rate of return that the suppliers of capital—bondholders and owners—require as compensation for their contribution of capital. Another way of looking at the cost of capital is that it is the opportunity cost of funds for the suppliers of capital: A potential supplier of capital will not voluntarily invest in a company unless its return meets or exceeds what the supplier could earn elsewhere in an investment of comparable risk.

A company typically has several alternatives for raising capital, including issuing equity, debt, and instruments that share characteristics of debt and equity. Each source selected becomes a component of the company's funding and has a cost (required rate of return) that may be called a **component cost of capital**. Because we are using the cost of capital in the evaluation of investment opportunities, we are dealing with a *marginal* cost—what it would cost to raise additional funds for the potential investment project. Therefore, the cost of capital that the investment analyst is concerned with is a marginal cost.

Let us focus on the cost of capital for the entire company (later we will address how to adjust that for specific projects). The cost of capital of a company is the required rate of return that investors demand for the average-risk investment of a company. The most common way to estimate this required rate of return is to calculate the marginal cost of each of the various sources of capital and then calculate a weighted average of these costs. This weighted average is referred to as the **weighted average cost of capital** (**WACC**). The WACC is also referred to as the **marginal cost of capital** (**MCC**) because it is the cost that a company incurs for additional capital. The weights in this weighted average are the proportions of the various sources of capital that the company uses to support its investment program. Therefore, the WACC, in its most general terms, is

$$WACC = w_d r_d (1 - t) + w_p r_p + w_e r_e \qquad \textbf{(48-1)}$$

where

w_d is the proportion of debt that the company uses when it raises new funds
r_d is the before-tax marginal cost of debt
t is the company's marginal tax rate
w_p is the proportion of preferred stock the company uses when it raises new funds
r_p is the marginal cost of preferred stock
w_e is the proportion of equity that the company uses when it raises new funds
r_e is the marginal cost of equity

Example 48-1

Computing the Weighted Average Cost of Capital

Assume that ABC Corporation has the following capital structure: 30 percent debt, 10 percent preferred stock, and 60 percent equity. ABC Corporation wishes to maintain these proportions as it raises new funds. Its before-tax cost of debt is 8 percent, its cost of preferred stock is 10 percent, and its cost of equity is 15 percent. If the company's marginal tax rate is 40 percent, what is ABC's weighted average cost of capital?

▶ **Solution.** The weighed average cost of capital is

$$\begin{aligned} WACC &= (0.3)(0.08)(1 - 0.40) + (0.1)(0.1) + (0.6)(0.15) \\ &= 11.44 \text{ percent.} \end{aligned}$$

There are important points concerning the calculation of the WACC as shown in Equation 48-1 that the analyst must be familiar with. The next two sections address two key issues: taxes and the selection of weights.

2.1 Taxes and the Cost of Capital

Notice that in Equation 48-1 we adjust the expected before-tax cost on new debt financing, r_d, by a factor of $(1 - t)$. In the United States and many other tax jurisdictions, the interest on debt financing is a deduction to arrive at taxable income. Taking the tax deductibility of interest as the base case, we adjust the pre-tax cost of debt for this tax shield. Multiplying r_d by $(1 - t)$ results in an estimate of the after-tax cost of debt.

For example, suppose a company pays €1 million in interest on its €10 million of debt. The cost of this debt is not €1 million because this interest expense reduces taxable income by €1 million, resulting in a lower tax. If the company is subject to a tax rate of 40 percent, this €1 million of interest costs the company (€1 million)(1 − 0.4) = €0.6 million because the interest reduces the company's tax bill by €0.4 million. In this case, the before-tax cost of debt is 10 percent, whereas the after-tax cost of debt is (€0.6 million)/(€10 million) = 6 percent.

Estimating the cost of common equity capital is more challenging than estimating the cost of debt capital. Debt capital involves a stated legal obligation on the part of the company to pay interest and repay the principal on the borrowing. Equity entails no such obligation. Estimating the cost of conventional preferred equity is rather straightforward because the dividend is generally stated and fixed, but estimating the cost of common equity is challenging. There are several methods available for estimating the cost of common equity, and we discuss two in this reading. The first method uses the capital asset pricing model, and the second method uses the dividend discount model, which is based on discounted cash flows. No matter the method, there is no need to make any adjustment in the cost of equity for taxes because the payments to owners, whether in the form of dividends or the return on capital, are not tax deductible for the company.

Example 48-2

Incorporating the Effect of Taxes on the Costs of Capital

Jorge Ricard, a financial analyst, is estimating the costs of capital for the Zeale Corporation. In the process of this estimation, Ricard has estimated the before-tax costs of capital for Zeale's debt and equity as 4 percent and 6 percent, respectively. What are the after-tax costs of debt and equity if Zeale's marginal tax rate is

1. 30 percent?

2. 48 percent?

▶ **Solution.**

Marginal Tax Rate	After-Tax Cost of Debt	After-Tax Cost of Equity
1. 30 percent	$0.04(1 - 0.30) = 2.80$ percent	6 percent
2. 48 percent	$0.04(1 - 0.48) = 2.08$ percent	6 percent

Note: There is no adjustment for taxes in the case of equity; the before-tax cost of equity is equal to the after-tax cost of equity.

2.2 Weights of the Weighted Average

How do we determine what weights to use? Ideally, we want to use the proportion of each source of capital that the company would use in the project or company. If we assume that a company has a target capital structure and raises capital consistent with this target, we should use this target capital structure. The **target capital structure** is the capital structure that a company is striving to obtain.[1] If we know the company's target capital structure, then, of course, we should use this in our analysis. Someone outside the company, however, such as an analyst,

---

[1] In Reading 49 on capital structure and leverage, we will discuss the capital structure decision in greater detail, including a look at how it relates to the value of the company.

typically does not know the target capital structure and must estimate it using one of several approaches:

1. Assume the company's current capital structure, at market value weights for the components, represents the company's target capital structure.

2. Examine trends in the company's capital structure or statements by management regarding capital structure policy to infer the target capital structure.

3. Use averages of comparable companies' capital structures as the target capital structure.

In the absence of knowledge of a company's target capital structure, we may take Method 1 as the baseline. Note that in applying Method 3, we use unweighted, arithmetic average, as is often done for simplicity. An alternative is to calculate a weighted average, which would give more weight to larger companies.

Suppose we are using the company's current capital structure as a proxy for the target capital structure. In this case, we use the market value of the different capital sources in the calculation of these proportions. For example, if a company has the following market values for its capital

Bonds outstanding	$5 million
Preferred stock	1 million
Common stock	14 million
Total capital	$20 million

the weights that we apply would be

$$w_d = 0.25$$
$$w_p = 0.05$$
$$w_e = 0.70$$

Example 48-3 illustrates the estimation of weights. Note that a simple way of transforming a debt-to-equity ratio D/E into a weight—that is, $D/(D + E)$—is to divide D/E by $1 + D/E$.

Example 48-3

Estimating the Proportions of Capital

Fin Anziell is a financial analyst with Analytiker Firma. Anziell is in the process of estimating the cost of capital of Gewicht GmbH. The following information is provided:

Gewicht GmbH
    Market value of debt   €50 million
    Market value of equity   €60 million

Primary competitors and their capital structures (in millions):

Competitor	Market Value of Debt	Market Value of Equity
A	€ 25	€ 50
B	€ 101	€ 190
C	£ 40	£ 60

What are Gewicht's proportions of debt and equity that Anziell would use if estimating these proportions using the company's

1. current capital structure?
2. competitors' capital structure?

Suppose Gewicht announces that a debt-to-equity ratio of 0.7 reflects its target capital structure.

3. What weights should Anziell use in the cost of capital calculations?

▶ **Solution to 1.** Current capital structure

$$w_d = \frac{\text{€50 million}}{\text{€50 million} + \text{€60 million}} = 0.4545$$

$$w_e = \frac{\text{€60 million}}{\text{€50 million} + \text{€60 million}} = 0.5454$$

▶ **Solution to 2.** Competitors' capital structure[2]

$$w_d = \frac{\left(\dfrac{\text{€25}}{\text{€25} + \text{€50}}\right) + \left(\dfrac{\text{€101}}{\text{€101} + \text{€190}}\right) + \left(\dfrac{\text{£40}}{\text{£40} + \text{£60}}\right)}{3} = 0.3601$$

$$w_e = \frac{\left(\dfrac{\text{€50}}{\text{€25} + \text{€50}}\right) + \left(\dfrac{\text{€190}}{\text{€101} + \text{€190}}\right) + \left(\dfrac{\text{£60}}{\text{£40} + \text{£60}}\right)}{3} = 0.6399$$

▶ **Solution to 3.** A debt-to-equity ratio of 0.7 represents a weight on debt of $0.7/1.7 = 0.4118$ so that $w_d = 0.4118$ and $w_e = 1 - 0.4118 = 0.5882$. These would be the preferred weights to use in a cost of capital calculation.

2.3 Applying the Cost of Capital to Capital Budgeting and Security Valuation

With some insight now into the calculation of the cost of capital, let us continue to improve our understanding of the roles it plays in financial analysis. A chief use of the marginal cost of capital estimate is in capital-budgeting decision making. What role does the marginal cost of capital play in a company's investment program, and how do we adapt it when we need to evaluate a specific investment project?

A company's marginal cost of capital (MCC) may increase as additional capital is raised, whereas returns to a company's investment opportunities are generally believed to decrease as the company makes additional investments, as

---

[2] These weights represent the arithmetic average of the three companies' debt proportion and equity proportion, respectively. If instead we chose to use a weighted average, we would calculate the debt proportion as the sum of the debt for all three companies, divided by the sum of the total capital for all three; we would calculate the equity proportion in the same manner. The weighted average proportions are 0.3562 and 0.6438, respectively.

represented by the **investment opportunity schedule** (IOS).[3] We show this relation in Figure 48-1, graphing the upward-sloping marginal cost of capital schedule against the downward-sloping investment opportunity schedule. In the context of a company's investment decision, the optimal capital budget is that amount of capital raised and invested at which the marginal cost of capital is equal to the marginal return from investing. In other words, the optimal capital budget occurs when the marginal cost of capital intersects with the investment opportunity schedule as seen in Figure 48-1.

The relation between the MCC and the IOS provides a broad picture of the basic decision-making problem of a company. However, we are often interested in valuing an individual project or even a portion of a company, such as a division or product line. In these applications, we are interested in the cost of capital for the project, product, or division as opposed to the cost of capital for the company overall. The cost of capital in these applications should reflect the riskiness of the future cash flows of the project, product, or division. For an average-risk project, the opportunity cost of capital is the company's WACC. If the systematic risk of the project is above or below average relative to the company's current portfolio of projects, an upward or downward adjustment, respectively, is made to the company's WACC. Companies may take an *ad hoc* or a systematic approach to making such adjustments. The discussion of a systematic approach is a somewhat advanced topic that we defer to Section 4.1.

The WACC or MCC corresponding to the average risk of the company, adjusted appropriately for the risk of a given project, plays a role in capital-budgeting decision making based on the **net present value** (**NPV**) of that project. Recall from the capital-budgeting reading that the NPV is the present value of all the project cash flows. It is useful to think of it as the difference between the present value of the cash inflows, discounted at the opportunity cost of capital applicable to

FIGURE 48-1   Optimal Investment Decision

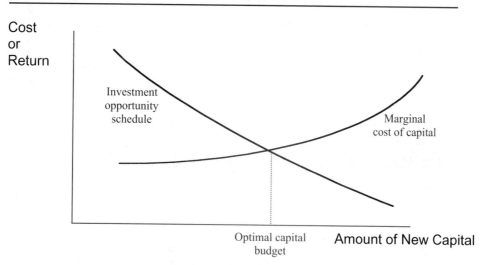

[3] The investment opportunity schedule originates with Fisher's production opportunities [Irving Fisher, *The Theory of Interest* (New York: MacMillan Co.), 1930] and was adapted to capital budgeting by John Hirshleifer ["On the Theory of Optimal Investment Decision," *Journal of Political Economy*, Vol. 66, No. 4 (August 1958), pp. 329–352.]

the specific project, and the present value of the cash outflows, discounted using that same opportunity cost of capital:

$$\text{NPV} = \text{Present value of inflows} - \text{Present value of outflows}$$

If an investment's NPV is positive, the company should undertake the project. If we choose to use the company's WACC in the calculation of the NPV of a project, we are assuming that the project

▶ has the same risk as the average-risk project of the company, and

▶ will have a constant target capital structure throughout its useful life.[4]

These may not be realistic or appropriate assumptions and are potential drawbacks to using the company's WACC in valuing projects. However, alternative approaches are subject to drawbacks as well, and the approach outlined has wide acceptance.[5]

For the analyst, the second key use of the marginal cost of capital is in security valuation using any one of several discounted cash flow valuation models available.[6] For a particular valuation model, if these cash flows are cash flows to the company's suppliers of capital (that is, free cash flow to the firm), the analyst uses the weighted average cost of capital of the company in the valuation.[7] If these cash flows are strictly those belonging to the company's owners, such as the **free cash flow to equity**, or dividends, the analyst uses the cost of equity capital to find the present value of these flows.[8]

In the next section, we discuss how an analyst may approach the calculation of the component costs of capital, focusing on debt, preferred stock, and common equity.

3 COSTS OF THE DIFFERENT SOURCES OF CAPITAL

Each source of capital has a different cost because of the differences among the sources, such as seniority, contractual commitments, and potential value as a tax shield. We focus on the costs of three primary sources of capital: debt, preferred equity, and common equity.

---

[4] WACC is estimated using fixed proportions of equity and debt. The NPV method assumes a constant required rate of return, whereas a fluctuating capital structure would cause WACC to fluctuate. The importance of this issue is demonstrated by James A. Miles and John R. Ezzell, "The Weighted Average Cost of Capital, Perfect Capital Markets, and Project Life: A Clarification," *Journal of Financial and Quantitative Analysis*, Vol. 15, No. 3 (September 1980), pp. 719–730.

[5] See Reading 47 on capital budgeting for a discussion.

[6] See John Stowe, Thomas Robinson, Jerald Pinto, and Dennis McLeavey, *Analysis of Equity Investments: Valuation* (AIMR 2002) for a presentation of such models.

[7] **Free cash flow to the firm** (**FCFF**) is the cash flow available to the company's suppliers of capital after all operating expenses (including taxes) have been paid and necessary investments in working capital (e.g., inventory) and fixed capital (e.g., plant and equipment) have been made.

[8] **Free cash flow to equity** (**FCFE**) is the cash flow available to holders of the company's common equity after all operating expenses, interest, and principal payments have been paid and necessary investments in working capital and fixed capital have been made. See John Stowe, Thomas Robinson, Jerald Pinto, and Dennis McLeavey, *Analysis of Equity Investments: Valuation* (AIMR 2002) for more details on FCFF and FCFE and valuation models based on those concepts.

3.1 Cost of Debt

The **cost of debt** is the cost of debt financing to a company when it issues a bond or takes out a bank loan. We discuss two methods to estimate the before-tax cost of debt, r_d: the yield-to-maturity approach and debt-rating approach.

3.1.1 Yield-to-Maturity Approach

The **yield to maturity** (**YTM**) is the annual return that an investor earns on a bond if the investor purchases the bond today and holds it until maturity. In other words, it is the yield, r_d, that equates the present value of the bond's promised payments to its market price:

$$
\begin{aligned}
P_0 &= \frac{PMT_1}{\left(1 + \dfrac{r_d}{2}\right)} + \ldots + \frac{PMT_n}{\left(1 + \dfrac{r_d}{2}\right)^n} + \frac{FV}{\left(1 + \dfrac{r_d}{2}\right)^n} \\
&= \left(\sum_{t=1}^{n} \frac{PMT_i}{\left(1 + \dfrac{r_d}{2}\right)^t}\right) + \frac{FV}{\left(1 + \dfrac{r_d}{2}\right)^n}
\end{aligned}
$$

(48-2)

where

P_0 is the current market price of the bond
PMT_t is the interest payment in period t
r_d is the yield to maturity[9]
n is the number of periods remaining to maturity
FV is the maturity value of the bond

This valuation equation assumes the bond pays semi-annual interest and that any intermediate cash flows (in this case the interest prior to maturity) are reinvested at the rate $r_d/2$.

Example 48-4 illustrates the calculation of the after-tax cost of debt.

Example 48-4

Calculating the After-Tax Cost of Debt

Valence Industries issues a bond to finance a new project. It offers a 10-year, 5 percent semi-annual coupon bond. Upon issue, the bond sells at $1,025. What is Valence's before-tax cost of debt? If Valence's marginal tax rate is 35 percent, what is Valence's after-tax cost of debt?

---

[9] r_d is expressed as an annual rate and is divided by the number of payment periods per year. Because most corporate bonds pay semi-annual interest, we divided r_d by 2 in this calculation. The interest payment for each period thus corresponds with the bond's semi-annual coupon payment.

> ▶ **Solution.**
> Given:
>
> $$
> \begin{aligned}
> PV &= \$1,025 \\
> FV &= \$1,000 \\
> PMT &= 5 \text{ percent of } 1,000 \div 2 = \$25 \\
> n &= 10 \times 2 = 20
> \end{aligned}
> $$
>
> $$\$1,025 = \left(\sum_{t=1}^{20} \frac{\$25}{(1+i)} \right) + \frac{\$1,000}{(1+i)^{20}}$$
>
> Use a financial calculator to solve for i, the six-month yield. Because $i = 2.342$ percent, the before-tax cost of debt is $r_d = 2.342$ percent $\times$ 2 = 4.684 percent, and Valence's after-tax cost of debt is $r_d(1-t) = 0.04684$ $(1 - 0.35) = 0.03045$ or 3.045 percent.

3.1.2 Debt-Rating Approach

When a reliable current market price for a company's debt is not available, the **debt-rating approach** can be used to estimate the before-tax cost of debt. Based on a company's debt rating, we estimate the before-tax cost of debt by using the yield on comparably rated bonds for maturities that closely match that of the company's existing debt.

Suppose a company's capital structure includes debt with an average maturity (or duration) of 10 years and the company's marginal tax rate is 35 percent. If the company's rating is AAA and the yield on debt with the same debt rating and similar maturity (or duration) is 4 percent, the company's after-tax cost of debt is[10]

$$r_d = 4 \text{ percent}(1 - 0.35) = 2.6 \text{ percent}$$

A consideration when using this approach is that debt ratings are ratings of the debt issue itself, with the issuer being only one of the considerations. Other factors, such as debt seniority and security, also affect ratings and yields, so care must be taken to consider the likely type of debt to be issued by the company in determining the comparable debt rating and yield. The debt-rating approach is a simple example of pricing on the basis of valuation-relevant characteristics, which in bond markets has been known as evaluated pricing or **matrix pricing**.

3.1.3 Issues in Estimating the Cost of Debt

3.1.3.1 Fixed-Rate Debt versus Floating-Rate Debt Up to now, we have assumed that the interest on debt is a fixed amount each period. We can observe market yields of the company's existing debt or market yields of debt of similar risk in estimating the before-tax cost of debt. However, the company may also issue floating-rate debt in which the interest rate adjusts periodically according to a prescribed index, such as the prime rate or LIBOR, over the life of the instrument.

Estimating the cost of a floating-rate security is difficult because the cost of this form of capital over the long term depends not only on the current yields but also

---

[10] Duration is a more precise measure of a bond's interest rate sensitivity than maturity.

on the future yields. The analyst may use the current term structure of interest rates and term structure theory to assign an average cost to such instruments.

3.1.3.2 Debt with Optionlike Features   How should an analyst determine the cost of debt when the company used debt with optionlike features, such as call, conversion, or put provisions? Clearly, options affect the value of debt. For example, a callable bond would have a yield greater than a similar noncallable bond of the same issuer because bondholders want to be compensated for the call risk associated with the bond. In a similar manner, the put feature of a bond, which provides the investor with an option to sell the bond back to the issuer at a predetermined price, has the effect of lowering the yield on a bond below that of a similar nonputable bond.

If the company already has debt outstanding incorporating optionlike features that the analyst believes are representative of the future debt issuance of the company, the analyst may simply use the yield to maturity on such debt in estimating the cost of debt.

If the analyst believes that the company will add or remove option features in future debt issuance, the analyst can make market value adjustments to the current YTM to reflect the value of such additions and/or deletions. The technology for such adjustments is an advanced topic that is outside the scope of this reading.[11]

3.1.3.3 Nonrated Debt   If a company does not have any debt outstanding or if the yields on the company's existing debt are not available, the analyst may not always be able to use the yield on similarly rated debt securities. It may be the case that the company does not have rated bonds. Though researchers offer approaches for estimating a company's "synthetic" debt rating based on financial ratios, these methods are imprecise because debt ratings incorporate not only financial ratios but also information about the particular bond issue and the issuer that are not captured in financial ratios.

3.1.3.4 Leases   A lease is a contractual obligation that can substitute for other forms of borrowing. This is true whether the lease is an operating lease or a capital lease, though only the capital lease is represented as a liability on the company's balance sheet.[12] If the company uses leasing as a source of capital, the cost of these leases should be included in the cost of capital. The cost of this form of borrowing is similar to that of the company's other long-term borrowing.

3.2 Cost of Preferred Stock

The **cost of preferred stock** is the cost that a company has committed to pay preferred stockholders as a preferred dividend when it issues preferred stock. In the

---

[11] See, for example, *Fixed Income Analysis for the Chartered Financial Analyst® Program*, by Frank Fabozzi, for an introduction. Fabozzi discusses the estimation of an option-adjusted spread (OAS) to price the call option feature of a callable bond.

[12] In the United States, an operating lease is distinguished from a capital lease in Statement of Financial Accounting Standards No. 13, *Accounting for Leases* (FASB, November 1976). (IAS 17 similarly distinguishes between operating and finance leases, another term for capital-type leases.) These two forms of leases are distinguished on the basis of ownership transference, the existence of a bargain purchase option, the term of the lease relative to the economic life of the asset, and the present value of the lease payments relative to the value of the asset. In either case, however, the lease obligation is a form of borrowing, even though it is only in the case of a capital lease that the obligation appears as a liability on the company's balance sheet. The discount rate applied in the valuation of a capital lease is the rate of borrowing at the time of the lease commencement; therefore, it is reasonable to apply the company's long-term borrowing rate when estimating the cost of capital for leasing.

case of nonconvertible, noncallable preferred stock that has a fixed dividend rate and no maturity date (**fixed rate perpetual preferred stock**), we can use the formula for the value of a preferred stock:

$$P_p = \frac{D_p}{r_p}$$

where

P_p is the current preferred stock price per share
D_p is the preferred stock dividend per share
r_P is the cost of preferred stock

We can rearrange this equation to solve for the cost of preferred stock:

$$r_p = \frac{D_p}{P_p} \qquad\qquad\text{(48-3)}$$

Therefore, the cost of preferred stock is the preferred stock's dividend per share divided by the current preferred stock's price per share. Unlike interest on debt, the dividend on preferred stock is not tax deductible by the company; therefore, there is no adjustment to the cost for taxes.[13]

A preferred stock may have a number of features that affect the yield and hence the cost of preferred stock. These features include a call option, cumulative dividends, participating dividends, adjustable-rate dividends, or convertibility into common stock. When estimating a yield based on current yields of the company's preferred stock, we must make appropriate adjustments for the effects of these features on the yield of an issue. For example, if the company has callable, convertible preferred stock outstanding, yet it is expected that the company will issue only noncallable, nonconvertible preferred stock in the future, we would have to either use the current yields on comparable companies' noncallable, nonconvertible preferred stock or estimate the yield on preferred equity using methods outside the scope of this reading.[14]

Example 48-5

Calculating the Cost of Preferred Equity

Alcoa has one class of preferred stock outstanding, a $3.75 cumulative preferred stock, for which there are 546,024 shares outstanding.[15] If the price of this stock is $72, what is the estimate of Alcoa's cost of preferred equity?

▶ **Solution.** Cost of Alcoa's preferred stock = $3.75/$72.00 = 5.21 percent.

---

[13] This is not to be confused, however, with the dividends received deduction, which reduces the effective tax on intercorporate preferred dividends received.

[14] A method for estimating this yield involves first estimating the option-adjusted spread (OAS). For further information on the OAS, see, for example, Frank Fabozzi's *Fixed Income Analysis for the Chartered Financial Analyst® Program.*

[15] Alcoa Annual Report 2004, footnote R, p. 56.

> **Example 48-6**
>
> ### Choosing the Best Estimate of the Cost of Preferred Equity
>
> Wim Vanistendael is finance director of De Gouden Tulip N.V., a leading Dutch flower producer and distributor. He has been asked by the CEO to calculate the cost of preferred equity and has recently obtained the following information:
>
> ▶ The issue price of preferred stock was €3.5 million and the preferred dividend is 5 percent.
>
> ▶ If the company issued new preferred stock today, the preferred coupon rate would be 6.5 percent.
>
> ▶ The company's marginal tax rate is 30.5 percent.
>
> What is the cost of preferred equity for De Gouden Tulip N.V.?
>
> ▶ **Solution.** If De Gouden Tulip were to issue new preferred stock today, the coupon rate would be close to 6.5 percent. The current terms thus prevail over the past terms when evaluating the actual cost of preferred stock. The cost of preferred stock for De Gouden Tulip is, therefore, 6.5 percent. Because preferred dividends offer no tax shield, there is no adjustment made based upon the marginal tax rate.

3.3 Cost of Common Equity

The cost of common equity, (r_e), usually referred to simply as the cost of equity, is the rate of return required by a company's common shareholders. A company may increase common equity through the reinvestment of earnings—that is, retained earnings—or through the issuance of new shares of stock.

As we discussed earlier, the estimation of the cost of equity is challenging because of the uncertain nature of the future cash flows in terms of the amount and timing. Commonly used approaches for estimating the cost of equity include the capital asset pricing model, the dividend discount model, and the bond yield plus risk premium method.

3.3.1 Capital Asset Pricing Model Approach

In the capital asset pricing model (CAPM) approach, we use the basic relationship from the capital asset pricing model theory that the expected return on a stock, $E(R_i)$, is the sum of the risk-free rate of interest, R_F, and a premium for bearing the stock's market risk, $\beta(R_M - R_F)$:

$$E(R_i) = R_F + \beta_i [E(R_M) - R_F] \tag{48-4}$$

where

$\beta_i =$ the return sensitivity of stock i to changes in the market return

$E(R_M) =$ the expected return on the market

$E(R_M) - R_F =$ the expected market risk premium

A risk-free asset is defined here as an asset that has no default risk. A common proxy for the risk-free rate is the yield on a default-free government debt instrument. In general, the selection of the appropriate risk-free rate should be guided by the duration of projected cash flows. If we are evaluating a project with an estimated useful life of 10 years, we may want to use the rate on the 10-year Treasury bond.

Example 48-7

Using the CAPM to Estimate the Cost of Equity

Valence Industries wants to know its cost of equity. Its CFO believes the risk-free rate is 5 percent, equity risk premium is 7 percent, and Valence's equity beta is 1.5. What is Valence's cost of equity using the CAPM approach?

▶ **Solution.** Cost of common stock = 5 percent + 1.5(7 percent) = 15.5 percent.

The expected market risk premium, or $E(R_M - R_F)$, is the premium that investors demand for investing in a market portfolio relative to the risk-free rate. When using the CAPM to estimate the cost of equity, in practice we typically estimate beta relative to an equity market index. In that case, the market premium estimate we are using is actually an estimate of the **equity risk premium** (ERP).

An alternative to the CAPM to accommodate risks that may not be captured by the market portfolio alone is a **multifactor model** that incorporates factors that may be other sources of **priced risk** (risk for which investors demand compensation for bearing), including macroeconomic factors and company-specific factors. In general

$$E(R_i) = R_F + \beta_{i1}(\text{Factor risk premium})_1 \\ + \beta_{i2}(\text{Factor risk premium})_2 + \ldots \\ + \beta_{ij}(\text{Factor risk premium})_j \tag{48-5}$$

where

β_{ij} is stock i's sensitivity to changes in the jth factor
(Factor risk premium)$_j$ is expected risk premium for the jth factor

The basic idea behind these multifactor models is that the CAPM beta may not capture all the risks, especially in a global context, which include inflation, business-cycle, interest rate, exchange rate, and default risks.[16, 17]

---

[16] An example of the multi-factor model is the three-factor Fama and French model [Eugene Fama and Kenneth French, "The Cross-Section of Expected Stock Returns," *Journal of Finance*, Vol. 47, No. 2 (1992), pp. 427–465], which includes factors for the market, equity capitalization, and the ratio of book value of equity to the market value of equity.

[17] These models are discussed in more detail by Robert F. Bruner, Robert M. Conroy, Wei Li, Elizabeth O'Halloran, and Miquel Palacios Lleras [*Investing in Emerging Markets*, AIMR Research Foundation monograph (August 2003)] and by Eugene F. Fama and Kenneth R. French, ["The Capital Asset Pricing Model: Theory and Evidence," *Journal of Economic Perspectives*, Vol. 18, No. 3 (Summer 2004), pp. 3–24.]

There are several ways to estimate the equity risk premium, though there is no general agreement as to the best approach. The three we discuss are the historical equity risk premium approach, the dividend discount model approach, and the survey approach.

The **historical equity risk premium approach** is a well-established approach based on the assumption that the realized equity risk premium observed over a long period of time is a good indicator of the expected equity risk premium. This approach requires compiling historical data to find the average rate of return of a country's market portfolio and the average rate of return for the risk-free rate in that country. For example, an analyst might use the historical returns to the TOPIX Index to estimate the risk premium for Japanese equities. The exceptional bull market observed during the second half of the 1990s, and the bursting of the technology bubble that followed during the years 2000–2002, reminds us that the time period for such estimates should cover complete market cycles.

Elroy Dimson, Paul Marsh, and Mike Staunton conduct an analysis of the equity risk premiums observed in markets located in 16 countries, including the United States, over the period 1900–2002.[18] These researchers found that the annualized U.S. equity risk premium relative to U.S. Treasury bills was 5.3 percent (geometric mean) and 7.2 percent (arithmetic mean). They also found that the annualized U.S. equity risk premium relative to bonds was 4.4 percent (geometric mean) and 6.4 percent (arithmetic mean).[19] Note that the arithmetic mean is greater than the geometric mean as a result of the significant volatility of the observed market rate of return and of the observed risk-free rate. Under the assumption of an unchanging distribution of returns through time, the arithmetic mean is the unbiased estimate of the expected single-period equity risk premium, but the geometric mean better reflects growth rate over multiple periods.[20] In Table 48-1 we provide historical estimates of the equity risk premium for 16 developed markets from Dimson, Marsh, and Staunton's study. To illustrate the historical method as applied in the CAPM, suppose that we use the historical geometric mean for U.S. equity of 4.8 percent to value Citibank Inc. (NYSE: C) as of early January 2006. According to Standard & Poor's, Citibank had a beta of 1.32 at that time. Using the 10-year U.S. Treasury bond yield of 4.38 percent to represent the risk-free rate, the estimate of the cost of equity for Citibank is 4.38 percent + 1.32(4.8 percent) = 10.72 percent.

The historical premium approach has several limitations. One limitation is that the level of risk of the stock index may change over time. Another is that the risk aversion of investors may change over time. And still another limitation is that the estimates are sensitive to the method of estimation and the historical period covered.

---

[18] Elroy Dimson, Paul Marsh, and Mike Staunton, "Global Evidence on the Equity Risk Premium," *Journal of Applied Corporate Finance* (Fall 2003), pp. 27–38.

[19] Jeremy Siegel presents a longer time series of market returns, covering the period from 1802 through 2004, and observes an equity return of 6.82 percent and an equity risk premium in the range of 3.31 to 5.36 percent. See Jeremy J. Siegel, "Perspectives on the Equity Risk Premium," *Financial Analysts Journal*, Vol. 61, No. 6 (November/December 2005), pp. 61–73. The range depends on the method of calculation (compounded or arithmetic) and the benchmark (bonds or bills).

[20] Aside from the method of averaging (geometric versus arithmetic), estimates of the historical equity risk premium differ depending on the assumed investment horizon (short versus intermediate versus long), whether conditional on some variable or unconditional, whether U.S. or global markets are examined, the source of the data, the period observed, and whether nominal or real returns are estimated.

TABLE 48-1   Equity Risk Premiums Relative to Bonds (1900 to 2001)

	Mean	
Country	Geometric	Arithmetic
Australia	6.3%	7.9%
Belgium	2.8	4.7
Canada	4.2	5.7
Denmark	1.8	3.1
France	4.6	6.7
Germany	6.3	9.6
Ireland	3.1	4.5
Italy	4.6	8.0
Japan	5.9	10.0
The Netherlands	4.4	6.4
South Africa	5.4	7.1
Spain	2.2	4.1
Sweden	4.9	7.1
Switzerland	2.4	3.9
United Kingdom	4.2	5.5
United States	4.8	6.7
World	4.3	5.4

Note: Germany excludes 1922–23. Switzerland commences in 1911.

Source: Dimson, Marsh, and Staunton (2003).

Example 48-8

Estimating the Equity Risk Premium Using Historical Rates of Return

Suppose that the arithmetic average T-bond rate observed over the last 100 years is an unbiased estimator for the risk-free rate and amounts to 5.4 percent. Likewise, suppose the arithmetic average of return on the market observed over the last 100 years is an unbiased estimator for the expected return for the market. The average rate of return of the market was 9.3 percent. Calculate the equity risk premium.

▶ **Solution.**

$$\text{ERP} = \overline{R}_M - \overline{R}_F = 9.3 \text{ percent} - 5.4 \text{ percent} = 3.9 \text{ percent}.$$

A second approach for estimating the equity risk premium is the **dividend discount model based approach** or **implied risk premium approach**, which is implemented using the Gordon growth model (also known as the constant-growth dividend discount model). For developed markets, corporate earnings often meet, at least approximately, the model's assumption of a long-run trend growth rate. We extract the premium by analyzing how the market prices an index. That is, we use the relationship between the value of an index and expected dividends, assuming a constant growth in dividends:

$$P_0 = \frac{D_1}{r_e - g}$$

where P_0 is the current market value of the equity market index, D_1 are the dividends expected next period on the index, r_e is the required rate of return on the market, and g is the expected growth rate of dividends. We solve for the required rate of return on the market as

$$r_e = \frac{D_1}{P_0} + g \qquad \textbf{(48-6)}$$

Therefore, the expected return on the market is the sum of the dividend yield and the growth rate in dividends.[21] The equity risk premium thus is the difference between the expected return on the equity market and the risk-free rate.

Suppose the expected dividend yield on an equity index is 5 percent and the expected growth rate of dividends on the index is 2 percent. The expected return on the market according to the Gordon growth model is

$$E(R_m) = 5 \text{ percent} + 2 \text{ percent} = 7 \text{ percent}$$

A risk-free rate of interest of 3.8 percent implies an equity risk premium of 7 percent − 3.8 percent = 3.2 percent.

Another approach to estimate the equity risk premium is quite direct: Ask a panel of finance experts for their estimates and take the mean response. This is the **survey approach**. For example, one set of U.S. surveys found that the expected U.S. equity risk premium over the next 30 years was 5.5 percent to 7 percent forecasting from 2001 as the baseline year and 7.1 percent using 1998 as the baseline year.

Once we have an estimate of the equity risk premium, we fine-tune this estimate for the particular company or project by adjusting it for the specific systematic risk of the project. We adjust for the specific systematic risk by multiplying the market risk premium by beta to arrive at the company's or project's risk premium, which we then add to the risk-free rate to determine the cost of equity within the framework of the CAPM.[22]

3.3.2 *Dividend Discount Model Approach*

Earlier we used the Gordon growth model to develop an estimate of the equity risk premium for use in the CAPM. We can also use the Gordon growth model directly to obtain an estimate of the cost of equity. To review, the dividend

---

[21] We explain Equation 48-6 in more detail in Section 3.3.2.

[22] Some researchers argue that the equity risk premium should reflect a country risk premium. For example, a multinational company or project may have a higher cost of capital than a comparable domestic company because of political risk, foreign exchange risk, or higher agency costs. In most cases, this risk is unsystematic and hence does not affect the cost of capital estimate.

discount model in general states that the intrinsic value of a share of stock is the present value of the share's expected future dividends:

$$V_0 = \sum_{t=1}^{\infty}\left(\frac{D_t}{(1 + r_e)^t}\right) = \frac{D_1}{(1 + r_e)} + \frac{D_2}{(1 + r_e)^2} + \ldots$$

where

V_0 is the intrinsic value of a share
D_t is the share's dividend at the end of period t
r_e is the cost of equity

Based on Gordon's constant growth formulation, we assume dividends are expected to grow at a constant rate, g.[23] Therefore, if we assume that price reflects intrinsic value ($V_0 = P_0$), we can rewrite the valuation of the stock as

$$P_0 = \frac{D_1}{r_e - g}$$

We can then rewrite the above equation and estimate the cost of equity as we did for Equation 48-6 in Section 3.3.1:

$$r_e = \frac{D_1}{P_0} + g$$

Therefore, to estimate r_e, we need to estimate the dividend in the next period and the assumed constant dividend growth rate. The current stock price, P_0, is known, and the dividend of the next period, D_1, can be predicted if the company has a stable dividend policy. (The ratio D_1/P_0 may be called the forward annual dividend yield.) The challenge is estimating the growth rate.

There are at least two ways to estimate the growth rate. The first is to use a forecasted growth rate from a published source or vendor. A second is to use a relationship between the growth rate, the retention rate, and the return on equity. In this context, this is often referred to as the **sustainable growth rate** and is interpretable as the rate of dividend (and earnings) growth that can be sustained over time for a given level of return on equity, keeping the capital structure constant and without issuing additional common stock. The relationship is given in Equation 48-7:

$$g = (1 - {}^{D}/_{EPS})\,ROE \qquad\qquad \textbf{(48-7)}$$

where D/EPS represents the assumed stable dividend payout ratio and ROE is the historical return on equity. The term $(1 - D/EPS)$ is the company's earnings retention rate.

Consider Citigroup, Inc. Citigroup has an earnings retention rate of 59 percent. As of early January 2006, Citigroup had a forward annual dividend yield of 3.9 percent, a trailing return on equity of approximately 20 percent, but an estimated average return on equity going forward of approximately 16.6 percent. According to Equation 48-7, Citigroup's sustainable growth rate is 0.59(16.6 percent) = 9.79 percent. The dividend discount model estimate of the cost of equity is, therefore, 9.79 percent + 3.9 percent = 13.69 percent.

[23] Myron J. Gordon, *The Investment, Financing, and Valuation of the Corporation*, Homewood, IL: Irwin, 1962.

3.3.3 Bond Yield Plus Risk Premium Approach

The **bond yield plus risk premium approach** is based on the fundamental tenet in financial theory that the cost of capital of riskier cash flows is higher than that of less risky cash flows. In this approach, we sum the before-tax cost of debt, r_d, and a risk premium that captures the additional yield on a company's stock relative to its bonds. The estimate is, therefore,

$$r_e = r_d + \text{Risk premium} \qquad \text{(48-8)}$$

The risk premium compensates for the additional risk of equity compared with debt.[24] Ideally, this risk premium is forward looking, representing the additional risk associated with the stock of the company as compared with the bonds of the same company. However, we often estimate this premium using historical spreads between bond yields and stock yields. In developed country markets, a typical risk premium added is in the range of 3 to 5 percent.

Looking again at Citigroup, as of early January 2006, the yield to maturity of the Citigroup 5.3s bonds maturing in 2016 was approximately 4.95 percent. Adding an arbitrary risk premium of 3.5 percent produces an estimate of the cost of equity of 4.95 + 3.5 = 8.45 percent. This estimate contrasts with the higher estimates of 10.72 percent, under the CAPM approach, and 13.69 percent, under the dividend discount model approach. Such disparities are not uncommon and reflect the difficulty of cost of equity estimation.

TOPICS IN COST OF CAPITAL ESTIMATION

4

When calculating a company's weighted average cost of capital (WACC), it is essential to understand the risk factors that have been considered in determining the risk-free rate, the equity risk premium, and beta to ensure a consistent calculation of WACC and avoid the double counting or omission of pertinent risk factors.

4.1 Estimating Beta and Determining a Project Beta

When the analyst uses the CAPM to estimate the cost of equity, he or she must estimate beta. The estimation of beta presents many choices as well as challenges.

One common method of estimating the company's stock beta is to use a market model regression of the company's stock returns (R_i) against market returns (R_m) over T periods:[25]

$$R_{it} = \hat{a} + \hat{b} R_{mt} \quad t = 1, 2, \ldots T$$

---

[24] This risk premium is not to be confused with the equity risk premium. The equity risk premium is the difference between the cost of equity and the *risk-free rate of interest*. The risk premium in the bond yield plus risk premium approach is the difference between the cost of equity and the *company's cost of debt*.

[25] This equation is commonly referred to as the *market model* and was first introduced by Michael C. Jensen in "The Performance of Mutual Funds in the Period 1945–1964," *Journal of Finance*, Vol. 23, No. 2 (1969), pp. 389–416.

where â is the estimated intercept and $\hat{b}$ is the estimated slope of the regression that is used as an estimate of beta. However, beta estimates are sensitive to the method of estimation and data used. Consider some of the issues:

▶ *Estimation period.* The estimated beta is sensitive to the length of the estimation period, with beta commonly estimated using data over two to nine years. Selection of the estimation period is a trade-off between data richness captured by longer estimation periods and company-specific changes that are better reflected with shorter estimation periods. In general, longer estimation periods are applied to companies with a long and stable operating history, and shorter estimation periods are used for companies that have undergone significant structural changes in the recent past (such as restructuring, recent acquisition, or divestiture) or changes in financial and operating leverage.

▶ *Periodicity of the return interval* (e.g., daily, weekly, or monthly). Researchers have observed smaller standard error in beta estimated using smaller return intervals, such as daily returns.[26]

▶ *Selection of an appropriate market index.* The choice of market index affects the estimate of beta.

▶ *Use of a smoothing technique.* Some analysts adjust historical betas to reflect the tendency of betas to revert to 1.[27] As an example, the expression $\beta_{i,adj} = 0.333 + 0.667\beta_i$ adjusts betas above and below 1.0 toward 1.0.

▶ *Adjustments for small-capitalization stocks.* Small-capitalization stocks have generally exhibited greater risks and greater returns than large-capitalization stocks over the long run. Roger Ibbotson, Paul Kaplan, and James Peterson argue that betas for small-capitalization companies be adjusted upward.[28]

Arriving at an estimated beta for publicly traded companies is generally not a problem because of the accessibility of stock return data, the ease of use of estimating beta using simple regression, and the availability of estimated betas on publicly traded companies from financial analysis vendors, such as Barra, Bloomberg, Thompson Financial's Datastream, Reuters, and Value Line. The challenge is to estimate a beta for a company that is not publicly traded or to estimate a beta for a project that is not the average or typical project of a publicly traded company. Estimating a beta in these cases requires proxying for the beta by using the information on the project or company combined with a beta of a publicly traded company.

The beta of a company or project is affected by the systematic components of business risk and by financial risk. Both of these factors affect the uncertainty of the cash flows of the company or project. The **business risk** of a company or project is the risk related to the uncertainty of revenues, referred to as **sales risk**, and to **operating risk**, which is the risk attributed to the company's operating cost structure. Sales risk is affected by the elasticity of the demand of the product, the cyclicality of the revenues, and the structure of competition in the industry.

---

[26] Phillip R. Daves, Michael C. Ehrhardt, and Robert A. Kunkel, "Estimating Systematic Risk: The Choice of Return Interval and Estimation Period," *Journal of Financial and Strategic Decisions*, Vol. 13, No. 1 (Spring 2000), pp. 7–13.

[27] Marshall Blume, "On the Assessment of Risk," *Journal of Finance*, Vol. 26, No. 1, (March 1971), pp. 1–10.

[28] Roger G. Ibbotson, Paul D. Kaplan, and James D. Peterson, "Estimates of Small Stock Betas Are Much Too Low," *Journal of Portfolio Management* (Summer 1997), pp. 104–110.

Operating risk is affected by the relative mix of fixed and variable operating costs: the greater the fixed operating costs, relative to variable operating costs, the greater the uncertainty of income and cash flows from operations.

Financial risk is the uncertainty of net income and net cash flows attributed to the use of financing that has a fixed cost, such as debt and leases. The greater the use of fixed-financing sources of capital, relative to variable sources, the greater the financial risk. In other words, a company that relies heavily on debt financing instead of equity financing is assuming a great deal of financial risk.

How does a financial analyst estimate a beta for a company or project that is not publicly traded? One common method is the **pure-play method**, which requires using a comparable publicly traded company's beta and adjusting it for financial leverage differences.

A **comparable company** is a company that has similar business risk. The reason it is referred to as the *pure-play* method is that one of the easiest ways of identifying a comparable for a project is to find a company in the same industry that is in that *single* line of business. For example, if the analyst is examining a project that involves drug stores, appropriate comparables in the United States may be Walgreens, CVS Corporation, and Rite Aid Corporation.

In estimating a beta in this way, the analyst must make adjustments to account for differing degrees of financial leverage. This requires a process of "unlevering" and "levering" the beta. The beta of the comparable is first "unlevered" by removing the effects of its financial leverage.[29] The unlevered beta is often referred to as the **asset beta** because it reflects the business risk of the assets. Once we determine the unlevered beta, we adjust it for the capital structure of the company or project that is the focus of our analysis. In other words, we "lever" the asset beta to arrive at an estimate of the equity beta for the project or company of interest.

For a given company, we can unlever its equity beta to estimate its asset beta. To do this, we must determine the relationship between a company's asset beta and its equity beta. Because the company's risk is shared between creditors and owners, we can represent the company's risk, β_{asset}, as the weighted average of the company's creditors' market risk, β_{debt}, and the market risk of the owners, β_{equity}:

$$\beta_{asset} = \beta_{debt}\, w_d + \beta_{equity}\, w_e$$

or

$$\beta_{asset} = \beta_{debt}\left(\frac{D}{D+E}\right) + \beta_{equity}\left(\frac{E}{D+E}\right)$$

where

E = market value of equity
D = market value of debt
w_d = proportion of debt = $D/D+E$
w_e = proportion of equity = $E/D+E$

But interest on debt is deducted by the company to arrive at taxable income, so the claim that creditors have on the company's assets does not cost the company the full amount but, rather, the *after-tax* claim; the burden of debt financing is

---

[29] The process of unlevering and levering a beta was developed by Robert S. Hamada ["The Effect of the Firm's Capital Structure on the Systematic Risk of Common Stocks," *Journal of Finance* (May 1972), pp. 435–452] and is based on the capital structure theories of Franco Modigliani and Merton Miller.

actually less due to interest deductibility. We can represent the asset beta of a company as the weighted average of the betas of debt and equity after considering the effects of the tax deductibility of interest:

$$\beta_{asset} = \beta_{debt}\frac{(1-t)D}{(1-t)D+E} + \beta_{equity}\frac{E}{(1-t)D+E}$$

where t is the marginal tax rate.

We generally assume that a company's debt does not have market risk, so $\beta_{debt} = 0$. This means that the returns on debt do not vary with the returns on the market, which we generally assume to be true for most large companies. If $\beta_{debt} = 0$, then[30]

$$\beta_{asset} = \beta_{equity}\left[\frac{1}{1 + \left((1-t)\dfrac{D}{E}\right)}\right] \qquad \textbf{(48-9)}$$

Therefore, the market risk of a company's equity is affected by both the asset's market risk, β_{asset}, and a factor representing the nondiversifiable portion of company's financial risk, $[1 + (1-t)D/_E]$:

$$\beta_{equity} = \beta_{asset}\left[1 + \left((1-t)\dfrac{D}{E}\right)\right] \qquad \textbf{(48-10)}$$

Suppose a company has an equity beta of 1.5, a debt-to-equity ratio of 0.4, and a marginal tax rate of 30 percent. Using Equation 48-9, the company's asset beta is 1.3393:

$$\beta_{asset} = 1.5\left[\frac{1}{1 + ((0.3(0.4))}\right] = 1.5\,[0.8929] = 1.3393$$

In other words, if the company did not have any debt financing, its $\beta_{asset} = \beta_{equity} = 1.3393$; however, the use of debt financing increases its β_{equity} from 1.3393 to 1.5. What would the company's equity beta be if the company's debt-to-equity ratio were 0.5 instead of 0.4? In this case, we apply Equation 48-10, using the debt-to-equity ratio of 0.5:

$$\beta_{equity} = 1.3393\,[1 + (0.3(0.5))] = 1.5402$$

Therefore, the unlevering calculation produces a measure of market risk for the assets of the company—ignoring the company's capital structure. We use the levering calculation in Equation 48-10 to estimate the market risk of a company given a specific asset risk, marginal tax rate, and capital structure.

We can use the same unlevering and levering calculations to estimate the asset risk and equity risk for a project. We start with the equity beta of the comparable company, which is the levered beta, $\beta_{L,comparable}$, and then convert it

---

[30] The first step is $\beta_{asset} = \beta_{equity}\left[\dfrac{E}{(1-t)D+E}\right]$, which we simplify to arrive at Equation 48-9.

into the equivalent asset beta for the unlevered company, $\beta_{U,comparable}$. Once we have the estimate of the unlevered beta, which is the company's asset risk, we then can use the project's capital structure and marginal tax rate to convert this asset beta into an equity beta for the project, $\beta_{L,project}$.

Estimating a Beta Using the Pure-Play Method

Step 1: Select the comparable   Determine comparable company or companies. These are companies with similar business risk.

$\downarrow$

Step 2: Estimate comparable's beta   Estimate the equity beta of the comparable company or companies.

$\downarrow$

Step 3: Unlever the comparable's beta   Unlever the beta of the comparable company or companies, removing the financial risk component of the equity beta, leaving the business risk component of the beta.

$\downarrow$

Step 4: Lever the beta for the project's financial risk   Lever the beta of the project by adjusting the asset beta for the financial risk of the project.

We begin by estimating the levered beta of the comparable company, $\beta_{L,comparable}$. Using the capital structure and tax rate of the levered company, we estimate the asset beta for the comparable company, $\beta_{U,comparable}$:

$$\beta_{U,comparable} = \frac{\beta_{L,comparable}}{\left[1 + \left((1 - t_{comparable})\dfrac{D_{comparable}}{E_{comparable}}\right)\right]} \qquad \textbf{(48-11)}$$

We then consider the financial leverage of the project or company and calculate its equity risk, $\beta_{L,project}$:

$$\beta_{L,project} = \beta_{U,comparable}\left[1 + \left((1 - t_{project})\dfrac{D_{project}}{E_{project}}\right)\right] \qquad \textbf{(48-12)}$$

To illustrate the use of these equations, suppose we want to evaluate a project that will be financed with debt and equity in a ratio of 0.4:1 (a debt-to-equity ratio of 0.4, corresponding to approximately $0.4/(0.4 + 1.0) = €0.286$ for each euro of capital needed). We find a comparable company operating in the same line of business as the project. The marginal tax rate for the company sponsoring the project and the comparable company is 35 percent. The comparable company has a beta of 1.2 and a debt-to-equity ratio of 0.125. The unlevered beta of the comparable is 1.1098:

$$\beta_{U,comparable} = \frac{1.2}{\left[1 + ((1 - 0.35)\ 0.125)\right]} = 1.1098$$

The levered beta for the project is 1.3983:

$$\beta_{L,project} = 1.1098\left[1 + ((1 - 0.35)\ 0.4)\right] = 1.3983$$

We then use the 1.3983 as the beta in our CAPM estimate of the component cost of equity for the project and, combined with the cost of debt in a weighted average, provide an estimate of the cost of capital for the project.[31]

---

[31] In this example, the weights are $w_d = 0.4/1.4 = 0.2857$ and $w_e = 1/1.4 = 0.7143$.

Example 48-9

Inferring an Asset Beta

Suppose that the beta of a publicly traded company's stock is 1.3 and that the market value of equity and debt are, respectively, C$540 million and C$720 million. If the marginal tax rate of this company is 40 percent, what is the asset beta of this company?

▶ **Solution.**

$$\beta_U = \frac{1.3}{\left[1 + \left((1 - 0.4)\dfrac{720}{540}\right)\right]} = 0.72$$

Example 48-10

Calculating a Beta Using the Pure-Play Method

Raymond Cordier is the business development manager of Aerotechnique S.A., a private Belgian subcontractor of aerospace parts. Although Aerotechnique is not listed on the Belgian stock exchange, Cordier needs to evaluate the levered beta for the company. He has access to the following information:

▶ The average levered and average unlevered betas for the group of comparable companies operating in different European countries are 1.6 and 1.0, respectively.

▶ Aerotechnique's debt-to-equity ratio, based on market values, is 1.4.

▶ Aerotechnique's corporate tax rate is 34 percent.

▶ **Solution.** The beta for Aerotechnique is estimated on the basis of the average unlevered beta extracted from the group of comparable companies. On that basis, and applying the financing structure of Aerotechnique, the estimated beta for Aerotechnique is

$$\beta_{Aerotechnique} = 1.0\left[1 + ((1 - 0.34)(1.4))\right] = 1.924$$

Example 48-11

Estimating the Weighted Average Cost of Capital

Georg Schrempp is the CFO of Bayern Chemicals KgaA, a large German manufacturer of industrial, commercial, and consumer chemical products. Bayern Chemicals is privately owned, and its shares are not listed on an exchange. The CFO has appointed Markus Meier, CFA, of Crystal Clear Valuation Advisors, a third-party valuator, to perform a stand-alone valuation of Bayern Chemicals. Meier had access to the following information to calculate Bayern Chemicals' weighted average cost of capital:

▶ The nominal risk-free rate is represented by the yield on the long-term 10-year German bund, which at the valuation date was 4.5 percent.

▶ The average long-term historical equity risk premium in Germany is assumed at 5.7 percent.[32]

▶ Bayern Chemicals' corporate tax rate is 38 percent.

▶ Bayern Chemicals' target debt-to-equity ratio is 0.7. Bayern is operating at its target debt-to-equity ratio.

▶ Bayern Chemicals' cost of debt has an estimated spread of 225 basis points over the 10-year bund.

▶ Table 48-2 supplies additional information on comparables for Bayern Chemicals.

TABLE 48-2   Information on Comparables

Comparable companies	Country	Tax rate	Market capitalization in millions	Net debt in millions	D/E	Beta
British Chemicals Ltd.	UK	30.0%	4,500	6,000	1.33	1.45
Compagnie Petrochimique S.A.	France	30.3%	9,300	8,700	0.94	0.75
Rotterdam Chemie N.V.	Netherlands	30.5%	7,000	7,900	1.13	1.05
Average					1.13	1.08

Based only on the information given, calculate Bayern Chemicals' WACC.

▶ **Solution.** To calculate the cost of equity, the first step is to "unlever" the betas of the comparable companies and calculate an average for a company with business risk similar to the average of these companies:

Comparable companies	Unlevered beta
British Chemicals Ltd.	0.75
Compagnie Petrochimique S.A.	0.45
Rotterdam Chemie N.V.	0.59
Average	0.60

---

[32] Dimson, Marsh, and Staunton, *ibid.*

Levering the average unlevered beta for the peer group average, applying Bayern Chemicals' target debt-to-equity ratio and marginal tax rate, results in a beta of 0.86:

$$\beta_{\text{Bayern Chemical}} = 0.60\,\{1 + [(1 - 0.38)\,0.7]\} = 0.86$$

The cost of equity of Bayern Chemicals (r_e) can be calculated as follows:

$$r_e = 4.5 \text{ percent} + (0.86)(5.7 \text{ percent}) = 9.4 \text{ percent}$$

The weights for the cost of equity and cost of debt may be calculated as follows:

$$w_d = \frac{D/E}{\left(\dfrac{D}{E} + 1\right)} = \frac{0.7}{1.7} = 0.41$$
$$w_e = 1 - w_d = 1 - 0.41 = 0.59$$

The before-tax cost of debt of Bayern Chemicals (r_d) is 6.75 percent:

$$r_d = 4.5 \text{ percent} + 2.25 \text{ percent} = 6.75 \text{ percent}.$$

As a result, Bayern Chemicals' WACC is 7.27 percent:

$$\text{WACC} = [(0.41)(0.0675)(1 - 0.38)] + [(0.59)(0.094)]$$
$$= 0.0726 \text{ or } 7.26 \text{ percent.}$$

4.2 Country Risk

The use of a stock's beta to capture the country risks of a project is well supported in empirical studies that examine developed nations. However, beta does not appear to adequately capture **country risk** for companies in developing nations.[33] A common approach for dealing with this problem is to adjust the cost of equity estimated using the CAPM by adding a **country spread** to the market risk premium.[34] The country spread is also referred to as a **country equity premium**.

Perhaps the simplest estimate of the country spread is the **sovereign yield spread**, which is the difference between the government bond yield in that country, denominated in the currency of a developed country, and the Treasury bond yield on a similar maturity bond in the developed country.[35] However, this approach may be too coarse for the purposes of equity risk premium estimation.

---

[33] Campbell R. Harvey, "The International Cost of Capital and Risk Calculator," Duke University working paper (July 2001).

[34] Adding the country spread to the market risk premium for a developing country and then multiplying this sum by the market risk of the project is making the assumption that the country risk premium varies according to market risk. An alternative method calculates the cost of equity as the sum of three terms: (1) the risk-free rate of interest, (2) the product of the beta and the developed market risk premium, and (3) the country risk premium. This latter method assumes that the country risk premium is the same, regardless of the project's market risk.

[35] Jorge O. Mariscal and Rafaelina M. Lee, "The Valuation of Mexican Stocks: An Extension of the Capital Asset Pricing Model," New York: Goldman Sachs (1993).

Another approach is to calculate the country equity premium as the product of the sovereign yield spread and the ratio of the volatility of the developing country equity market to that of the sovereign bond market denominated in terms of the currency of a developed country:[36]

$$\text{Country equity premium} = \text{Sovereign yield spread}\left(\frac{\text{Annualized standard deviation of equity index}}{\text{Annualized standard deviation of the sovereign bond market in terms of the developed market currency}}\right) \qquad \textbf{(48-13)}$$

The logic of this calculation is that the sovereign yield spread captures the general risk of the country, which is then adjusted for the volatility of the stock market relative to the bond market. This country equity premium is then used in addition to the equity premium estimated for a project in a developed country. Therefore, if the equity risk premium for a project in a developed country is 4.5 percent and the country risk premium is 3 percent, the total equity risk premium used in the CAPM estimation is 7.5 percent. If the appropriate beta is 1.2 and the risk-free rate of interest is 4 percent, the equity risk premium is

Equity risk premium = 0.04 + 1.2(0.045 + 0.03) = 0.13 or 13 percent

Example 48-12

Estimating the Country Equity Premium

Miles Avenaugh, an analyst with the Global Company, is estimating a country equity premium to include in his estimate of the cost of equity capital for Global's investment in Argentina. Avenaugh has researched yields in Argentina and observed that the Argentinean government's 10-year bond is 9.5 percent. A similar maturity U.S. Treasury bond has a yield of 4.5 percent. The annualized standard deviation of the Argentina Merval stock index, a market value index of stocks listed on the Buenos Aires Stock Exchange, during the most recent year is 40 percent. The annualized standard deviation of the Argentina dollar-denominated 10-year government bond over the recent period was 28 percent.

What is the estimated country equity premium for Argentina based on Avenaugh's research?

▶ **Solution.** Country risk premium = $0.05\left(\dfrac{0.40}{0.28}\right)$ = 0.05(1.4286) = 0.0714, or 7.14 percent

---

[36] Aswath Damodaran, "Estimating Equity Risk Premiums," New York University working paper (1999) and Aswath Damodaran, "Measuring Company Exposure to Country Risk: Theory and Practice," New York University working paper (September 2003).

Still another approach is to use country credit ratings to estimate the expected rates of returns for countries that have credit ratings but no equity markets.[37] This method requires estimating reward to credit risk measures for a large sample of countries for which there are both credit ratings and equity markets and then applying this ratio to those countries without equity markets based on the country's credit rating.

4.3 Marginal Cost of Capital Schedule

As we noted in Section 2.3, as a company raises more funds, the costs of the different sources of capital may change, resulting in a change in the weighted average cost of capital for different levels of financing. The result is the marginal cost of capital (MCC) schedule, which we often depict in graphical form as the weighted average cost of capital for different amounts of capital raised, as we showed earlier in Figure 48-1.[38]

Why would the cost of capital change as more capital is raised? One source of a difference in cost depending on the amount of capital raised is that a company may have existing debt with a bond covenant that restricts the company from issuing debt with similar seniority as existing debt. Or, a **debt incurrence test** may restrict a company's ability to incur additional debt at the same seniority based on one or more financial tests or conditions. For example, if a company issues senior debt such that any additional debt at that seniority violates the debt incurrence test of an existing bond covenant, the company may have to issue less senior debt or even equity, which would have a higher cost.

Another source of increasing marginal costs of capital is a deviation from the target capital structure. In the ideal, theoretical world, a company has a target capital structure and goes to the market each period and raises capital in these proportions. However, as a practical matter, companies do not necessarily **tap** the market in these ideal proportions because of considerations for economies of scale in raising new capital and market conditions. Because of such perceived economies of scale, companies tend to issue new securities such that in any given period, it may deviate from the proportions dictated by any target or optimal capital structure. In other words, these short-run deviations are due to the "lumpiness" of security issuance. As the company experiences deviations from the target capital structure, the marginal cost of capital may increase, reflecting these deviations.

The amount of capital at which the weighted average cost of capital changes—which means that the cost of one of the sources of capital changes—is referred to as a **break point**. The reality of raising capital is that the marginal cost of capital schedule is not as smooth as we depicted in Figure 48-1 but, rather, is a step-up cost schedule as shown in Figure 48-2.

[37] Claude Erb, Campbell R. Harvey, and Tadas Viskanta, "Expected Returns and Volatility in 135 Countries," *Journal of Portfolio Management* (Spring 1996), pp. 46–58.

[38] In the section on capital structure and leverage, we will discuss cases where a company's WACC may actually decrease as additional capital is raised. For example, if a company financed solely with common equity raises additional capital via debt, then the tax advantages provided by debt will result in a lower WACC under the new capital structure. For this discussion, we are assuming that the company is already operating at or near its optimum balance of debt versus equity.

FIGURE 48-2 Marginal Cost of Capital Schedule

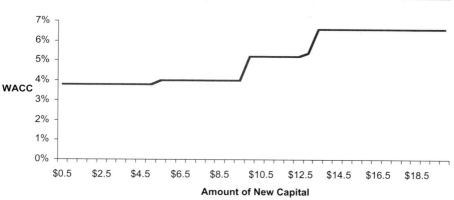

Consider the case of a company facing the costs of capital given in Table 48-3.

TABLE 48-3 Schedule of the Costs of Debt and Equity

Amount of new debt (in millions)	After-tax cost of debt	Amount of new equity (in millions)	Cost of equity
new debt ≤ €2	2.0 percent	new equity ≤ €6	5.0 percent
€2 < new debt ≤ €5	2.5 percent	€6 < new equity ≤ €8	7.0 percent
€5 < new debt	3.0 percent	€8 < new equity	9.0 percent

If the company raises capital according to its target capital structure proportions of 40 percent debt and 60 percent equity, this company faces a marginal cost of capital schedule that is upward sloping, with break points at €5 million, €10 million, €12.5 million, and €13.3 million, as depicted in Figure 48-2. These break points are determined from the amounts of capital at which the cost changes, calculated as

$$\text{Break point} = \frac{\text{Amount of capital at which the source's cost of capital changes}}{\text{Proportion of new capital raised from the source}} \tag{48-14}$$

For example, the first break point for debt financing is reached with €2 million/0.4 = €5 million of new capital raised. The first break point attributed to a change in equity cost occurs at €6 million/0.6 = €10 million. Example 48-13 illustrates a marginal cost of capital schedule with break points and also how the WACC figures in the choice of an optimal capital structure.

Example 48-13

Marginal Cost of Capital Schedule

Alan Conlon is the CFO of Allied Canadian Breweries Ltd. He wants to determine the capital structure that will result in the lowest cost of capital for Allied. He has access to the following information:

▶ The minimum rate at which the company can borrow for 12 months is 12-month LIBOR +200 basis points until it reaches a debt to total capital ratio of 30 percent. For debt to total capital ratios above 30 percent, the spread over 12-month LIBOR increases according to the following schedule given in Table 48-4.

TABLE 48-4   Spreads over LIBOR for Alternative Debt-to-Equity Ratios

$\dfrac{D}{D + E}$	Spread (bps)
0.4	300
0.5	400
0.6	600
0.7	800
0.8	1000
0.9	1200

▶ The current 12-month LIBOR is 4.5 percent.
▶ The equity risk premium is 4 percent, and unleveraged beta is 0.9.
▶ The company's tax rate is 36 percent.

1. Determine the WACC for levels of the debt-to-equity ratio given in Table 48-4.
2. Recommend a target capital structure given that the company is concerned with achieving the lowest possible cost of capital.

▶ **Solution to 1.** The WACC expressed as a function of the capital structure is shown in Table 48-5.

TABLE 48-5 WACC for Alternative Capital Structures

$\dfrac{D}{D+E}$	β	r_d (percent)	r_e (percent)	WACC (percent)
0.1	0.96	6.5	10.4	9.7
0.2	1.04	6.5	10.7	9.4
0.3	1.15	6.5	11.1	9.0
0.4	1.28	7.5	12.6	9.5
0.5	1.48	8.5	14.4	9.9
0.6	1.76	10.5	17.6	11.1
0.7	2.24	12.5	21.5	12.0
0.8	3.20	14.5	27.3	12.9
0.9	6.08	16.5	40.8	13.6

▶ **Solution to 2.** The optimal capital structure is 30 percent debt, which corresponds to an optimal D/E of 0.43.

4.4 Flotation Costs

When a company raises new capital, it generally seeks the assistance of investment bankers. Investment bankers charge the company a fee based on the size and type of offering. This fee is referred to as the **flotation cost**. In the case of debt and preferred stock, we do not usually incorporate flotation costs in the estimated cost of capital because the amount of these costs is quite small, often less than 1 percent.[39]

However, with equity issuance, the flotation costs may be substantial, so we should consider these when estimating the cost of external equity capital. For example, Inmoo Lee, Scott Lochhead, Jay Ritter, and Quanshui Zhao observe average flotation costs for new equity in the United States of 7.11 percent.[40] The flotation costs in other countries differ from the U.S. experience: Thomas Bühner and Christoph Kaserer observe flotation costs around 1.65 percent in Germany, Seth Armitage estimates an average issuance cost of 5.78 percent in the United Kingdom, and Christoph Kaserer and Fabian Steiner observe an average cost of 4.53 for Swiss capital offerings.[41] A large part of the differences in costs among these studies is likely attributed to the type of offering; cash underwritten

[39] We can incorporate them for these sources by simply treating the flotation costs as an outlay, hence reducing proceeds from the source.

[40] Inmoo Lee, Scott Lochhead, Jay R. Ritter, and Quanshui Zhao, "The Costs of Raising Capital," *Journal of Financial Research*, Vol. 19 (Spring, 1996), pp. 59–71.

[41] Thomas Bühner and Christoph Kaserer, "External Financing Costs and Economies of Scale in Investment Banking: The Case of Seasoned Equity Offerings in Germany," *European Financial Management*, Vol. 9 (June 2002), p. 249; Seth Armitage, "The Direct Costs of UK Rights Issues and Open Offers," *European Financial Management*, Vol. 6 (2000), pp. 57–68; Christoph Kaserer and Fabian Steiner, "The Cost of Raising Capital—New Evidence from Seasoned Equity Offerings in Switzerland," Technische Universität München working paper (February 2004).

offers, typical in the United States, are generally more expensive than rights offerings, which are common in Europe.

Should we incorporate flotation costs into the cost of capital? There are two views on this topic. One view, which you can find often in textbooks, is to incorporate the flotation costs into the cost of capital. The other view is that flotation costs should not be included in the cost of capital but, rather, incorporated into any valuation analysis as an additional cost of the project.

Consistent with the first view, we can specify flotation costs in monetary terms, as an amount per share or as a percentage of the share price. With flotation costs in monetary terms on a per share basis, F, the cost of external equity is

$$r_e = \left(\frac{D_1}{P_0 - F}\right) + g \tag{48-15}$$

As a percentage applied against the price per share, the cost of external equity is

$$r_e = \left(\frac{D_1}{P_0(1 - f)}\right) + g \tag{48-16}$$

where f is the flotation cost as a percentage of the issue price.

Suppose a company has a current dividend of $2 per share, a current price of $40 per share, and an expected growth rate of 5 percent. The cost of internally generated equity would be 10.25 percent:

$$r_e = \left(\frac{\$2\ (1 + 0.05)}{\$40}\right) + 0.05 = 0.0525 + 0.05 = 0.1025, \text{ or } 10.25 \text{ percent}$$

If the flotation costs are 4 percent of the issuance, the cost of externally generated equity would be slightly higher at 10.469 percent:

$$r_e = \left(\frac{\$2\ (1 + 0.05)}{\$40(1 - 0.04)}\right) + 0.05 = 0.05469 + 0.05 = 0.1047, \text{ or } 10.47 \text{ percent}$$

The problem with this approach is that the flotation costs are a cash flow at the initiation of the project and affect the value of any project by reducing the initial cash flow. Adjusting the cost of capital for flotation costs is incorrect because by doing so, we are adjusting the present value of the future cash flows by a fixed percentage—in the above example, a difference of 22 basis points, which does not necessarily equate to the present value of the flotation costs.[42]

The alternative and recommended approach is to make the adjustment to the cash flows in the valuation computation. For example, consider a project that requires a €60,000 initial cash outlay and is expected to produce cash flows of €10,000 each year for 10 years. Suppose the company's marginal tax rate is 40 percent and that the before-tax cost of debt is 5 percent. Furthermore, suppose that the company's dividend next period is €1, the current price of the stock is €20, and the expected growth rate is 5 percent so that the cost of equity using the

---

[42] This argument is made by John R. Ezzell and R. Burr Porter ["Flotation Costs and the Weighted Average Cost of Capital," *Journal of Financial and Quantitative Analysis*, Vol. 11, No. 3 (September 1976), pp. 403–413]. They argue that the correct treatment is to deduct flotation costs as part of the valuation as one of the initial-period cash flows.

dividend discount model is (€1/€20) + 0.05 = 0.10 or 10 percent. Assume the company will finance the project with 40 percent debt and 60 percent equity. Table 48-6 summarizes the information on the component costs of capital.

TABLE 48-6 After-Tax Costs of Debt and Equity

Source of capital	Amount raised	Proportion	Marginal after-tax cost
Debt	€24,000	0.40	0.05(1 − 0.4) = 0.03
Equity	€36,000	0.60	0.10

The weighted average cost of capital is 7.2 percent calculated as 0.40(3 percent) + 0.60(10 percent). Ignoring flotation costs for the moment, the net present value (NPV) of this project is

$$\text{NPV} = €69,591 − €60,000 = €9,591$$

If the flotation costs are, say, 5 percent of the new equity capital, the flotation costs are €1,800. The net present value considering flotation costs is

$$\text{NPV} = €69,591 − €60,000 − €1,800 = €7,791$$

If, instead of considering the flotation costs as part of the cash flows, we adjust the cost of equity, the cost of capital is 7.3578 percent and the NPV is

$$\text{NPV} = €69,089 − €60,000 = €9,089$$

As you can see, we arrive at difference assessments of value using these two methods.

So, if it is preferred to deduct the flotation costs as part of the net present value calculation, why do we see the adjustment in the cost of capital so often in textbooks? The first reason is that it is often difficult to identify particular financing associated with a project. Using the adjustment for the flotation costs in the cost of capital may be useful if specific project financing cannot be identified. Second, by adjusting the cost of capital for the flotation costs, it is easier to demonstrate how costs of financing a company change as a company exhausts internally generated equity (i.e., retained earnings) and switches to externally generated equity (i.e., a new stock issue).

4.5 What Do CFOs Do?

In this reading, we have introduced you to methods that may be used to estimate the cost of capital for a company or a project. What do companies actually use when making investment decisions? In a survey of a large number of U.S. company CFOs, John Graham and Campbell Harvey asked about the methods that companies actually use.[43] Their survey revealed the following:

▶ The most popular method for estimating the cost of equity is the capital asset pricing model.

---

[43] John Graham and Campbell Harvey, "How Do CFOs Make Capital Budgeting and Capital Structure Decisions," *Journal of Applied Corporate Finance*, Vol. 15, No. 1 (Spring 2002), pp. 8–23.

▶ Few companies use the dividend cash flow model to estimate a cost of equity.

▶ Publicly traded companies are more likely to use the capital asset pricing model than are private companies.

▶ In evaluating projects, the majority use a single company cost of capital, but a large portion apply some type of risk adjustment for individual projects.

The survey also reveals that the single-factor capital asset pricing model is the most popular method for estimating the cost of equity, though the next most popular methods, respectively, are average stock returns and multifactor return models. The lack of popularity of the dividend discount model indicates that this approach, which was once favored, has lost its following in practice.[44]

In a survey of publicly traded multinational European companies, Franck Bancel and Usha Mittoo provide evidence consistent with the Graham and Harvey survey.[45] They find that over 70 percent of companies use the CAPM to determine the cost of equity; this compares with the 73.5 percent of U.S. companies that use the CAPM. In a survey of both publicly traded and private European companies, Dirk Brounen, Abe de Jong, and Kees Koedijk confirm the result of Graham and Harvey that larger companies are more likely to use the more sophisticated methods, such as CAPM, in estimating the cost of equity.[46] Brounen, Jong, and Koedijk find that the popularity of the use of CAPM is less for their sample (ranging from 34 percent to 55.6 percent, depending on the country) than for the other two surveys, which may reflect the inclusion of smaller, private companies in the latter sample.

We learn from the survey evidence that the CAPM is a popular method for estimating the cost of equity capital and that it is used less by smaller, private companies. This latter result is not surprising because of the difficulty in estimating systematic risk in cases in which the company's equity is not publicly traded.

---

[44] A survey published in 1982 by Lawrence Gitman and V. Mercurio ["Cost of Capital Techniques Used by Major U.S. Firms: Survey and Analysis of Fortune's 1000," *Financial Management*, Vol. 14, No. 4 (Winter 1982), pp. 21–29] indicated that fewer than 30 percent used the CAPM model in the estimation of the cost of equity.

[45] Franck Bancel and Usha Mittoo, "The Determinants of Capital Structure Choice: A Survey of European Firms," *Financial Management*, Vol. 44, No. 4 (Winter 2004).

[46] Dirk Brounen, Abe de Jong, and Kees Koedijk, "Corporate Finance in Europe: Confronting Theory with Practice," *Financial Management*, Vol. 44, No. 4 (Winter 2004).

SUMMARY

In this reading, we provided an overview of the techniques used to calculate the cost of capital for companies and projects. We examined the weighted average cost of capital, discussing the methods commonly used to estimate the component costs of capital and the weights applied to these components. The international dimension of the cost of capital, as well as key factors influencing the cost of capital, were also analyzed.

▶ The weighted average cost of capital is a weighted average of the after-tax marginal costs of each source of capital: $\text{WACC} = w_d r_d (1 - t) + w_p r_p + w_e r_e$

▶ An analyst uses the WACC in valuation. For example, the WACC is used to value a project using the net present value method:

$$\text{NPV} = \text{Present value of inflows} - \text{Present value of the outflows}$$

▶ The before-tax cost of debt is generally estimated by means of one of the two methods: yield to maturity or bond rating.

▶ The yield-to-maturity method of estimating the before-tax cost of debt uses the familiar bond valuation equation. Assuming semi-annual coupon payments, the equation is

$$P_0 = \frac{PMT_1}{\left(1 + \frac{r_d}{2}\right)} + \ldots + \frac{PMT_n}{\left(1 + \frac{r_d}{2}\right)^n} + \frac{FV}{\left(1 + \frac{r_d}{2}\right)^n} = \left(\sum_{t=1}^{n} \frac{PMT_i}{\left(1 + \frac{r_d}{2}\right)^t}\right) + \frac{FV}{\left(1 + \frac{r_d}{2}\right)^n}$$

We solve for the six-month yield $(r_d/2)$ and then annualize it to arrive at the before-tax cost of debt, r_d.

▶ Because interest payments are generally tax deductible, the after-tax cost is the true, effective cost of debt to the company. If a current yield or bond rating is not available, such as in the case of a private company without rated debt or a project, the estimate of the cost of debt becomes more challenging.

▶ The cost of preferred stock is the preferred stock dividend divided by the current preferred stock price:

$$r_p = \frac{D_p}{P_p}$$

▶ The cost of equity is the rate of return required by a company's common stockholders. We estimate this cost using the CAPM (or its variants) or the dividend discount method.

▶ The CAPM is the approach most commonly used to calculate the cost of common stock. The three components needed to calculate the cost of common stock are the risk-free rate, the equity risk premium, and beta:

$$E(R_i) = R_F + \beta_i [E(R_M) - R_F]$$

▶ When estimating the cost of equity capital using the CAPM when we do not have publicly traded equity, we may be able to use the pure-play method in which we estimate the unlevered beta for a company with similar business risk, β_U,

$$\beta_{U,comparable} = \frac{\beta_{L,comparable}}{\left[1 + \left((1 - t_{comparable}) \dfrac{D_{comparable}}{E_{comparable}} \right) \right]}$$

and then lever this beta to reflect the financial risk of the project or company:

$$\beta_{L,project} = \beta_{U,comparable} \left[1 + \left((1 - t_{project}) \dfrac{D_{project}}{E_{project}} \right) \right]$$

▶ It is often the case that country and foreign exchange risk are diversified so that we can use the estimated β in the CAPM analysis. However, in the case in which these risks cannot be diversified away, we can adjust our measure of systematic risk by a country equity premium to reflect this nondiversified risk:

$$\text{Country equity premium} = \text{Sovereign yield spread} \left(\frac{\text{Annualized standard deviation of equity index}}{\text{Annualized standard deviation of the sovereign bond market in terms of the developed market currency}} \right)$$

▶ The dividend discount model approach is an alternative approach to calculating the cost of equity, whereby the cost of equity is estimated as follows:

$$r_e = \frac{D_1}{P_0} + g$$

▶ We can estimate the growth rate in the dividend discount model by using published forecasts of analysts or by estimating the sustainable growth rate:

$$g = (1 - D/EPS)\ ROE$$

▶ In estimating the cost of equity, an alternative to the CAPM and dividend discount approaches is the bond yield plus risk premium approach. In this approach, we estimate the before-tax cost of debt and add a risk premium that reflects the additional risk associated with the company's equity.

▶ The marginal cost of capital schedule is a graph plotting the new funds raised by a company on the x-axis and the cost of capital on the y-axis. The cost of capital is level to the point at which one of the costs of capital changes, such as when the company bumps up against a debt covenant, requiring it to use another form of capital. We calculate a break point using information on when the different sources' costs change and the proportions that the company uses when it raises additional capital:

$$\text{Break point} = \frac{\text{Amount of capital at which the source's cost of capital changes}}{\text{Proportion of new capital raised from the source}}$$

► Flotation costs are costs incurred in the process of raising additional capital. The preferred method of including these costs in the analysis is as an initial cash flow in the valuation analysis.

► Survey evidence tells us that the CAPM method is the most popular method used by companies in estimating the cost of equity. The CAPM is more popular with larger, publicly traded companies, which is understandable considering the additional analyses and assumptions required in estimating systematic risk for a private company or project.

PROBLEMS FOR READING 48

1. The cost of equity is equal to the

   A. expected market return.

   B. rate of return required by stockholders.

   C. cost of retained earnings plus dividends.

   D. risk the company incurs when financing.

2. Which of the following statements is correct?

   A. The appropriate tax rate to use in the adjustment of the before-tax cost of debt to determine the after-tax cost of debt is the **average tax rate** because interest is deductible against the company's entire taxable income.

   B. For a given company, the after-tax cost of debt is less than both the cost of preferred equity and the cost of common equity.

   C. For a given company, the investment opportunity schedule is upward sloping because as a company invests more in capital projects, the returns from investing increase.

   D. The target capital structure is the average ratio of debt to equity for the most recent fiscal years.

3. Using the dividend discount model, what is the cost of equity capital for Zeller Mining if the company will pay a dividend of C$2.30 next year, has a payout ratio of 30 percent, a return on equity of 15 percent, and a stock price of C$45?

   A. 5.11 percent

   B. 9.61 percent

   C. 10.50 percent

   D. 15.61 percent

4. Dot.Com has determined that it could issue $1,000 face value bonds with an 8 percent coupon paid semi-annually and a five-year maturity at $900 per bond. If Dot.Com's marginal tax rate is 38 percent, its after-tax cost of debt is *closest* to

   A. 6.2 percent

   B. 6.4 percent.

   C. 6.6 percent.

   D. 6.8 percent.

5. The cost of debt can be determined using the yield-to-maturity and the bond rating approaches. If the bond rating approach is used, the

   A. coupon is the yield.

   B. yield is based on the interest coverage ratio.

   C. company is rated and the rating can be used to assess the credit default spread of the company's debt.

   D. after-tax cost of the debt is not known.

6. Morgan Insurance Ltd. issued a fixed-rate perpetual preferred stock three years ago and placed it privately with institutional investors. The stock was issued at $25 per share with a $1.75 dividend. If the company were to issue preferred stock today, the yield would be 6.5 percent. The stock's current value is

   A. $25.00

   B. $26.92

C. $37.31

D. $40.18

7. A financial analyst at Buckco Ltd. wants to compute the company's weighted average cost of capital (WACC) using the dividend discount model. The analyst has gathered the following data:

Before-tax cost of new debt	8 percent
Tax rate	40 percent
Target debt-to-equity ratio	0.8033
Stock price	$30
Next year's dividend	$1.50
Estimated growth rate	7 percent

Buckco's WACC is *closest* to

A. 8 percent

B. 9 percent

C. 12 percent

D. 20 percent

8. The Gearing Company has an after-tax cost of debt capital of 4 percent, a cost of preferred stock of 8 percent, a cost of equity capital of 10 percent, and a weighted average cost of capital of 7 percent. Gearing intends to maintain its current capital structure as it raises additional capital. In making its capital-budgeting decisions for the average-risk project, the relevant cost of capital is

A. 4 percent

B. 7 percent

C. 8 percent

D. 10 percent

9. Fran McClure of Alba Advisers is estimating the cost of capital of Frontier Corporation as part of her valuation analysis of Frontier. McClure will be using this estimate, along with projected cash flows from Frontier's new projects, to estimate the effect of these new projects on the value of Frontier. McClure has gathered the following information on Frontier Corporation:

	Current year	Forecasted for next year
Book value of debt	$50	$50
Market value of debt	$62	$63
Book value of shareholders' equity	$55	$58
Market value of shareholders' equity	$210	$220

The weights that McClure should apply in estimating Frontier's cost of capital for debt and equity are, respectively

A. $w_d = 0.200$; $w_e = 0.800$

B. $w_d = 0.185$; $w_e = 0.815$

C. $w_d = 0.223$; $w_e = 0.777$

D. $w_d = 0.228$; $w_e = 0.772$

4⅝ 4⅜   −⅜
    5½ 5½ −
5½ 21³⁄₁₆ −¼
20⅝ 18⅛ +⅞
17⅜ 6½ −½
6½ 6½ −
7¼ 31⁄₃₂ −⅛
15⁄₁₆
9⁄₁₆
9⁄₁₆
7¹⁵⁄₁₆
7¹³⁄₁₆ 7¹⁵⁄₁₆
7¹⁵⁄₁₆ 2½ +
2⅝ 2¹¹⁄₃₂
2¾ 2¼ 2¼
11⅜ 11¼ +
61⅛ 12¹⁄₁₆ 11⅜
87 33¾ 33 33¹⁄₁₆ −
602 25⅝ 24⁹⁄₁₆ 25⅝ +
833 12 11⅝ 11⅞ +
16 10½ 10½ 10⅛ −
78 15⅞ 15¹³⁄₁₆ 15⅛ −
4508 9¹⁄₁₆ 8¼ 8⅛ +
430 11¼ 10⅛

CAPITAL STRUCTURE AND LEVERAGE

by Raj Aggarwal, Cynthia Harrington, Adam Kobor, and Pamela P. Peterson

LEARNING OUTCOMES

The candidate should be able to:

a. define and explain leverage, business risk, sales risk, operating risk, and financial risk;

b. calculate and interpret the degree of operating leverage, the degree of financial leverage, and the degree of total leverage;

c. characterize the operating leverage, financial leverage, and total leverage of a company given a description of it;

d. calculate the breakeven quantity of sales and determine the company's net income at various sales levels;

e. describe the effect of financial leverage on a company's net income and return on equity;

f. compare and contrast the risks of creditors and owners.

INTRODUCTION   1

This reading presents capital structure and leverage. **Leverage** is the use of fixed costs in a company's cost structure. The fixed costs that are operating costs (such as depreciation or rent) create operating leverage. Fixed costs that are financial costs (such as interest expense) create financial leverage. Analysts need to understand a company's use of leverage for three main reasons.

First, the degree of leverage is an important component in assessing a company's risk and return characteristics. Second, analysts may be able to discern a company's prospects from management's decisions about financing choices. Knowing how to interpret these signals also helps the analyst evaluate the quality of management's decisions. Third, the valuation of a company requires forecasting future cash flows and assessing the risk associated with those cash flows. The cost structure of a company affects its risk: The greater the company's fixed costs relative to its variable costs, the greater the potential volatility in its future earnings and, hence, cash flows. We refer to the use of fixed costs as leverage because these fixed costs act as a fulcrum for the company's earnings. Leverage can magnify earnings both up and down. The profits of highly leveraged companies might soar with small upturns in sales. But the reverse is also true: Small drops in revenue can rapidly lead to losses.

This reading also discusses the choice about how to finance (i.e., raise money for) a company's operations, which is the capital structure decision. Senior management makes the capital structure decision. The capital structure that is chosen will very often include the use of debt, which will affect the company's financial leverage. Thus, it is natural to discuss capital structure and leverage together. In this reading, therefore, we will

► discuss and illustrate the business risk and financial risk of a company,
► show how to quantify these risks for a company or division using degrees of leverage,
► view how leverage affects a company's value, and
► learn how to evaluate a company's capital structure.

The reading is organized as follows: In Section 2, we introduce the concept of leverage. In Section 3, we discuss the sources of earnings volatility, including sales risk, operating risk, and financial risk, and explain quantitative measures of leverage. In Section 4, we discuss the company's capital structure decision and the choice of alternative sources of financing. In Section 5, we present important issues for the analyst, such as the role of debt rating in the capital structure decision and international differences in capital structure policies. We summarize this at the end of the reading.

2   LEVERAGE

Leverage increases the potential volatility of a company's earnings and cash flows and increases the risk of lending to or owning a company. Additionally, the valuation of a company and its equity is affected by the degree of leverage: The greater the leverage, the greater the risk and hence, the greater the discount rate applied in its valuation. Further, highly leveraged companies have a greater chance of incurring significant losses during downturns, thus accelerating conditions that lead to financial distress and bankruptcy.

Consider the simple example of two companies, Impulse Robotics, Inc., and Malvey Aerospace, Inc. These companies have the following performance for the period of study:[1]

---

[1] We are ignoring taxes for this example, but when taxes are included, the general conclusions remain the same.

TABLE 49-1 Impulse Robotics and Malvey Aerospace		
	Impulse Robotics	**Malvey Aerospace**
Revenues	$1,000,000	$1,000,000
Operating costs	700,000	750,000
Operating income	$300,000	$250,000
Financing expense	100,000	50,000
Net income	$200,000	$200,000

These companies have the same net income, but are they identical in terms of financial characteristics? Would we appraise these two companies at the same value? Not necessarily.

The risk associated with future earnings and cash flows of a company are affected by the company's cost structure. The **cost structure** of a company is the mix of variable and fixed costs. **Variable costs** fluctuate with the level of production and sales. Some examples of variable costs are the cost of goods purchased for resale, costs of materials or supplies, shipping charges, delivery charges, wages for hourly employees, sales commissions, and sales or production bonuses. **Fixed costs** are expenses that are the same regardless of the production and sales of the company. These costs include depreciation, rent, interest on debt, insurance, and wages for salaried employees.

Suppose that the cost structures of the companies differ in the following manner:

TABLE 49-2 Impulse Robotics and Malvey Aerospace		
	Impulse Robotics	**Malvey Aerospace**
Number of units produced and sold	100,000	100,000
Sales price per unit	$10	$10
Variable cost per unit	$2	$6
Fixed operating cost	$500,000	$150,000
Fixed financing expense	$100,000	$50,000

The risk associated with these companies is different, although, as we saw in Table 49-1, they have the same net income. They have different operating and financing cost structures, resulting in differing potential volatility of net income.

For example, if the number of units produced and sold is different from 100,000, the net income of the two companies diverges. If 50,000 units are produced and sold, Impulse Robotics has a loss of $200,000 and Malvey Aerospace has $0 earnings. If, on the other hand, the number of units produced and sold is 200,000, Impulse Robotics earns $1 million whereas Malvey Aerospace earns $600,000. In other words, the swing in net income is greater for Impulse Robotics, which has higher fixed costs in terms of both fixed operating costs and fixed financing costs.

Impulse Robotics' cost structure results in more leverage than that of Malvey Aerospace. We can see this effect when we plot the net income of each company against the number of units produced and sold, as in Figure 49-1. The greater

FIGURE 49-1   Net Income for Different Numbers of Units Produced and Sold

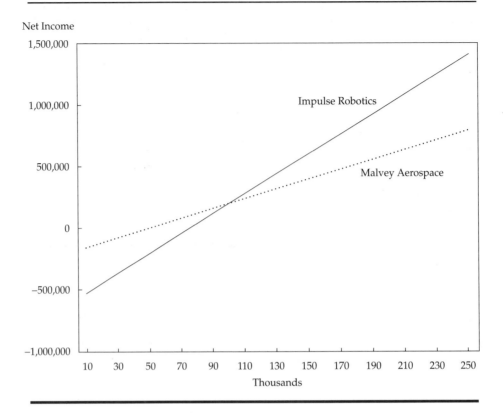

leverage of Impulse Robotics is reflected in the greater slope of the line representing net income. This means that as the number of units sold changes, Impulse Robotics experiences a greater change in net income than does Malvey Aerospace for the same change in units sold.

Companies that have more fixed costs relative to variable costs in their cost structures have greater variation in net income as revenues fluctuate and, hence, more risk.

3   BUSINESS RISK AND FINANCIAL RISK

Risk arises from both the operating and financing activities of a company. In the following, we address how that happens and the measures available to the analyst to gauge the risk in each case.

3.1 Business Risk and Its Components

Business risk is the risk associated with operating earnings. Operating earnings are uncertain because total revenues and many of the expenditures contributed to produce those revenues are uncertain. Revenues are affected by a large number of factors, including economic conditions, the actions of competitors, governmental regulation, and demographics. Therefore, prices of the company's goods or services or the quantity of sales may be different from what is expected. We refer to the uncertainty with respect to the price and quantity of goods and services as **sales risk**.

Operating risk is the risk attributed to the operating cost structure, in particular the use of fixed costs in operations. The greater the fixed operating costs relative to variable operating costs, the greater the operating risk. Business risk is therefore the combined risk of sales and operations. Companies that operate in the same line of business generally have similar business risk.

3.2 Sales Risk

Consider Impulse Robotics once again. Suppose that the forecasted number of units produced and sold in the next period is 100,000 but that the standard deviation of the number of units sold is 20,000. And suppose the price that the units sell for is expected to be $10 per unit but the standard deviation is $2. Contrast this situation with that of a company named Tolley Aerospace, Inc., which has the same cost structure but a standard deviation of units sold of 40,000 and a price standard deviation of $4.

If we assume, for simplicity's sake, that the fixed operating costs are known with certainty and that the units sold and price per unit follow a normal distribution, we can see the impact of the different risks on the operating income of the two companies through a simulation; the results are shown in Figure 49-2. Here, we see the

FIGURE 49-2   Operating Income Simulations for Impulse Robotics and Tolley Aerospace

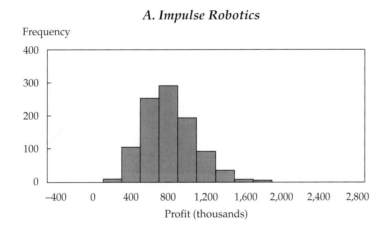

A. Impulse Robotics

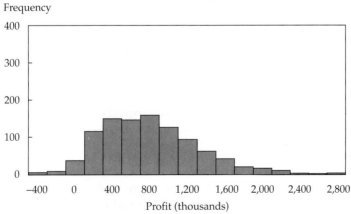

B. Tolley Aerospace

differing distributions of operating income that result from the distributions of units sold and price per unit. So, even if the companies have the same cost structure, differing *sales risk* affects the potential variability of the company's profitability. In our example, Tolley Aerospace has a wider distribution of likely outcomes in terms of operating profit. This greater potential volatility in operating earnings means that Tolley Aerospace has more sales risk than Impulse Robotics.

3.3 Operating Risk

The greater the fixed component of costs, the more difficult it is for a company to adjust its operating costs to changes in sales. The mixture of fixed and variable costs depends largely on the type of business. Even within the same line of business, companies can vary their fixed and variable costs to some degree. We refer to the risk arising from the mix of fixed and variable costs as **operating risk**. The greater the fixed operating costs relative to variable operating costs, the greater the operating risk.

Next, we will look at how operating risk affects the variability of cash flows. A concept taught in **microeconomics** is **elasticity**, which is simply a measure of the sensitivity of changes in one item to changes in another. We can apply this concept to examine how sensitive a company's operating income is to changes in demand, as measured by unit sales. We will calculate the operating income elasticity, which we refer to as the **degree of operating leverage (DOL)**.

The degree of operating leverage is the ratio of the percentage change in operating income to the percentage change in units sold. We will simplify things and assume that the company sells all that it produces in the same period. Then,

$$\text{DOL} = \frac{\text{Percentage change in operating income}}{\text{Percentage change in units sold}} \qquad \textbf{(49-1)}$$

Returning to Impulse Robotics, the price per unit is \$10, the variable cost per unit is \$2, and the total fixed costs are \$500,000. If Impulse Robotics' output changes from 100,000 units to 110,000 units—an increase of 10 percent in the number of units sold—operating income changes from \$300,000 to \$380,000:[2]

TABLE 49-3   Operating Leverage of Impulse Robotics

Item	Selling 100,000 units	Selling 110,000 units	Percentage change
Revenues	\$1,000,000	\$1,100,000	+10.00%
less variable costs	200,000	220,000	+10.00%
less fixed costs	500,000	500,000	0.00%
Operating income	\$300,000	\$380,000	+26.67%

---

[2] We provide the variable and fixed operating costs for our sample companies used in this reading to illustrate the leverage and breakeven concepts. In reality, however, the financial analyst does not have these breakdowns but rather is faced with interpreting reported account values that often combine variable and fixed costs and costs for different product lines.

Operating income increases by 26.67 percent when units sold increases by 10 percent. What if the number of units *decreases* by 10 percent, from 100,000 to 90,000? Operating income is $220,000, representing a *decline* of 26.67 percent.

What is happening is that for a 1 percent change in units sold, the operating income changes by 2.67 times that percentage, in the same direction. If units sold increases by 10 percent, operating income increases by 26.7 percent; if units sold decreased by 20 percent, operating income would decrease by 53.3 percent.

We can represent the degree of operating leverage as given in Equation 49-1 in terms of the basic elements of the price per unit, variable cost per unit, number of units sold, and fixed operating costs. Operating income is

$$\begin{matrix} \text{Operating} \\ \text{income} \end{matrix} = \left[\left(\begin{matrix} \text{Price} \\ \text{per unit} \end{matrix} \right) \left(\begin{matrix} \text{Number of} \\ \text{units sold} \end{matrix} \right) \right] - \left[\left(\begin{matrix} \text{Variable cost} \\ \text{per unit} \end{matrix} \right) \left(\begin{matrix} \text{Number of} \\ \text{units sold} \end{matrix} \right) \right] \\ - \left[\begin{matrix} \text{Fixed operating} \\ \text{costs} \end{matrix} \right]$$

or

$$\begin{matrix} \text{Operating} \\ \text{income} \end{matrix} = \left(\begin{matrix} \text{Number of} \\ \text{units sold} \end{matrix} \right) \underbrace{\left[\left(\begin{matrix} \text{Price} \\ \text{per unit} \end{matrix} \right) - \left(\begin{matrix} \text{Variable cost} \\ \text{per unit} \end{matrix} \right) \right]}_{\text{Contribution margin}} - \left[\begin{matrix} \text{Fixed operating} \\ \text{costs} \end{matrix} \right]$$

The **per unit contribution margin** is the amount that each unit sold contributes to covering fixed costs—that is, the difference between the price per unit and the variable cost per unit. That difference multiplied by the quantity sold is the **contribution margin**, which equals revenue minus variable costs.

How much does operating income change when the number of units sold changes? Fixed costs do not change; therefore, operating income changes by the contribution margin. The percentage change in operating income for a given change in units sold simplifies to

$$\text{DOL} = \frac{Q(P - V)}{Q(P - V) - F} \qquad \textbf{(49-2)}$$

where Q is the number of units, P is the price per unit, V is the variable operating cost per unit, and F is the fixed operating cost. Therefore, $P - V$ is the per unit contribution margin and $Q(P - V)$ is the contribution margin.

Applying the formula for DOL using the data for Impulse Robotics, we can calculate the sensitivity to change in units sold from 100,000 units:

$$\begin{matrix} \text{DOL @} \\ \text{100,000 units} \end{matrix} = \frac{100,000(\$10 - \$2)}{100,000(\$10 - \$2) - \$500,000} = 2.67$$

A DOL of 2.67 means that a 1 percent change in units sold results in a $1\% \times 2.67 = 2.67\%$ change in operating income; a DOL of 5 means that a 1 percent change in units sold results in a 5 percent change in operating income, and so on.

Why do we specify that the DOL is at a particular quantity sold (in this case, 100,000 units)? Because the DOL is different at different numbers of units produced and sold. For example, at 200,000 units,

$$\begin{matrix} \text{DOL @} \\ \text{200,000 units} \end{matrix} = \frac{200,000(\$10 - \$2)}{200,000(\$10 - \$2) - \$500,000} = 1.45$$

We can see the sensitivity of the DOL for different numbers of units produced and sold in Figure 49-3. When operating profit is negative, the DOL is negative. At positions just below and just above the point where operating income is $0, operating income is at its most sensitive on a percentage basis to changes in units produced and sold. At the point at which operating income is $0 (at 62,500 units produced and sold in this example), the DOL is undefined because the denominator in the DOL calculation is $0. After this point, the DOL gradually declines as more units are produced and sold.

We will now look at a similar situation in which the company has shifted some of the operating costs away from fixed costs and into variable costs. Malvey Aerospace has a unit sales price of $10, a variable cost of $6 a unit, and $150,000 in fixed costs. A change in units sold from 100,000 to 110,000 (a 10 percent change) changes operating profit from $250,000 to $290,000, or 16 percent. The DOL in this case is 1.6:

$$\text{DOL @ } 100{,}000 \text{ units} = \frac{100{,}000(\$10 - \$6)}{100{,}000(\$10 - \$6) - \$150{,}000} = 1.6$$

and the change in operating income is 16 percent:

$$\text{Percentage change in operating income} = \text{DOL}\left(\text{Percentage change in units sold}\right) = 1.6(10\%) = 16\%$$

We can see the difference in leverage in the case of Impulse Robotics and Malvey Aerospace companies in Figure 49-4. In Panel A, we see that Impulse Robotics has higher operating income than Malvey Aerospace when both companies produce

FIGURE 49-3   Impulse Robotics' Degree of Operating Leverage for Different Number of Units Produced and Sold

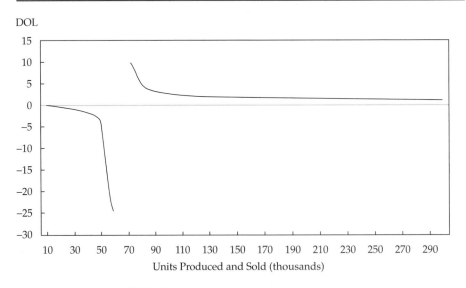

Units Produced and Sold (thousands)

$P = \$10; V = \$2; F = \$500{,}000$

and sell more than 87,500 units, but lower operating income than Malvey when both companies produce and sell less than 87,500 units.[3]

This example confirms what we saw earlier in our reasoning of fixed and variable costs: The greater the use of fixed, relative to variable, operating costs, the more sensitive operating income is to changes in units sold and, therefore, the more operating risk. Impulse Robotics has more operating risk because it has more operating leverage. However, as Panel B of Figure 49-4 shows, the degrees

FIGURE 49-4   Profitability and the DOL for Impulse Robotics and Malvey Aerospace

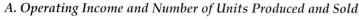

A. Operating Income and Number of Units Produced and Sold

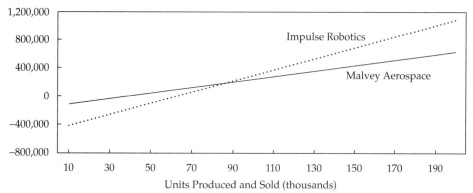

B. Degree of Operating Leverage

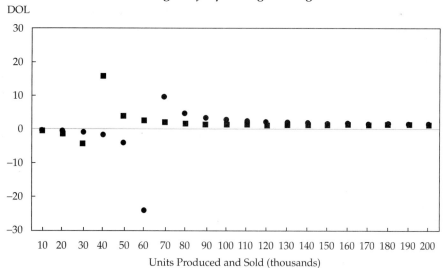

Impulse Robotics: $P = \$10$; $V = \$2$; $F = \$500{,}000$
Malvey Aerospace: $P = \$10$; $V = \$6$; $F = \$150{,}000$

---

[3] We can calculate the number of units that produce the same operating income for these two companies by equating the operating incomes and solving for the number of units. Let X be the number of units. The X at which Malvey Aerospace and Impulse Robotics generate the same operating income is the X that solves the following: $10X - 2X - 500{,}000 = 10X - 6X - 150{,}000$; that is, $X = 87{,}500$.

of operating leverage are similar for the two companies for larger numbers of units produced and sold.

Both sales risk and operating risk influence a company's business risk. And both sales risk and operating risk are determined in large part by the type of business the company is in. But management has more opportunity to manage and control operating risk than sales risk.

Suppose a company is deciding which equipment to buy to produce a particular product. The sales risk is the same no matter what equipment is chosen to produce the product. But the available equipment may differ in terms of the fixed and variable operating costs of producing the product. Financial analysts need to consider how the operating cost structure of a company affects the company's risk.

Example 49-1

Calculating the Degree of Operating Leverage

Arnaud Kenigswald is analyzing the potential impact of an improving economy on earnings at Global Auto, one of the world's largest car manufacturers. Global is headquartered in Berlin. Two Global Auto divisions manufacture passenger cars and produce combined revenues of €93 billion. Kenigswald projects that sales will improve by 10 percent due to increased demand for cars. He wants to see how Global's earnings might respond given that level of increase in sales. He first looks at the degree of leverage at Global, starting with operating leverage.

Global sold 6 million passenger cars in 2003. The average price per car was €24,000, fixed costs associated with passenger car production total €15 billion per year, and variable costs per car are €14,000. What is the degree of operating leverage of Global Auto?

▶ **Solution**

$$
\text{DOL @ 6 million units} = \frac{6 \text{ million} (€24,000 - €14,000)}{6 \text{ million} (€24,000 - €14,000) - €15 \text{ billion}}
$$

$$
= 1.333
$$

For a 10 percent increase in cars sold, operating income increases by $1.333 \times 10\% = 13.33\%$.

Industries that tend to have high operating leverage are those that invest up front to produce a product but spend relatively little on making and distributing it. Software developers and pharmaceutical companies fit this description. Alternatively, retailers have low operating leverage because much of the cost of goods sold is variable.

Because most companies produce more than one product, the ratio of variable to fixed costs is difficult to obtain. We can get an idea of the operating leverage of a company by looking at the change in operating income in relation to changes in sales for the entire company. Although this approach does not provide a precise measure of operating risk, it can help provide a general idea of the sensitivity of operating earnings. For example, compare the relation between operating earnings and revenues for Abbott Laboratories, a pharmaceutical company, and Wal-Mart Stores, a discount retailer, as shown in Figure 49-5. Not only is the slope of a least-squares regression line greater for Abbott, but also note the higher volatility of observations around the regression.[4] We can see that operating earnings are more sensitive to changes in revenues for the higher-operating-leveraged Abbott as compared to the lower-operating-leveraged Wal-Mart Stores.

3.4 Financial Risk

We can expand on the concept of risk to accommodate the perspective of owning a security. A security represents a claim on the income and assets of a business;

FIGURE 49-5   Relation between Operating Earnings and Revenues

A. Abbott Laboratories Operating Earnings and Revenues, 1990-2004

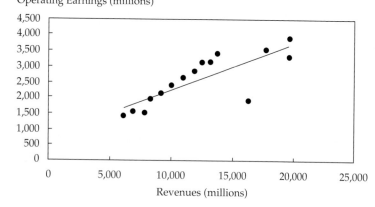

B. Wal-Mart Stores Operating Earnings and Revenues, 1990-2004

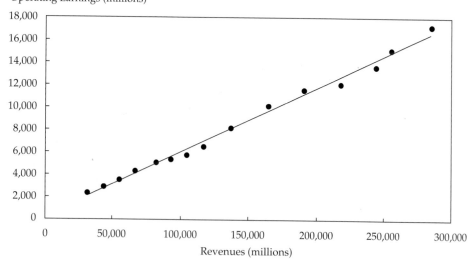

Sources: Abbott Laboratories 10-K filings and Wal-Mart Stores 10-K filings, various years

---

[4] A least-squares regression is a procedure for finding the best-fitting line through a set of data points by minimizing the squared deviations from the line. For more information on regression analysis, see the readings on quantitative methods.

therefore, the risk of the security goes beyond the variability of operating earnings to include how the cash flows from those earnings are distributed among the claimants—the creditors and owners of the business. The risk of a security is therefore affected by both business risk and financial risk.

Financial risk is the risk associated with how a company finances its operations. If a company finances with debt, it is legally obligated to pay the amounts that make up its debts when due. By taking on fixed obligations, such as debt and long-term leases, the company increases its financial risk. If a company finances its business with equity, generated either from operations (retained earnings) or from issuing new equity, it does not incur fixed obligations. The more fixed-cost obligations (e.g., debt) incurred by the company, the greater its financial risk.

We can quantify this risk in the same way we did for operating risk, looking at the sensitivity of the cash flows available to owners when operating income changes. This sensitivity, which we refer to as the **degree of financial leverage (DFL)**, is

$$ DFL = \frac{Percentage\ change\ in\ net\ income}{Percentage\ change\ in\ operating\ income} \qquad \textbf{(49-3)} $$

Net income is equal to operating income, less interest and taxes.[5] If operating income changes, how does net income change? Consider Impulse Robotics. Suppose the interest payments are $100,000 and, for simplicity and wishful thinking, the tax rate is 0 percent: If operating income changes from $300,000 to $360,000, net income changes from $200,000 to $260,000:

TABLE 49-4   Financial Risk of Impulse Robotics (1)

	Operating income of $300,000	Operating income of $360,000	Percentage change
Operating income	$300,000	$360,000	+20%
less interest	100,000	100,000	0%
Net income	$200,000	$260,000	+30%

A 20 percent increase in operating income increases net income by $60,000, or 30 percent. What if, instead, the fixed financial costs are $150,000? A 20 percent change in operating income results in a 40 percent change in the net income, from $150,000 to $210,000:

TABLE 49-5   Financial Risk of Impulse Robotics (2)

	Operating income of $300,000	Operating income of $360,000	Percentage change
Operating income	$300,000	$360,000	+20%
less interest	150,000	150,000	0%
Net income	$150,000	$210,000	+40%

---

[5] More complex entities than we have been using for our examples may also need to account for other income (losses) and extraordinary income (losses) together with operating income as the basis for earnings before interest and taxes.

Using more debt financing, which results in higher fixed costs, increases the sensitivity of owners' income. We can represent the sensitivity of owners' cash flows to a change in operating income, continuing the notation from before and including the fixed financial cost, C, and the tax rate, t, as

$$\text{DFL} = \frac{[Q(P - V) - F](1 - t)}{[Q(P - V) - F - C](1 - t)} = \frac{[Q(P - V) - F]}{[Q(P - V) - F - C]} \qquad \textbf{(49-4)}$$

As you can see in Equation 49-4, the factor that adjusts for taxes, $(1 - t)$, cancels out of the equation. In other words, the DFL is not affected by the tax rate.

In the case in which operating income is \$300,000 and fixed financing costs are \$100,000, the degree of financial leverage is

$$\text{DFL @ \$300,000 operating income} = \frac{\$300,000}{\$300,000 - \$100,000} = 1.5$$

If, instead, fixed financial costs are \$150,000, the DFL is equal to 2.0:

$$\text{DFL @ \$300,000 operating income} = \frac{\$300,000}{\$300,000 - \$150,000} = 2.0$$

Again, we need to qualify our degree of leverage by the level of operating income because DFL is different at different levels of operating income.

The greater the use of financing sources that require fixed obligations, such as interest, the greater the sensitivity of net income to changes in operating income.

Example 49-2

Calculating the Degree of Financial Leverage

Global Auto also employs debt financing. If Global can borrow at 8 percent, the interest cost is €40 billion. What is the degree of financial leverage of Global Auto if 6 million cars are produced and sold?

▶ **Solution:** At 6 million cars produced and sold, operating income = €45 billion. Therefore:

$$\text{DFL @ €45 billion operating income} = \frac{€45 \text{ billion}}{€45 \text{ billion} - €40 \text{ billion}} = 9.0$$

For every 1 percent change in operating income, net income changes 9 percent due to financial leverage.

Unlike operating leverage, the degree of financial leverage is most often a choice by the company's management. Whereas operating costs are very similar among companies in the same industry, competitors may decide on differing capital structures.

Companies with a higher ratio of tangible assets to total assets may have higher degrees of financial leverage because lenders may feel more secure that their claims would be satisfied in the event of a downturn. In general, "old economy" businesses with plants, land, and equipment use more financial leverage than "new economy" businesses in technology and pharmaceuticals.

3.5 Total Leverage

The degree of operating leverage gives us an idea of the sensitivity of operating income to changes in revenues. And the degree of financial leverage gives us an idea of the sensitivity of owners' income to changes in operating income. But often we are concerned about the combined effect of both operating leverage and financial leverage. Owners are concerned about the combined effect because both factors contribute to the risk associated with their future cash flows. And financial managers, making decisions intended to maximize owners' wealth, need to be concerned with how investment decisions (which affect the operating cost structure) and financing decisions (which affect the capital structure) affect lenders' and owners' risk.

Look back on the example of Impulse Robotics. The sensitivity of owners' cash flow to a given change in units sold is affected by both operating and financial leverage. Consider using 100,000 units as the base number produced and sold. A 10 percent increase in units sold results in a 27 percent increase in operating income and a 40 percent increase in net income; a like decrease in units sold results in a similar decrease in operating income and net income.

TABLE 49-6   Total Leverage of Impulse Robotics

	Units Produced and Sold:		
	90,000	**100,000**	**110,000**
Revenues	$900,000	$1,000,000	$1,100,000
less variable costs	180,000	200,000	220,000
less fixed costs	500,000	500,000	500,000
Operating income	$220,000	$300,000	$380,000
less interest	100,000	100,000	100,000
Net income	$120,000	$200,000	$280,000
Relative to 100,000 units produced and sold			
Percentage change in units sold	−10%		+10%
Percentage change in operating profit	−27%		+27%
Percentage change in net income	−40%		+40%

Combining a company's degree of operating leverage with its degree of financial leverage results in the **degree of total leverage** (**DTL**), a measure of the sensitivity of the cash flows to owners to changes in the number of units produced and sold. Once again making the simplifying assumption that a company sells all that it produces in the same period,

$$DTL = \frac{\text{Percentage change in net income}}{\text{Percentage change in the number of units sold}} \quad (49\text{-}5)$$

or

$$DTL = \frac{Q(P-V)}{Q(P-V)-F} \times \frac{[Q(P-V)-F](1-t)}{[Q(P-V)-F-C](1-t)}$$

$$= \frac{Q(P-V)}{Q(P-V)-F-C} = DOL \times DFL$$

(49-6)

Suppose

Number of units sold $= Q = 100,000$
Price per unit $= P = \$10$
Variable cost per unit $= V = \$2$
Fixed operating cost $= F = \$500,000$
Fixed financing cost $= C = \$100,000$

Then,

$$DTL = \frac{100,000(\$10-\$2)}{100,000(\$10-\$2)-\$500,000-\$100,000} = 4.0$$

which we could also have determined by multiplying the DOL, 2.67, by the DFL, 1.5. This means that a 1 percent increase in units sold will result in a 4 percent increase in net income; a 50 percent increase in units produced and sold results in a 200 percent increase in net income; a 5 percent decline in units sold results in a 20 percent decline in income to owners; and so on.

Because the DOL is relative to the base number of units produced and sold and the DFL is relative to the base operating earnings, DTL is different depending on the number of units produced and sold. We can see the DOL, DFL, and DTL for Impulse Robotics for different numbers of units produced and sold, beginning at the number of units for which the degrees are positive, in Figure 49-6.

In the case of operating leverage, the fixed operating costs act as a fulcrum. The greater the proportion of operating costs that are fixed, the more sensitive operating income is to changes in sales. In the case of financial leverage, the fixed

FIGURE 49-6 DOL, DFL, and DTL for Different Numbers of Units Produced and Sold

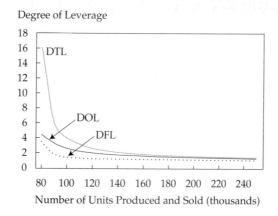

$P = \$10, V = \$2, F = \$500,000, C = \$100,000$

financial costs, such as interest, act as a fulcrum. The greater the proportion of financing with fixed cost sources, such as debt, the more sensitive cash flows available to owners are to changes in operating income. Combining the effects of both types of leverage, we see that fixed operating and financial costs together increase the sensitivity of earnings to owners.

Example 49-3

Calculating the Degree of Total Leverage

Continuing from Example 49-2, Global Auto's total leverage is

$$\underset{\text{6 million units}}{\text{DTL@}} = \underset{\text{6 million units}}{\text{DTL@}} \times \underset{\text{€45 million operating income}}{\text{DTL@}}$$

$$\underset{\text{6 million units}}{\text{DTL@}} = \frac{6 \text{ million}(€24{,}000 - €14{,}000)}{6 \text{ million }(€24{,}000 - €14{,}000) - €15 \text{ billion}}$$

$$\times \frac{€45 \text{ billion}}{€45 \text{ billion} - €40 \text{ billion}}$$

$$\underset{\text{6 million units}}{\text{DTL@}} = 1.333 \times 9.0 = 12$$

Given Global Auto's operating and capital structures, a 1 percent change in unit sales changes net income by 12 percent.

3.6 Breakeven Rates and Expected Return

Looking back at Figure 49-1, we see that there is a number of units at which the company goes from being unprofitable to being profitable—that is, the number of units at which the net income is zero. This number is referred to as the breakeven point. The **breakeven point** is the number of units produced and sold at which the company's net income is zero—the point at which revenues are equal to costs.

Plotting revenues and total costs against the number of units produced and sold, as in Figure 49-7, indicates that the breakeven is at 75,000 units. At this number of units produced and sold, revenues are equal to costs and, hence, profit is zero.

We can calculate this breakeven point for Impulse Robotics and Malvey Aerospace. Consider that net income is zero when the revenues are equal to the expenses. We can represent this equality of revenues and costs as the following:

$$PQ = VQ + F + C$$

where

P is the price per unit
Q is the number of units produced and sold
V is the variable cost per unit
F is the fixed operating costs
C is the fixed financial cost

FIGURE 49-7   Impulse Robotics Break-Even

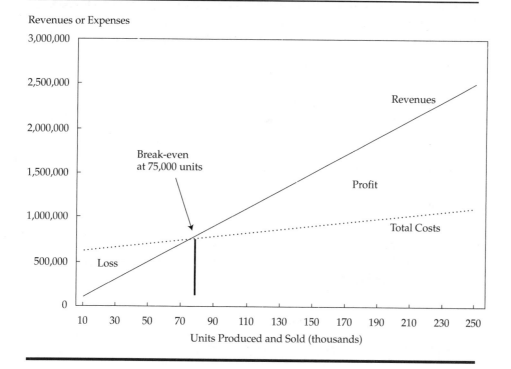

Therefore,

$$PQ_{BE} = VQ_{BE} + F + C$$

and the breakeven number of units, Q_{BE}, is[6]

$$Q_{BE} = \frac{F + C}{P - V}$$

(49-7)

In the case of Impulse Robotics and Malvey Aerospace, Impulse Robotics has a higher breakeven point:

Impulse Robotics: $Q_{BE} = \dfrac{\$500,000 + \$100,000}{\$10 - \$2} = 75,000 \text{ units}$

Malvey Aerospace: $Q_{BE} = \dfrac{\$150,000 + \$50,000}{\$10 - \$6} = 50,000 \text{ units}$

---

[6] You will notice that we did not consider taxes in our calculation of the breakeven point. This is because at the point of breakeven, taxable income is zero.

This means that Impulse Robotics must produce and sell more units to achieve a profit. So, while the higher-leveraged Impulse Robotics has a greater breakeven point relative to Malvey Aerospace, the profit that Impulse Robotics generates beyond this breakeven point is greater than that of Malvey Aerospace. Therefore, leverage has its rewards in terms of potentially greater profit, but it also increases risk.

We can also specify the breakeven in terms of the operating profit, which we refer to as the **operating breakeven**, Q_{OBE}. In this case, the equality is set for revenues and operating costs and the breakeven number of units, Q_{OBE}, is

$$PQ_{OBE} = VQ_{OBE} + F$$

$$Q_{OBE} = \frac{F}{P - V}$$

For the two companies in our example, Impulse Robotics and Malvey Aerospace, the operating breakevens are 62,500 and 37,500 units, respectively:

Impulse Robotics: $Q_{OBE} = \dfrac{\$500,000}{\$10 - \$2} = 62,500$ units

Malvey Aerospace: $Q_{OBE} = \dfrac{\$150,000}{\$10 - \$6} = 37,500$ units

Again, Impulse Robotics has a higher breakeven point in terms of the number of units produced and sold.

Example 49-4

Calculating the Breakeven Point

Continuing with his analysis, Kenigswald considers the effect of a possible downturn on Global Auto's earnings. He divides the fixed costs of €15 billion by the per unit contribution margin:

$$Q_{OBE} = \frac{€15 \text{ billion}}{€24,000 - €14,000} = 1,500,000 \text{ cars}$$

The operating breakeven for Global is 1,500,000 cars, or €36 billion in revenues. We calculate the total breakeven by dividing fixed operating costs, plus interest costs, by the contribution margin:

$$Q_{BE} = \frac{€15 \text{ billion} + €40 \text{ billion}}{€24,000 - €14,000} = \frac{€55 \text{ billion}}{€10,000} = 5,500,000 \text{ cars}$$

Considering the degree of total leverage, Global's total breakeven is 5.5 million cars, or revenues of €132 billion.

We can verify these calculations by constructing an income statement for the breakeven sales (in € billions):

	1,500,000 cars	5,500,000 cars
Revenues	€36	€132
Variable operating costs	21	77
Fixed operating costs	15	15
Operating income	**€0**	€40
Fixed financial costs	40	40
Net income	−€40	**€0**

As business expands or contracts beyond or below breakeven points, fixed costs do not change. The breakeven points for companies with low operating and financial leverage are less important than those for companies with high leverage. Companies with greater total leverage must generate more revenue to cover fixed operating and financing costs. The farther unit sales are from the breakeven point for high-leverage companies, the greater the magnifying effect of this leverage.

Example 49-5

The Leveraging Role of Debt

Consider the Capital Company, which is expected to generate $1.5 million in revenues and $0.5 million in operating earnings next year. Currently, the Capital Company does not use debt financing and has assets of $2 million.

Suppose Capital were to change its capital structure, buying back $1 million of stock and issuing $1 million in debt. If we assume that interest on debt is 5 percent and income is taxed at a rate of 30 percent, what is the effect of debt financing on Capital's net income and return on equity if operating earnings may vary as much as 40 percent from expected earnings?

TABLE 49-7 Return of Equity of Capital Company

No Debt Shareholders' Equity = $2 million	Expected Operating Earnings, less 40%	Expected Operating Earnings	Expected Operating Earnings, plus 40%
Earnings before interest and taxes	$300,000	$500,000	$700,000
Interest expense	0	0	0
Income before taxes	$300,000	$500,000	$700,000
Taxes	90,000	150,000	210,000
Net income	$210,000	$350,000	$490,000
Return on equity[7]	10.5%	17.5%	24.5%

---

[7] Recall that ROE is calculated as Net income/Shareholders' equity.

(*Table continued on next page …*)

TABLE 49-7   Return of Equity of Capital Company (continued)

Debt to Total Assets = 50% Shareholders' Equity = $1 million	Expected Operating Earnings, less 40%	Expected Operating Earnings	Expected Operating Earnings, plus 40%
Earnings before interest and taxes	$300,000	$500,000	$700,000
Interest expense	50,000	50,000	50,000
Income before taxes	$250,000	$450,000	$650,000
Taxes	75,000	135,000	195,000
Net income	$175,000	$315,000	$455,000
Return on equity	17.5%	31.5%	45.5%

Depicting a broader array of capital structures and operating earnings, ranging from an operating loss of $500,000 to operating earnings of $2 million, Figure 49-8 shows the effect of leverage on the return on equity for Capital Company:

FIGURE 49-8   Return on Equity of Capital Corporation for Different Levels of Operating Earnings and Different Financing Choices

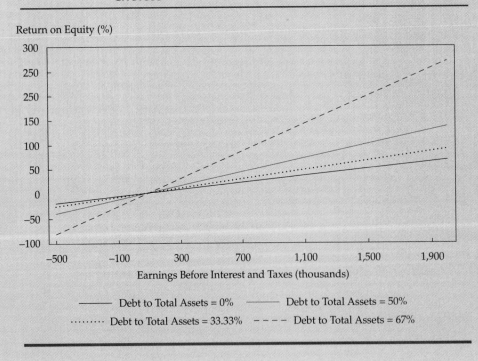

Business is generally an uncertain venture. Changes in the macroeconomic and competitive environments that influence sales and profitability are typically hard to discern and forecast. The larger the proportion of debt in the financing mix of a business, the greater is the likelihood that it will face default. Similarly, the greater the proportion of debt in the capital structure, the more earnings are magnified upward in improving economic times. The bottom line? The greater the leverage, the greater the risk of ownership for equityholders.

3.7 The Risks of Creditors and Owners

As we discussed earlier, business risk refers to the effect of economic conditions as well as the level of operating leverage. Uncertainty about demand, output prices, and costs are among the many factors that affect business risk. When conditions change for any of these factors, companies with higher business risk experience more volatile earnings. Financial risk is the additional risk that results from the use of debt and preferred stock. The degree of financial risk grows with greater use of debt. Who bears this risk?

The risk for providers of equity and debt capital differs because of the relative rights and responsibilities associated with the use of borrowed money in a business. Lenders have priority claims on assets, so they have greater security. In return for lending money to a business, lenders require the payment of interest and principal when due. These contractual payments to lenders must be made regardless of the profitability of the business. A business must satisfy these claims in a timely fashion or face the pain of bankruptcy should it default. In return for their higher priority in claims, lenders get predefined yet limited returns.

In contrast, equity providers claim whatever is left over after all expenses, including debt service, have been paid. So, unlike the fixed and known commitments to the lenders, what is left over for the owners may be a great deal or may be nothing. In exchange for this risk, providers of equity capital exercise the decision-making power over the business, including the right to hire, guide, and if necessary, fire managers. Equityholders also have the right to declare what portion of the business earnings they will take out as dividends. In public companies, ownership rights are usually exercised through an elected board of directors.

Legal codes in most countries provide for these rights, as well as conditions for companies to file for bankruptcy. Most bankruptcy codes provide in some form for two categories of bankruptcies. One form provides for a temporary protection from creditors so that a viable business may reorganize. In the United States, the U.S. Bankruptcy Code sets the terms for the form of negotiated **reorganization** of a company's capital structure that allows it to remain a going concern in Chapter 11.[8] For businesses that are not viable, the second form of bankruptcy process allows for the orderly satisfaction of the creditors' claims. In the United States, this form of bankruptcy is referred to as **liquidation**.[9] Whereas both types of bankruptcy lead to major dislocations in the rights and privileges of owners, lenders, employees, and managers, it is in this latter category of bankruptcy that the original business ceases to exist.

The difference between a company that reorganizes and emerges from bankruptcy and one that is liquidated is often the difference between operating and financial leverage. Companies with high operating leverage have less flexibility in making changes, and bankruptcy protection does little to help reduce operating costs. Companies with high financial leverage use bankruptcy laws and protection to change their capital structure and, once the restructuring is complete, can emerge as ongoing concerns.

---

[8] U.S. Code, Title 11 – Bankruptcy, Chapter 11 – Reorganization. Companies filing for bankruptcy under this code are referred to as having filed for Chapter 11 bankruptcy.

[9] U.S. Code, Title 11 – Bankruptcy, Chapter 7 – Liquidation.

Example 49-6

Chapter 11 Reorganization and Owens Corning

The world's largest manufacturer of glass fiber insulation, Owens Corning Corporation of Toledo, Ohio, filed for Chapter 11 bankruptcy on 5 October 2000, as it faced growing asbestos liability claims. With revenues exceeding $6 billion per year, Owens Corning was one of the largest corporations ever afforded bankruptcy protection by the U.S. courts.

From 1952 to 1972, Owens Corning produced an asbestos-containing high-temperature pipe coating called Kaylo, and at the time of its bankruptcy filing, it had received more than 460,000 asbestos personal injury claims and had paid or agreed to pay more than $5 billion for asbestos-related awards and settlements, legal expenses, and claims processing fees. While the company had assets of $7 billion and liabilities of $5.7 billion, the trust fund it set aside to pay those claims appeared inadequate.

The company's stock traded at between $15 and $25 per share in the year prior to the announcement; the price fell to $1 per share when Owens Corning declared bankruptcy and admitted that it had been overwhelmed by the asbestos liabilities.

Example 49-7

Chapter 7 and Webvan Do Not Deliver

Since the peak of the NASDAQ in March of 2000, many technology companies have found either that they cannot raise enough capital to implement their business plans or that they have an untenable business plan. Some have simply shut their doors and gone out of business, while others have filed for bankruptcy. Either way, these companies have left many unsatisfied creditors.

For example, Webvan.com was a start-up company in the late 1990s that raised over $1.2 billion in equity, $375 million of which came from an IPO in November 1999. It had very ambitious business plans to build a series of warehouses and deliver groceries to fulfill customer orders placed over the Internet. Webvan.com, however, faced a number of challenges, including a downturn in the economy, and quickly ran through its capital.

Webvan.com filed for Chapter 11 bankruptcy protection in July 1999 and reported that it owed $106 million to creditors. By the time it began liquidation under Chapter 7 in January 2002, it reported that the value of its liquidated assets totaled only $25 million, leaving its creditors to receive pennies on the dollar and its investors to receive little or nothing for their $1.2 billion investment in the company.

Whereas the ability to file for bankruptcy is important to the economy, the goal of the analyst is to avoid ownership of companies that are heading toward this extreme step, as well as to be able to evaluate opportunities among companies already in bankruptcy. Under both Chapter 7 and Chapter 11, providers of equity capital generally lose all value during the bankruptcy. On the other hand, debtholders typically receive at least a portion of their capital, but the payments of principal and interest are delayed during the period of bankruptcy protection.

THE CAPITAL STRUCTURE DECISION

4

A company's **capital structure** is the mix of debt and equity that a company uses to finance its business. The goal of a company's capital structure decision is to determine the financial leverage or capital structure that maximizes the value of the company by minimizing the average cost of capital. The weighted average cost of capital (WACC) is given by the average of the marginal costs of financing for each type of financing used. For a company with both debt and equity in its capital structure for which interest expense is tax deductible at a rate t, the WACC is

$$WACC = \left(\frac{D}{V}\right)r_d(1 - t) + \left(\frac{E}{V}\right)r_e$$

where r_e is the cost of equity, r_d is the before-tax cost of debt, and t is the marginal tax rate.[10] Variables E and D denote the market value of the shareholders' equity and the outstanding debt, respectively, and the value of the company is given by $V = D + E$. You will notice that we use the term "marginal" with respect to both the cost of capital and the tax rate. The cost of capital is a marginal cost: what it costs the company to raise additional capital. Therefore, the cost of equity, the cost of debt, and the tax rate that we use throughout the remainder of this reading are marginal: the cost or tax rate for additional capital.

In this section, we first consider the theoretical relationship between leverage and a company's value. We then examine the practical relationship between leverage and company value in equal depth.

4.1 Proposition I without Taxes: Capital Structure Irrelevance

In now-classic papers, Nobel Prize–winning economists Franco Modigliani and Merton Miller argued the important theory that, given certain assumptions, a company's choice of capital structure does not affect its value.[11] The assumptions relate to expectations and markets:

1. Investors agree on the expected cash flow from a given investment.[12]

2. Bonds and shares of stock are traded in a perfect capital market.[13]

Implicit in the perfect market assumption is that bankruptcy has no costs.

Consider the capital of a company to be a pie you can split any number of ways, but the size of the pie remains the same. Likewise, Modigliani and Miller reason, the amount and risk of the aggregate returns to debtholders and equityholders of a company do not change with changes in capital structure. They use

---

[10] For simplicity, this discussion ignores preferred stock. Additionally, (D/V) and (E/V) have been substituted for w_d and w_e, respectively.

[11] Modigliani and Miller (1958, 1963).

[12] All investors have the same expectations with respect to the cash flows from an investment in bonds or stocks. In other words, expectations are homogeneous.

[13] A perfect capital market is one in which any two investments with identical cash flow streams must trade for the same price.

the concept of arbitrage to demonstrate their point: If the value of an unlevered company—that is, a company without any debt—is not equal to that of a levered company, investors could make an arbitrage profit and this profit taking would force the values to be equivalent.

The importance of the Modigliani and Miller theory is that it demonstrates that managers cannot create value simply by changing the company's capital structure. Consider why this might be true. The operating earnings of a business are available to the providers of its capital. In an all-equity company (that is, a company with no debt), all of the operating earnings are available to the equity-holders and the value of the company is the present value of these operating earnings. If, on the other hand, a company is partially financed by debt, these operating earnings are split between the providers of capital: the equityholders and the debtholders. Under market equilibrium, the sum of the values of debt and equity in such a case should equal the value of the all-equity company. In other words, the value of a company is determined solely by its cash flows, not by the relative reliance on debt and equity capital.

This principle does not change the fact of the relative risks of leverage to debtholders versus equityholders. Adding leverage does increase the risk faced by the equityholders. In such a case, equityholders are compensated for this extra risk by receiving a larger proportion of the operating earnings, with the debtholders receiving a smaller portion, as they face less risk. Indeed, in equilibrium, the increase in equity returns is exactly offset by increases in the risk and the associated increase in the required rate of return on equity, so that there is no change in the value of the company.

Modigliani and Miller (MM) first illustrated the capital structure irrelevance proposition under the condition of no taxes:

> <u>MM Proposition I</u>:
> The market value of a company is not affected by the capital structure of the company.

In other words, the value of the company levered (V_L) is equal to the value unlevered (V_U), or $V_L = V_U$.

To understand this proposition, we can think about two companies with the same expected, perpetual cash flows and uncertainty and, hence, the same discount rate applied to value these cash flows. Even if the companies have different capital structures, these two companies must have the same present value using discounted cash flow models. If capital structure changes were to have any effect on a company's value, there would exist an arbitrage opportunity to make endless profits.

In a perfect market, investors can substitute their own leverage for a company's leverage by borrowing or lending appropriate amounts in addition to holding shares of the company. Because this process is costless for investors (remember, we assumed no transaction costs), a company's financial leverage should have no impact on its value. Therefore, a company's capital structure is irrelevant in perfect markets if taxes are ignored.

4.2 Proposition II without Taxes: Higher Financial Leverage Raises the Cost of Equity

Modigliani and Miller's second proposition focuses on the cost of capital of the company:

> <u>MM Proposition II</u>:
> The cost of equity is a linear function of the company's debt to equity ratio.

Assuming that financial distress has no costs and that debtholders have prior claim to assets and income relative to equityholders, the cost of debt is less than the cost of equity. According to this proposition, as the company increases its use of debt financing, the cost of equity rises. The net effect of the increased use of a cheaper source of capital and the rising cost of equity is that there is *no* change in the company's overall cost of capital. Again, Modigliani and Miller argue that the relative amount of debt versus equity does not affect the overall value of the company. This is because despite the low cost of using debt financing, the more debt in the capital structure, relative to equity, the riskier the equity capital.

The risk of the equity depends on two factors: the risk of the company's operations (business risk) and the degree of financial leverage (financial risk). Business risk determines the cost of capital, whereas the capital structure determines financial risk.

The **weighted average cost of capital** (**WACC**), *ignoring taxes*, is

$$r_a = \left(\frac{D}{V}\right)r_d + \left(\frac{E}{V}\right)r_e$$

where

- r_a is the weighted average cost of capital of the company
- r_d is the before-tax marginal cost of debt capital
- r_e is the marginal cost of equity capital
- D is the value of debt
- E is the value of equity
- V is the value of the company, which is equal to $D + E$

We can rearrange the weighted average cost of capital to solve for the cost of equity:

$$r_e = r_a + (r_a - r_d)\left(\frac{D}{E}\right)$$

More than four decades later, the MM theory still provides the foundation for discussions about company value as it relates to capital structure. Higher leverage does not create value. As shown in the above equation, as the debt/equity ratio increases, the cost of equity capital also increases.

Just as we can express the beta of any investment portfolio as a market-value weighted average of the betas of the investments in that portfolio, we can express the systematic risk of each of the sources of a company's capital in a similar manner.[14] In other words, we can represent the systematic risk of the assets of the entire company as a weighted average of the systematic risk of the company's debt and equity:

$$\beta_a = \left(\frac{D}{V}\right)\beta_d + \left(\frac{E}{V}\right)\beta_e$$

where β_a is the asset's systematic risk, or **asset beta**, β_d is the beta of debt, and β_e is the equity beta. The asset beta represents the amount of the risk that cannot be diversified away by investing in assets that are not perfectly correlated with one another.

[14] Hamada (1972).

According to Modigliani and Miller, the company's cost of capital does not depend on its capital structure but rather is determined by the business risk of the company. On the other hand, as the level of debt rises, the risk of the company's defaulting on its debt increases. These costs are borne by the equityholders. So, as the proportionate use of debt rises, the equity's beta, β_e also rises. By reordering the formula of β_a to solve for β_e we get

$$\beta_e = \beta_a + (\beta_a - \beta_d)\left(\frac{D}{E}\right)$$

In the next section, we look at the decision to use debt financing given the taxes and market imperfections found in the real world.

4.3 Taxes, the Cost of Capital, and the Value of the Company

Taxes are the first practical consideration in modifying the results of the MM propositions. Because interest is deductible from income for tax purposes in most countries, the use of debt provides a tax shield that translates into savings that enhance the value of a company. Indeed, ignoring other practical realities of costs of financial distress and bankruptcy, the value of the company increases with increasing levels of debt. In effect, by making the interest costs deductible for income taxes, the government subsidizes companies' use of debt. The actual cost of debt is reduced by the level of the company's tax benefit:

After-tax cost of debt = Before-tax cost of debt × (1 − Marginal tax rate)

Or, representing the after-tax cost of debt as r_d^*,

$$r_d^* = r_d(1 - t)$$

where t is the marginal tax rate. By introducing corporate tax, we adjust the weighted average cost of capital formula to reflect the impact of the tax benefit:

$$r_a = \left(\frac{D}{V}\right)r_d(1 - t) + \left(\frac{E}{V}\right)r_e$$

or

$$r_a\left(\frac{D}{V}\right)r_d^* + \left(\frac{E}{V}\right)r_e$$

We can rearrange this equation to solve for the cost of equity:

$$r_e = r_a + (r_a - r_d)\left(\frac{D}{E}\right)(1 - t)$$

Therefore, the cost of equity is equal to the return on the company as a whole, plus an adjustment for financial leverage.

This tax shield afforded by debt financing adds value to a company. In fact, the value of a levered company is the value of an unlevered (i.e., all-equity) company plus the value of the tax shield, td:[15]

$$V_L = V_U + td$$

Therefore, if taxes are considered but financial distress and bankruptcy costs are not, debt financing is highly advantageous, and in the extreme, a company's optimal capital structure is all debt.

We can see the effect of taxes on the cost of capital in Figure 49-9. Here, we see that if there are no taxes, as shown in Panel B, the cost of capital is constant at r_a. If, on the other hand, interest is tax deductible, the cost of capital declines for ever-increasing use of debt financing, as shown in Panel C.

Figure 49-9   Modigliani and Miller Propositions

A. Value of the Company and Cost of Capital for Propositions Without and With Taxes

	Without Taxes	With Taxes
Proposition I	$V_L = V_U$	$V_L = V_U + {}_tD$
Proposition II	$R_A = \left(\dfrac{D}{V}\right)R_D + \left(\dfrac{E}{V}\right)R_E$	$R_A = \left(\dfrac{D}{V}\right)R_D(1-t) + \left(\dfrac{E}{V}\right)R_E$

B. Costs of Capital if There Are no Taxes

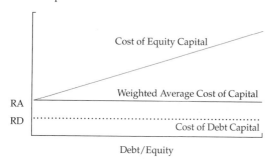

C. Costs of Capital if There are Taxes

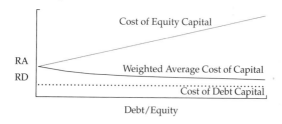

[15] Note that the annual tax saving is $r_d \cdot td$. Expressing its present value in the form of an annuity, we get PV(tax saving) $= r_d \cdot td / r_d = td$.

Example 49-8

The After-Tax Cost of Debt

Payment People, a provider of temporary accounting workers, is considering an $85 million acquisition. The company could raise capital by selling either debt or equity. If the company finances the acquisition with debt at 8 percent interest, what is the after-tax cost of issuing debt if the company's marginal tax rate is 34 percent?

▶ **Solution:** Annual interest expense on $85 million at 8 percent is $6.8 million. The $6.8 million is deducted from income, saving $2,312,000 in taxes. The after-tax interest cost is $6.8 million − $2.312 million = $4.488 million. The before-tax cost of debt is 8 percent; the after-tax cost of debt is

After-tax cost of debt = $4.488 million / $85 million = 5.28%, or $0.08(1 − 0.34) = 0.0528$, or 5.28%.

Example 49-9

The Cost of Equity

Hotel chain Hostales Vacaciones finances land purchases for new hotels through debt financing. The company is opening in ten locations for a total cost of 500 million pesos. The company is considering the cost of equity versus debt for its financing needs. The company has a cost of capital of 13 percent, a debt to equity ratio of 0.5, debt costs of 9 percent, and a tax rate of 32 percent. What is the company's cost of equity with and without the consideration of taxes?

▶ **Solution**
Without taxes

$$r_e = r_a + (r_a - r_d)\left(\frac{D}{E}\right)$$
$$r_e = 13\% + [(13\% - 9\%)(0.5)] = 0.15, \text{ or } 15\%$$

With taxes

$$r_e = r_a + (r_a - r_d)\left(\frac{D}{E}\right)(1 - t)$$
$$r_e = 13\% + [(13\% - 9\%)(0.5)(1 - 0.32)] = 0.1436, \text{ or } 14.36\%$$

Miller (1977) introduced another aspect into the benefit from tax deductibility of interest on debt. He argued that if investors face different tax rates on dividend and interest income for their personal taxes, this situation may reduce the advantage of debt financing somewhat. If investors face a higher rate of tax on income from debt investments relative to stock investments, they will demand a higher return on debt—and, hence, a higher cost of debt—than if there were no differential personal taxes in order to compensate for the personal tax on the income from the bond investment.[16]

From these examples with taxes, we can see that the more a company borrows, the greater the company's value. In practice, however, the value of a levered company is affected by more than the interest due on the debt. Things get more complicated once we introduce factors such as the cost of financial distress, agency costs, and asymmetric information. We address these additional factors next.

4.4 Costs of Financial Distress

The downside of operating and financial leverage is that earnings are magnified downward during economic slowdowns. Lower or negative earnings put companies under stress, and this **financial distress** adds costs—both explicit and implicit costs—to a company. Even before taking the drastic step of filing for bankruptcy, companies under stress may lose customers, creditors, suppliers, and valuable employees to more secure competitors.

Example 49-10

Costs of Financial Distress

Enron is an extreme example of the loss of value due to financial distress. Up until its demise in 2001, Enron was a large player in the natural gas industry. Events leading up to the eventual bankruptcy protection filing caused investors to flee the common stock as creditors refused new lending. Enron went from a favored to a disdained company in record time.

According to a company presentation made ten days after its 2 December 2001 bankruptcy filing, the company's common stock price plunged from $80 per share to $1 per share prior to the bankruptcy announcement, losing $25 billion in market value.[17] This loss in value was due to a number of factors, including

► investors' and creditors' lost confidence,

► financial market reaction from a lack of access to capital markets,

► current maturities greatly exceeding operating cash flow because of the inability to refinance debt,

► nervous trade creditors,

► Dynegy pulling out of the merger on 28 November 2001, and

► the bond ratings downgrade on 28 November 2001.

Cash bankruptcy expenses listed in the bankruptcy filing documents totaled $17.3 million, though the bankruptcy costs including accountants', advisors', and lawyers' fees were over $500 million by November of 2003.[18]

---

[16] It can be argued that there is a higher personal tax on debt income because debt instruments typically provide investors with taxable interest periodically, whereas taxable income from stock investments could, conceivably, be lower because the tax consequences of investing in non-dividend-paying stocks are deferred until the stock is sold.

[17] Enron Corporation Organizational Meeting, 12 December 2001.

[18] *Houston Business Journal*, 19 November 2003.

The expected cost of financial distress is composed of two key ingredients: (1) the costs of financial distress and bankruptcy and (2) the likelihood of financial distress. We can classify the costs of financial distress into direct and indirect costs. Direct costs of financial distress include the actual cash expenses associated with the bankruptcy process, such as legal and administrative fees. Indirect costs of financial distress include forgone investment opportunities, impaired ability to conduct business, and agency costs associated with the debt during periods in which the company is near or in bankruptcy.

Companies whose assets have a ready secondary market have lower costs associated with financial distress. Companies with safe, tangible assets, such as airlines, shipping companies, and steel manufacturers, incur lower costs from financial distress because such assets are usually more readily marketable. On the other hand, companies with few tangible assets, such as high-tech growth companies, pharmaceutical companies, information technology companies, and others in the service industry, have less to liquidate and therefore have a higher cost associated with financial distress.

The probability of bankruptcy increases as the degree of leverage increases. The probability of bankruptcy for a given company depends on how the fixed costs of debt service interact with the instability of the business environment and the reserves available to the company to delay bankruptcy. In other words, the probability of bankruptcy depends, in part, on the company's business risk. Other factors that affect the likelihood of bankruptcy include the company's corporate governance structure and the management of the company.

4.5 Agency Costs

Agency costs are the costs associated with the fact that all public companies and the larger private companies are managed by nonowners. Agency costs result from the inherent conflicts of interest between managers and equity owners. The smaller the stake that managers have in the company, the less is their share in bearing the cost of excessive perquisite consumption or not giving their best efforts in running the company. This conflict has been called the **agency costs of equity**. Given that outside shareholders are aware of this conflict, they will take actions to minimize the loss, such as requiring audited financial statements. The **net agency costs of equity** therefore have three components:[19]

1. **Monitoring costs**. These are the costs borne by owners to monitor the management of the company and include the expenses of the annual report, board of director expenses, and the cost of the annual meeting.

2. **Bonding costs**. These are the costs borne by management to assure owners that they are working in the owners' best interest. These include the implicit cost of noncompete employment contracts and the explicit cost of insurance to guarantee performance.

3. **Residual loss**. This consists of the costs that are incurred even when there is sufficient monitoring and bonding, because monitoring and bonding mechanisms are not perfect.

The better a company is governed, the lower the agency costs. Good governance practices translate into higher shareholder value, reflecting the fact that managers' interests are better aligned with those of shareholders. Additionally, agency theory posits that a reduction in net agency costs of equity results from an increase in the use of debt versus equity. That is, there is an agency cost savings

---

[19] Jensen and Meckling (1976) provide this breakdown of agency costs.

associated with the use of debt. Similarly, the more financially leveraged a company is, the less freedom managers have to either take on more debt or untowardly spend cash. This is the foundation of Michael Jensen's **free cash flow hypothesis**.[20] Higher debt levels discipline managers by forcing them to make fixed debt service payments and by reducing the company's free cash flow.[21]

4.6 Costs of Asymmetric Information

Asymmetric information arises from the fact that managers have more information about a company's performance and prospects (and future investment opportunities) than do outsiders such as owners and creditors. Whereas all companies have a certain level of insider information, companies with comparatively high asymmetry in information are those with complex products like high-tech companies, companies with little transparency in financial accounting information, or companies with lower levels of institutional ownership. Providers of both debt and equity capital demand higher returns from companies with higher asymmetry in information because there is a greater likelihood of agency costs in companies with higher asymmetry in information.

Some degree of asymmetric information always exists because investors never know as much as managers and other insiders. Consequently, investors often closely watch manager behavior for insight into insider opinions on the company's future prospects. Being aware of this scrutiny, managers take into account how their actions might be interpreted by outsiders. The signaling model of capital structure suggests a pecking order to financing decisions. When a company is presented with a new investment opportunity, management must choose the best way to pay for the project. Management wants to optimize return on the investment at the lowest risk.

The **pecking order theory**, developed by Myers and Majluf, suggests that managers choose methods of financing that range from the least visible signals up the scale to the most visible—public offerings of equity.[22] The least visible form of financing is no external financing at all—that is, internally generated funds. If internal financing is insufficient, managers next prefer debt, and finally equity. Another implication of the work of Myers and Majluf is that financial managers tend to issue equity when they believe the stock is overvalued but are reluctant to issue equity if they believe the stock is undervalued. Hence, the issuance of stock is interpreted by investors as a negative signal.

We can read the signals that managers provide in their choice of financing method. For example, commitments to fixed payments, such as dividends and debt service payments, may be interpreted as the company's management having confidence in the company's future prospects of making payments. Such signals are considered too costly for poorly performing companies to afford. Alternatively, the signal of raising money at the top of the pecking order and issuing equity at the bottom of the pecking order holds other clues. If, for instance, the company's cost of capital increases after an equity issuance, we may interpret this effect as an indication that management needed capital beyond what comes cheaply; in other words, this is a negative signal regarding the company's future prospects.

---

[20] Jensen (1986).

[21] Harvey, Lins, and Roper (2004) observe that this discipline is especially important in emerging markets, in which there is a tendency to overinvest.

[22] Myers and Majluf (1984).

4.7 The Optimal Capital Structure According to the Static Trade-Off Theory

Companies make decisions about financial leverage that weigh the value-enhancing effects of leverage from the tax deductibility of interest against the value-reducing impact of the costs of financial distress or bankruptcy, agency costs, and asymmetric information. Putting together all the pieces of the theory of Modigliani and Miller, along with the taxes, costs of financial distress, agency costs, and asymmetric information, we see that as financial leverage is increased, there comes a point beyond which further increases in value from value-enhancing effects are offset completely by value-reducing effects. This point is known as the **optimal capital structure**. In other words, the optimal capital structure is that capital structure at which the value of the company is maximized.

Considering only the tax shield provided by debt and the costs of financial distress, the expression for the value of a leveraged company becomes

$$V_{\mathrm{L}} = V_{\mathrm{U}} + td - \mathrm{PV}(\text{Costs of financial distress}) \qquad \textbf{(49-8)}$$

Equation 49-8 represents the **static trade-off theory of capital structure**. It results in an optimal capital structure such that debt composes less than 100 percent of a company's capital structure. We diagram this optimum in Figure 49-10.

FIGURE 49-10 Tradeoff Theory with Taxes and Cost of Financial Distress

A. Value of the Company and the Debt-Equity Ratio

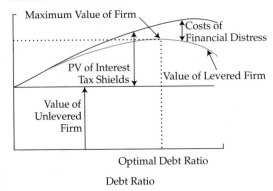

B. Cost of Capital and the Debt-Equity Ratio

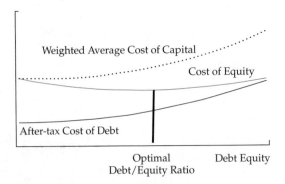

The static trade-off theory of capital structure is based on balancing the expected costs from financial distress against the tax benefits of debt service payments, as shown in Panel A of Figure 49-10. Unlike the Modigliani and Miller proposition of no optimal capital structure, or a structure with almost all debt when the tax shield is considered, static trade-off theory puts forth an optimal capital structure with an optimal proportion of debt. Optimal debt usage is found at the point where any additional debt would cause the costs of financial distress to increase by a greater amount than the benefit of the additional tax shield.

We cannot say precisely at which level of debt financing a company reaches its optimal capital structure. The optimal capital structure depends on the company's business risk, combined with its tax situation, corporate governance, and financial accounting information transparency, among other factors. However, what we can say, based on this theory, is that a company should consider a number of factors, including its business risk and the possible costs of financial distress, in determining its capital structure.

A company's management uses these tools to decide the level of debt appropriate for the company. The tax benefit from the deductibility of the interest expense on debt must be balanced against the risk associated with the use of debt. The extent of financial leverage used should thus depend on owners' and management's appetites for risk, as well as the stability of the company's business environment. Indeed, as we show in Panel B of Figure 49-10, as the proportion of debt in a business rises, the costs of both debt and equity are likely to rise to offset the higher risks associated with higher levels of debt. These cost increases reduce or even negate the cost savings due to the greater use of debt, the cheaper source of financing. The result is a U-shaped weighted average cost of capital curve.

When the company does indeed recognize that it has a most appropriate or best capital structure, it may adopt this as its **target capital structure**. Because management may exploit short-term opportunities in one or another financing source and because market-value fluctuations continuously affect the company's capital structure, a company's capital structure at any point in time may differ from the target. Nevertheless, so long as the assumptions of the analysis and the target are unchanged, analysts and management should focus on the target capital structure.

Example 49-11

Financial Leverage and the Cost of Capital

The Chuang Ho Company provides copper wired components for cellular telephone manufacturers globally. Chuang Ho currently has no debt and has assets of 3 billion SGD. The company's business has matured and it now expects operating earnings of 20,000 SGD per year, indefinitely. Alex Ahn, the company's CFO, wants to evaluate a target leverage structure and uses a scenario approach to evaluate the cost of capital for the present 0 percent debt and possible 50 percent debt or 80 percent debt. Chuang Ho's marginal tax rate is 35 percent. Ahn has gathered the following information regarding costs of capital:

▶ The cost of equity rises with increased levels of debt from 15 percent to 18 percent to 24 percent.

▶ The company can borrow at 12 percent on 50 percent debt, or at 16 percent on 80 percent debt.

Which capital structure is expected to have the lowest cost of capital?

▶ **Solution:** First, calculate the cost of capital under the three scenarios:

TABLE 49-8 Chuang Ho Company

	Leverage		
	No Debt	**50% Debt**	**80% Debt**
Assets	$3,000,000,000	$3,000,000,000	$3,000,000,000
Debt	$0	$1,500,000,000	$2,400,000,000
Equity	$3,000,000,000	$1,500,000,000	$600,000,000
Debt/equity ratio	0	1	4
Proportion of debt	0%	50%	80%
Proportion of equity	100%	50%	20%
Before-tax cost of debt	—	12%	16%
Cost of equity	15%	18%	24%
After-tax cost of debt	—	7.8%	10.4%
Weighted average cost of capital	15.0%	12.9%	13.1

Of the three capital structures that we are evaluating, the cost of capital is lowest for 50 percent debt.

PRACTICAL ISSUES IN CAPITAL STRUCTURE POLICY

5

5.1 Debt Ratings

Debt ratings are an important consideration in the practical management of leverage. As leverage rises, rating agencies tend to lower the ratings of the company's debt to reflect the higher credit risk resulting from the increasing leverage. Lower ratings signify higher risk to both equity and debt capital providers, who therefore demand higher returns.

Most large companies pay one or more rating services to rate their bonds. Debt issues are rated for creditworthiness by public rating agencies. The rating agencies include Moody's, Standard & Poor's, and Fitch. Rating agencies perform a financial analysis of the company's ability to pay the promised cash flows, as well as an analysis of the bond's indenture, the set of complex legal documents associated with the issuance of debt instruments.

These agencies evaluate the wealth of information about the issuer and the bond, including the bond's characteristics and indenture, and provide investors with an assessment of the company's ability to pay the interest and principal on the bond as promised. We provide the bond rating classifications in Figure 49-11. Though there is significant agreement in ratings among the three major services, some disagreements do occur. For example, Standard & Poor's reduced the credit rating of General Motors to speculative grade in early May of 2005, but Moody's did not do so until late August of 2005.

In practice, most managers consider the company's debt rating in their policies regarding capital structure. Managers must be mindful of their company's bond ratings because the cost of capital is tied closely to bond ratings. Consider the difference in the yields on Aaa and Baa rated corporate bonds, as shown in Figure 49-12. Typically, a difference of 100 basis points exists between the yields of Aaa and Baa bonds, though this spread widens in economic recessions.[23] The cost of debt increases significantly when a bond's rating drops from investment grade to speculative. For example, when the rating of General Motors' unsecured 7.2 percent bond maturing in 2011 was changed by Moody's from Baa to Ba, the bond's price fell by over 7.5 percent and its yield rose from 7.541 percent to 9.364 percent.

5.2 Evaluating Capital Structure Policy

In evaluating a company's capital structure, the financial analyst must look at the capital structure of the company over time, the capital structure of competitors

FIGURE 49-11 Bond Ratings by Moody's, Standard & Poor's, and Fitch

	Moody's	Standard & Poor's	Fitch	
Highest quality	Aaa	AAA	AAA	⎫
High quality	Aa	AA	AA	Investment grade
Upper medium grade	A	A	A	
Medium grade	Baa	BBB	BBB	⎭
Speculative	Ba	BB	BB	⎫
Highly speculative	B	B	B	
Substantial risk	Caa	CCC	CCC	Speculative grade
Extremely speculative	Ca			
Possibly in default	C			
Default		D	DDD-D	⎭

---

[23] The Board of Governors of the Federal Reserve System H15 series of Aaa and Baa corporate yields shows an average spread of 119 basis points between Aaa and Baa rated bonds, on average, from 1919 to mid-2005. The largest spread occurred in 1932, with 565 bps, and the lowest spread occurred in 1966, with a 32 bp difference.

FIGURE 49-12   Yields on Aaa and Baa Rated Corporate Bonds, 1984–2005

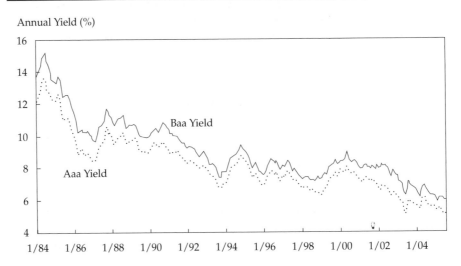

Source: Board of Governors of the Federal Reserve System, release H.15.

that have similar business risk, and company-specific factors, such as the quality of corporate governance, that may affect agency costs, among other factors.[24] The financial analyst is not privy to the company's target capital structure but rather can evaluate the company's ability to handle its financial obligations and the potential role of costs of financial distress in determining how much financial leverage a company can handle.

A common goal of capital structure decisions is to finance at the lowest cost of capital. Analysts can use a scenario approach to assess this point for a particular company, starting with the current cost of capital for a company and considering various changes to answer the following questions:

1. What happens to the cost of capital as the debt ratio is changed?
2. At what debt ratio is the cost of capital minimized and company value maximized?
3. What will happen to the company value and stock price if the company moves toward its optimal capital structure?

5.3 Leverage in an International Setting

Despite the fact that Modigliani and Miller tell us that under several conditions the market value of a company is independent of its capital structure, we know that a company's capital structure is indeed relevant in the real world due to the effects of taxation, the costs of financial distress, and agency costs. The static trade-off theory suggests that the optimal level of leverage should be the level at which the value of the company is maximized; this is the level of debt financing

---

[24] Good corporate governance should lower the net agency costs of equity.

at which any additional debt increases the costs of financial distress by an amount greater than the benefit from interest deductibility.

A company's capital structure largely depends on company-specific factors such as the probability of bankruptcy, profitability, quality and structure of assets, and growth opportunities. Beyond these factors, the company's industry affiliation, as well as the characteristics of the country where the company operates, can account for differences in capital structure also.

The general business environment differs from one country to another, and researchers show that country-specific factors have explanatory power that is similar to or even greater than that of the company's industry affiliation in determining a company's capital structure.[25] Drawing conclusions from the comparison of financial leverage indicators of a U.S.-based energy company and a Japanese energy company is not meaningful if we do not take country-specific differences into account. Tradition, tax policy, and regulation may largely explain the different degrees of leverage in the two countries.

In examining the capital structure and debt maturity structure of corporations in an international context, researchers generally find that differences in the capital structures exist between developed and emerging markets, as well as across the developed countries. Moreover, the debt maturity structure—another important capital structure decision—also tends to vary across the international setting. Therefore, when analysts focus on the capital structure of companies in an international setting, they must consider both the relative use of debt and the maturity structure of debt. In fact, short-term and long-term debt ratios follow very different patterns in an international comparison:

► Taking total debt into account, companies in France, Italy, and Japan tend to be more highly levered than companies in the United States and the United Kingdom.

► Focusing on the use of long-term debt, on the other hand, a different picture emerges: North American companies tend to use more long-term debt than do Japanese companies.

► Companies in developed markets typically use more long-term debt and tend to have higher long-term debt to total debt ratios compared to their emerging market peers.

Beyond the pure comparison of the capital structures, it is equally or even more important to identify and understand the country-specific factors that explain the cross-country differences.[26] Three major types of factors may be used to explain most capital structure differences in an international comparison:

1. *Institutional and legal environment:* These factors represent the legal and regulatory environment in which companies operate, as well as the requirements related to financial reporting. These institutional factors—including taxation, accounting standards, and even the presence or lack of corruption—may affect a company's optimal capital structure.

---

[25] See, for example, Fan, Titman, and Twite (2004).

[26] We should note, however, that the conclusions drawn in different studies are not always consistent with each other. The results of empirical studies, in fact, may depend on several factors, such as the set of countries and companies taken into the data sample, the analyzed historical period, the hypotheses that the researchers intended to test, and even the definition of leverage that they considered.

2. *Financial markets and banking sector.* These factors include characteristics of the banking sector, as well as the size and activity of the financial markets. Financial institutions are crucial for companies' access to financing.

3. *Macroeconomic environment.* These factors capture the general economic and business environment, addressing the influence of economic growth and inflation on the capital structure.

5.3.1 Institutional and Legal Environment

Taxation, financial legislation, the content of laws (e.g., bankruptcy law), and the quality of their enforcement all differ from one country to another. These differences may influence the capital structures of companies and explain many of the differences that we observe across countries.

The apparent conflict of interest between the companies' management and outside investors has already been addressed as the agency problem. This problem is, in fact, one of the key determinants of a company's ability to obtain capital; hence, agency costs are one of the major factors determining the capital structure. This conflict may be mitigated by carefully prepared contracts. The quality of investors' legal protections depends on both the content and the enforcement of the contracts and laws. As a result, we expect to see higher financial leverage in those countries that have weaker legal systems. Further, in countries with weaker legal systems, we expect a greater use of short-term debt financing versus long-term debt financing. Researchers find that companies operating in countries with an efficient legal system tend to use more long-term debt than short-term debt and exhibit lower leverage than comparable companies in countries with weaker legal systems.

Some researchers assume that legal systems based on common law offer external capital providers (both equity and debt providers) with better protection compared to the legal systems of civil-law countries. Common law originated in England and is also followed in other countries, such as the United States, Canada, Australia, New Zealand, Singapore, India, and Malaysia. Civil law, on the other hand, has origins going back to ancient Rome; the countries of continental Europe and most of the rest of the world have legal systems based on this tradition. Researchers find mixed and limited evidence that companies operating in common-law countries tend to have longer debt maturity structures compared to their peers in civil-law countries and use less debt and more equity in their capital structure.

Similar to the rationale described in the case of legal system efficiency, a high level of information asymmetry between insiders and outsiders encourages a greater use of debt relative to equity, as well as a greater reliance on short-term debt than on long-term debt in the capital structure. This is likely due to the fact that enforcing the debt contract is easier than enforcing the less clearly contracted shareholders' rights. Auditors and financial analysts can help in reducing information asymmetries and increase the level of transparency.[27] Researchers confirm that the presence of auditors and analysts is associated with lower financial leverage. The importance of auditors is usually strongest in emerging markets, whereas the presence of analysts is more important in developed markets.

As we discussed earlier, taxes affect the capital structure decision by lowering the cost of debt financing to the issuer in those jurisdictions in which interest expense is tax deductible. In the absence of agency and bankruptcy costs, the benefit from the tax deductibility of interest encourages companies to use debt financing instead of equity financing. However, if dividend income is taxed at

---

[27] Fan et al.

lower rates than interest income, some of the advantage of debt versus equity financing may be reduced from the corporate perspective because the price at which equity can be sold should reflect that advantage. Taxes are an important factor in a company's capital structure decision.

Researchers find mixed results on the effect of the corporate tax rate on capital structures, but they find that personal tax rates do matter. Because the tax treatment of dividends differs across countries, researchers can examine the importance of different tax treatments of dividend income.[28] They find that companies in countries that have lower tax rates on dividend income also have less debt in their capital structures.[29]

5.3.2 Financial Markets and Banking Sector

The size, activity, and liquidity of capital markets are crucial for corporations' access to capital. Several researchers have analyzed the impact of capital markets' characteristics on companies' capital structures. Some find that liquid and active capital markets affect companies' debt maturity structure. Specifically, they find that companies in countries that have liquid and active capital markets tend to use more long-term debt with longer debt maturity. Researchers attribute this finding to the heightened external monitoring of companies by market participants in active markets.[30]

The banking sector is one of the primary sources of funds for the corporate sector in many countries, and its role is especially significant in countries that do not have a corporate bond market. The importance of the banking sector relative to the capital markets can vary from one country to another, however. Countries with a common-law tradition, where the shareholders' rights are stronger, tend to be more market-based, whereas civil-law countries tend to be more bank-based. Because the relationship between a bank and a company is stronger and closer than between a company and a bondholder, banks can handle information asymmetries more efficiently. This effect may partly explain why civil-law countries are more bank-oriented.

However, researchers' findings are mixed regarding the effect of the banking system. Some researchers claim that banks have no effect on companies' financial leverage and that the difference between the bank-oriented and market-oriented countries is more reflected by the relative importance of public financing (i.e., stock and bonds) and private financing (i.e., bank loans).[31] On the other hand, some researchers find that companies in bank-based countries exhibit higher financial leverage compared to those that operate in market-based countries.[32]

The presence of institutional investors may also affect the companies' capital structure choice. Some institutional investors may have preferred habitats, and this preference may affect companies' debt maturity structure. Insurance companies and pension plans, for example, may prefer investing in long-term debt securities in order to match the interest rate risk of their long-term liabilities. Researchers find limited results regarding the influence of preferred habitats; companies in countries that have more institutional investors in their markets

---

[28] Fan et al.

[29] A lower dividend tax burden can be achieved in countries that apply dividend tax relief (e.g., Austria, Belgium, Thailand, and Turkey) or dividend imputation (e.g., Canada, France, Germany, Italy, United Kingdom, and Mexico).

[30] See Demirguc-Kunt and Maksimovic (1998).

[31] Rajan (1995).

[32] See, for example, Claessens, Djankov, and Nevova (2001).

FIGURE 49-13   Country-Specific Factors and Their Assumed Impacts on the Companies' Capital Structure

Country-specific factor	If a country	... then D/E ratio is potentially	... and debt maturity is potentially
Institutional framework			
Legal system efficiency	is more efficient	Lower	Longer
Legal system origin	has common law as opposed to civil law	Lower	Longer
Information intermediaries	has auditors and analysts	Lower	Longer
Taxation	has taxes that favor equity	Lower	
Banking system, financial markets			
Equity and bond markets	has active bond and stock markets		Longer
Bank-based or market-based country	has a bank-based financial system	Higher	
Investors	has large institutional investors	Lower	Longer
Macroeconomic environment			
Inflation	has high inflation	Lower	Shorter
Growth	has high GDP growth		Longer

tend to have less short-term and more long-term debt and somewhat lower debt to equity ratios.[33]

5.3.3 Macroeconomic Environment

Inflation is a widely recognized macroeconomic indicator. High inflation has a negative impact on both the level of the debt financing and the desired debt maturity.[34] Companies in higher-inflation countries usually exhibit lower levels of financial leverage, rely more on equity financing, and have a shorter debt maturity structure compared to their peers in lower-inflation countries.

Researchers have also found that the growth in gross domestic product is associated with longer debt maturity in developed markets. In addition, researchers

---

[33] See, for example, Fan et al. and Domowitz, Glen, and Madhavan (2000).

[34] See, for example, Demirguc-Kunt and Maksimovic (1999), Domowitz et al., and Fan et al.

focusing on developing countries find that companies in countries with high growth rely more on equity financing.[35]

5.3.4 Conclusions

Financial analysts must consider country-specific factors when analyzing and comparing companies that operate in different countries. We have summarized these factors in Figure 49-13.

These factors include the differences in the business and legal environments in other countries, taxes, and macroeconomic factors, among others. Companies' optimal capital structures may differ simply as a consequence of these many country-specific differences. In addition to presenting challenges for international financial and credit analysis, these international differences in debt ratios present some challenges in developing debt policies for the foreign subsidiaries of multinational companies. Theory provides little guidance, and corporate practices in this area seem to vary widely.

---

[35] See Domowitz et al.

SUMMARY

In this reading, we have reviewed the fundamentals of business risk, financial risk, and selection of sources of financing.

▶ Leverage is the use of fixed costs in a company's cost structure. Business risk is the risk associated with operating earnings, including sales risk (uncertainty with respect to the price and quantity of sales) and operating risk (the risk related to the use of fixed costs in operations). Financial risk is the risk associated with how a company finances its operations.

▶ The degree of operating leverage (DOL) is the ratio of the percentage change in operating income to the percentage change in units sold. We can use the following formula to measure the degree of operating leverage:

$$\text{DOL} = \frac{Q(P-V)}{Q(P-V)-F}$$

▶ The degree of financial leverage (DFL) is the percentage change in net income for a given percentage change in operating income. We can use the following formula to measure the degree of financial leverage:

$$\text{DFL} = \frac{[Q(P-V)-F](1-t)}{[Q(P-V)-F-C](1-t)} = \frac{[Q(P-V)-F]}{[Q(P-V)-F-C]}$$

▶ The degree of total leverage (DTL) is a measure of the sensitivity of the cash flows to owners to changes in unit sales, which is equivalent to DTL = DOL × DFL.

▶ The breakeven point, Q_{BE}, is the number of units produced and sold at which the company's net income is zero, which we calculate as

$$Q_{BE} = \frac{F+C}{P-V}$$

▶ A high debt ratio increases the risk of bankruptcy where debtholders' claims have priority over equityholders' claims.

▶ The goal of the capital structure decision is to determine the financial leverage that maximizes the value of the company (or minimizes the weighted average cost of capital).

▶ The deductibility of interest lowers the cost of debt and the cost of capital for the company as a whole. Adding the tax shield provided by debt to the Modigliani and Miller framework suggests that the optimal capital structure is nearly all debt.

▶ In the Modigliani and Miller propositions with and without taxes, increasing a company's relative use of debt in the capital structure increases the risk for equity providers and, hence, the cost of equity capital.

▶ Using more debt in a company's capital structure reduces the net agency costs of equity.

▶ The costs of asymmetric information increase as more equity is used versus debt, suggesting the pecking order theory of leverage, in which new equity issuance is the least preferred method of raising capital.

▶ According to the static trade-off theory of capital structure, in choosing a capital structure, a company balances the value of the tax benefit from deductibility of interest with the present value of the costs of financial distress. At the optimal target capital structure, the incremental tax shield benefit is exactly matched by the incremental costs of financial distress.

▶ A company may identify its target capital structure, but its capital structure at any point in time may not be equal to its target for many reasons, including that management may exploit tactical opportunities in financing sources, market-value fluctuations in its securities, and the uncertainty regarding future retained earnings.

▶ Many companies have goals for maintaining a certain credit rating, and these goals are influenced by the relative costs of debt financing among the different rating classes.

▶ In evaluating a company's capital structure, the financial analyst must look at the capital structure of the company over time, the capital structure of competitors that have similar business risk, and company-specific factors, such as the quality of corporate governance, that may affect agency costs, among other factors.

▶ Good corporate governance and accounting transparency should lower the net agency costs of equity.

▶ When comparing capital structures of companies in different countries, an analyst must consider a variety of characteristics that might differ and affect both the typical capital structure and the debt maturity structure. The major characteristics fall into three categories: institutional and legal environment, financial markets and banking sector, and macroeconomic environment.

PROBLEMS FOR READING 49

1. If two companies have identical operating risk, they also have identical
   A. business risk.
   B. sales risk.
   C. total leverage.
   D. sensitivity of operating earnings to changes in the number of units produced and sold.

2. Operating leverage is a measure of the
   A. sensitivity of net earnings to changes in operating earnings.
   B. sensitivity of net earnings to changes in sales.
   C. sensitivity of fixed operating costs to changes in variable costs.
   D. sensitivity of earnings before interest and taxes to changes in the number of units produced and sold.

3. The Fulcrum Company produces decorative swivel platforms for home televisions. If Fulcrum produces 40 million units, it estimates that it can sell them for $100 each. The variable production costs are $65 per unit, whereas the fixed production costs are $1.05 billion. Which of the following statements is true?
   A. The Fulcrum Company produces a positive operating income if it produces and sells more than 25 million swivel platforms.
   B. The Fulcrum Company's degree of operating leverage is 1.333.
   C. If the Fulcrum Company increases production and sales by 5 percent, its operating earnings are expected to increase by 20 percent.
   D. Increasing the fixed production costs by 10 percent will result in a lower sensitivity of operating earnings to changes in units produced and sold.

4. Increases and decreases in the level of sales are due to business risk. The business risk of a particular company is characterized by
   A. the ratio of debt to equity in the capital structure.
   B. the level of risk assumed by the debt providers.
   C. operating leverage and uncertainty about demand, output prices, and competition.
   D. uncertainty about credit ratings, government debt, interest rates, and the demand for the domestic currency.

5. Consider two companies that operate in the same line of business and have the same degree of operating leverage: the Basic Company and the Grundlegend Company. The Basic Company has no debt in its capital structure, but the Grundlegend Company has a capital structure that consists of 50 percent debt. Which of the following statements is true?
   A. The Grundlegend Company has a degree of total leverage that exceeds that of the Basic Company by 50 percent.
   B. The Grundlegend Company has the same sensitivity of net earnings to changes in earnings before interest and taxes as the Basic Company.
   C. The Grundlegend Company has the same sensitivity of earnings before interest and taxes to changes in sales as the Basic Company.
   D. The Grundlegend Company has the same sensitivity of net earnings to changes in sales as the Basic Company.

6. Myundia Motors now sells 1 million units at ¥3,529 per unit. Fixed operating costs are ¥1,290 million and variable operating costs are ¥1,500 per unit. If the company pays ¥410 million in interest, the levels of sales at the operating and total breakeven points are, respectively

Operating	Total
A. ¥1,500,000,000	¥2,257,612,900
B. ¥2,243,671,760	¥2,956,776,737
C. ¥2,975,148,800	¥3,529,000,000
D. ¥2,257,612,900	¥3,529,000,000

7. Juan Alavanca is evaluating the risk of two companies in the machinery industry: The Gearing Company and Hebelkraft, Inc. Alavanca used the latest fiscal year's financial statement and interviews with managers of the espective companies to gather the following information:

	The Gearing Company	Hebelkraft, Inc.
Number of units produced and sold	1 million	1.5 million
Sales price per unit	$200	$200
Variable cost per unit	$120	$100
Fixed operating cost	$40 million	$90 million
Fixed financing expense	$20 million	$20 million

Based upon this information, the total breakeven points for The Gearing Company and Hebelkraft, Inc. are

A. 0.75 million and 1.1 million units, respectively.

B. 1 million and 1.5 million units, respectively.

C. 1.5 million and 0.75 million units, respectively.

D. 1.0 million units for both companies.

8. If there are homogeneous expectations, an efficient market, and no taxes, transactions costs, or bankruptcy costs, the Modigliani and Miller Proposition I states that

A. bankruptcy risk rises with more leverage.

B. managers cannot increase the value of the company by adding debt.

C. the value of a company is the product of leverage, taxes, and imperfect markets.

D. managers cannot add value by employing tax-saving strategies.

9. If managers justified a choice of optimal capital structure using Modigliani and Miller's Proposition II without taxes, they would contend that

A. taxes increase the value of debt.

B. taxes increase the value of equity.

C. debt is riskier than equity, so it is more costly.

D. the cost of equity increases with increasing proportionate use of debt in the capital structure.

10. Suppose the cost of capital of the Gadget Company is 10 percent. If Gadget has a capital structure that is 50 percent debt and 50 percent equity, its before-tax cost of debt is 5 percent, and its marginal tax rate is 20 percent, then its cost of equity capital is *closest* to

A. 10 percent

B. 12 percent

C. 14 percent

D. 16 percent

DIVIDENDS AND DIVIDEND POLICY

by George H. Troughton and Catherine E. Clark

LEARNING OUTCOMES

The candidate should be able to:

a. review cash dividends, stock dividends, stock splits, and reverse stock splits and calculate and discuss their impact on a shareholder;

b. compare the impact on shareholder wealth of a share repurchase and a cash dividend of equal amount;

c. calculate the earnings per share effect of a share repurchase when the repurchase is made with borrowed funds and the company's after-tax cost of debt is greater (less) than its earnings yield;

d. calculate the book value effect of a share repurchase when the market value of a share is greater (less) than book value per share;

e. compare and contrast share repurchase methods;

f. review dividend payment chronology including declaration, holder-of-record, ex-dividend, and payment dates and indicate when the share price will most likely reflect the dividend;

g. summarize the factors affecting dividend payout policy;

h. calculate the effective tax rate on a dollar of corporate earnings distributed as a dividend using the double-taxation, split-rate, and tax imputation systems;

i. discuss the types of information that dividend initiations, increases, decreases, and omissions may convey, and cross-country differences in the signalling content of dividends.

INTRODUCTION   1

One of the longest running and most debated issues in corporate finance is whether a company's decision about the level of its dividends has an impact on the value of its equity. Essentially, a company has three choices with respect to its earnings in any given year: 1) It could reinvest the earnings back into the business, 2) It could pay the earnings out to the shareholders in the form of dividends, 3) It could repurchase outstanding shares. In reality, most large companies do some combination of the three. For example, in recent decades, large companies in Germany, Great Britain, and the United States paid out dividends that often ranged from 20 percent to 60 percent of their earnings. Japan and some other developing nations had significantly lower dividend payout ratios.

We emphasize in this reading that the overriding consideration in determining a company's dividend payout policy is whether it has positive net present value (NPV) reinvestment opportunities. In addition, a country's income taxes on corporate profits, shareholder income, and capital gains play an important role. Furthermore, traditions, transaction costs for new share issues, and shareholder preferences enter the picture. Finally, dividends are often read in the market place as sending a signal regarding the company's short- and long-term prospects.

This reading is organized as follows: In Section 2, we discuss how cash and stock dividends are paid and how shares are repurchased. In Section 3, we present the chronology of dividend payment procedures, including record date, ex-dividend date, and payment date. In Section 4, we discuss the factors affecting a company's payout policy including taxation, flotation costs, debt covenants and other institutional restrictions, the clientele effect, and the information content of dividends. This leads to a discussion in Section 5 of alternative dividend policies once a company is committed to paying a dividend. We look at the residual, stable, and target cash dividend approaches, as well as whether companies appear to be changing dividend policies. In Section 6, we explore the question of whether dividends matter or are irrelevant, and in Section 7, we touch briefly on the valuation implications of dividends. The last section summarizes the reading.

2   FORMS OF DIVIDENDS

Companies can pay dividends in a number of ways. Cash dividends can be distributed to shareholders through regular, extra, special, or liquidating dividends. Other forms include stock dividends, stock splits, and share repurchases. In this section, we will explore the different forms that dividends can take and their impact on both the shareholder and the issuing company.

2.1. Regular Dividends

Many companies choose to distribute dividends on a regular schedule. Most U.S. and Canadian companies pay quarterly dividends. Some non-North American companies, such as Samsung (Korea), Bayer AG (Germany), and Sony (Japan) distribute regular dividends either semi-annually or annually. In each case, the intention is to distribute among shareholders a portion of a company's profits on a regularly recurring basis.

Most companies that pay regular dividends strive to maintain—or better yet, increase—their dividends on a regular basis. A record of consistent dividends over a very long period of time is important to many companies and many shareholders. The higher standard of consistently increasing dividends is a goal that a substantial number of companies seek to attain and a significant portion of shareholders value.

Regular dividends, and especially increasing regular dividends, also signal to investors that their company is growing and willing to share the gains with their shareholders. Perhaps more importantly, management can use dividend announcements to communicate confidence in the future. An increase in the regular dividend (especially if it is unexpected) will likely have a more positive effect on the share price than could be explained by the increased monetary value of the dividend.

However, some interpret rising dividends or the payment of any dividends as a tacit sign of lack of sufficient growth opportunities, that is, as a sign that the company is unable to profitably reinvest all its earnings. In general, though, failing to increase a regular dividend over a long period of time, or worse yet, cutting it, is often an indication that all is not well at the company.

2.1.1 Dividend Reinvestment Plans (DRIPs)

Some companies have in place a system that allows shareholders to automatically reinvest their dividends into the purchase of additional company shares. Shareholders must register to sign up for the dividend reinvestment plan. The advantages for the company are numerous: It retains the cash otherwise sent out to the shareholder; it reduces the transaction costs of making the payments; and it accumulates more equity capital while saving the underwriting costs of a new share issue. The advantages to the shareholder are twofold: It allows accumulation of shares using cost averaging, and the shareholder's additional investments are in a company he has already deemed a good investment. The additional shares are purchased with no transaction costs, and some companies offer the additional benefit of purchasing shares at a discount (usually 3–5 percent) to the market price.

A disadvantage to the shareholder is the extra bookkeeping involved in jurisdictions in which capital gains are taxed. Shares purchased through a dividend reinvestment plan change the average cost basis for capital gains tax purposes. If the share price is higher (lower) than the original purchase price, it will increase (decrease) the average cost basis. Either way, the average shareholder is left with an accounting situation that is complicated. A further perceived disadvantage to the shareholder is that the cash dividend is fully taxed in the year received even when reinvested, which means the shareholder is paying tax on cash not actually received.

2.2 Extra (or Special) Dividends

Extra (or special) dividends occur when a company does not have a regular dividend policy or rate or it wants to make a one-time extra payment.[1] Extra dividends are generally viewed as nonrecurring payments to shareholders brought about by special circumstances. Typically, companies in more cyclical industries

---

[1] In *The Wall Street Journal's* Dividend News Section, extra or special dividends are referred to as irregular dividends.

would be likely to use this form of dividend payment. When times are bad and earnings are down, cash that would otherwise have gone to dividends can be conserved. But when times are good and earnings are up, the companies can "share the wealth" with their shareholders by issuing a special dividend. Some companies in cyclical industries choose to declare a small regular dividend and then, when circumstances warrant, declare an extra dividend at the end of the year. While "extra" implies that this dividend is in addition to a more regular base of dividends, extra dividend, irregular dividend, and special dividend are terms used interchangeably. In the past, certain automobile companies were among those that regularly used the extra dividend. Ford and GM declared moderate regular quarterly dividends and used the "extra dividend" at the end of the year to reflect particularly good earnings years.

2.3 Liquidating Dividends

A liquidating dividend occurs when a company dissolves its business and distributes the proceeds to its shareholders. Alternatively, a liquidating dividend could refer to the sale of part of a company's business for cash that is distributed to the shareholders. In either case, the distribution would be treated as a capital gain for tax purposes.

2.4 Stock Dividends

Another form of dividend used by some companies is the stock dividend. Here the company does not send cash to its shareholders, but distributes a certain percentage (typically 2–10 percent) of additional shares to each shareholder. The shareholders' total cost basis remains the same but the cost per share held is reduced. For example, if a shareholder owns 100 shares at a price of $10 per share, the total cost base would be $1,000. After a 5 percent stock dividend, the total cost basis would be the same $1,000 but the cost basis per share would become (approximately) $9.52 on the 105 shares now held ($9.52 = $1,000/105).

Superficially, the stock dividend might seem an improvement on the cash dividend from both the shareholders' and the company's point of view. Each shareholder ends up with more shares, which didn't have to be paid for, and the company didn't have to spend any actual money issuing a dividend. Furthermore, the shareholder postpones any tax due until the stock is ultimately sold. However, the stock dividend does nothing to change the value of each shareholder's ownership position in the company since along with shares outstanding, earnings per share (and other per share data) are also adjusted. For example, a company with a billion dollar market capitalization before issuing a stock dividend will still be a company with a billion dollar market capitalization after the stock dividend: The decrease in the share price should be exactly offset by the increase in the number of shares outstanding.

Table 50-1 shows the impact of a 3 percent stock dividend to a shareholder who owns 10 percent of a company with a market value of $20 million.[2] As one can see, the market value of the shareholder's wealth does not change, assuming an unchanged P/E. In addition, a stock dividend and, as the reader will see shortly, a stock split do not alter a company's asset base or earning power.

---

[2] The table rounds intermediate calculations to only four decimal places. Final results ignore rounding errors.

TABLE 50-1 Illustration of the Effect of a Stock Dividend		
	Before Dividend	**After Dividend**
Shares outstanding	1,000,000	1,030,000
Earnings per share	$1.00	$0.97 (1/1.03)
Stock price	$20.00	$19.4175 (20 × 0.9709)
P/E	20	20
Total market value	$20 million	$20 million (1,030,000 × $19.4175)
Shares owned	100,000 (10% × 1,000,000)	103,000 (10% × 1,030,000)
Ownership value	$2,000,000 (100,000 × $20)	$2,000,000 (103,000 × $19.4175)

In contrast to financial theorists, companies that regularly pay stock dividends see some advantages to this form of dividend payment. From the company's point of view, more shares outstanding broaden the shareholder base. With more shares outstanding, there is a higher probability that more individual shareholders will own the stock, almost always a plus for companies. Market folklore has it that a lower stock price will attract more investors, all else equal. U.S. companies often view the optimal share price as $20 to $80. Assuming a growing company, a systematic stock dividend will be more likely to keep the stock in the "optimal" range. For example, Tootsie Roll Industries has issued a 3 percent dividend every year since 1966 in addition to its regular quarterly dividend. When the company pays the same dividend rate on the new shares as they did on the old shares, a shareholder's dividend income has increased.

A stock dividend has no effect on a company's capital structure (its mix of sources of financing) because it leaves the market values of equity and debt unchanged. This is a difference between cash and stock dividends. Cash dividends transfer assets from the company to shareholders, thereby reducing the assets of the company and the market value of its equity. As a result, cash dividends increase leverage (i.e., the proportion of financing provided by debt) from what it was before the payment of the dividend. An increase in leverage could decrease the market value of existing bonds, and bondholders usually seek to protect their position through certain restrictions on the payment of cash dividends, as discussed in more detail in Section 4.3.

Another difference between a cash dividend and a stock dividend is its accounting treatment on the books of the corporation. By shifting retained earnings (equal to the market value of the additional stock being distributed) to the capital account, a stock dividend merely reclassifies certain amounts of shareholders' equity on the balance sheet, whereas a cash dividend represents a cash outflow and a reduction in shareholders' equity.

2.5 Stock Splits

Stock splits are similar to stock dividends, in that each shareholder ends up with more shares but no change in his percent ownership of the company. For example, if a company announces a three-for-one stock split, each shareholder will be issued two additional shares for each share owned, so that the end result will be three shares for each one share previously owned. In the process, though, earnings and dividends (and all other per share data) will decline by two thirds, leaving the P/E, dividend yield, and market value all unchanged. While two-for-one and three-for-one stock splits are the most common, unusual splits such as five-for-four or seven-for-three are not unheard of. It is important for each shareholder to recognize that their wealth is unchanged by the stock split (just as it was for a stock dividend, all else equal). Following is an example of a six-for-five split and its impact on stock price, earnings per share, dividends per share, dividend yield, P/E, and market value.

TABLE 50-2   Before and After a Six-for-Five Stock Split

	Before Split	After Split
Number of shares outstanding	4 million	4.8 million
Stock price	$40.00	$33.33 [$40 / (6/5)]
Earnings per share	$1.50	$1.25 [$1.50 / (6/5)]
Dividends per share	$0.50	$0.4167 [$0.50 / (6/5)]
Dividends yield	1.25%	1.25% ($0.4167/$33.33)
P/E	26.7	26.7 ($33.33 / $1.25)
Market value of company	$160 million	$160 million

As one can see, a six-for-five stock split is basically the same as a 20 percent stock dividend, since all per share data have been reduced by 20 percent. The only difference is in the accounting treatment on the books of the company: Stock splits are accounted for as a reduction in the par value of the shares, whereas stock dividends are a transfer from retained earnings to equity capital. A company may announce a stock split at any time. Typically it is after a period in which the stock has risen either for reasons specific to that company or, just as likely, during a general rise in the stock market in which the company's stock has done well. Investor folklore has it that an announcement of a stock split is viewed as a positive sign for future stock gains by some investors. However, announced stock splits more often merely recognize that the stock has risen enough to justify a stock split, and return the stock price to the "optimal" range of $20 to $80 per share.

In mid 1999 when its stock was selling for about $90 per share, Enron announced a two-for-one stock split. Over the next year the stock doubled before the company plunged into bankruptcy in 2001. Ameritrade had two stock splits in 1999, a two-for-one in March and a three-for-one in August. The stock commenced to fall from over $60 per share (adjusted) to less than $3 per share in 2002. Even two of the largest companies in the world (as measured by market value), General Electric and Microsoft, saw their stocks decline significantly during the three years after their 1999 stock splits. In each of these above cases, the stock was split after a significant rise but was not, in and of itself, a meaningful predictor of future price action.

Much less common than stock splits are reverse stock splits. A **reverse stock split** increases share price and reduces the number of shares outstanding—again, with no change to the underlying fundamentals. Just as a rising stock price might indicate an upcoming stock split, so, too, a dramatically falling stock price might signal a forthcoming reverse stock split. Reverse stock splits are typically one-for-a much larger number, with the objective of getting the stock closer (this time *up*) to the optimal $20 to $80 range. Reverse stock splits are perhaps most common for companies coming out of bankruptcy (where a one-for-thirty or one-for-fifty reverse stock split would not be unusual) or when the share price declines to a low value (for example, in the United States many institutional investors do not regard stocks selling below $5 per share as investment grade). AT&T Corporation had a 1-for-5 reverse split in November 2002 that brought its stock price up from approximately $5 (adjusting for a liquidating dividend paid on the same date) to about $28.

2.6 Share Repurchases

A **share repurchase** (or buyback) is a transaction in which a company buys back its own shares. Unlike stock dividends and stock splits, share repurchases use corporate cash. Hence, share repurchases can be viewed as an alternative to cash dividends. Shares that have been issued and subsequently repurchased become **treasury shares** (**treasury stock**), which are not considered for dividends, voting, or computing earnings per share. Treasury shares may be reissued later, typically for employee stock options. When used for stock options, repurchased shares reduce or prevent earnings per share dilution but do not increase earnings per share.

Share repurchases have been around for a long time, but it is only in the last twenty years that they have been used extensively. In the early 1980s, cash dividends were approximately five times greater than the market value of share repurchases. For a number of years in the bull market of the late 1990s, the value of share repurchases was greater than the value of cash dividends in the United States.

A share repurchase should be equivalent to the payment of cash dividends of equal amount in their effect on shareholders' wealth, all other things being equal. "All other things being equal" in this context is shorthand for assumptions that the taxation and information content of cash dividends and share repurchases do not differ. (We shall discuss the information content of dividends in a subsequent section.) Understanding this baseline equivalence result permits more advanced analysis to explore the result's sensitivity to various modifications to the "all other things being equal" assumption. For example, in Section 5.4 we will discuss the advantage share repurchases may have over cash dividends when the tax rate on dividend income is higher than that on capital gains. Example 50-1 demonstrates the claim of equivalence in the "all other things being equal" case.

Example 50-1

The Equivalence of Share Repurchases and Cash Dividends

Waynesboro Chemical Industries, Inc. (WCII) has 10,000,000 shares outstanding with a current market value of $20 per share. WCII's Board of Directors is considering two ways of distributing WCII's current $50,000,000 free cash flow to equity. The first method involves paying a cash dividend of $50,000,000/10,000,000 = $5 per share. The second method involves repurchasing $50,000,000 worth of shares. For simplicity, we make the assumptions that dividends are received when the shares go ex-dividend and that any quantity of shares can be bought at the market price of $20 per share. We also assume that the taxation and information content of cash dividends and share repurchases do not differ. How would the wealth of a shareholder be affected by WCII's choice of method in distributing the $50,000,000?

Cash Dividend. After the shares go ex-dividend, a shareholder of a single share would have $5 in cash (the dividend) and a share worth $20 − $5 = $15. The ex-dividend value of $15 can be demonstrated as the market value of equity after the distribution of $50,000,000, divided by the number shares outstanding after the dividend payment, or [(10,000,000) ($20) − $50,000,000]/10,000,000 = $150,000,000/10,000,000 = $15. (The payment of a cash dividend of course has no effect on the number of shares outstanding.) Total wealth from ownership of one share is therefore $5 + $15 = $20.

Share Repurchase. With $50,000,000 WCII could repurchase $50,000,000/$20 = 2,500,000 shares. The post-repurchase share price would be unchanged at $20, which can be calculated as the market value of equity after the $50,000,000 share repurchase, divided by the shares outstanding after the share repurchase, or [(10,000,000)($20) − $50,000,000]/(10,000,000 − 2,500,000) = $150,000,000/7,500,000 = $20. Total wealth from ownership of one share is therefore $20, exactly the same as in the case of a cash dividend. It is irrelevant for a shareholder's wealth whether the shareholder actually sold the share back to the WCII in the share repurchase: If the one share was sold, $20 in cash would be realized; if the share was not sold, its market value of $20 would count equally towards the shareholder's wealth.

The assumption made in Example 50-1 that the company repurchases shares at the market price is an important one. Example 50-2 illustrates that if a company repurchases shares from an individual shareholder at a negotiated price representing a premium over the market price, the remaining shareholders' wealth is reduced.

Example 50-2

A Share Repurchase that Transfers Wealth

While considering the choice between cash dividends and a share repurchase at the market price of $20 per share, WCII becomes aware that Kirk Parent recently purchased a major position in its outstanding shares with the intention of influencing the business operations of WCII in ways the current board does not approve. An advisor to the board has suggested approaching Parent privately with an offer to buy back $50,000,000 worth of shares from him at $25 per share, which is a $5 premium over the current market price. The board of WCII declines to do so because of the effect of such a repurchase on its other shareholders. Determine the effect of the proposed share repurchase on the wealth of shareholders other than Parent.

▶ **Solution:** With $50,000,000 WCII could repurchase $50,000,000/$25 = 2,000,000 shares from Parent. The post-repurchase share price would be $18.75, which can be calculated as the market value of equity after the $50,000,000 share repurchase divided by the shares outstanding after the share repurchase, or [(10,000,000)($20) − $50,000,000]/

$(10,000,000 - 2,000,0000) = \$150,000,000/8,000,000 = \$18.75$. Shareholders other than Parent would lose $\$20 - \$18.75 = \$1.25$ for each share owned. Although this share repurchase would conserve total wealth (including Parent's), it effectively transfers wealth to Parent from the other shareholders.

The theme of Example 50-1 was that, as the baseline result, a company should not expect to create or destroy shareholder wealth merely by its choice of method in distributing money to shareholders. In Example 50-1, the market price per share of $20 was not affected by the share repurchase. We can interpret $20 as the product of expected EPS and a forward price-to-earnings ratio, or as the product of book value per share and the price-to-book ratio. A share repurchase may affect the terms in these products (e.g., EPS and price-to-earnings) but, if it does, Example 50-1 suggests that the changes should be offsetting. Examples 50-3 and 50-4 illustrate the types of analysis we can conduct on the effect of share repurchases on EPS and book value per share (BVPS).

Example 50-3

Share Repurchases Using Borrowed Funds: The Effect on EPS When the After-Tax Cost of Borrowing Equals E/P

Jensen Industries plans to borrow $12 million which it will use to repurchase shares. The following information is given:

- Share price at time of buyback: $60
- EPS before buyback = $3
- Earnings yield (E/P) = $3/$60 = 5%
- After-tax cost of borrowing = 5%
- Planned buyback: 200,000 shares

Calculate the EPS after the buyback.

▶ **Solution:**

EPS after buyback = Earnings less After-tax cost of funds / Shares outstanding after buyback

$= [\$6.6 \text{ million} - (200,000 \text{ shares} \times \$60 \times 0.05)]/2 \text{ million shares}$
$= [\$6.6 \text{ million} - (\$0.6 \text{ million})]/2 \text{ million shares}$
$= \$6.0 \text{ million}/2 \text{ million shares}$
$= \$3.00$

With the after-tax cost of borrowing equal to the earnings yield (E/P) of the shares, the share repurchase has no effect on the company's EPS.

In Example 50-3, the share repurchase produced no change in EPS because the shares' earnings yield of 5% equaled its after-tax cost of borrowing. We can also see that if the after-tax cost of borrowing were greater than 5%, earnings after the buyback would be less than $6 million so that EPS after the buyback would be less than $3.00. On the other hand, after-tax cost of borrowing less than 5% would increase EPS to a level above $3.00. In summary, a share repurchase may increase, not affect, or reduce EPS, depending on whether the after-tax cost of the funds used to accomplish the repurchase is less than, equal to, or greater than the earnings yield of the shares (E/P) before the repurchase. A share repurchase may cause the price-to-earnings ratio to change as well. For example, if a share repurchase causes a company's financial leverage to change, the financial risk of the company's earnings stream changes and the price-to-earnings ratio post-repurchase may change from its pre-repurchase level to reflect the change in risk.

Example 50-4

The Effect of Share Repurchase on Book Value per Share

Company A and Company B stocks sell at $20 a share and each company has 10 million shares outstanding. Both companies have announced a $5 million buyback. The only difference is that Company A has a market price per share greater than its book value per share, while Company B has a market price per share less than its book value per share:

► Company A has book value of equity of $100 million and BVPS of $100 million/10 million shares = $10. *The market price per share of $20 is greater than BVPS of $10.*

► Company B has a book value of equity of $300 million and BVPS of $300 million / 10 million shares = $30. *The market price per share of $20 is less than BVPS of $30.*

Both companies

► buy back 250,000 shares at the market price per share ($5 million buyback/$20 per share = 250,000).

► are left with 9.75 million shares outstanding (10 million pre-buyback shares − 0.25 million repurchased = 9.75 million shares).

After the share repurchase:

► Company A's shareholders' equity at book value falls to $95 million ($100 million − $5 million) and its *book value per share decreases* from $10 to $9.74 (shareholders' equity/shares outstanding = $95 million/9.75 million shares = $9.74).

► Company B's shareholders' equity at book value falls to $295 million ($300 million − $5 million) and its *book value per share increases* from $30 to $30.26 (shareholders' equity/shares outstanding = $295 million/9.75 million = $30.26).

Example 50-4 shows that book value per share will either increase or decrease depending on whether share price is higher or lower than BVPS. When share price is greater than BVPS, BVPS will decrease after a share repurchase; when share price is less than BVPS, BVPS will increase after a share repurchase. Still worth underlining is that if shares are repurchased at market price, we would not expect the balance sheet effect just illustrated to affect shareholders' wealth, all other things being equal.

2.7 Repurchase Methods

There are three main ways that companies repurchase shares:

1. **Buy in the open market**. This is the most common method of repurchase, with the company buying "from time to time, as conditions warrant in the open market." This gives the company optimum flexibility and, in many shareholders' minds, acts to set a floor on the price of the shares. The latter is not always the case, but all other things being equal, an outstanding authorized share repurchase probably does function as a support for the share price.

2. **Buy back a fixed number of shares at a fixed price**. Sometimes a company will make a *tender offer* to repurchase a specific number of shares, typically at a premium to the current market. Shareholders may subscribe to the offer agreeing to sell their shares at the pre-determined price. If more shares are subscribed than the total repurchase, the company will typically buy back a pro rata amount from each shareholder.

3. **Repurchase by direct negotiation**. On occasion a company will negotiate with a major shareholder to buy back its shares, often at a premium to the market price. Example 50-2 illustrated this practice. The company may do this to keep a large block of shares from overhanging the market (and thus acting to dampen the share price). In some of the more infamous cases, unsuccessful takeover attempts have ended with the company buying back the would-be suitor's shares in what is referred to as a greenmail transaction, often to the detriment of remaining shareholders.[3]

2.8 Dividend Forms Outside the United States

To provide a perspective on dividends, our discussion thus far has been limited to the United States. Laws, customs, and other considerations, all of which can vary from country to country, influence the forms that dividends take. Legal restrictions affect some forms of dividends. Stock repurchases, so common in recent years in the United States, are discouraged or even prohibited in some countries. Repurchases in the open market could be viewed as an attempt at company manipulation of its own stock. In fact, the U.S. Securities and Exchange Commission (SEC) held such a view until it adopted a safe harbor for company repurchases in 1982.

Companies may also consider their competitive environment when contemplating dividends and the form that a prospective dividend might take. In smaller capitalization markets, a company may feel that returning cash to its shareholders

---

[3] **Greenmail** is the purchase of the accumulated shares of a hostile investor by a company that is targeted for takeover by that investor, usually at a substantial premium over market price.

is not in its best interest. Some managements worry that a shareholder would take the cash (from either a cash dividend or repurchased shares) and invest it in a competitor of the company, thus possibly hurting the company's competitive position.

3   DIVIDEND PAYMENT CHRONOLOGY

In the previous section, we saw that dividends can take several forms. Once a company's Board of Directors votes a dividend, a fairly standard dividend chronology is set in motion. Below we provide an explanation of dividend payment chronology in the United States. Since the payment chronology is determined by rules set by exchanges in various countries, there are some country-to-country differences; but declaration dates, ex-dividend dates, and record dates are common on most exchanges. Furthermore, the shares of most large non-U.S. companies trade on the New York Stock Exchange (NYSE) and thus must meet the chronology described below. For example, the five largest publicly held non-U.S. companies, BP (UK), DaimlerChrysler (Germany), Toyota (Japan), Royal Dutch (Netherlands/UK) and Total (France), as well as 354 other global companies, trade on the NYSE as American Depository Securities (ADS). Canadian companies such as Royal Bank of Canada, Alcan, Nortel Networks, EnCana, and Canadian National Railway trade like U.S. shares on the NYSE.

3.1 Declaration Date

The first date on the time line is the **declaration date**, the day that the corporation issues a statement declaring a specific dividend. Whether it is a regular, irregular, special, liquidating, or stock dividend, all begin with a company's Board of Directors authorizing its payment. In Japan and several European countries, the company's shareholders must approve the payment. At the time of the declaration, the company will state the **holder-of-record date** and the **payment date**. Typically, business publications will list dividends declared during the previous day (for daily publications) or week (for weekly publications) under the heading "Dividends Reported" including the period for which the dividend applies (e.g. monthly, quarterly, special), the dollar amount of the dividend (to six decimal points if applicable), the payable date, and the record date.

3.2 Ex-Dividend Date

After the declaration date, the next pertinent date is the **ex-dividend date** (also referred to as the **ex-date**). This is the first date that a share trades without (i.e. "ex") the dividend. For a share traded on the ex-dividend date, the seller will receive the dividend. In order to have a claim on that dividend, the share must be bought no later than the last business day *before* the ex-dividend date. This is the last day a share trades "cum dividend," or with the dividend, and the last day that the buyer of the share will receive the dividend. For example, in the United States, if the ex-date is Tuesday, December 26th, shares must be bought by Friday, December 22nd, to receive the dividend (markets are closed on Christmas Day, Monday, December 25th, and are not open on Saturday and Sunday). Trading **ex-dividend** refers to shares that no longer carry the right to the next dividend payment. This trading day is often designated in the share price tables of business publications with an x in the volume column. This indicates that the money value of the upcoming dividend has been subtracted from the previous day's closing price. For example, if a share closed at $20 on the day before the ex-date and the upcoming dividend is $0.25, then on the ex-date (all other things being equal) the shares will start the trading day at $19.75. If it closes at $20 for that day, it will show a gain of $0.25 for the day, even though the closing price is the same as it was the day before.

3.3 Holder-of-Record Date

The **holder-of-record date** (also called the **owner-of-record date**, **shareholder-of-record date**, **record date**, or **date of record**) is two business days after the ex-dividend date. This is the date that a shareholder listed on the corporation's books will be deemed to have ownership of the shares for purposes of receiving the upcoming dividend. While the shareholder-of-record date is determined by the corporation, the ex-date is determined by the exchange on which the shares trade. Currently, the ex-date is two business days before the record date. In our example above, if the ex-date were Tuesday, December 26th, the record date would be Thursday December 28th. Not too many years ago, there were four or five business days between the ex- and the record dates. The shorter time frame no doubt is due to technological improvements in handling share transactions and mirrors the fewer number of days stipulated between trade and settlement dates for share transactions.

3.4 Payment Date

The final pertinent date on the dividend chronology is the **payment date** (also called the **payable date**). This is the day that the company actually mails out (or, more recently, electronically transfers) the dividend payment. As discussed earlier, the company typically states the payment date when the dividend declaration is made. Unlike other pertinent dates, such as the ex-date and record date which are only on business days, the payment date is just as likely to be on a weekend or holiday as not. For example, a company may list its payment dates as March 15th, June 15th, September 15th, and December 15th even though some of those dates will inevitably fall on a Saturday, Sunday, or holiday.

3.5 Interval between Key Dates in the Dividend Payment Chronology

The time between the ex-date and the record date is fixed (currently at two days) but the time between the other pertinent dates is determined by each company and can vary substantially. For example, record dates are typically anywhere from a week to a month after the declaration date for most normal dividends, but can be much longer for less-commonly occurring dividends such as irregular dividends, special dividends, liquidating dividends, and stock dividends. Likewise, the time between the record date and the payment date is typically anywhere from a few days to a month or more. However, most companies follow a fairly set routine for their dividends, especially for regular quarterly dividends. Some business publications such as *Value Line* include in their individual company reports the approximate dates of a company's next dividend meeting, its ex-date, and payment date. Exhibit 50-1 portrays a typical time-line for dividend chronology.

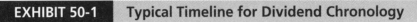

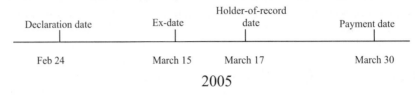

EXHIBIT 50-1   Typical Timeline for Dividend Chronology

Typical Timeline for Dividend Chronology

Declaration date		Ex-date	Holder-of-record date		Payment date
Feb 24		March 15	March 17		March 30

2005

3.5.1 Impact on Indirect Shareholders

For those who own shares through open-end, closed-end, and exchange-traded funds (ETFs), the dividend chronology is generally the same as for those who own shares directly. That is, on the ex-dividend date for any shares in the fund portfolio, the price of those shares will nominally fall by the value of the dividend, and on the payment date the company will send an electronic transfer for the value of the dividend to the fund. However, most funds only declare their dividends (the total dividends and interest received by the portfolio less management fees and expenses) to fund owners on a periodic basis. No doubt, this is for logistical purposes, because accounting for each fund's shareholder payments on a frequent pro-rata basis would not be cost effective. Therefore, equity funds typically distribute dividend income on a periodic basis, usually quarterly or annually. For example, for the Vanguard funds, those with a relatively higher dividend yield (the Wellington Balanced Fund, Index 500, and Value Index Fund) generally distribute dividends quarterly, while those funds with a relatively lower dividend yield (the small-cap, growth, and international funds) generally distribute dividends once a year, usually in December. Paralleling the ex-dividend concept, on the dividend distribution date, the price of the fund will be decreased by the value of the dividends being distributed. The fund owner can then either receive the dividends in cash or reinvest them in additional shares of the fund. For example, if a fund has a net asset value of $20 on January 15th and is distributing $1 in dividends on the 16th, the net asset value of the fund will drop $1 to $19 (all other things being equal) on the 16th. The total value to each fund shareholder is still $20 ($19 in share value and $1 in dividends) although the dividend distribution is a taxable event to the fund shareholder. Under U.S. tax law, regulated investment companies are not taxed on fund income as long as 90 percent of such income (after fees) is passed on to the fund shareholder.

4   FACTORS AFFECTING DIVIDEND PAYOUT POLICY

In this section we explore six factors affecting a company's decision to pay dividends—its **dividend payout policy**. Some factors are external to the company, such as taxation, while other factors are more company-specific, such as possible restrictions on dividend payments and flotation costs. Shareholder preference for current income versus capital gains and the so-called clientele effect are also discussed. We also look at the information content of dividends—how dividends can be used as a signaling device by management.

4.1 Taxation of Dividends

Taxation is an important factor in all investment decisions, because it is the after-tax return that is most relevant to investors. Different countries tax corporate dividends in a wide variety of ways, and even within a single country it can be quite complex. In addition, as a major fiscal policy tool that is subject to politics, governments have a tendency to "re-address" tax issues, sometimes with great frequency, thereby complicating the issue even more. As with other aspects of taxation, governments use the taxation of dividends to address a variety of goals: either to encourage or discourage the retention or distribution of corporate earnings; to redistribute income; or to address other political, social, and/or investment goals.

Most developed markets tax shareholder investment income. Some tax both capital gains and dividend income. Others tax dividends but not capital gains. Hong Kong is an exception in that it levies no tax on either dividends or capital gains.

For the global investor, foreign taxes can be just as important as domestic taxes. Foreign tax credits in the investor's home country also may figure importantly into the overall taxation issue. For example, GlaxoSmithKline PLC (GSK) is a giant pharmaceutical company based in the United Kingdom. In 2003, the United Kingdom withheld approximately 5 percent of GSK's dividend, but U.S. shareholders were generally able to claim a tax credit for the amount withheld by the United Kingdom on their U.S. tax return.

4.1.1 Taxation Methods

We will look at three main systems of taxation that impact dividends: the **double taxation**, **split-rate**, and **imputation** tax systems. Other tax systems can be a combination of these.

The United States is often described as an example of a *double taxation* system. Corporate earnings are taxed regardless of whether they will be distributed as dividends or retained at the corporate level, and dividends are taxed again at the individual shareholder level. (In fact, for many U.S. investors, there is triple taxation of dividends because many states also levy a tax on dividend income.) In 2003, taxes on the shareholders' dividends were lowered from a maximum of 39.6 percent (the highest marginal income tax rate) to a maximum of 15 percent. At the same time, the tax on long-term capital gains was also reduced to the same 15 percent (from a 20 percent maximum rate). Table 50-3 depicts the double taxation system using the highest marginal rate on dividends in the United States both before and after the 2003 tax law change.[4]

---

[4] Under current U.S. tax law both dividend and capital gains tax rates are scheduled to return to pre-2003 levels in 2009.

TABLE 50-3 Double Taxation of Dividends at Different Personal Tax Rates (per $100)

	39.6%	15%
Net income before taxes	$100	$100
Corporate tax rate	35%	35%
Net income after tax	$65	$65
Dividend assuming 100% payout	$65	$65
Shareholder tax	$25.74	$9.75
Net dividend to Shareholder	$39.26	$55.25
Double tax rate per $ of dividend	60.7%	44.8%

While there is still double taxation of dividends in the example, the net tax rate on a dollar of income distributed in dividends has declined from 61 percent to 45 percent: a decline of about 26 percent. Though U.S. investors clearly prefer the lower preferential tax rate for dividends, it is not clear whether they would prefer a higher or lower payout, because the current tax rate is the same on both dividends and long-term capital gains for most shareholders. Later we will discuss a company's decision with respect to the dividend payout ratio.

Other countries, such as Germany, have a *split-rate* system of corporate taxes. A split-rate system taxes earnings to be distributed as dividends at a different rate than earnings to be retained. Corporate profits distributed as dividends are taxed at a lower rate than those retained in the business. This offsets the higher taxation of dividends at the individual level compared with taxation of capital gains. The following table depicts this split-rate tax system for dividends.

TABLE 50-4 Taxation of Dividends Based on Split Rate System (per €100)

Pretax earnings	€200
Pretax earnings retained	100
35% tax on retained earnings	35
Pretax earnings allocated to dividends	100
20% tax on earnings allocated to dividends	20
Dividends distributed	80
Shareholder tax rate	35%
After tax dividend to shareholder	$[(1 - 0.35) \times 80] = 52$
Effective tax rate on dividend	$[20\% + (80 \times 0.35)] = 48\%$

The split-rate tax system would lead shareholders in a low tax bracket to prefer a higher payout, since distributed income is taxed less. Alternatively, those shareholders in higher brackets would prefer a lower payout, with more funds retained, since capital gains receive a preferential tax treatment. Canada and Japan have a tax credit system that would have a similar effect.

A third major taxation system is the *imputation* tax system, which imputes, or attributes, taxes at only one level of taxation. The United Kingdom, New Zealand, and Australia have a form of the imputation system. For countries using an imputation tax system, taxes on dividends are effectively levied only at the shareholder rate. Taxes are paid at the corporate level but they are *attributed* to the shareholder. Shareholders deduct from their tax bill their portion of taxes paid by the company. If the shareholder's tax bracket were lower than the company's, the shareholder would receive a tax credit equal to the difference between the two rates. If the shareholder's tax bracket is higher than the company's, the shareholder pays the difference between the two rates. The following table depicts the taxation of dividends based on the tax imputation system for both a low marginal-rate shareholder and a high marginal-rate shareholder.

TABLE 50-5   Taxation of Dividends Based on Tax Imputation System ($Australian)

	Marginal Shareholder Tax Rate	
	15%	**47%**
Pretax income	$100	$100
Taxes at 30% corporate tax rate	30	30
Net income after tax	70	70
Dividend assuming 100% payout	70	70
Shareholder taxes	15	47
Less tax credit for corporate payment	30	30
Tax due from shareholder	(15)	17
Effective tax rate on dividend	15/100 = 15%	47/100 = 47%

Here, as with the split-rate system, shareholders in lower tax brackets would prefer higher payouts, since they actually receive a tax credit for the difference between the corporate rate and their individual rate.

4.1.2 Shareholder Preference for Current Income versus Capital Gains

All other things being equal, one could expect that the lower the tax rate on dividends the higher the level of dividends. But other tax issues also impinge on this issue. As mentioned earlier, the trade-off between taxes on dividends and taxes on capital gains is an important part of the equation. Even if dividends were to be taxed at a lower rate than capital gains, it is not clear that shareholders would necessarily prefer higher dividends. After all, capital gains taxes don't have to be paid until the shares are sold, whereas taxes on dividends must be paid in the year received, even if reinvested. In addition, in some countries such as the United States, shares held at the time of death benefit from a *step-up* valuation to the death date. Finally, tax-exempt institutions such as pension funds and endowment funds are major shareholders in most industrial countries. Such institutions are typically exempt from both taxes on dividends and taxes on capital gains. Hence, all other things being equal, they are indifferent as to whether their return comes in the form of current dividends or capital gains.

4.2 Flotation Costs on New Issues vs. Retaining Earnings

Another factor affecting a company's decision to pay dividends is the flotation costs on new issues versus retained earnings. **Flotation cost** is the percentage cost of new common share issuance, and reflects the fees paid to investment bankers as well as other costs of share issuance. It is typically higher for smaller companies and smaller share issues. Because of flotation costs, the cost of new equity capital is always higher than the cost of retained earnings. Therefore, many companies will not pay a dividend while issuing new shares in order to fund projects with positive NPVs. Issuing shares to fund the payment of dividends would be unprofitable.

Example 50-5

A Company that Needs to Reinvest All Profits

Boar's Head Spirits Ltd., based in the United Kingdom, has estimated profits of £500 million. The company's financial analyst has calculated its cost of capital as 12 percent. The same analyst has evaluated modernization and expansion projects with a positive NPV that would require £800 million. The cost of positive NPV projects exceeds estimated profits by £300 million (£800 million − £500 million). Boar's Head does not want to increase its long-term debt in the next year. Hence, in this simplified example, the company would not pay dividends because free cash flow is not positive.

Because the company has unfunded positive NPV projects, it should consider issuing new shares incurring flotation costs of perhaps 5–7 percent of the new issue. The company would not, however, issue shares to fund the payment of dividends.

4.3 Restrictions on Dividend Payments

The ability of a company to even consider paying a dividend is often affected by restrictions, both formal and informal. In some countries there is a legal restriction, known as the **impairment of capital rule**, which states that dividends cannot exceed retained earnings. More typical are formal restrictions resulting from debt covenants, which can be anything that the company and the lender agree to. Here, certain minimum figures are set for such constraints as interest coverage, current ratio, and net worth, before any dividend payments may be considered.

Informal restrictions can also figure into a company's decision to pay dividends. Cash flow is an important one. Some companies will continue to pay a regularly scheduled dividend even when earnings are down and the payout ratio exceeds the company's target payout ratio. It is also not unusual for a company's dividend to exceed its earnings for a brief period. But most companies are loath to pay out dividends that exceed their cash flow from operations unless the company is in a liquidation mode.

Industry life cycle may also act as an implicit restriction on dividend payments. Many companies in the technology-related industries have negative net income, although positive EBITDA (earnings before interest, taxes, depreciation, and amortization). Even profitable biotechnology companies, or any company with an assumed high growth rate, might well be viewed negatively for instituting a dividend, because shareholders could interpret a dividend as a lack of investment opportunities for the company. Banks, on the other hand, typically have a dividend yield that exceeds that of the overall market. For example, in late 2004 the shares of Barclay's Bank (U.K.), Citigroup (U.S.), and UBS (Switzerland) yielded 4.3 percent, 3.4 percent, and 2.8 percent, respectively.

4.4 Clientele Effect

Another factor affecting a company's decision to pay dividends is the clientele effect. The **clientele effect** is the preference some investors have for shares that exhibit certain characteristics. For example, investors with low or no tax exposure are assumed to be attracted to companies with high or relatively high dividend yields. Retired investors typically have a preference for higher current income; they usually prefer to hold stocks with a higher dividend yield. On the other hand, other investor groups, such as younger workers with a long time horizon, might favor industries and companies that reinvest a high proportion of their earnings for long term capital growth and therefore prefer stocks with little or no dividends.

The tax status of the investor is an important component of this clientele effect. As discussed earlier, tax-exempt entities such as pension funds, university endowments, or charitable foundations would reasonably have a higher preference for current income (and, therefore, dividends) than would higher-taxed individuals who would rather defer tax payments through capital gains.

Institutional investors, including certain mutual funds, banks, and insurance companies, will only invest in companies that pay at least some dividend. Some even require (either officially or unofficially) a specific minimum dividend yield. As dividend yields fell during the bull market of the 1990s, this requirement was often altered to accept stocks with dividend yields in the top quartile (or half) of their stock universe. Trusts and foundations may be under a restriction that stipulates that only income (i.e. interest and dividends) may be distributed to beneficiaries.

Some individual investors use a self-control device of "only spending the dividends, not the principal" in order to preserve their capital.[5] Furthermore, in some jurisdictions, there are *legal lists* or *approved lists of equity investments* for institutions such as insurance companies and trusts for individuals. Such legal lists typically mandate that permissible investments consist of only companies that pay dividends. Often, such restrictive lists are intended to serve as a proxy discouraging high-risk stocks. All of this suggests that a clientele effect does exist and that a preference for dividends is one way in which the equity market can be segmented.

The question of whether different industries attract different investors can be partially addressed by looking at the dividend yield of major industry groups. Exhibit 50-2 shows the dividend yield for five of the S&P 500 industry groups: Utilities, Financial, Energy, Health Care, and Information Technology.

---

[5] See Hersh Shefrin and Meir Statman, "Explaining Investor Preference for Cash Dividends," *Journal of Financial Economics,* 1984.

EXHIBIT 50-2	Dividend Yield of Major Standard & Poor's Industry Groups September 2004 (in percent)

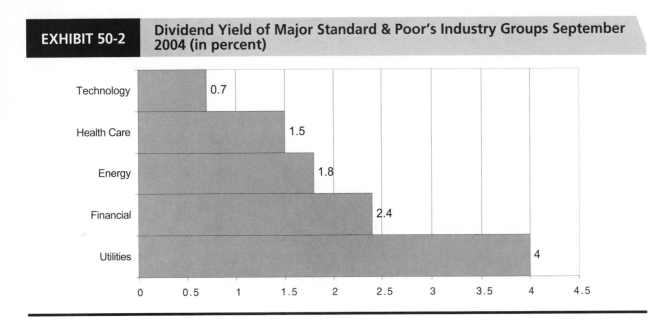

As is evident, there is a dramatic difference in dividend yields for these five industries, with Utilities having the highest yield and Technology having a miniscule one. The clientele effect would suggest that certain investors might be drawn to certain industry groups because of the dividend yield.

4.5 Signaling Effect: The Information Content of Dividends

A final factor affecting dividend payout policy is the information content of dividends. The implication is that a company's board of directors and/or management uses its dividend policy to signal investors about how the company is *really* doing. Empirical studies support the thesis that dividend initiation or increases are associated with future earnings growth, and a dividend omission or reduction are associated with future earnings problems.[6] Members of both the board and management are, after all, the ultimate insiders, and it is likely that no other group has better information about future earnings and cash flow. A dividend declaration can help resolve some of the information asymmetry between insiders and outsiders. Therefore, a company's decision to initiate, maintain, increase, or cut a dividend can often convey much more information than could words alone.

Good examples of this are companies that regularly increase their dividend. Many companies take pride in their record of consistently increasing dividends on a regular basis over a long period of time. It is an important tool to let shareholders know that the future is good and that the company has a desire to share its increasing fortunes with its shareholders. For example, ExxonMobil has consistently increased its dividend on a yearly basis over the past two decades. While the company's earnings, cash flow, payout, and yield have fluctuated over this

---

[6] For example, see Harry DeAngelo, Linda DeAngelo, and Douglas Skinner, "Reversal of Fortune: Dividend Signals and the Disappearance of Sustained Earnings Growth," *Journal of Financial Economics*, 1986.

time, dividends have continued to increase each year, signaling to the market that the company's long-term outlook is intact. Unlike other companies in its peer group whose dividends have more closely reflected current movements in the fortunes of the oil industry, for ExxonMobil to cut dividends, or even fail to increase the yearly dividend, would send a meaningful (and negative) signal to investors about the future of the company. Anecdotal evidence for a signaling effect is also found on the Standard & Poor's web site. As of September 2004, S&P found 58 companies in the S&P 500 Index that are "Dividend Aristocrats" in that they have increased their dividend for 25 consecutive years. These companies span various industries and include General Electric, Pfizer, Procter & Gamble, and Wal-Mart. Mergent has established a list of Canadian and European companies that are called Dividend Achievers. These companies include Novartis (Switzerland), Barclays (U.K.), Unilever (Netherlands), Imperial Oil (Canada), and Thompson (Canada).[7] Companies that consistently increase their dividends seem to share certain characteristics:

▶ Dominant or niche positions in their industry; in Michael Porter's terms they have a competitive advantage.

▶ Global operations.

▶ Relatively high returns on assets.

▶ Relatively low debt ratios (unlikely to be affected by debt covenants).

Dividend cuts or omissions present a powerful signaling component. For many companies under financial or operating stress, the dividend declaration date is viewed with more than usual interest. Will they cut the dividend? Will they omit the dividend altogether? In these instances, merely holding the dividend or not cutting it as much as expected is viewed as good news, although in retrospect there are plenty of instances where the dividend should have been cut or omitted and was not. Some companies hang in to the bitter end and only omit the dividend as they file for bankruptcy, sending what turned out to be a most erroneous signal to the market.

In some instances, though, management can attempt to send a positive signal by cutting the dividend (this, admittedly, is more difficult). In 1993, IBM, long the giant of mainframe computers and having maintained an enviable record of dividend increases over the years, announced a more than 50 percent cut in its dividend, explaining that their intention was to shift its business by strongly investing in non-mainframe technology and consulting services to improve future returns. While the message was met with varying reactions, it was, in retrospect, a positive signal, and those who paid attention were richly rewarded. Likewise, in 2003 Schering-Plough, a leading U.S. based pharmaceutical company, suffered a triple blow to its worldwide position including loss of patent on its leading drug, Claritin; a U.S. Food and Drug Administration (FDA) consent degree; and legal actions by government prosecutors related to sales and marketing. In April 2003 Fred Hassan was appointed Chairman and CEO. Mr. Hassan is generally credited with the turnaround in Pharmacia that was later merged in Pfizer. He announced a six to eight year plan to transform Schering-Plough that included a 68 percent cut in the quarterly dividend. As of late 2004, the jury is still out regarding Schering-Plough's prospective turnaround.

Another even more complicated example of the signaling content of dividends can be found in Microsoft's initial dividend declaration. As we saw from

[7] *Barron's*, November 1, 2004, p.37.

Exhibit 50-2, technology companies have among the lowest dividend yields. This makes sense. By their very nature (most would argue), technology companies are on the cutting edge; they have high R&D requirements, and those that are profitable have high returns on assets. All of this would suggest low (or no) dividend payments, because funds would much better be spent on investing in new product development that will maintain high returns. But in the mid 1990s, as Microsoft's phenomenal growth and dominance of its industry continued, net cash grew to tens of billions of dollars and many wondered if the company could effectively use its cash "hoard," and if it were time for Microsoft to pay a dividend.

In late 2003, Microsoft declared its first annual dividend of $0.06 per share, equaling about 7 percent of its yearly cash flow, less than two percent of its net cash position, and representing a yield of 0.3 percent. Then, in the summer of 2004, the company increased its annual dividend to $0.32 per share and announced a special year-end dividend of $3.00 a share. Clearly, the signaling effect was more important than the actual cash impact on either the company or its investors. The stock market viewed these declarations with mixed feelings. Some viewed that Microsoft was signaling an interest in broadening its investor focus and in sharing its wealth with shareholders. The clientele effect, discussed earlier, would suggest that Microsoft's dividend opened up a whole new group of potential shareholders, possibly increasing demand for the company's shares. On the other hand, others viewed the dividend declaration as an admission that it was becoming a mature company—that it could no longer reap the high returns from reinvesting. The future growth prospects for the stock, they would argue, had been diminished. In any event, few could argue that the 2003–2004 dividend declarations by Microsoft were not signals of some importance. It is interesting to speculate that taxes had some impact on Microsoft's dividend decision. Bill Gates and other Microsoft insiders were among those who had their tax rate on dividend income reduced from 39.6 percent in 2002 to 15 percent in 2003 and 2004.

4.5.1 Cross-Country Differences in Signaling Content

It should be noted that there is often a cultural or country-specific element to the signaling aspect of dividends. For example, where U.S. investors often infer significant signals in long-term expectations from even minute changes in a dividend, Japanese investors are much less likely to regard even large changes in dividend policy as a message from management about future prospects. U.S. companies are typically reluctant to reduce a regular dividend, because it almost always gives a signal that "all is not well." However, in some Asian markets, a dividend cut is not necessarily viewed as an unfavorable sign and therefore companies are freer to raise and lower their dividends depending on circumstances.

Furthermore, dividends are larger and considered more important in some markets than in others. When investing in the global marketplace, investors will find that the contribution of dividends to total return will vary considerably. As discussed earlier in this reading, most of the world's largest companies trade on the New York Stock Exchange either as American depository shares (ADS) or ordinary shares. For example, the five largest non-U.S. companies had the following dividend yields (in US$) in October 2004: BP (UK) 2.9 percent, DaimlerChrysler (Germany) 4.3 percent, Toyota (Japan) 1.5 percent, Royal Dutch (Holland/UK) 4.0 percent and Total (France) 2.7 percent. Canadian companies trade as ordinary shares. Representative Canadian dividend yields (in US$) were Bank of Nova Scotia 3.7 percent, Thomson 2.2 percent, and EnCana 0.8 percent.

An investor who wanted to gain some insight into the relative importance of dividends around the world might look at the gross dividend yield on the FTSE Global Equity Indexes.

TABLE 50-6	Gross Dividend Yield on Selected FTSE Index Funds (October 2004)
Regions	
FTSE Global Large Cap	2.1%
FTSE North America Large Cap	1.9%
FTSE Developed Europe Large Cap	2.8%
FTSE Asia Pacific Large Cap (ex-Japan)	2.9%
FTSE All Emerging Large Cap	2.7%
Specific Countries	
FTSE U.K. All Cap	3.1%
FTSE U.S.A. All Cap	1.7%
FTSE Japan (Large/Mid Cap)	0.9%

Source: Financial Times, 12 October 2004, p. 30.

4.6 Conclusion

There are several factors affecting a company's decision to pay dividends. We have examined some of them in this section, but it is not possible to argue that one is more dominant than another. Indeed, it is more likely that multiple factors affect dividend policy, with customs, laws, taxes, shareholder preferences, and management signaling interacting to affect a given company's actions.

DIVIDEND POLICIES

In the last section, we considered factors affecting a company's decision to pay dividends or not. In this section we look more closely at how the amount of the dividend is actually determined. **Dividend payout policy** is the strategy that companies follow in determining the amount and timing of dividend payments over time to shareholders. Our starting point is the residual dividend approach, one of the gold standards of corporate finance theory. Next we consider a dividend policy that results in a more stable dividend over time. The target payout ratio is then examined as an approach to dividend policy. We then discuss share repurchase as an alternative to the payment of dividends.

5.1 Residual Dividend Approach

The **residual dividend approach** is perhaps the most logical and intuitively appealing of all possible dividend policies, and can be defined as the payment of dividends resulting from earnings less funds necessary to finance the equity portion company's capital budget.

Recall that the NPV for any potential investment project is the net present value of all cash inflows minus the net present value of all cash outflows. When the NPV is positive, the investment should be undertaken, and when the NPV is negative, the project should be rejected. The company uses its weighted average cost of capital (WACC) as its discount rate. The company's optimal capital budget will include all positive NPV projects. The company then finances these projects with retained earnings. What is left over—the residual—is distributed to shareholders as a dividend. In essence, a company should reinvest earnings only when it can earn a higher rate of return on the shareholder's money than the shareholder could earn on his own by investing in equivalent-risk assets. If the company cannot earn such a return, the company should pay the earnings out in the form of dividends.

The following table depicts how the residual dividend approach might work. We look at the implied residual dividend given a company with earnings of $100 million, a target debt/equity ratio of 30/70, and three prospective capital spending plans of $50 million, $100 million, and $150 million.

TABLE 50-7   Residual Dividend Approach for a Target Debt/Equity Ratio of 30/70 (dollars in millions)

	$50 in Capital Spending	$100 in Capital Spending	$150 in Capital Spending
Earnings	$100	$100	$100
Target D/E	30/70	30/70	30/70
Capital spending	$50	$100	$150
Financed from new debt	0.3×50 $= \$15$	0.3×100 $= \$30$	0.3×150 $= \$45$
Financed from retained earnings	0.7×50 $= \$35$	0.7×100 $= \$70$	$(0.7 \times 150 > 100)$ $= \$100$
Financed from new equity	$0	$0	$5
Residual cash flow = residual dividend	$100 - \$35$ $= \$65$	$100 - \$70$ $= \$30$	$100 - \$100$ $\$0$
Implied payout ratio	$65/100 = 65\%$	$30/100 = 30\%$	$0/100 = 0\%$

It should be pointed out that under the residual dividend approach, the only retained earnings the company has available are from the current year's operations, since all previous years' earnings have been either spent on capital projects or paid out as dividends to shareholders. Also, it can be noted that in the final column of the above table, the $150 million in capital spending is greater than the total earnings of $100 million. Therefore, financing from new equity and debt would be required. If the target debt/equity ratio were maintained, new equity issues would incur flotation costs. The cost of capital would be higher, and fewer projects would have a positive NPV.

As can be seen from the above table, various capital spending plans result in dramatically different implied dividend payments. Payout ratios, too, range from a zero payment of dividends under the highest capital spending plan, to a 65 percent payout ratio under the lowest capital spending plan.

Example 50-6

Determining Dividends Using the Residual Dividend Approach

Acree Products uses the residual dividend approach in determining its dividend policy. Using the following information, calculate the expected dividend:

▶ Earnings: $1.6 million
▶ Debt: $20 million
▶ Capital budget: $1 million
▶ Optimal capital structure: 25/75 Debt/Equity

▶ **Solution:**

$$
\begin{aligned}
\text{Expected dividend} \quad &= \text{Earnings} - (\text{Capital budget} \times \text{Equity percent}) \\
&= 1.6 \text{ mil} - (1.0 \text{ mil} \times 0.75) \\
&= \$850{,}000
\end{aligned}
$$

The residual dividend approach definitely has advantages to the company. It is intuitively appealing to use funds generated to profitably maintain and grow the business, and only return what is left over—the residual—to the owners of the company. The residual dividend approach also allows the company to more freely determine attractive investments independent of dividend considerations.

A major disadvantage of the residual dividend approach is that it results in widely fluctuating dividends. Not only will earnings vary with the economic cycle and innumerable company-specific events, but also the optimal capital budget will fluctuate with interest rates, investment opportunities, and a plethora of other investment inputs. This uncertainty about future dividend levels implies a higher level of perceived risk by the investor, thereby increasing the investor's required rate of return (k) and lowering the expected value of the stock, as can be seen in the following familiar constant growth dividend discount model equation:

$$V = D_1 / (k - g)$$

where

V = the value of a share of common stock today
D_1 = the expected dividend per share for Year 1, assumed to be paid at the end of the year
k = the required rate of return on the stock
g = the expected growth rate of dividends

The implication is that if future annual dividends are uncertain, as they would be under the residual dividend approach, then the value of the share (V) might decline (all other things being equal) as k increases.

To take advantage of the benefits of the residual approach while reducing its negative implications, many companies will forecast their optimal capital budget for the next five or ten years. The residual from that process will be allocated to dividends and paid out on a steadier, more even basis over the same period. A relatively new approach over the last twenty years is for companies to use this

longer-term residual approach to allocate all funds designated for shareholders—including both cash dividends and share repurchases—paying out a more stable cash dividend to shareholders and allocating a more flexible amount to share repurchases.

5.2 Stable Dividend Policy

In many instances, both management and shareholders prefer more stability in their stream of dividends than strict adherence to the residual dividend approach would allow. Companies that employ a stable dividend approach are likely to look more toward a forecast of their long-run sustainable earnings in determining their dividend policy. In addition, over the last three decades when inflation has become a more important consideration, dividend stability has come to mean stability *in the rate of increase* in dividends.

Many companies pride themselves on a long record of gradually and consistently rising dividends. For example, following is the earnings and dividend record of La-Z-Boy Inc. since 1993.

TABLE 50-8	Earnings and Dividends of La-Z-Boy Inc. 1993–2004			
	Earnings Per share	**Change in Earnings**	**Dividends Per share**	**Change in Dividends**
1993	$0.63	26%	$0.21	5%
1994	$0.67	6%	$0.23	10%
1995	$0.71	6%	$0.25	9%
1996	$0.83	17%	$0.26	4%
1997	$0.91	10%	$0.28	8%
1998	$1.24	36%	$0.30	7%
1999	$1.60	29%	$0.32	7%
2000	$1.19	(26%)	$0.35	9%
2001	$1.23	3%	$0.36	3%
2002	$1.67	36%	$0.39	8%
2003	$1.09	(35%)	$0.40	3%
2004e	$0.99	(9%)	$0.44	10%

Source: Value Line

As one can see from the above example, dividends over this period have increased at a fairly consistent, real rate, even while earnings have experienced considerable variability.

5.3 Target Payout Ratio

Many companies have a target payout ratio as the basis for their dividend policy. A **payout ratio** is the percentage of total earnings paid out in dividends in any given year (in per-share terms, DPS/EPS). A **target payout ratio** is a strategic corporate goal representing the long-term proportion of earnings that the company intends to distribute to shareholders as dividends.

Companies may, on occasion, state publicly their target payout ratio. What is more likely is that the company will use its dividend policy to move toward a dividend payout target.

In a classic study on this subject in the mid 1950s, John Lintner[8] drew three basic conclusions: 1) Companies have a target payout ratio, based on long-run, sustainable earnings; 2) they prefer to move toward this goal in smaller, incremental steps; and 3) cutting or eliminating a dividend should only be done in extreme circumstances or as a last resort.

While the resulting Lintner regression model has many variables, a simplified version can be used to show how a company in certain circumstances could incrementally move toward its target payout ratio.[9] In instances when the payout ratio is below the target payout ratio and earnings are expected to increase, the product of the increase in earnings, the target payout ratio, and the adjustment factor (1 divided by the number of years over which the adjustment in dividends should take place) will result in an estimated increase in the dividend. For example, given a current dividend of $0.40, a target payout ratio of 50 percent, an adjustment factor of 0.2 (i.e. the adjustment is to occur over five years), and an earnings increase from $1.00 to $1.50, the expected increase in dividends would be

= Increase in earnings × Target payout ratio × Adjustment factor
= $0.50 × 0.5 × 0.2
= $0.05 Increase in dividends

Therefore, even though earnings increased 50 percent from $1.00 to $1.50, the dividend would only incrementally increase by about 13 percent from $0.40 to $0.45.

Using this example, it can be noted that if in the following year earnings fell from $1.50 to $1.00, the dividend might well be increased by up to $0.05 per share, as the implied new dividend of $0.50 would still be moving the company toward its target payout ratio of 50 percent. Even if earnings were to fall further or even experience a loss, the company would be reluctant to cut or eliminate the dividend (unless its estimate of sustainable earnings or target payout ratio were lowered) opting, rather, to maintain the current dividend until future earnings increases justified an increase in the dividend.

Example 50-7

Determining Dividend Using a Target Payout Adjustment Approach

Last year Luna Inc. had earnings of $2.00 per share and paid a regular dividend of $0.40. For the current year, the company anticipates earnings of $2.80. It has a 30 percent target payout ratio and uses a 5-year period to adjust the dividend. Compute the expected dividend for the current year.

---

[8] John Lintner, "Distribution of Incomes of Corporations Among Dividends, Retained Earnings, and Taxes," *American Economic Review*, 1956.

[9] Ronald Lease et al., *Dividend Policy Its Impact on Firm Value*, Boston: Harvard Business School Press, 2000, p. 124.

▶ **Solution**

$$\text{Expected dividend} = \text{Last dividend} + (\text{Expected increase in earnings} \\ \times \text{Target payout ratio} \times \text{Adjustment factor})$$
$$= \$0.40 + [(\$2.80 - \$2.00) \times 0.3 \times (1/5)]$$
$$= \$0.40 + (\$0.80 \times 0.3 \times 0.2)$$
$$= \$0.45$$

Thus, while earnings are expected to increase by 40 percent, the increase in the dividend would be 12.5 percent.

5.4 Share Repurchase

In earlier parts of this reading we discussed the mechanics of share repurchase and showed that share repurchases were equivalent to cash dividends of equal amount in their effect on shareholders' wealth, all other things being equal. For some companies, share repurchase is intended to prevent the earnings per share dilution that would result from the exercise of employee stock options. Whether stated or not, many companies endeavor to buy back at least as many shares as were issued in the exercise of stock options—even though the options are exercised at lower prices than the repurchase price. Otherwise, share repurchase can be considered part of a company's dividend policy. In this section we consider the advantages and disadvantages of substituting a share repurchase program for the payment of a regular or extra cash dividend.

The main advantage of share repurchase over cash dividend occurs in those jurisdictions that tax shareholder dividends at higher rates than shareholder capital gains. This argument is now much less powerful in the United States as its tax code now taxes shareholder dividends and capital gains at the same rate. Furthermore, the U.S. tax code prohibits "routine" repurchase, as it could be tax avoidance. Other countries tax share repurchases at the same rate as dividends. Some jurisdictions have actually prohibited company share repurchase. An analyst should evaluate a company's share repurchase policy based on the tax circumstances of the company's home country as well as the investor's home country.

In principle, share repurchase sends the same signal to shareholders as does a cash dividend: Your company does not have sufficient reinvestment opportunities for the amount of cash flow generated. Shareholders have to consider why a company is shrinking its equity base. An alternative view is that management thinks its company's shares are undervalued.

5.4.1 Reasons for Share Repurchase

A company may decide to repurchase its shares for a variety of reasons. Perhaps the best reason is that the company views its own shares as an excellent investment. While the company's stock market judgment can be just as good or bad as any other market participant, there is no question that the company has more information about itself than does any other entity, and is therefore the ultimate insider. For many years, the oil industry has been a large purchaser of its own shares, as investment returns in their current operations (through a share purchase) were an attractive alternative to drilling for new sources of oil. In one five-year period, ExxonMobil spent more than $30 billion in repurchasing its own shares while it has also paid out $30 billion in cash dividends.

Another closely related reason for announcing a share repurchase is to signal to the investment community that the outlook for the company is good even if the share price is declining. Management has confidence in the company's future and believes that its stock is undervalued. An unexpected announcement of a meaningful buyback can often have the same positive impact on share price as would a better-than-expected earnings report or other similarly encouraging event. In the days following the global stock market crash of October 1987, a number of prominent companies announced huge buybacks in an effort to halt the slide in the price of their shares and show confidence in the future. It may have been an important aspect in the relatively quick stock market rebound. As indicated earlier, some investment analysts take issue with the notion that share repurchase sends positive signals.

A third reason for buying back shares is to alter the company's capital structure by decreasing the equity component. Borrowing money to buy back shares intensifies this shift.

Example 50-8

Share Repurchase to Increase Financial Leverage

Canadian Holdings Inc. (CHI) is evaluating the impact of a buyback of $C7 million or 10 percent of the market value of its common stock. The estimated impact on CHI's capital structure depends on whether it has the cash on hand to make the buyback or if it has to borrow to finance the purchase:

TABLE 50-9 Estimated Impact on Capital Structure (in millions of $C)

| | Before Buyback | | After Buy-back | | | |
| | | | All Cash | | All Debt | |
	$C	%	$C	%	$C	%
Debt	$ 30	30%	$30	32%	$ 37	37%
Equity (at market)	$ 70	70%	$63	68%	$ 63	63%
Total Cap	$100	100%	$93	100%	$100	100%

Canadian Holdings' beginning debt/equity ratio was 30/70. If Canadian Holdings uses borrowed funds to repurchase equity, the debt/equity ratio at market will increase to 37/63, which is significantly more than if it used excess cash (32/68).

Finally, a company could use both a regular cash dividend and a periodic share repurchase policy as a supplement to cash dividends. This policy is particularly apt in years where there are large and extraordinary increases in cash flow that are not expected to continue in future years. In this way, share repurchase becomes a substitute for an extra cash dividend. Such a policy could smooth out dividends similar to the target payout policy. Grullon and Michaely found that U.S. companies used repurchases as a substitute for cash dividends and that companies often initiate payouts through repurchases rather than cash dividends.[10] Share buybacks are more flexible than cash dividends, as repurchases are not a long-term commitment.

While all of the preceding can be the stated or unstated reasons for share repurchases, in general, buybacks are larger when the economy is strong and companies have more cash. During recessions, when company coffers are not as full, buybacks typically fall. This is perhaps the biggest disadvantage of share repurchases: They occur in the greatest number when times are good, and concurrently, when share prices are relatively high. Were shareholders' interests best served in 2000–2001 when high technology companies bought back their shares when the NASDAQ was at 5000? To carry this one step further, some companies may actually endanger their future viability by embarking on a highly leveraged repurchase endeavor. This is most likely for companies that have been threatened with large holdings by "aggressive" shareholders. More than one company has been eased into bankruptcy by increasing its debt burden to repurchase the shares of a potential hostile takeover suitor.

Example 50-9, in which a company initiates a cash dividend, integrates a number of themes related to cash dividends, stock dividends, and share repurchases.

Example 50-9

Scottsville Instruments' Dividend Policy Decision

Scottsville Instruments, Inc., (SCII) is a U.S.-based emerging leader in providing medical testing equipment to the pharmaceutical and biotechnology industries. SCII's primary markets are growing and the company is spending $100 million a year on research and development to enhance its competitive position. SCII is highly profitable and has substantial positive free cash flow after funding positive NPV projects. During the past three years, SCII has made significant share repurchases. Subsequent to the reduction in the tax rate on cash dividends to 15 percent in the United States, SCII management has begun to consider the initiation of an annual dividend of $0.40 per share. Based on estimated earnings per share of $3.20, this dividend would represent a payout ratio (DPS/EPS) of 0.125 or 12.5 percent. The proposal that will be brought before the Board is the following:

> "Proposed: Scottsville Instruments, Inc. will institute a $0.40 per share annual dividend to be paid quarterly beginning in the next fiscal year."

The company's Board of Directors will formally consider the dividend proposal at its next meeting in one month's time. Although some directors favor the dividend initiation proposal, other directors, led by William Marshall, are skeptical of it. Marshall has stated:

> "The initiation of a cash dividend will suggest to investors that SCII is no longer a growth company."

---

[10] Gustavo Grullon and Roni Michaely, "Dividends, Share Repurchases, and the Substitution Hypothesis," *Journal of Finance*, 2002.

As a counterproposal, Marshall has offered his support for the initiation of an annual 2 percent stock dividend. Elise Tashman, a director who is neutral to both the cash and stock dividend ideas, has told Marshall the following:

"The initiation of a cash dividend will have no effect on the value of the firm to shareholders. Likewise, a 2 percent stock dividend should also be value neutral to our shareholders."

Table 50-10 presents selected *pro forma* financials of SCII, if the directors approve the initiation of a cash dividend.

**TABLE 50-10 Scottsville Instruments, Inc.
Pro Forma Financial Data Assuming Cash Dividend
(in millions, except for ratios and percentages)**

Income Statement		Statement of Cash Flows	
Sales	$1,200	Cash flow from operations	$135
Earnings before Taxes	140	Cash flow from investing activities:	(84)
Taxes	35	Cash flow from financing activities:	
Net income	105	Debt repayment	(4)
		Share repurchase	(32)
		Proposed dividend	(15)
		Estimated change in cash	0

Ratios		Five Year Forecasts	
Current ratio	2.1	Sales growth	8% annually
Debt/Equity (at market)	0.27	Earnings growth	11% annually
Interest Coverage	10.8x	Projected cost of capital	10%
ROA	10.0%		
ROE	19.3%		
P/E	20x		
E/P	5.0%		

Using the proceeding information, address the following.

1. Critique Marshall's statement.
2. Justify Tashman's statement concerning stock dividends.
3. Identify and explain the dividend policy approach that the proposed $0.40 a share cash dividend reflects.

▶ **Solution to 1.** The following points argue against the thesis of Marshall's statement:

▶ As discussed in the text, dividend initiations and increases are on average associated with higher future earnings growth.

▶ Forecasted sales and earnings growth are relatively high.

▶ SCII still has considerable positive NPV projects available to it, as shown by the cash flow from investing activities of negative $84 million. This fact is consistent with a company with substantial current growth opportunities.

▶ For several years SCII has been making share repurchases, so investors are already cognizant that management is distributing cash to shareholders. The initiation of a dividend as a continuation of that policy is less likely to be interpreted as an information signaling event.

▶ **Solution to 2.** A stock dividend has no effect on shareholder wealth. A shareholder owns the same percentage of the company and its earnings as it did before the stock dividend. All other things being equal, the price of a stock will decline to reflect the stock dividend, but the decline will be exactly offset by the greater number of shares owned.

▶ **Solution to 3.** As shown in the Statement of Cash Flows, the $0.40 annual dividend reflects a total amount of $15 million, fully using SCII's free cash flow after acceptance of positive NPV projects, as shown in the Statement of Cash Flows. This reflects a residual dividend policy approach.

5.5 Are Dividend Policies Changing?

In the late 1990s, some financial analysts claimed that the historical role of dividends was "disappearing." This was a period characterized by its enthusiasts as the "New Era Economy," and by its critics as "Irrational Exuberance." It was highlighted in most of the developed world by several years of rising share prices, particularly in the more speculative industries. Companies that were barely profitable (and sometimes unprofitable) obtained larger market capitalizations than very profitable companies in unglamorous industries. At its peak, almost 40 percent of the S&P Index's market value was composed of companies in the technology and telecommunications sectors. This phenomenon was not limited to the United States, as Nortel Networks had the highest market capitalization in Canada in 2000 and companies such as Nokia in Finland and SAP in Germany were market leaders.

Proponents of New Era investing argued that dividends were a trivial, if not an unwelcome component of total return for investors more interested in capital gains. Investor preference for or aversion to dividends is a mercurial argument. The more interesting issue is whether corporations were changing their dividend policies. Fama and French[11] investigated the case for disappearing dividends. They found a large decline in the number of U.S. based industrial companies that paid dividends from 1978 to 1998. But the aggregate payout ratio in the 1990s was about 40 percent; within the 40–60 percent range typical of the 1960–1998 period. Fama and French argued that the decline in dividends was related to the large number of relatively unprofitable companies that were assuming prominence in the stock market. The exhibit below shows the relatively stable dividend payout range for all U.S. corporations from 1979–2003. In fact, the graph would seem to argue that companies follow the target payout approach.

---

[11] Eugene Fama and Kenneth French, "Disappearing Dividends: Changing firm Characteristics or Lower Propensity to Pay?" *Journal of Financial Economics*, 2001.

EXHIBIT 50-3

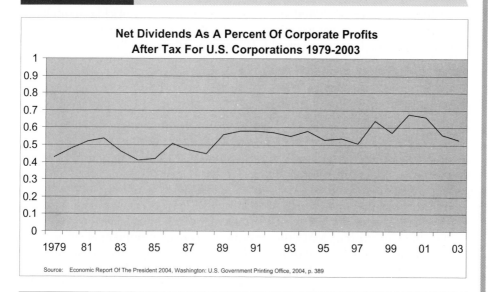

Net Dividends As A Percent Of Corporate Profits After Tax For U.S. Corporations 1979-2003

Source: Economic Report Of The President 2004, Washington: U.S. Government Printing Office, 2004, p. 389

DeAngelo, DeAngelo, and Skinner[12] enhanced Fama and French's argument by showing that even though fewer corporations were paying dividends, the largest 100 companies in the United States increased their inflation-adjusted dividends by 23 percent from 1978 to 2000. What appears to be happening is that there are two tiers of companies. The first tier is composed of approximately 100 large, extremely profitable companies that have a fairly stable payout ratio of around 42 percent. The second tier is composed of two types of non-dividend payers: financially troubled marginally profitable or money losing companies, and/or companies related to technology where companies typically use share repurchase as a substitute for dividends.

In the period following the severe developed-country stock market decline in the early 2000s, investors began to question reported earnings, balance sheets, and cash flows as corporate scandals revealed management shenanigans to over inflate revenues, use accruals to understate expenses, and hide liabilities off-balance sheet. An argument can be made that dividends are more important than ever since it is the one number that a shareholder can trust. Earnings per share and even cash flow per share can be manipulated by management, but dividend checks can be cashed.

THE DIVIDEND CONTROVERSY: DO DIVIDENDS MATTER?

6

For the last forty years, leading financial theorists have argued over whether dividends and dividend policy matter to a company's shareholders. The first school of thought is that dividends are irrelevant. The second school says that dividends do matter because investors prefer them and higher dividend payouts are likely to increase the value of a company's shares. The third school says that dividends do matter, but a company's high dividend payout ratio will lead to a lower share price because dividend income is often taxed at a higher rate than capital gains.

---

[12] Harry DeAngelo, Linda DeAngelo, and Douglas Skinner, "Are Dividends Disappearing? Dividend Concentration and the Consolidation of Earnings," *Journal of Financial Economics*, 2004.

6.1 Dividends Are Irrelevant

In a 1961 paper, Miller and Modigliani (MM) argued that in a world without taxes and transaction costs, a company's dividend policy would have no impact on its cost of capital or shareholder wealth.[13] Their argument begins by assuming a company has a given capital budget (e.g., it accepts all projects with a positive NPV), and that its current capital structure and debt ratio are optimal. Hence, if the company decided to pay out all its earnings in dividends, it would have to issue new shares of common stock to finance its capital budget. The value of the newly issued shares would exactly offset the value of the dividend. So if the company paid out a dividend that represented a 5 percent dividend yield (dividend per share/price per share), its share price would drop 5 percent to represent the dilution resulting from the new shares. If a common stock in Australia were priced at A$20 before an A$1 dividend, the implied new price would be A$19. The shareholder has assets worth A$20 if the dividend were not paid, and assets worth A$20 if the stock drops to A$19 and a A$1 dividend is paid.

Further embellishing MM's theory is the concept of a "homemade dividend." If a shareholder really wanted or needed income, he or she could construct their own dividend policy by selling sufficient shares to create their own dividend. Using the Australian example above, assume the company did not pay the A$1 dividend and the stock remained at A$20. A holder of 1000 shares who desired A$1000 in income could sell 50 shares at A$20 reducing his/her holdings to 1950 shares.

In the real world, there are market imperfections that create some problems for MM's dividend irrelevance propositions. First, there are transaction costs because a company issuing new shares would incur flotation costs (typically 4 percent to 10 percent of the capital raised, depending on the size of the company and the size of the issue). Second, a shareholder selling shares to create a homemade dividend would incur transaction costs and, in some countries, capital gains taxes (of course, he would also incur taxes on cash dividends in most countries). Furthermore, selling shares on a periodic basis to create a stream of dividends over time can be problematic when equities are volatile. Some shareholders will be reluctant to create a dividend when share price is low because they would have to sell off more shares.

6.2 Dividends Matter: Investors Prefer Dividends

Traditionalists such as Myron Gordon,[14] John Lintner,[15] and Benjamin Graham argued that investors prefer a dollar of dividends to a dollar of reinvested earnings. Graham's viewpoint was that ". . . the typical dollar of reinvestment has less economic value to the shareholder than a dollar paid in dividends."[16] Gordon, Lintner, and Graham's argument is similar to the "bird in the hand" analogy. Because a dollar of dividends is more certain than a dollar of capital gains, a company that pays dividends will have a lower cost of equity capital. As indicated in the section on the residual dividend approach, in the constant growth dividend discount, investors will often use a lower discount rate for a company that pays dividends than a company that does not pay dividends.

---

[13] Merton H. Miller and Franco Modigliani, "Dividend Policy, Growth, and the Valuation of Shares," *Journal of Business,* October 1961.

[14] Myron Gordon, "Optimal Investment and Financing Policy," *Journal of Finance*, May 1963.

[15] John Lintner, "Dividends, Earnings, Leverage, Stock Prices and the Supply of Capital to Corporations," *Review of Economics and Statistics,* August 1962.

[16] Benjamin Graham, David Dodd, et al. *Security Analysis,* 4th edition, New York: McGraw-Hill, 1962, p. 486.

Example 50-10

Dividends and P/Es

Splashco Inc. is an international oil service company headquartered in Calgary, Alberta, Canada. It has a good record of earnings growth over the last 20 years, albeit subject to the ups and downs of oil and gas production. It has never paid dividends but has used its considerable cash flow to repurchase shares. Institutional investors in both Canada and the United States have indicated that they think Splashco would sell at a price/earnings multiple more similar to its competitors if it instituted regular dividend payments. John Petrowitz, CFA of Splashco's Treasurer's office has been asked to present the case for a dividend to the company's Board of Directors. He starts his analysis with the fact that Splashco typically sells at a P/E of 12–15x current earnings per share as compared to 17–20x for its competitors. He decides to use the Gordon constant growth discounted dividend model to make his case.[17]

$$P = D_1/(k-g)$$

where

P = share price (at fair value)
D_1 = the expected dividend for Year 1
k = the required rate of return on the stock
g = the expected growth rate of dividends

Dividing both sides of the equation by E_1 where E_1 = next year's estimated earnings per share, the result is

$$P/E_1 = (D_1/E_1)/(k-g)$$

Constant growth is estimated at 8 percent. The implied required rate of return for Splashco has been 12 percent, but Petrowitz thinks the initiation of a dividend would lower the required rate of return to 11 percent, close to the average of its competitors. If Splashco had a target payout ratio of 50 percent and next year's earnings were C$2.00, the P/E_1 would be

$$
\begin{aligned}
P/E_1 &= (1.00/2.00)/(0.11 - 0.08) \\
&= 0.50/0.03 \\
&= 16.7x
\end{aligned}
$$

Petrowitz concludes that if Splashco initiated a C$1.00 dividend, it might alleviate some investor concern about what the company would do with its earnings and its P/E might increase from 12–15x to 16–17x.

---

[17] Frank Reilly and Keith Brown, *Investment Analysis and Portfolio Management*, 7th edition, Mason, OH: 2003, pp. 388–391.

Real world market imperfections also bolster the "higher payouts lead to higher share prices" argument. There appear to be specific clienteles who desire to live off their wealth, but selling off shares periodically to produce homemade dividends is cumbersome and a taxable event. In some jurisdictions, trusts and institutions are precluded from spending principal. Miller and Modigliani would rebut this argument by saying that different dividend policies will attract different clienteles and assuming both types of clients are active in the market place, the value of the company will be unaffected by dividend policy.

6.3 Dividends Matter: Investors Are Tax Averse to Dividends

In the United States and several other countries, dividend income has traditionally been taxed at higher rates than capital gains. In the 1970s, tax rates on dividend income in the United States were as high as 70 percent while the long-term capital gains rate was 35 percent. Even as recently as 2002, U.S. tax rates were as high as 39.1 percent on dividends and 20 percent on long-term capital gains. A good argument could be that in a high dividend tax country, investors would prefer companies that pay low dividends and reinvest earnings in growth opportunities. Presumably, any growth in earnings would translate into a higher P/E. If a company lacked growth opportunities sufficient to consume its annual retained earnings, it should repurchase shares. Taken to its extreme, this school of thought would advocate a *zero* payout ratio. Here again some real world market imperfections muddy the waters, as tax law often precludes companies from the accumulation of excess earnings and restricts share repurchase if it appears to be an ongoing event such as in lieu of payment of dividends.

As already discussed, effective in 2003 the playing field between dividends and long-term capital gains in the United States was leveled, with both dividends and long-term capital gains being taxed at 15 percent. This neutralized tax environment should provide financial researchers with a fertile laboratory to clarify some of the dividend controversy.

7   VALUATION IMPLICATIONS OF DIVIDENDS

In a world without market imperfections, Miller and Modigliani describe a market where both corporations and shareholders would be unconcerned with dividend policies. In an MM world there are no valuation implications of dividends. Shareholder value is created by investing in profitable projects, not by manipulating the debt/equity ratio on the balance sheet or by financing dividend payments with new equity issues. But looking at the real world, this reading has established the existence of market imperfections. In addition, some investors are led, by logic or custom, to prefer dividends. When valuing equities in various countries, investors should factor both market imperfections and market preferences into the valuation process.[18]

First and foremost on the list of market imperfections is taxation, and in particular any differential in the way dividends are taxed as compared to capital gains. Almost all countries tax corporate profits and some tax them twice when profits

---

[18] For practical application of how analysts use dividends and dividend policy in equity valuation, see John Stowe, Thomas Robinson, Jerald Pinto and Dennis McLeavey, *Analysis of Equity Investments: Valuation*, Charlottesville, VA: AIMR, 2002.

are paid out in dividends. If a government taxes dividends at high rates, it encourages low payouts. At the limit, a 100 percent tax on dividends would lead to a zero payout ratio. The United States reduced the highest tax rate on dividends from 39.1 percent to 15 percent and equalized the tax rate on dividends and long term capital gains. Researchers are already finding evidence that more companies have initiated dividend payments, and existing dividend payers have increased dividends more than would be associated with a typical period of profit recovery.[19]

In some countries, there are restrictions on the payment of dividends and de facto requirements to pay dividends in order to obtain admission to institutional legal lists or screens. Some investors become part of a clientele for dividend paying shares, while others have no preference for dividends.

We discussed the information content of dividends (signaling effect). Boards of directors and management send important information about the future prospects of their company by increasing and decreasing the dividend. In a world where the quality of accounting information is suspect, investors would do well to heed management's signals.

Finally, ownership structure and ensuing agency problems provide a possible explanation of country differences in dividend policy.[20] Dividends assume a larger role in the valuation process in certain jurisdictions. Dividend payments are higher in Canada, Great Britain, the United States, and some parts of Europe. They are lower in Japan and in developing countries. There may be more than tradition to explain these differences. For example, ownership of public corporations in the United States, Canada, and Great Britain tends to be diffuse rather than concentrated; corporations finance operations through capital markets. Companies in Asia and developing markets often have large family shareholder control and finance operations using banks and insurance companies rather than through capital markets. There is a natural conflict of interest between owners and management in countries that have dispersed ownership. This agency cost can be alleviated by the payment of dividends. Payment of dividends restricts management's ability to reinvest earnings in negative NPV projects just to build empires. Dividends thus discipline management to be more careful with the shareholders' money. In countries where founding families still control large blocks of shares and there are close links between financial institutions and industrial corporations, there is less need of discipline because the "insiders" are less likely to act imprudently with their own money.

So what can we conclude about the link between dividends and valuation? Unfortunately, the evidence is contradictory as shown by a myriad of studies over the years. It is difficult to show an exact relationship between dividends and value because there are so many variables affecting value. In the paragraphs above, we have presented factors that would seem to explain why some companies put emphasis on dividends and others do not. Financial theory proclaims that reinvestment opportunities should be the dominant factor. Indeed, no matter where they are located in the world, smaller, fast-growing companies pay out little or none of their earnings. Regardless of jurisdiction, more mature companies with fewer reinvestment opportunities tend to pay dividends. For these mature companies, taxes, laws, tradition, signaling, ownership structure, and attempts to reconcile agency conflicts all seem to play a role in determining the dividend payout ratio. At a minimum, in looking at a company, an analyst should evaluate whether a given company's dividend policy matches its reinvestment opportunities, clientele preferences, and legal/financial environment.

---

[19] Raj Chetty and Emmanuel Saez, "Do Dividends Respond to Taxes? Preliminary Evidence from the 2003 Dividend Tax Cut" NBER Working Paper 10572, June 2004.

[20] William Megginson, *Corporate Finance Theory*, Reading, MA: Addison-Wesley, 1997, pp. 374–378.

ENDS

SUMMARY

The dividend policy of a company affects the form in which shareholders receive the return on their investment and is a prominent decision of a company's board of directors. This reading has made the following points:

▶ Dividends can take the form of regular or special cash payments, stock dividends, or stock splits. Only cash dividends are payments to shareholders. Stock dividends and splits merely carve equity into smaller pieces.

▶ A share repurchase is equivalent to the payment of a cash dividend of equal amount in its effect on shareholders' wealth, all other things being equal.

▶ If a company has to fund a share repurchase with debt and its after-tax cost of debt is greater than the earning yield, earnings per share will decline. If the buyback market price is greater than the book value, the book value will decline.

▶ Share repurchases can be accomplished in the open market, through a tender offer to all shareholders, or by a direct negotiation with a major shareholder. The latter is not likely to positively affect share price.

▶ The key dates for a cash dividend are the declaration date, the ex-date, the shareholder-of-record date, and the payment date. Share price will reflect the dividend as of record date and, all else being equal, share price will be reduced by the amount of the dividend on the ex-date.

▶ Under double taxation systems, dividends are taxed at both the corporate and shareholder level. Under split rate taxation systems, corporate profits are taxed at different rates depending on whether the profits are retained or paid out in dividends. Under tax imputation systems, a shareholder receives a credit on dividends for the tax paid on corporate profits.

▶ Companies with debt outstanding often are restricted in the amount of dividends they can pay because of debt covenants, and formal and informal traditions in industries and countries. Some institutions require that a company pay a dividend in order to be on their "approved" list. If a company funds capital expenditures by borrowing while paying earnings out in dividends, it will incur flotation costs on new issues.

▶ The clientele effect assumes that different classes of investors have differing preferences for dividend income. Those who prefer dividends will tend to invest in higher yielding shares.

▶ The signaling effect assumes that declaration of dividends provide information to current and prospective shareholders as to the prospects of the company. Initiating a dividend or increasing a dividend sends a positive signal, while cutting a dividend or omitting a dividend sends a negative signal.

▶ Using a residual dividend approach, a company first compares its capital expenditure requirements to its net income and whatever is left is paid out to shareholders in the form of cash dividends. An advantage of the residual approach is that all positive NPV opportunities have the first priority.

▶ In a strict residual approach, the amount of the annual dividend is equal to annual earnings minus the capital budget times the percent of the capital budget to be financed through retained earnings.

▶ Using a stable dividend approach, a company tries to align its dividend growth rate to the company's long-term earnings growth rate. Dividends may increase even in years when earnings decline, and dividends will increase at a lower rate than earnings in boom years. A longer-term residual approach is a combination of residual and stable policies, where the company maintains the dividend at some level and increases the dividend periodically. With a target approach, the company has a goal of maintaining the dividend payout within a range; the dividend will increase with the company's long-term sustainable growth rate, but the increase will be in incremental steps.

▶ In the target payout adjustment approach, the expected dividend is equal to last year's dividend per share, plus [(this year's expected increase in earnings per share) × (the target payout ratio) × (an annual adjustment factor)].

▶ Companies can repurchase shares in lieu of increasing cash dividends. This policy is often justified in jurisdictions where dividends are taxed at higher rates than capital gains. Companies can also pay regular cash dividends supplemented by share repurchases. In years of extraordinary increases in earnings, share repurchase becomes a substitute for increasing dividends, smoothing out potentially volatile payout ratios.

▶ Share repurchases can signal that company officials think their shares are undervalued. On the other hand, share repurchases could send a negative signal that the company has few positive NPV opportunities. Share repurchases can also lower debt ratings.

▶ Considering aggregate corporate dividend payout ratios, dividend policy has remained within historical levels in recent years. A large number of companies with little or no earnings and/or questionable financials make it appear that dividends are "disappearing."

▶ There are three general theories on investor preference for dividends. The first, MM, argues that in a no-tax, no-market world, dividends are irrelevant. The "bird-in-the-hand" theory contends that investors value a dollar of dividends today more than uncertain capital gains in the future. The third theory argues that investors are tax averse to cash dividends and would prefer companies buy back shares, especially when the tax rate on dividends is greater than the tax rate on capital gains.

▶ Miller and Modigliani demonstrate that shareholders who want dividends could create their own homemade dividends by periodically selling off part of their holdings.

▶ According to those who argue that dividends do matter, a company could increase its price/earnings ratio by initiating a cash dividend. The initiation of a dividend results in a higher P/E by reducing the spread between the company's required rate of return and its expected growth rate using a constant growth dividend discount model.

PROBLEMS FOR READING 50

1. Would a cash dividend, compared to a stock dividend, most likely result in a higher

	Debt/equity ratio?	Current ratio?
A.	No	No
B.	No	Yes
C.	Yes	No
D.	Yes	Yes

2. In a recent presentation, Doug Pearce made two statements about dividends:

▶ "A stock dividend should increase share price, all other things being equal."

▶ "One practical concern with a stock split is that it will reduce the firm's price-to-earnings ratio."

Are Pearce's comments about the effects of the stock dividend and stock split correct or incorrect?

	Stock Dividend	Stock Split
A.	Correct	Correct
B.	Correct	Incorrect
C.	Incorrect	Correct
D.	Incorrect	Incorrect

3. Devon Ltd. common shares sell at $40 a share and its estimated price/earnings ratio (P/E) is 32x. If Devon borrows funds to repurchase shares at its cost of capital of 5 percent, its EPS will

A. increase.

B. decrease.

C. remain the same.

D. increase initially, but decline in future years.

4. The following calendar dates in Column 1 are potentially significant dates in a typical dividend chronology. Column 2 lists descriptions of these potentially significant dates (in random order).

Column 1	Column 2
Friday, 10 June	A. Holder-of-record date
Thursday, 23 June	B. Declaration date
Friday, 24 June	C. Payment date
Sunday, 26 June	D. Not a significant date
Tuesday, 28 June	E. Ex-date
Sunday, 10 July	F. Last day shares trade cum dividend

Match the significance of these typical dividend chronology dates by placing the correct letter of the description by the appropriate date. Use the template for your answer.

Dividend Chronology

Friday, 10 June	
Thursday, 23 June	
Friday, 24 June	
Sunday, 26 June	
Tuesday, 28 June	
Sunday, 10 July	

---

5. Assume that a company is based in a country that has no taxes on dividends and capital gains. The company is considering either paying a special dividend or repurchasing its own shares. Shareholders of the company would have

   A. greater wealth if the company paid a special cash dividend.

   B. greater wealth if the company repurchased its shares.

   C. the same wealth under either a cash dividend or share repurchase program.

   D. less wealth under either a cash dividend or share repurchase program.

6. Aiken Instruments (AIK) has recently declared a regular quarterly dividend of $0.50, payable on 12 November, to holders of record on 1 November. 28 October is the ex-date. Which date below would be the last day an investor purchasing AIK shares would receive the quarterly dividend?

   A. 27 October

   B. 28 October

   C. 1 November

   D. 12 November

7. WL Corporation is located in a jurisdiction that has a 40 percent corporate tax rate on pretax income and a 30 percent personal tax rate on dividends. WL distributes all its after-tax income to shareholders. What is the effective tax rate on WL pretax income distributed in dividends?

   A. 42 percent

   B. 52 percent

   C. 58 percent

   D. 70 percent

8. The clientele effect implies that

   A. high tax bracket investors are indifferent to dividends.

   B. investors prefer high dividend paying shares.

   C. investors have varying preferences regarding dividends.

   D. low tax bracket investors are indifferent to dividends.

9. Which of the following factors would *not* tend to be associated with a company having a low dividend payout ratio?

  A. Restrictive debt covenants.

  B. High flotation costs on new equity issues.

  C. High tax rates on dividends.

  D. Low growth prospects.

10. Which of the following is *most* likely to signal negative information concerning a firm?

  A. Share repurchase.

  B. Increase in the payout ratio.

  C. Decrease in the quarterly dividend rate.

  D. A two-for-one stock split.

11. Berkshire Gardens Inc. uses a target payout adjustment approach in paying its annual dividend. Last year Berkshire had earnings per share of $3.00 and paid a dividend of $0.60 a share. This year it estimates earnings at $4.00 a share. Find its dividend per share for this year if it has a 25 percent target payout ratio and uses a five-year period to adjust its dividend.

  A. $0.65

  B. $0.72

  C. $0.80

  D. $0.85

12. Investors may prefer companies which repurchase their shares instead of paying a cash dividend when

  A. capital gains are taxed at higher rates than dividends.

  B. capital gains are taxed at lower rates than dividends.

  C. capital gains are taxed at the same rate as dividends.

  D. the company needs more equity to finance capital expenditures.

13. Sophie Chan owns 100,000 shares of PAT Company. PAT is selling for €40 per share, so her investment is worth €4,000,000. Chan reinvests the gross amount of all dividends received to purchase additional shares. If PAT pays a €1.50 dividend, Chan's new share ownership after reinvesting dividends at the ex-dividend price is closest to

  A. 103,450.

  B. 103,600.

  C. 103,750.

  D. 103,900.

14. Mary Young intends to take a position in Megasoft Industries once Megasoft begins paying regular dividends with a special dividend of C$4 on 2 December. The ex-date for the dividend is 10 November, and the holder-of-record date is 12 November. What is the last possible date for Young to purchase her shares if she wants to receive the dividend?

  A. 9 November

  B. 10 November

  C. 11 November

  D. 12 November

THE CORPORATE GOVERNANCE OF LISTED COMPANIES: A MANUAL FOR INVESTORS

LEARNING OUTCOMES

The candidate should be able to:

a. define corporate governance;

b. discuss and critique characteristics and practices related to board and committee independence, experience, compensation, external consultants and frequency of elections and determine whether they are supportive of shareowner protection;

c. define board independence and explain the importance of independent board members in corporate governance;

d. identify factors that indicate a board and its members possess the experience required to govern the company for the benefit of its shareowners;

e. explain the provisions that should be included in a strong corporate code of ethics and the implications of a weak code of ethics with regard to related-party transactions and personal use of company assets;

f. state the key areas of responsibility for which board committees are typically created and explain the criteria for assessing whether each committee is able to adequately represent shareowner interests;

g. evaluate, from a shareowner's perspective, company policies related to voting rules, shareowner sponsored proposals, common stock classes and takeover defenses.

The Purpose of This Manual

Some of the most spectacular corporate collapses and losses in recent memory have highlighted the role that corporate governance practices play in maintaining viable entities, and safeguarding Investors' interests. The governance failures at Enron, Parmalat and others since 2001 are harsh examples of the risks posed by corporate governance breakdowns. Losses of tens of billions of dollars of Investors' capital proved that the existing set of corporate checks and balances on insiders' activities could not protect Shareowners from the misplaced priorities of Board Members and the manipulation and misappropriation of Company resources by management and other groups that exercised significant and improper influence over the Company's affairs.

Thus, it is with the goal of educating and empowering the Investor that this manual endeavors to provide Investors a way of assessing a Company's corporate governance policies, and the associated risks. It is our hope that all Investors—be they existing Shareowners, potential Investors, or analysts—can use this information as part of their analyses and valuations, in light of their particular investment perspectives, objectives, and risk-tolerance levels, to evaluate a Company. In particular, we hope that use of this manual will help Investors better recognize, understand and analyze how corporate governance may affect the value of their investments, and thus help them in making more informed investment decisions.

In response to wide-ranging effects of recent corporate failures on the global markets, many countries, industry groups and other constituencies have proposed or created new or amended corporate governance codes. Many of these codes seek to establish internal controls or set an ethical tone that focus on Investors' interests. While these government-mandated and voluntary industry codes may help to restore a degree of Investor confidence in the markets, they provide only part of the answer. Investors also must take the initiative to evaluate the presence—or absence—of corporate governance safeguards of Companies in which they invest, as well as their corporate cultures.

To this end, the CFA Centre for Financial Market Integrity ("CFA Centre"), through the work of its Global Corporate Governance Task Force, has prepared this manual. While suggesting issues for Investors to consider, the manual does not provide a set of best practices, nor attempt to decide what corporate governance structures are best for Investors. Instead, its purpose is to alert Investors to the primary corporate governance issues and risks affecting Companies, and to highlight some of the factors they should consider. It will evolve over time as listed Companies and financial markets change, and will serve as a starting point from which the CFA Centre can address revisions to this manual necessitated by such change.

Issuers of financial securities may also find this manual useful as a reference tool for determining what corporate governance issues are important to Investors. We hope that this manual will raise awareness of their governance standards within the investment community.

The Importance of Corporate Governance to Investors

For corporate governance structures to work effectively, Shareowners must be active and prudent in the use of their rights. In this way, Shareowners must act like owners and continue to exercise the rights available to them. Benjamin Graham and David Dodd stated in the 1930s that:

> *The choice of a common stock is a single act, its ownership is a continuing process. Certainly there is just as much reason to exercise care and judgment in being a shareholder as in becoming one.*[1]

A number of studies published in recent years have shown a strong link between good corporate governance and strong profitability and investment performance measures. For example, a joint study of Institutional Shareholder

---

[1] Benjamin Graham and David Dodd, *Security Analysis,* 1st ed. (New York: McGraw Hill, 1934)

Services ("ISS") and Georgia State University[2] found that the best-governed Companies—as measured by ISS's Corporate Governance Quotient—had mean returns on investment and equity that were 18.7 % and 23.8% better, respectively, than those of poorly governed companies during the year reviewed. Research carried out by employees of the California Public Employees Retirement System ("CalPERS") on the effects of the system's "Focus List" suggests that efforts by investment funds to improve the governance of Companies which are considered poorly governed also produces good returns in excess of market performance.[3]

On this basis, one would expect Investors to reward Companies that have superior governance with higher valuations. Indeed, a study of U.S. markets by Paul Gompers of Harvard University and colleagues from Harvard and the University of Pennsylvania[4] found that portfolios of Companies with strong share-owner-rights protections outperformed portfolios of Companies with weaker protections by 8.5% per year. A similar study in Europe found annual disparities of 3.0%.[5] Another study establishing and testing a governance rating system in the German market for the period from March 1998 to February 2002 shows that a portfolio consisting of the best governed Companies outperformed a portfolio of the worst governed Companies by a statistically significant average of 2.33% per month.[6]

This phenomenon is neither new nor limited to developed markets. Even before the collapse of Enron, Amar Gill, an analyst in Malaysia, found that Investors in emerging markets experienced higher investment returns from Companies with good governance.[7] Of the 100 largest emerging markets Companies his firm followed, those with the best governance—based on management discipline, transparency, Independence, accountability, responsibility, fairness and social responsibility—generated five-year returns well above average.[8]

The conclusion is that good corporate governance leads to better results for Companies and for Investors. Corporate governance, therefore, is a factor that Investors cannot ignore but should consider in seeking the best possible results for themselves or their clients.

---

[2] Brown, Lawrence D., and Caylor, Marcus, "Corporate Governance Study: The Correlation between Corporate Governance and Company Performance," Institutional Shareholder Services (2004).

[3] Anson, Mark, Ted White, and Ho Ho, "Good Corporate Governance Works: More Evidence from CalPERS," *Journal of Asset Management*, Vol. 5, 3 (February 2004), 149-156. Also see "The Shareholder Wealth Effects of CalPERS' Focus List" by the same authors, published in the *Journal of Applied Corporate Finance*, (Winter 2003), 8-17. The authors found that between 1992 and 2002, publication of the CalPERS' "Focus List" and efforts to improve the corporate governance of companies on that list generated one-year average cumulative excess returns of 59.4%. Cumulative excess return is the cumulative "return earned over and above the risk-adjusted return required for each public corporation."

[4] Gompers, Paul A., Joy L. Ishii, and Andrew Metrick, "Corporate Governance and Equity Prices," *Quarterly Journal of Economics*, 118(1) (February 2003), 107-155. The authors compared the investment performance of some 1,500 U.S.-listed companies against a corporate governance index the authors constructed from 24 distinct governance rules. Also see Lucian Bebchuk, Alma Cohen, and Allen Ferrell, "What Matters in Corporate Governance," (2004), The John M. Olin Center for Law, Economics and Business of Harvard University.

[5] Bauer, Rod, and Nadja Guenster, "Good Corporate Governance Pays Off!: Well-governed companies perform better on the stock market," (2003). This study used Deminor Ratings as the basis for determining which companies relative to corporate governance quality. (www.deminor-rating.com).

[6] Wolfgang Drobetz, Andreas Schillhofer, and Heinz Zimmermann, "Ein Corporate Governance Rating für deutsche Publikumsgesellschaften," WWZ/Department of Finance, Working Paper No. 5/03 (2003) (in German.) (www.unibas.ch/wwz/finanz/publications/researchpapers/5).

[7] Gill, Amar, "Corporate Governance in Emerging Markets—Saints and Sinners: Who's Got Religion?", CLSA Emerging Markets, April 2001. Gill points out that CLSA assigned corporate governance ratings to 495 companies in 25 markets.

[8] The five-year returns reported by Gill amounted to 930% for the well-governed large-cap companies in emerging markets, versus the total average return of 388% for large-cap companies in emerging markets during that period.

SUMMARY CORPORATE GOVERNANCE CONSIDERATIONS

The Board

Investors and Shareowners should:

► *determine whether a Company's Board has, at a minimum, a majority of Independent Board Members.*

► *determine whether Board Members have the qualifications the Company needs for the challenges it faces.*

► *determine whether the Board and its committees have budgetary authority to hire Independent third-party consultants without having to receive approval from management.*

► *determine whether Board Members are elected annually, or whether the Company has adopted an election process that staggers the terms of Board Member elections.*

► *investigate whether the Company engages in outside business relationships with management or Board Members, or individuals associated with them, for goods and services on behalf of the Company.*

► *determine whether the Board has established a committee of Independent Board Members, including those with recent and relevant experience of finance and accounting, to oversee the audit of the Company's financial reports.*

► *determine whether the Company has a committee of Independent Board Members charged with setting executive remuneration/compensation.*

► *determine if the Company has a nominations committee of Independent Board Members that is responsible for recruiting Board Members.*

► *determine whether the Board has other committees that are responsible for overseeing management's activities in select areas, such as corporate governance, mergers and acquisitions, legal matters, or risk management.*

Management

Investors and Shareowners should:

► *determine whether the Company has adopted a code of ethics, and whether the Company's actions indicate a commitment to an appropriate ethical framework.*

► *determine whether the Company permits Board Members and management to use Company assets for personal reasons.*

► *analyze both the amounts paid to key executives for managing the Company's affairs, and the manner in which compensation is provided to determine whether compensation paid to its executives is commensurate with the executives' level of responsibilities and performance, and provides appropriate incentives.*

► *inquire into the size, purpose, means of financing and duration of share-repurchase programs and price stabilization efforts.*

Shareowner Rights

Investors and Shareowners should:

▶ *determine whether the Company permits Shareowners to vote their shares by proxy regardless of whether they are able to attend the meetings in person.*

▶ *determine whether Shareowners are able to cast confidential votes.*

▶ *determine whether Shareowners can cast the cumulative number of votes allotted to their shares for one or a limited number of Board nominees ("cumulative voting").*

▶ *determine whether Shareowners can approve changes to corporate structures and policies that may alter the relationship between Shareowners and the Company.*

▶ *determine whether and under what circumstances Shareowners can nominate individuals for election to the Board.*

▶ *determine whether and under what circumstances Shareowners can submit proposals for consideration at the Company's annual general meeting.*

▶ *determine whether the Board and management are required to implement proposals that Shareowners approve.*

▶ *examine the Company's ownership structure to determine whether it has different classes of common shares that separate the voting rights of those shares from their economic value.*

▶ *determine whether the corporate governance code and other legal statutes of the jurisdiction in which the Company is headquartered permit Shareowners to take legal or seek regulatory action to protect and enforce their ownership rights.*

▶ *carefully evaluate the structure of existing or proposed takeover defenses and analyze how they could affect the value of shares in a normal market environment and in the event of a takeover bid.*

DEFINITIONS

Corporate Governance

Corporate governance is the system of internal controls and procedures by which individual Companies are managed. It provides a framework that defines the rights, roles and responsibilities of different groups—management, Board, controlling Shareowners and minority or non-controlling Shareowners—within an organization. This system and framework is particularly important for Companies with a large number of widely dispersed minority Shareowners.

At its core, corporate governance is the arrangement of checks, balances, and incentives a Company needs to minimize and manage the conflicting interests between insiders and external Shareowners. Its purpose is to prevent one group from expropriating the cash flows and assets of one or more other groups.

In general, good corporate governance practices seek to ensure that:

▶ Board Members act in the best interests of Shareowners;

▶ The Company acts in a lawful and ethical manner in their dealings with all stakeholders and their representatives;

▶ All Shareowners have the same right to participate in the governance of the Company and receive fair treatment from the Board and management, and all rights of Shareowners and other stakeholders are clearly delineated and communicated;

> ▶ The Board and its committees are structured to act independently from management, individuals or entities that have control over management, and other non-Shareowner groups;

> ▶ Appropriate controls and procedures are in place covering management's activities in running the day-to-day operations of the Company; and

> ▶ The Company's operating and financial activities, as well as its governance activities, are consistently reported to Shareowners in a fair, accurate, timely, reliable, relevant, complete and verifiable manner.

How well a Company achieves these goals depends, in large part, on the adequacy of the Company's corporate governance structure and the strength of the Shareowner's voice in corporate governance matters, through Shareowner voting rights. The success of the Board in safeguarding Shareowner interests depends on these factors.

This manual focuses on these two areas as a means of evaluating the corporate governance practices of Companies.

Independence

A number of new national corporate governance codes and exchange-based rules prescribe factors to consider in determining the Independence of Board and Board committee Members. Generally, to be considered Independent under these codes and rules, a Board Member must not have a material business or other relationship with the following individuals or groups:

> ▶ The Company and its subsidiaries or members of its group, including former employees and executives and their family members;

> ▶ Individuals, groups or other entities—such as controlling families and governments—that can exert significant influence on the Company's management;

> ▶ Executive management, including their family members;

> ▶ Company advisers (including external auditors) and their families; or

> ▶ Any entity which has a cross-directorship relationship with the Company.

Board Members

The term "Board Member"—in some jurisdictions called "directors"—in this Manual refers to all individuals who sit on the Board (defined below), including Executive Board Members, Independent Board Members, and Non-Executive Board Members.

Executive Board Members

This term refers to the members of executive management. In a Unitary Board, or Committees System, Executive Board Members also serve as part of the Board in a Unitary Board Structure. In a Two-Tier Board, these individuals only would be part of the Management Board. These individuals are not considered Independent.

Independent Board Members

An Independent Board Member refers to an individual who meets the qualifications listed under "Independence."

Non-Executive Board Members

Non-Executive Board Members are neither Executive Board Members nor Independent Board Members. Individuals in this category may represent interests that may conflict with those of other Shareowners. These may include Board Members who are affiliated with individuals or entities that have control over management, who are part of a cross-directorship arrangement with another listed Company, or are representatives of labor organizations.

Board

The term "Board" in this manual refers to both the Supervisory Board—or a Board of Corporate Auditors in Japan—in countries with a Two-Tier Board Structure, and the Board of Directors in countries that use a Unitary Board. In most cases, corporate structures take the form of one or the other of these, but in some countries such as in France and Japan, Companies have the option of choosing which of the two structures they wish to use.

Two-Tier (Dual) Board

Common in some parts of Europe, particularly in Germany, the Netherlands, Austria and Denmark, this structure has two elements, the Management Board and the Supervisory Board, both of which are described further below:

Management Board

The Management Board consists exclusively of executive management and is charged with running the Company on a daily basis and setting the corporate strategy for the Company, in consultation with the Supervisory Board. Its Members do not sit on the Company's Supervisory Board.

Supervisory Board

The Supervisory Board is charged with overseeing and advising the Company's Management Board and includes only Independent and Non-Executive Board Members.

Corporate Auditors System

In Japan, the Two-Tier Board structure is called the Corporate Auditors System and is used by most large Japanese Companies. It includes a Board—including either Independent Board Members or Non-Executive Board Members who are elected by Shareowners and are responsible for business decisions—and a Board of Corporate Auditors—consisting of corporate auditors, including at least one full-time corporate auditor, and at least half the Members must be outside auditors. These corporate auditors are elected separately by Shareowners and are charged with auditing the performance of the Board.

Unitary Board

In a Unitary Board structure, the Board may include Executive, Non-Executive and Independent Board Members. It oversees and advises management and helps set corporate strategy, though in many jurisdictions it does not engage in corporate decision-making, except in matters such as mergers, acquisitions, divestitures and sales. Jurisdictions increasingly require Independent Board Members to comprise at least a majority of the Board.

Committees System

This is the Unitary Board structure in Japan which uses a Board consisting of Executive Board Members, Independent Board Members and Non-Executive Board Members. The system gets its name because the Board must establish three committees—the audit, nominations and compensation committees—all of which must have at least three members, a majority of whom are either Independent Board Members or Non-Executive Board Members.

Company

The Company is the firm in which the Shareowners have an ownership position, and in which Investors are considering an investment.

Investors

This term refers to all individuals or institutions who are considering investment opportunities in shares and other securities of the Company.

Shareowners

The term "Shareowners" is distinguished from the term Investors by referring only to those individuals, institutions or entities that own shares of common or ordinary stock in the Company in question.

THE BOARD

Board Members owe a duty to make decisions based on what ultimately is best for the long-term interests of Shareowners. In order to do this effectively, Board Members need a combination of three things: Independence, experience and resources.

First, a Board should be composed of at least a majority of Independent Board Members with the autonomy to act Independently from management. Board Members should bring with them a commitment to take an unbiased approach in making decisions that will benefit the Company and long-term Shareowners, rather than simply voting with management. **Second**, Board Members who have appropriate experience and expertise relevant to the Company's business are best able to evaluate what is in the best interests of Shareowners. Depending on the nature of the business, this may require specialized expertise by at least some Board Members. **Third**, there need to be internal mechanisms to support the Independent work of the Board, including the authority to hire outside consultants without management's intervention or approval. This mechanism alone provides the Board with the ability to obtain expert help in specialized areas, to circumvent potential areas of conflict with management, and to preserve the integrity of the Board's Independent oversight function.

These three areas, and how Investors can evaluate them, are discussed in more detail below.

Board Independence

Investors should determine whether a Company's Board has, at a minimum, a majority of Independent Board Members.

What is Independence? Independence, as it relates to Board Members, refers to the degree to which they are not biased or otherwise controlled by Company management or other groups who exert control over management. Factors to consider in determining whether a Board Member meets this definition are provided in the "Definitions" section at the front of this Manual.

Implications for Investors. A Board that is not predominantly Independent, or a committee that is not completely Independent, may be more likely to make decisions that unfairly or improperly benefit the interests of management and those who have influence over management. These decisions may also be detrimental to the long-term interests of Shareowners.

Things to Consider. Investors should determine whether:

▶ Independent Board Members constitute, at a minimum, a majority of the Board. A Board with this makeup and one which is diverse in its composition is more likely to limit undue influence of management and others over the affairs of the Board.

▶ Independent Board Members regularly meet without the presence of management and report on their activities at least annually to Shareowners. Such meetings permit these Board Members to discuss issues facing the Company without influence from Executive Board Members.

▶ the Board chair also holds the title of chief executive. Combining the two positions may give too much influence to Executive Board Members and impair the ability and willingness of Independent Board Members to exercise their Independent judgment. A number of national corporate governance codes require the separation of these two positions.

▶ Independent Board Members have a lead Member if the Board chair is not Independent.

▶ the Board chair is a former chief executive of the Company. If so, Investors run the risk that this arrangement could impair the Board's ability to act Independently of undue management influence and in the best interests of Shareowners. Such a situation also increases the risk that the chair may hamper efforts to undo the mistakes made by him/her as chief executive.

▶ individuals who are aligned with a Company supplier or customer, or are aligned with a manager or adviser to the Company's share-option or pension plan, are Members of the Board. In some cases, a Company with a large number of suppliers, customers and advisers may need to nominate individuals to the Board who are aligned with these entities to ensure that it has the expertise it needs to make reasoned decisions. Investors should determine whether such Board Members recuse themselves on issues that may create a conflict.

Where to find information about the Independence of the Board and its committees:

▶ In most jurisdictions, Companies disclose the names, credentials and Company affiliations of existing Board Members either in their annual reports to Shareowners, or in their annual proxy statements to Shareowners.

> ▶ Companies often devote a special section in their annual reports to a discussion of the issues confronted by the Board and Board committees during the past year.

> ▶ The websites of many listed Companies provide information about Board Members' Independence.

Board Member Qualifications

Investors should determine whether Board Members have the qualifications the Company needs for the challenges it faces.

Implications for Investors. Investors should assess whether individual Board Members have the knowledge and experience that is required to advise management in light of the particularities of that Company, its businesses, and the competitive environment. Board Members who lack the skills, knowledge and expertise to conduct a meaningful review of the Company's activities are more likely to defer to management when making decisions. Such reliance on management not only threatens the duty to consider Shareowner interests first, but also could threaten the Company's overall performance if Board Members are not capable of in-depth evaluations of the issues affecting the Company's business. (See also the discussion relating to the nominations committee, on page 225.)

Other Things to Consider. Among the factors Investors should consider when analyzing Board Members'[9] qualifications are whether the Board Members:

> ▶ are able to make informed decisions about the Company's future.
> ▶ are able to act with care and competence as a result of relevant expertise or understanding of:
>> ▶ the principal technologies, products or services offered in the Company's business,
>> ▶ financial operations,
>> ▶ legal matters,
>> ▶ accounting,
>> ▶ auditing,
>> ▶ strategic planning, and
>> ▶ the risks the Company assumes as part of its business operations.
> ▶ have made public statements that can provide an indication of their ethical perspectives.
> ▶ have had legal or regulatory problems as a result of working for, or serving on, the Board of another Company.
> ▶ have experience serving on other Boards, particularly with Companies known for having good corporate governance practices.
> ▶ serve on a number of Boards for other Companies, constraining the time needed to serve effectively.[10]
> ▶ regularly attend Board and committee meetings.

---

[9] The factors to consider are drawn from CFA Institute's upcoming textbook, "Corporate Finance for the CFA Program."

[10] Some corporate governance codes, including the code in Pakistan, put a limit on the number of Company Boards on which Board Members may participate. In Pakistan, for example, the limit is 10 Board mandates for a Board Member.

► have committed to the needs of Shareowners, for example by making significant investments in the Company or by avoiding situations or businesses that could create a conflict of interest with his or her position as a Board Member.

► have the background, expertise, and knowledge in specific subjects needed by the Board.

► have served individually on the Board for more than 10 years. Such long-term participation may enhance the individual Board Member's knowledge of the Company, but it also may cause the Board Member to develop a cooperative relationship with management that could impair his/her willingness to act in the best interests of Shareowners.

Investors should also review:

► disclosures made by the Company about the number of Board and committee meetings held during the past year, and individual Board Member attendance records.

► whether the Board and its committees performed a self-assessment and, if available, any information relating to this assessment. This review will help Investors determine whether the Board has the competence and Independence to respond to the competitive and financial challenges facing the Company.

► whether the Board voluntarily or under the requirement of a governance code provides adequate training for Board Members on their roles and responsibilities.

Where to find information about the qualifications of Board Members:

► Many listed Companies post the names and qualifications of Board Members on their websites. Companies also typically provide information about their Board Members in the annual report to Shareowners and, where applicable, in their annual proxy statements.

► In many countries, Companies report on the number of Board and Board committee meetings, as well as attendance by individual Board Members, in their annual reports, on their websites, or, where applicable, in their annual corporate governance reports and proxy statements.

► Some corporate governance codes in jurisdictions such as Australia, Canada, the United Kingdom, and the United States require listed Companies to disclose in their annual reports if they failed to comply with the codes' provisions and why they did not comply.

► The European Union has adopted a European Commission recommendation that the Board of listed Companies annually discuss their internal organizations, their procedures and the extent to which their self-assessments have led to material changes.

► In the United States, Companies typically list the names and qualifications of Board Members, together with the Board's report to Shareowners, in the annual proxy statement, as well as on their websites. The nominations committee also includes its report concerning its members and activities in the annual proxy statement.

Authority to Hire External Consultants

Investors should determine whether the Board and its committees have budgetary authority to hire Independent third-party consultants without having to receive approval from management.

Implications for Investors. It is important to recognize that Independent Board Members typically have limited time to devote to their Board duties. Consequently Board Members need support in gathering and analyzing a large amount of information relevant to managing and overseeing the Company.

The Board and its committees often need specialized and Independent advice as they consider various corporate issues and risks such as compensation, proposed mergers and acquisitions, legal, regulatory, financial matters and reputational concerns. The ability to hire external consultants without first having to seek management's approval provides the Board with an Independent means of receiving advice uninfluenced by management's interests.

It also ensures that the Board receives specialized advice on technical decisions that could affect Shareowner value.

Other Things to Consider. Among other issues, Investors should determine whether:

▶ at relevant periods in the past the Board hired external financial consultants to help it consider mergers, acquisitions, divestitures, and risk management issues.

▶ the nominations committee has used external advisers in the past to recruit qualified nominees for management or for the Board.

▶ the remuneration committee has hired external advisers in the past to help determine appropriate compensation for key executives.

Where to find information about the authority of the Board to hire external consultants: The most likely places to find information relating to the Board's authority to hire external consultants are:

▶ the corporate governance section of the Company's annual report;

▶ the annual corporate governance report to Shareowners;

▶ the corporate governance section of the Company's website; or

▶ the charter for the Board or its committees.

Other places to find this kind of information:

▶ the Company's articles of organization or by-laws; or

▶ national corporate governance codes or stock exchange-mandated corporate governance requirements.

Other Board Issues

Board Member Terms

Shareowners should determine whether Board Members are elected annually, or whether the Company has adopted an election process that staggers the terms of Board Member elections.

Reasons for Reviewing Board Member Terms. Investors need to understand the mechanisms that provide, limit, or eliminate altogether their ability to exercise their rights to vote on individual Board Members.

Implications for Investors. Companies that prevent Shareowners from approving or rejecting Board Members on an annual basis limit Shareowners' ability to change the Board's composition, for example, when Board Members fail to act on their behalf, or to elect individuals with needed expertise in response to a change in Company strategy.

Things to consider. When reviewing a Company's policy for the election of Board Members, Investors should consider whether:

► Shareowners may elect Board Members every year, or for staggered multiple-year terms (known as a classified Board). An annually elected Board may provide more flexibility to nominate new Board Members to meet changes in the marketplace, if needed, than a classified Board. Staggered Boards also may serve as an anti-takeover device.[11] On the other hand, a classified Board may provide better continuity of Board expertise.

  In Japan, Shareowners of a Company that uses a Corporate Auditors System elect Board Members for two-year terms, and Members of the Corporate Auditors Board for four-year terms. Shareowners of a Company using a Committees System elect Board Members every year.

► the Board has filled a vacancy for the remainder of a Board Member's term without receiving Shareowner approval at the next annual general meeting.

► Shareowners can vote to remove a Board Member under certain circumstances.

► the Board is the appropriate size for the facts and circumstances of the Company. A large Board may have difficulty coordinating its Members' views, be slow to act, and defer more frequently to the chief executive. A small Board may lack depth of experience and counsel, and may not be able to adequately spread the work load among its Members to operate effectively.

Where to find information about the mechanisms related to Board elections and structure:

► In most cases, the best place to find information regarding the election of Board Members is in the notice of the Company's annual general meeting. In the United States and Canada, this information is typically part of the annual proxy statement to Shareowners.

► Investors also should check the Company's by-laws and articles of organization to determine whether management and the Board can fill any vacancies without Shareowner approval.

Related-Party Transactions

Investors should investigate whether the Company engages in outside business relationships with management or Board Members, or individuals associated with them, for goods and services on behalf of the Company.

---

[11] See especially, "The Powerful Antitakeover Force of Staggered Boards: Theory, Evidence, and Policy," by Lucian A. Bebchuk, John C. Coates, IV, and Guhan Subramanian, *Stanford Law Review*, Vol. 54, Issue 5, pg. 887-952. The authors conclude that the ballot box route to a takeover is illusory for a company with an effective staggered Board because, in part, a bidder must foster interest and votes during two elections spread at least 14 months apart.

Reasons for Reviewing the Company's Policies on Related-Party Transactions. As they relate to Board Members, policies that cover related-party transactions attempt to ensure the Independence of Board Members by discouraging them from engaging in the following practices, among others:

▶ receiving consultancy fees for work performed on behalf of the Company;

▶ receiving finders' fees for bringing merger, acquisition or sale partners to the Company's attention;

Implications for Investors. Receiving personal benefits from the Company for which Board Members are supposed to make Independent decisions can create an inherent conflict of interest, when these benefits fall outside the role of a Board Member. Limitations on such transactions, either through the Company's ethical code or Board policies, reduce the likelihood that management can use Company resources to sway Board Members' allegiance away from Shareowners.

Other Things to Consider. When reviewing a Company's policies regarding related-party transactions, Investors should determine whether:

▶ the Company's ethical code or the Board's policies and procedures limit the circumstances in which insiders, including Board Members and their associates, can accept remuneration from the Company for consulting or other services outside of the scope of their positions as Board Members. The intent of such provisions is not only to discourage actions that could compromise Board Members' Independence, but also to discourage the Company from entering into contracts that may not provide the best value to the Company and its Shareowners.

▶ the Company has disclosed any material related-party transactions or commercial relationships with existing Board Members or Board nominees. (See a discussion of this issue under Board Independence on page 215.)

▶ Board Members or executive officers have lent, leased or otherwise provided property or equipment to the Company.

▶ the Company has paid Board Members finders' fees for their roles in acquisitions or other significant Company transactions.

Where to find information about business transactions between the Company and its Board Members, management, or controlling Shareowners:

▶ The annual reports of Companies in many countries include a discussion of insider transactions and fees paid to Board Members and controlling Shareowners, often under the heading of "Related-Party" transactions.

▶ In the United States, listed Companies are required to provide information relating to dealings with insiders in the annual proxy statement, often under the heading of "Related-Party Transactions."

▶ Investors also should review the prospectus of a Company preceding a public offering of securities for any related-party transactions disclosures. This document should inform Investors about transactions that permit insiders to purchase shares at a discount prior to an offering at a higher price.

Board Committees

<u>Audit Committee</u>

Investors should determine whether the Board has established a committee of Independent Board Members, including those with recent and relevant experience of finance and accounting, to oversee the audit of the Company's financial reports.

The Purpose of the Audit Committee. The audit committee's primary objective is to ensure that the financial information reported by the Company to Shareowners is complete, accurate, reliable, relevant and timely.

To this end, the audit committee is responsible for hiring and supervising the Independent external auditors, ensuring that the external auditors' priorities are aligned with the best interests of Shareowners, and ensuring that:

► the information included in the financial reports to Shareowners is complete, accurate, reliable, relevant, verifiable and timely;

► the financial statements are prepared in accordance with generally accepted accounting principles (GAAP) and regulatory disclosure requirements;

► the audit is conducted in accordance with generally accepted auditing standards (GAAS);

► that the external auditor is Independent of management influence;

► that all conflicts of interest between the external auditor and the Company are resolved in favor of the Shareowners; and

► that the Independent auditors have authority over the audit of the entire corporate group, including foreign subsidiaries and affiliated Companies.

Implications for Investors. If the Independence of the audit committee is undermined, it could compromise the integrity of the financial reporting process and raise doubts about the credibility of the Company's financial statements. Misrepresentations of, or other distortions about, the Company's performance and financial condition ultimately could have a detrimental affect on the Company's share valuation.

What to Consider. Investors should determine whether:

► all of the Board Members serving on the audit committee are Independent. Some jurisdictions permit Board Members who are not Independent to serve on the committee. Japan, for example, requires that the committee have three or more members, a majority of whom are either Independent Board Members or Non-Executive Board Members.[12]

► any of the Board Members serving on the audit committee are considered financial experts.[13]

---

[12] Japan's Commercial Code has similar requirements for remuneration/compensation and nominating committees.

[13] Under SEC rules developed in response to Sarbanes-Oxley, a financial expert is a director who: (i) understands GAAP and financial statements; (ii) can assess the application of GAAP for estimates, accruals and reserves; (iii) has prepared, audited, analyzed or evaluated financial statements similar to those of the Company, or has experience supervising those who performed these functions; (iv) understands internal controls and financial reporting procedures; and (v) understands audit committee functions. They may acquire these attributes through: education and experience as or supervising a principal financial officer, principal accounting officer, controller, public accountant or auditor; overseeing or assessing companies or public accountants in the preparation, auditing or evaluation of financial statements; or from other relevant experience. See: www.sec.gov/rules/final/33-8177.htm, under "Audit Committee Financial Experts."

► the Board submits the appointment of the external auditors to a vote of Shareowners.

► the audit committee has the authority to approve or reject other proposed non-audit engagements with the external audit firm. This should be based on a review of the committee's report on the services received from, and fees paid to, the external audit firm. Investors also should determine whether the audit committee has policies relating to any fees paid by the Company to the external auditor for non-audit consulting services and for resolving these types of potential conflicts of interest. Such non-audit fees may influence the auditors in a way that leads them to resolve conflicts regarding financial reporting issues in favor of management rather than for the benefit of Shareowners.

► the Company has procedures and provisions that determine to whom the internal auditor reports. Regardless of the reporting lines, the internal auditor should have unimpeded access to the audit committee in the case of concerns regarding the accuracy or integrity of the financial reports or accounting practices. Likewise, the audit committee should have unimpeded access to the internal auditor.

► there were any discussions between the committee and the external auditors resulting in a change in the financial reports as a result of questionable interpretations of accounting rules, fraud, or other accounting problems, and whether the Company has fired its external auditors as a result of such issues.

► the committee controls the audit budget to enable it to address unanticipated or complex issues.

Where to look for information about the audit committee:

Australia—Companies listed on the Australian Stock Exchange are required to disclose in their annual reports if they have not complied with the exchange's recommendations relating to the audit committee, together with an explanation of why they did not comply.

Canada—Pursuant to Multilateral Instruments 52-101, 102 and 110, listed Companies must report the following information about their audit committees in their Annual Information Form:

► the committee's charter and composition;

► relevant education and experience of each committee member; and

► whether the Company relied on an exemption.

In addition, Companies listed on Toronto Stock Exchange markets are required to disclose in their annual reports whether:

► they have an audit committee;

► its members are non-executive;

► the Board has defined its roles and responsibilities;

► it communicates directly with internal and external auditors; and

► it is responsible for overseeing management reporting and internal control systems.

European Union—The Prospectus Directive in the European Union follows the disclosure standards of the International Organization of Securities Commissioners by requiring that Companies provide the names of committee members and a summary "of the terms of reference under which the committee operates" in the Prospectus. Companies in the United Kingdom also are required to report on their systems of internal controls in the annual directors' report.

United States—Companies must disclose whether they have at least one financial expert on their audit committees and the name of at least one of the committee's financial experts. They also must disclose whether the named Board Members are Independent. If they disclose that they do not have at least one financial expert, they must explain why. Companies also must disclose the following in their annual proxy statements:

- whether there is a standing audit committee and, if so, the name of each committee member, the number of meetings held, and a description of the functions performed by the committee;

- whether the Board has adopted a written charter for the audit committee (if so, they must include a copy of the charter as an appendix to the proxy statement at least once every three years.[14] If this information is available, one will most likely find it on the Company's website.

- if their shares are quoted on the Nasdaq, American or New York stock exchanges, whether the audit committee members are "Independent" as defined in the applicable listing standards (together with certain information regarding any audit committee member who is not "Independent");

- whether the audit committee has reviewed and discussed the audited financial reports with management and the Independent auditors and whether the auditors made appropriate disclosures regarding their Independence; and

- a statement by the audit committee about whether it recommended to the Board that the audited financial statements be included in the annual report.

Remuneration/Compensation Committee

Investors should determine whether the Company has a committee of Independent Board Members charged with setting executive remuneration/compensation.

The Purpose of the Remuneration/Compensation Committee. The Remuneration Committee is responsible for ensuring that compensation and other awards encourage executive management to act in ways that enhance the Company's long-term profitability and value. It is also responsible for ensuring that the remuneration packages offered to management are commensurate with the level of responsibilities of the executive, and appropriate in light of the Company's performance. The committee can further these goals by:

- including only Independent Board Members on the committee,[15] and
- linking executive compensation to the long-term profitability of the Company and long-term increases in share value relative to competitors and other comparably situated Companies.

---

[14] See NYSE or NASDAQ rules relating to audit committee charters. Also see Regulation S-K, Item 401(h), 2004, www.sec.gov/divisions/corpfin/forms/regsk.htm.

[15] Please see a discussion of the independence of committees, particularly in Japan, under the discussion above concerning the Audit Committee.

Implications for Investors. The existence of the committee and its Independence from executive management bias help to ensure that the rewards and incentives offered to management are consistent with the best long-term interests of Shareowners. Committees that lack Independence could be overly pressured by management to award compensation that is excessive when compared with other comparably situated Companies, or to provide incentives for actions that boost short-term share prices at the expense of long-term profitability and value.

Other Things to Consider. As part of their analyses relating to this committee, Investors should determine whether:

▶ the composition of the compensation packages offered to senior management are appropriate.

▶ the Company provided loans or the use of Company property and equipment such as airplanes and real estate to Board Members.

▶ members of the committee regularly attended meetings during the past year.

▶ the committee has policies and procedures and, if so, what they are.

▶ the Company has provided detailed information to Shareowners in public documents relating to the compensation paid during the past year to the Company's five highest-paid executives and its Board Members. Investors also should review any disclosures about the major components and amounts paid to these individuals. Some jurisdictions only require Companies to provide summary information about the compensation of senior management and the Board.

▶ the terms and conditions of options granted to management and employees and whether the terms are reasonable.

▶ the Company intends to issue newly registered shares to fulfill its share-based remuneration obligations, or whether it intends to settle these options with shares repurchased in the open market.

▶ the Company and the Board are required to receive Shareowner approval for any share-based remuneration plans. Such plans affect the number of shares outstanding and, consequently, current Shareowners' ownership interests, as well as the basis on which earnings per share are reported and the market valuations of the Company's securities.

▶ senior executives from other Companies that have cross-directorship links with the Company are members of the committee. Executive remuneration is often based on compensation of similarly positioned individuals at other Companies, and if the committee has individuals who could benefit directly from reciprocal decisions on remuneration, those decisions may not be in the best interests of the subject Company's Shareowners. (Also see a discussion relating to Board Independence on page 215.)

Where to find information about the remuneration/compensation committee:

Australia—Companies that list on the Australian Stock Exchange are required to disclose in their annual reports if they did not comply with the exchange's recommendations for remuneration committees, together with an explanation of why they did not comply.

Canada—The Toronto Stock Exchange requires Companies listed on its markets to report in their annual reports or their management information and proxy circulars whether they have a compensation committee and, if so, whether it is comprised of Independent or Non-Executive Board Members, and whether a majority are Independent.

European Union—European Commission's non-binding recommendations state that Companies should report their remuneration policies and amounts paid to executive management in the annual report. Also, Companies listed in the United Kingdom are required to report in their annual reports on the frequency of, and attendance by, members at remuneration committee meetings. These Companies also must disclose the responsibilities delegated to the committee.

United States—Listed Companies report on whether there is a standing compensation committee in their annual proxy statements. These reports also include names of committee members, summaries of compensation strategies, and the policies and procedures of the committee.

Nominations Committee

Investors should determine if the Company has a nominations committee of Independent Board Members that is responsible for recruiting Board Members.

The purpose of the nominations committee. The nominations committee is responsible for:

- ▶ recruiting new Board Members with appropriate qualities and experience in light of the Company's business needs;
- ▶ regularly examining the performance, Independence, skills and expertise of existing Board Members to determine whether they meet the current and future needs of the Company and the Board;
- ▶ creating nominations policies and procedures;
- ▶ preparing for the succession of executive management and the Board.

Implications for Investors. The slate of candidates proposed by this committee will affect whether the Board works for the benefit of Shareowners. It is important for this committee to remain Independent[16] to ensure that it recruits individuals who can and will work on behalf of Shareowners, and to ensure that the performance assessment of current Board Members is fair and appropriate. (Also see Board Member Qualifications on page 216.)

Other Things to Consider. Investors may have to review Company reports over several years to adequately assess whether this committee has recruited Board Members who act in the interests of Shareowners. They also should review:

- ▶ the criteria for new Board Members.
- ▶ the composition, background and areas of expertise of existing Board Members, and whether new nominees complement the Board's current portfolio of talents.
- ▶ how the committee finds potential new Board Members. Among the considerations is whether the committee engages in a search for candidates, such as by using an executive search firm, or whether its members rely upon the advice of management or other Board Members.
- ▶ the attendance records of Board Members at regular and special meetings.
- ▶ whether the Company has a succession plan for executive management in the event of unforeseen circumstances, such as the sudden incapacitation of the chief operating and finance officers. Investors should examine the information provided by the Company about the plan and determine who is expected to lead and implement it.

---

[16] Please see a discussion of the Independence of committees, particularly in Japan, under the discussion above concerning the "Audit Committee."

▶ the report of the committee, including any discussion of its actions and decisions during the previous year (including the number of meetings held, attendance by committee members, and the committee's policies and procedures.)

Where to find information about the nominating committee:

▶ The annual reports of Companies in many countries include a general discussion of the actions taken by the committee during the previous year.

▶ The annual reports of Companies listed in some countries, such as Australia and the United Kingdom, are required to disclose and explain when a Company fails to comply with applicable nomination committee rules.

▶ The corporate governance report often includes an explanation of the Company's nominations process and whether they have a specially designated nominations committee.

▶ In some regions, such as North America, Investors should look in the annual proxy statement to Shareowners for indications about the work of this committee, including the name of each committee member and the number of meetings held.

▶ The websites of many listed Companies describe the activities and members of the committee and, in some countries, provide information about the committee's charter.

Other Board Committees

Investors should determine whether the Board has other committees that are responsible for overseeing management's activities in certain areas, such as corporate governance, mergers and acquisitions, legal matters or risk management.

Implications for Investors. Depending on the purpose, committees created by the Board can provide additional insight into the goals, focus and strategies of the Company. For example, a committee dedicated to risk management might consider the identification and quantification of risks faced by the Company, and determine its optimal risk exposure.

Whether these committees consist of only Independent Members is an important factor to weigh in evaluating the degree to which the committee is dedicated to achieving what is best for the Company and Shareowners, or may be improperly influenced by management and other insiders.

Other Things to Consider. Because such committees often are not covered by national corporate governance codes or exchange-mandated guidelines in the manner that audit, remuneration or nominations committees are, they are more likely to have members who are part of executive management. Consequently, the Independence of these committees may not, and possibly need not, achieve the levels of Independence expected of such committees as audit, nominations and remuneration.

Where to find information about other Board committees:
As in the case with the audit, compensation and nominations committees, there are four primary places to look for information about special-purpose committees, namely:

▶ The annual reports to Shareowners;

▶ The annual corporate governance report, where applicable; and

▶ In regions like the United States and Canada, the annual proxy statement to Shareowners.

▶ The websites of listed Companies.

MANAGEMENT

While the Board helps set the strategic, ethical and financial course for a Company in consultation with management, Investors ultimately must rely on management to implement that course. Management also has the responsibility to communicate to Investors and the public about the Company's performance, financial condition and any changes in strategy or corporate initiatives in an effective and timely manner.

Investors are familiar with the reports that management issues with regard to a Company's financial performance and condition. However, they may not be aware of other sources of information that may provide insight into the corporate culture or governance practices of a Company. In fact, there are various sources of information available to Investors for evaluating management's role in corporate governance practices, aside from the financial reports that Companies issue.

To help Investors better understand management's role and responsibilities in corporate governance matters, the following section provides a general discussion of a Company's code of ethics and corporate culture, followed by specific discussions of common areas of focus on ethical practices such as related-party transactions, executive compensation, contractual arrangements, share repurchase programs and takeover defenses.

Implementation of Code of Ethics

Investors should determine whether the Company has adopted a code of ethics, and whether the Company's actions indicate a commitment to an appropriate ethical framework.

The Purpose of a Code of Ethics. A Company's code of ethics sets standards for ethical conduct based on basic principles of integrity, trust, and honesty. It provides personnel with a framework for behavior while conducting the Company's business, as well as guidance for addressing conflicts of interest. In effect, it represents a part of the Company's risk management policies which are intended to prevent Company representatives from engaging in practices that could harm the Company, its products, or Shareowners.

Implications for Investors. Reported breaches of ethics in a Company often result in regulatory sanctions, fines, management turnover, and unwanted negative media coverage, all of which can adversely affect the Company's performance. Adoption and adherence to an appropriate corporate code of ethics indicates a commitment on the part of management to establish and maintain ethical practices. The existence of such a code may also be a mitigating factor from regulatory actions when breaches do occur.

Things to Consider. As part of their analyses of the Company's ethical climate, Investors should determine whether the Company:

- ► gives the Board access to relevant corporate information in a timely and comprehensive manner.

- ► is in compliance with the corporate governance code of the country where it is located, or the governance requirements of the stock exchange that lists its securities. Typically, Companies must disclose whether they have failed to adhere to such codes and, if so, give reasons for the failure. In some cases, non-compliance may result in fines or sanctions by regulators. The Company also may face informal sanctions, such as product boycotting from customers or political groups.

- ► has an ethical code and whether that code prohibits any practice that would provide advantages to Company insiders that are not also offered to

Shareowners. For example, a code might prohibit the Company from offering shares at discounted prices to management, Board Members and other insiders prior to a public offering of securities to prevent dilution of the value and interests of those who buy at the public offering price.

▶ has designated someone who is responsible for corporate governance.

▶ has an ethical code that provides waivers from its prohibitions to certain levels of management, and the reasons why.

▶ waived any of its code's provisions during recent periods, and why.

▶ regularly performs an audit of its governance policies and procedures to make improvements.

Where to find information about a Company's Code of Ethics and other ethical matters:

▶ The annual reports of Companies listed in some countries such as Australia disclose when and why a Company failed to meet applicable governance standards regarding the creation and implementation of a code of conduct.

▶ Companies with ethical codes typically post them on their public websites, in their annual reports to Shareowners, or, in countries that require them, in their annual corporate governance reports.

▶ Investors may check on the requirements of a country's national corporate governance code or exchange-mandated governance requirements.

Personal Use of Company Assets

Investors should determine whether the Company permits Board Members, management and their family members to use Company assets for personal reasons.

Reasons for Reviewing the Company's Policies on the Personal Use of Company Assets. As they relate to Board Members, policies that limit or prohibit the use of Company assets by insiders attempt to ensure that resources are used in the most efficient and productive manner for the purpose of generating returns for the Company and all of its Shareowners. Such policies and procedures also seek to preserve the Independence of Board Members by attempting to prevent the conflicts of interest that may result when Board Members or their families use Company assets.

Implications for Investors. When insiders such as Board Members, managers and their families use Company assets for personal reasons, those resources are not available for investment in productive and income-generating activities. Such use also creates conflicts of interest for Board Members.

Other Things to Consider. When reviewing a Company's policies regarding the personal use of Company assets, Investors should determine whether the Company:

▶ has an ethical code or policies and procedures that place strict limits on the ability of insiders to use Company assets for personal benefit.

▶ has lent cash or other resources to Board Members, management or their families.

▶ has purchased property or other assets such as houses or airplanes for the personal use of Board Members, management, or their family members.

▶ has leased assets such as dwellings or transportation vehicles to Board Members, management or their family members, and whether the terms of such contracts are appropriate given market conditions.

Where to find information about insider transactions involving Board Members, management and controlling Shareowners:

▶ Investors may find information about loans to Company executives, Board Members or their families in the "Related Party Transactions" sections of a Company's annual report, its annual corporate governance report, annual proxy statement to Shareowners, or its website.

▶ Investors also should review the prospectus of a Company preceding a public offering of securities for any related-party transactions disclosures. This document should inform Investors about transactions that permit insiders to purchase shares at a discount prior to an offering at a higher price.

Corporate Transparency

Executive Compensation

Investors should analyze both the amounts paid to key executives for managing the Company's affairs and the manner in which compensation is provided to determine whether compensation paid to its executives is commensurate with the executives' level of responsibilities and performance, and provides appropriate incentives.

Reasons for Reviewing Executive Compensation Disclosures. Disclosures of how much, in what manner, and on what basis executive management is paid shed light on the Board's stewardship of Shareowner assets. Furthermore, they allow Investors to evaluate whether the compensation is reasonable in light of the apparent return to the Company in terms of performance.

Implications for Shareowners. The manner in which executive management is compensated can affect Shareowner value in a number of ways. A flawed compensation program may encourage executives to make decisions that generate additional compensation to them through short-term gains, rather than implement an appropriate strategy that focuses on long-term growth. It also could dilute the ownership positions of existing Shareowners. On the other hand, an appropriately designed program can create incentives for Company executives to generate positive results for Shareowners.

Things to Consider. When reviewing a Company's executive compensation disclosures, Investors should examine the reported:

▶ Remuneration/Compensation strategy. An examination of the terms and conditions of the Company's executive compensation program, together with an analysis of summaries of agreements with executives, will help Investors determine whether the program rewards long-term growth, or short-term increases in share value. This review should include a determination of whether the remuneration/compensation committee uses consultants to set pay for Company executives, or whether it relies on internal sources. Investors also should focus on whether the rewards offered to management are based on the performance of the Company relative to its competitors or other peers, or on some other metric.

▶ Executive compensation. Analysis of the actual compensation paid to the Company's top executives during recent years and the elements of the compensation packages offered to key employees can help Investors determine whether the Company is receiving adequate returns for the investment it has made in executive management.

▶ Share-based compensation terms. Examination of the terms of this type of remuneration program, including the total shares offered to key executives and other employees, should alert Investors to how the program can affect shares outstanding, dilution of Shareowner interests, and share values. Investors also should determine whether the Company seeks Shareowner approval for creation or amendments to such plans. (See Shareowner Rights section beginning on page 232 for other issues that may require a vote of Shareowners.)

▶ Stock-option expensing. Compensation, regardless of whether it is paid in cash, shares or share options, involves payment for services received and should appear as an expense on the income statement. International Financial Reporting Standards (IFRS) and U.S. Generally Accepted Accounting Principles both require Companies to expense stock option grants.[17]

▶ Performance-based compensation. Investors should determine whether stock options and stock grants, as well as stock-appreciation rights and other performance-based compensation programs, are linked to the long-term profitability and share-price performance of the Company relative to its competitors and peers. The purpose of compensation is to reward management for gains attributable directly to superior performance, and linking pay to performance is one way to achieve this purpose.

▶ Option repricing. Investors should remain aware of efforts by the Company to reprice downward the **strike prices** of stock options previously granted. Changes in the strike price remove the incentives the original options created for management, and therefore reduce the link between long-term profitability and performance and management remuneration.

▶ Share ownership of management. Investors should determine whether members of management have share holdings other than those related to stock option grants. Such holdings may align the interests of Company executives with those of Shareowners.

Where to find information about executive compensation:

   ▶ In many jurisdictions, Companies report information about executive compensation in their annual reports. In some cases, disclosures about amounts paid to individual executives is voluntary, although accounting standards setters and securities regulators are increasingly making such disclosures compulsory.

   ▶ In the United States, executive compensation strategies and reports of actual compensation paid to key executives are included in the Company's annual proxy statement to Shareowners.

   ▶ Investors also may find such information posted on Companies' websites.

Share-Repurchase and Price Stabilization Programs

Shareowners should inquire into the size, purpose, means of financing and duration of share-repurchase programs and price stabilization efforts.

Reasons for Reviewing Disclosures of Share-Repurchase and Stabilization Programs. A Company will use a share-repurchase program to buy its own shares that are already trading on a public stock exchange. In a stabilization program, the Company has its investment bankers buy and sell shares following a public offering of shares as a means of reducing the price volatility of the shares.

---

[17] This requirement is applicable for U.S.-listed companies with fiscal years that end after 15 June 2005.

Implications for Investors. Buying shares on the open market can have a positive effect on share values by reducing the number of shares available and increasing the value for the remaining shares outstanding. Price-stabilization programs may reduce the volatility of a security's price following an offering and permit the market to achieve a balance between buyers and sellers, but may provide insiders with an opportunity to trade at a higher price in anticipation that the share price will decline—or to buy at a lower price in anticipation of future price gains.

Things to Consider. When reviewing share-repurchase and stabilization programs, Investors should determine the:

▶ Intention of the Program. Investors should determine whether the Board intends to use repurchased shares i) to reduce the number of shares outstanding to increase long-term valuations, ii) to fund the future exercise of management share options, or iii) to prevent a hostile takeover. Depending on the perspective of the Investor, the program may enhance or hurt long-term share value. Fixed-income Investors, for example, may view the use of cash to repurchase shares as detrimental to the ability of the Company to repay its outstanding debts.[18] Equity Investors, on the other hand, may see such actions as beneficial to their valuations.

▶ Size of and Financing for the Program. This information, together with disclosures about whether the Company plans to use internally generated cash from operations or issue debt to finance the purchases can help equity Investors determine how the program will affect the value of the Company's shares.

In addition, Investors should review:

▶ regular updates on the program's progress. In particular, Investors should review the prices at which open-market purchases of shares were made, the number of shares purchased, cumulative amounts of shares repurchased to date, and the average price paid to date. This information should help them anticipate completion of the program and how that may affect share value. It also should help them determine whether the program is proceeding as planned or exceeding original intentions for scope and cost.

▶ disclosures relating to stabilization activities. Following a public securities offering, a Company may contract with its securities underwriters to stabilize the price of the offering through the active purchase and sale of the securities in the open market. Investors should determine prior to investing in a public offering of securities whether the Company intends to use such stabilization services, and subsequently review updates about the number of shares purchased and sold under the program, the average price paid and received, and when the activities concluded. This information will indicate whether the Company and its advisers acted as proposed or whether they engaged in unintended or undisclosed activities.

Where to find information about share repurchase and stabilization programs:

▶ The annual and interim reports of Companies will, in most cases, provide the information relating to a share-repurchase program.

▶ The prospectus for an offering should include initial information relating

---

[18] Bond indentures may require that the Company repay outstanding debt securities or receive a waiver from bondholders prior to launching a share repurchase program.

to stabilization activities. Annual and interim financial reports should provide final information about the activities of stabilization programs.

▶ Investors should look to the prospectus of an offering to determine whether at the time of the offering the Company intended to use agents to perform price stabilization services following the issuance of the securities.

Post-stabilization disclosure. In the European Union, Companies are required by the Market Abuse Directive to disclose whether stabilization activities were undertaken and, if so, the dates the program began and ended, and the range of prices at which such activities were conducted. The ultimate disclosures will come from either the issuer or the lead underwriter.

The U.S. Securities and Exchange Commission currently does not require post-stabilization disclosures like those of the European Union, though it is considering implementation of one.[19] Currently Nasdaq requires market makers to attach a special symbol to an order for this purpose while other exchanges require underwriters to notify the exchange and provide disclosure to the recipient of the bid that such bids are part of a stabilization program.

Likewise, disclosure in many other jurisdictions is required to be made only to the Company and the exchange.

SHAREOWNER RIGHTS

The value of a financial security is determined not only by its claim on the Company's future earnings but also on the rights associated with those securities. Among the rights associated with shares of common stock is the right to elect Board Members and to vote on matters that may affect the value of their holdings, such as mergers or acquisitions. Other rights may include the right to apply the cumulative votes of one's shares to one or a limited number of Board nominees, the ability to nominate persons to the Board, or to propose changes to Company operations.

Shareowners may not have all these rights in all cases, and even when they do they may have difficulty exercising them. For example, Companies in some regions can restrict voting only to those owners who are present at scheduled meetings of Shareowners, or prevent Shareowners from trading for a designated period prior to the annual general meeting in return for exercising that vote. In other cases, individuals and institutions cannot confidentially cast their votes. In still other cases, founding-family members or government Shareowners may exercise disproportional influence over the Companies' affairs though the ownership of special classes of shares that grant them super-voting rights.

Shareowners may have powers to remedy situations in certain cases, though such remedies are not universal. Local laws and regulations also may provide legal or regulatory redress.

---

[19] "Amendments to Regulation M: Anti-Manipulation Rules Concerning Securities Offerings; Proposed Rule," 17 December 2004, (Federal Register, Vol. 69, No. 242, page 75782), under the third question: "Should the Commission consider, in addition to the proposed disclosure, revising Rule 104 to require a general notification to the market (e.g., through a press release, a website posting, or an administrative message sent over the Tape) that [the] activity has commenced (and another notification when [the activity] has ceased)?

Such issues are of interest not only to equity Investors, but also to Investors interested in **fixed-income investments**. For example, Companies that grant super-voting rights to a certain class of stock and Shareowners historically use debt financing more than equity financing to fund investments in new business opportunities.[20] Such a strategy may raise the financial risk of a Company and, ultimately, increase the possibility of default.

It is important for Investors to recognize what specific rights are attached to the securities they are considering and factor that information into any investment decisions. Doing so may avoid situations that result in reduced valuations and poor investment performance.

Following is a discussion of issues that Investors should consider in evaluating the Shareowner rights of different Companies.

Shareowner Voting

Proxy Voting

Investors should determine whether the Company permits Shareowners to vote their shares by proxy regardless of whether they are able to attend the meetings in person.

Reasons for evaluating a Company's voting rules. The ability to vote one's shares is a fundamental right of share ownership. In some jurisdictions, Shareowners may find it difficult to vote their shares because the Company accepts only those votes cast at its annual general meeting, and does not allow them the right to vote by proxy or imposes other constraints.

Implications for Investors. By making it difficult for Shareowners to vote their common shares, the Company limits a Shareowner's ability to choose Board Members or otherwise to express their views on other initiatives that could alter the Company's course.

Things to consider. In examining whether a Company permits proxy voting, Investors should consider whether the Company:

▶ limits Shareowners' ability to cast votes by conditioning the exercise of their right to vote on their presence at the annual general meeting.

▶ coordinates the timing of its annual general meeting with other Companies in its region to ensure that all of them hold their meetings on the same day but in different locations. In some regions that require Shareowners to attend such meetings to vote, such actions seek to prevent Shareowners from attending all the meetings, and, therefore, from exercising their voting rights.

▶ permits proxy voting by means of paper ballot, electronic voting, proxy voting services, or by some other remote mechanism.

▶ is permitted under its national governance code to use share blocking, whereby it prevents Investors that wish to exercise their voting rights to trade their shares during a period prior to the annual general meeting to permit the Company and various financial institutions certify who owns the shares.

Where to find information about the Company's proxy voting rules:

▶ Investors also can look to the Company's corporate governance statement for information about whether proxy voting is permitted.

---

[20] A December 2003 study by Gompers, et. al, found that companies with two classes of common shares that separated the voting rights from the cash flow rights resulted in underinvestment and lower valuations. See Gompers, et. al, "Incentives vs. Control: An Analysis of U.S. Dual-Class Companies," knowledge.wharton.upenn.edu/papers/1278.pdf.

> ► In the United States, the proxy statement will describe the mechanisms by which Shareowners can cast their votes by proxy.
>
> > ► Investors can look to the Company's articles of organization and by-laws to determine the mechanisms Shareowners can use to vote their shares.
>
> ► Also in the United States, state corporation law regulates issues relating to proxies. Consequently, Investors may have to determine the state in which a Company is incorporated—typically found in the Articles of Incorporation—to review the proxy regulations governing the Company.

Confidential Voting and Vote Tabulation

Investors should determine whether Shareowners are able to cast confidential votes.

Reasons for determining whether Shareowners are able to cast confidential votes. Shareowners are more likely to vote and to do so conscientiously if they are assured that Board Members and management will not find out how they voted.

Implications for Investors. Confidentiality of voting insures that all votes are counted equally, and that the Board Members and management cannot re-solicit the votes of individuals and institutions who vote against the positions of these insiders until the votes are officially recorded.[21]

Things to consider. In examining whether Shareowners can vote anonymously, Investors should consider whether:

> ► the Company uses a third-party entity to tabulate Shareowner votes.
>
> ► the Company or its third-party agent retains voting records.
>
> ► the vote tabulation performed by the Company or its third-party agent is subject to an audit to ensure accuracy.
>
> ► Shareowners are permitted to vote only if they are present at a scheduled Company meeting. (See "Proxy Voting" on page 233 for a discussion of this issue.)

Where to find information concerning confidentiality of voting rights:

> > ► Investors should look to the Company's by-laws or articles of organization to determine the procedures for counting and tabulating Shareowner votes.

Cumulative Voting

Shareowners should determine whether Shareowners can cast the cumulative number of votes allotted to their shares for one or a limited number of Board nominees ("cumulative voting").

Implications for Investors. The ability to use cumulative voting enables Shareowners to vote in a manner that enhances the likelihood that their interests are represented on the Board.

Things to Consider. In evaluating how a Company handles cumulative voting, Investors should consider whether:

---

[21] In the case of pooled investment funds, CFA Institute has taken the position that the funds should disclose to investors how they voted the shares of each company on behalf of the fund's beneficiaries. Such disclosures are different from disclosing those votes to management and the Board in that the investment fund is disclosing its voting record to the beneficiaries on whose behalf it is acting.

► the Company has a significant minority Shareowner group, such as a founding family, that might be able to use cumulative voting to elect Board Members that represent its specific interests at the expense of the interests of other Shareowners.

Where to find information about whether a Company permits cumulative voting:

► The articles of organization and by-laws frequently provide information regarding how a Company regards Shareowner initiatives and rights.

► The prospectus that a listed Company must file with the local regulator will typically describe the circumstances under which Shareowners can exercise their voting rights.

► In the United States, Investors also may look to the Form 8-A that listed Companies must file with the Securities and Exchange Commission for a description of the rights afforded a Company's common shares.

Voting for Other Corporate Changes

Shareowners should determine whether Shareowners can approve changes to corporate structures and policies that may alter the relationship between Shareowners and the Company.

Reasons for Considering Shareowner Input on Corporate Changes. Changes to certain corporate structures have the ability to affect the value, ownership percentage, and rights associated with the Company's securities. Among the issues Shareowners should review is the ability of Shareowners to effect changes to the Company's:

► articles of organization,

► by-laws,

► governance structures,

► voting rights and mechanisms,

► poison pills, and

► change-in-control provisions.

Implications for Investors. Certain changes to the Company's by-laws or articles of organization can affect the Shareowner's interests in the Company. For example, the introduction or modification of an anti-takeover mechanism might make a takeover too expensive for potential acquirers to consider, thereby denying Shareowners full market value for their shares. Likewise, providing large quantities of stock options to management and employees might dilute the value of shares held by existing Shareowners, while redistributing Company resources to insiders without Shareowner approval.

Things to Consider. In reviewing what issues require Shareowner approval, Investors should determine whether Shareowners:

► must approve such proposals with supermajority votes.

► will have an opportunity to vote on the sale of their Company, or a substantial portion of their Company, to a third-party buyer. Investors also may wish to consider whether Shareowners have an opportunity to vote on significant acquisitions and divestitures that could increase or reduce annual revenues by 10% or more and whether there is a threshold for approval of such transactions.

▶ will have the right to vote on certain aspects of executive compensation. (See the discussion of executive compensation on page 229.)

▶ have the right to approve a new anti-takeover measure, and whether such measures are subject to periodic review and retention by Shareowners. (See the discussion of anti-takeover measures on page 240.)

▶ have the ability to periodically reconsider and re-vote on rules that require supermajority voting to revise the Company's by-laws, articles of organization or other governance documents. While these supermajority requirements may have been useful in making unwanted changes more difficult at a particular time in the Company's development, they may not serve the same purpose in light of the Company's evolution. Such provisions can make even changes overwhelmingly supported by Shareowners more difficult to enact.

▶ have the ability to vote for changes to the Company's:
   ▶ articles of organization,
   ▶ by-laws,
   ▶ governance structures,
   ▶ voting rights and mechanisms.

▶ may attempt to use their ownership of a limited number of shares to force a vote on special interests that are unrelated to the Company's operations. Such actions could cause the Board to make it more difficult for other Shareowners to propose resolutions that are relevant to the Company's operations.

Investors also should review the following issues to determine whether or under what conditions Shareowners may vote on:

▶ share buy-back programs, particularly if their purpose is to fund share-based compensation grants. (See the discussion on share buy-backs on page 231.)

▶ Amendments, additions to, or revocation of, corporate charters and by-laws.

▶ Issuance of new capital stock, including both common shares, and instruments that convert into common shares.

Where to find information whether certain corporate changes require Shareowner approval:

   ▶ The Company will provide information to Shareowners that relates to specific issues requiring a vote. This will often occur as part of the Company's disclosures relating to the annual general meeting, or as part of disclosures related to a special meeting of Shareowners.

   ▶ A Company typically will provide information on which issues require Shareowner approval in the Company's by-laws and articles of organization. These documents will also provide information about whether management and the Board can fill any vacancies without Shareowner approval.

Shareowner Proposals

Shareowner-Sponsored Board Nominations

Investors should determine whether and under what circumstances Shareowners can nominate individuals for election to the Board.

Reasons for determining whether Shareowners can propose Board nominees. The ability to nominate one or more individuals to the Board can prevent erosion of Shareowner value. When a Board and management fail to remedy existing problems and to improve the Company's financial performance, Shareowners may use this power to ensure that at least one nominee is Independent of the existing Board and its nominations committee.

Implications for Investors. If Shareowners have the right to nominate Board Members, they have the ability to force the Board or management to take steps to address Shareowner concerns.

Things to Consider. In evaluating whether Shareowners can propose nominees to the Board, Investors should determine:

▶ under what circumstances Shareowners have the right to nominate Board Members, such as when the Board ignores a Shareowner initiative.[22]

▶ whether Shareowners can vote to remove a Board Member under certain circumstances.

▶ how the Company handles contested Board elections. At many Companies, particularly in the United States, a single vote cast in favor of a nominee is sufficient for an uncontested nominee to get elected to the Board. In cases where the nominations are contested by Shareowners, different rules for determining winners may apply.

Where to find information about the ability of Shareowners to nominate individuals for the Board:

▶ The notice of the annual general meeting also may provide information related to the election of Board Members.

▶ In the United States, Investors also may look to the Company's annual proxy statement.

▶ In most jurisdictions, the articles of organization and by-laws provide information regarding how a Company regards Shareowner initiatives and rights.

Shareowner-Sponsored Resolutions

Investors should determine whether and under what circumstances Shareowners can submit resolutions for consideration at the Company's annual general meeting.

Reasons for determining whether Shareowners can propose corporate initiatives. Investors need to understand what they can do if the Board and management fail to remedy existing problems or improve the Company's financial performance. Investors also need to understand the extent to which outside institutions or individuals with specific interests or biases are able to influence Company activity. The ability to propose needed changes can prevent erosion of Shareowner value.

Implications for Investors. The right to propose initiatives for consideration at the Company's annual general meeting is one way for Shareowners to send a message that they do not like the way the Board and/or management is handling one or more Company matters. If the proposal receives an overwhelming number of votes, it could pressure the Board and management either to make the changes called for or, if they fail to do so, to justify their inaction.

---

[22] Please see www.cfainstitute.org/advocacy/03commltr/03shd_nominations.html for a complete discussion of the position of CFA Institute on this issue. Also see the original SEC proposal at www.sec.gov/rules/proposed/34-48626.htm.

Things to Consider. In evaluating the ability of Shareowners to propose changes for the Company, Investors should determine whether:

▶ the Company requires a simple, two-thirds or other supermajority vote for passing a Shareowner resolution. By comparison, the Company may require a simple majority vote to pass Board- or management-sponsored initiatives.

▶ Shareowners can request a special Shareowner meeting to consider specific issues.

▶ initiatives proposed by Shareowners will benefit the long-term interests of all Shareowners, or whether they represent the narrow interests of those making the proposals.

Where to find information about Shareowner authority to propose voting initiatives:

▶ In the United States, Shareowners may look to the annual proxy statement for information about how to submit proxy initiatives.

▶ In most jurisdictions, the articles of organization and by-laws provide information regarding how a Company regards Shareowner-sponsored proposals.

Advisory or Binding Shareowner Proposals

Investors should determine whether the Board and management are required to implement proposals that Shareowners approve.

Reasons for determining whether Shareowner proposals are binding. Unless the Company is required to implement an initiative that Shareowners have approved, the Board and management may tend to ignore those and other Shareowner concerns.

Implications for Investors. Requirements that the Board and management must implement approved Shareowner-sponsored initiatives could make them more accountable to Shareowners.

Things to consider: When reviewing the Company's rules regarding Shareowner initiatives, Investors should determine whether:

▶ the Company has implemented or ignored approved Shareowner- sponsored proposals in the past.

▶ the Company requires a supermajority of votes to approve changes to its by-laws and articles of organization.

▶ national regulatory agencies have pressured Companies to act on the terms of approved Shareowner initiatives.

Where to find information about the enforceability of Shareowner-sponsored proposals:

▶ The articles of organization and by-laws typically provide information about whether Shareowner initiatives are binding and, if so, the size of the majority vote needed to enforce the measure.

▶ Investors also may look to the regulatory agency in the local market where the Company is headquartered to determine whether it has taken steps to enforce Shareowner initiatives in other cases.

Other Shareowner Rights Issues

Ownership Structure

Investors should examine the Company's ownership structure to determine whether it has different classes of common shares that separate the voting rights of those shares from their economic value.

Reasons for Examining the Ownership Structure of the Company. A Company that assigns one vote to each share is more likely to have a Board that considers and acts in the best interests of all Shareowners. Conversely, a Company with different classes of common shares in which the majority, or all, of the voting rights are given to one class of Shareowners is more likely to have a management team and Board that are focused on the interests of only those Shareowners. The rights of other Shareowners may suffer as a consequence.

Implications for Investors. Companies with dual classes of common equity could encourage potential acquirers to deal directly with those Shareowners who own the shares with super-voting rights. Moreover, studies have shown that Companies that separate the voting rights from the economic rights—which entitle a Shareowner to a pro-rata share of the earnings and residual asset value of the Company—of their common shares find it more difficult to raise equity capital to invest in capital improvements and product development than Companies that combine those rights.

Things to Consider. When analyzing the ownership structure of a Company, Investors should consider whether:

▶ the Company has safeguards in its articles of organization or by-laws that protect the rights and interests of those Shareowners whose shares have inferior voting rights.

▶ the Company was recently privatized by a government or governmental entity and whether the selling government has retained voting rights that could veto certain decisions of management and the Board. If so, it could prevent Shareowners from receiving full value for their shares.

▶ the super-voting rights granted to certain classes of Shareowners have impaired the Company's ability to raise equity capital for future investment. Investors may find the inferior class of shares unattractive, which could harm the Company's ability to finance future growth by means other than raising debt capital and increasing leverage.[23]

Where to find information about whether the Company has more than one class of shares:

▶ In certain jurisdictions and in certain Companies, Investors might find information about the different classes of shares in the annual proxy statement to Shareowners.

▶ The Company's website also is likely to describe the differences between shares of common stock and may provide hyperlinks to the Company's articles of organization, annual and interim financial reports, prospectuses, and proxy statements.

---

[23] Ibid.

> ► The prospectus relating to the initial or follow-on offerings of common shares to the public is likely to include a discussion about different classes of common shares, including whether any entity or group of Investors retains sufficient voting power to overrule certain management or Board decisions.
>
> ► The notes to the financial statements, particularly in the annual report, will likely disclose the existence of different classes of common shares.

Shareowner Legal Rights

Investors should determine whether the corporate governance code and other legal statutes of the jurisdiction in which the Company is headquartered permit Shareowners to take legal or seek regulatory action to protect and enforce their ownership rights.

Reasons for determining the legal remedies available to Shareowners. In situations where the Company has failed to fully recognize their rights, Shareowners may have to turn to the courts or national regulators to enforce their rights of ownership.

Things to consider: When reviewing the local governance code and legal statutes regarding legal and regulatory actions, Investors should determine whether:

> ► local legal statutes permit Shareowners to take derivative legal actions—which permit Shareowners to initiate legal actions against management or Board Members on behalf of the Company—and, if so, what conditions must be met.
>
> ► the regulator in the local market where the Company is headquartered has taken action in other cases to enforce Shareowner rights or to prevent the denial of Shareowner rights.
>
> ► Shareowners, either individually or as a class, are permitted to take legal or regulatory action to enforce fraud charges against management or the Board.
>
> ► Shareowners have "dissenters' rights" requiring the company to repurchase their shares at fair market value following such transactions.

Where to find information about legal and regulatory relief for Shareowners:

> ► The regulator in the local market of the Company's headquarters may provide information about the remedies available to Shareowners in a variety of legal regulatory matters.

Takeover Defenses

Shareowners should carefully evaluate the structure of an existing or proposed takeover defenses and analyze how they could affect the value of shares in a normal market environment and in the event of a takeover bid.

Reasons for Reviewing Disclosures Relating to Takeover Defenses. Such disclosures should provide Shareowners with information about the situations in which takeover defenses—such as so-called golden parachutes, poison pills and greenmail—could be used to counter a hostile bid.

Implications for Investors. By forcing an acquiring entity to deal directly with management and the Board, takeover defenses—often referred to as "Shareowner rights plans"—may reduce the potential for the acquirer to succeed, even in situations that would benefit Shareowners. Defenses against takeovers also may cause Investors to discount the value of the Company's shares in normal trading because of the conditions and barriers they create.

Things to Consider. When reviewing a Company's anti-takeover measures, Investors should:

- ▶ inquire whether the Company is required to receive Shareowner approval for such measures prior to implementation. It is likely that each Company will structure its measure differently from others. In some cases, Investors may find that the Board is permitted to implement an anti-takeover measure, subject to approval by Shareowners within a set period of time. Others may not require Shareowner approval at all.

- ▶ inquire whether the Company has received any formal acquisition overtures during the past two years.

- ▶ consider the possibility that the Board and management will use the Company's cash and available credit lines to pay a hostile bidder to forego a takeover. In general, Shareowners should take steps to discourage the Board from taking such actions. If the Company agrees to such payments, Shareowners should review any publicly available information about the terms of such so-called "greenmail" payments.[24]

- ▶ consider whether, in some cases, change of control issues are likely to invoke the interest of a national or local government, which might then pressure the seller to change the terms of a proposed acquisition or merger. In such cases, it is unlikely that the Investor will find specific government directives decreeing such defenses, although Investors may find indications about the likelihood of such actions by examining the government's past actions relating to the Company or relating to other companies in similar situations.

- ▶ consider whether change-in-control provisions will trigger large severance packages and other payments to Company executives.

Where to find information about takeover provisions:

- ▶ A Company's articles of organization are the most likely places to find information about existing takeover defenses.

- ▶ Newly created anti-takeover provisions may or may not require Shareowner approval. In either case, the Company may have to provide information to its Shareowners about any amendments to existing defenses.

---

[24] Greenmail is a premium paid by the object of a hostile takeover bid to the entity making that bid in return for an agreement that the bidding entity will halt its takeover bid for a certain period.

$4\frac{5}{8}$ $4\frac{11}{16}$ $-\frac{3}{8}$

$5\frac{1}{2}$ $5\frac{1}{2}$ $-\frac{3}{8}$

$20\frac{5}{8}$ $21\frac{3}{16}$ $-\frac{1}{16}$

$17\frac{3}{8}$ $18\frac{1}{8}$ $+\frac{7}{8}$

$6\frac{1}{2}$ $6\frac{1}{2}$ $-\frac{1}{2}$

$7\frac{1}{4}$ $31\frac{1}{32}$ $-\frac{1}{8}$

$\frac{15}{16}$ $\frac{9}{16}$

$\frac{9}{16}$

$7\frac{1}{16}$ $7\frac{13}{16}$ $7\frac{15}{16}$

$2\frac{5}{8}$ $2\frac{11}{32}$ $2\frac{1}{2}$ $+$

$2\frac{3}{4}$ $2\frac{1}{4}$ $2\frac{1}{4}$

$6\frac{1}{8}$ $12\frac{1}{16}$ $11\frac{3}{8}$ $11\frac{3}{4}$ $+$

87 $33\frac{3}{4}$ 33 $33\frac{1}{16}$ $-$

502 $25\frac{5}{8}$ $24\frac{9}{16}$ $25\frac{3}{8}$ $+$

833 12 $11\frac{5}{8}$ $11\frac{7}{8}$ $+$

16 $10\frac{1}{2}$ $10\frac{1}{2}$ $10\frac{1}{2}$ $-$

78 $15\frac{5}{8}$ $15\frac{13}{16}$ $15\frac{7}{8}$ $-$

4608 $9\frac{1}{16}$ $8\frac{1}{4}$ $8\frac{7}{8}$ $+$

430 $11\frac{1}{4}$ $10\frac{1}{8}$

PORTFOLIO MANAGEMENT

STUDY SESSION

Study Session 12   Portfolio Management

TOPIC LEVEL LEARNING OUTCOME

The candidate should be able to demonstrate a working knowledge of the key elements of the portfolio management process, including the investment setting, investment policy, and asset allocation.

4⅝ 4¹¹/₁₆ ⅜

5½ 5½ —

5½ 20⅝ 21¹³/₁₆ — ¹/₁₆

17⅜ 18⅛ + ⅞

15½ 6½ 6½ — ½

7¼ 6½ 3³/₃₂ —

15/16 ⅞

9/16

⁹/₃₂ 7¹⁵/₁₆ 7¹³/₁₆ 7¹⁵/₁₆

2⅝ 2¹¹/₃₂ 2½ —

2¾ 2¼ 2¼

6¹⁶ 12¼₁₆ 11⅜ 11¼ +

8T 33¾ 33 33¹/₈ —

8J2 25⅝ 24⁹/₁₆ 25⅝ +

12 11⅝ 11⅞ +

833 12 11⅝

16 10½ 10½ 10¼

78 15⅞ 15¹³/₁₆ 15⅞ —

4608 9¹/₁₆ 8¼ 8½

430 11¼ 10⅛

STUDY SESSION 12
PORTFOLIO MANAGEMENT

READING ASSIGNMENTS

Reading 52   The Asset Allocation Decision
Reading 53   An Introduction to Portfolio Management
Reading 54   An Introduction to Asset Pricing Models

As the first discussion within the CFA curriculum on portfolio management, this critical study session provides the framework and context for most of the following Level I study sessions that cover investments within equities, fixed income, derivatives, and alternative investments. Furthermore, this study session provides the underlying theories and tools for portfolio management in Level II and in Level III.

The first reading discusses the asset allocation decision and the portfolio management process, an integrated set of steps undertaken in a consistent manner to create and maintain an appropriate portfolio (combination of assets) to meet clients' stated goals. The last two readings build on the first reading to focus on the design of a portfolio of investments, introducing the capital asset pricing model (CAPM), a centerpiece of modern financial economics that provides a relationship between the risk of an asset and its expected return.

LEARNING OUTCOMES

Reading 52: The Asset Allocation Decision
The candidate should be able to:

a. describe the steps in the portfolio management process and explain the reasons for a policy statement;

b. explain why investment objectives should be expressed in terms of both risk and return and list the factors that may affect an investor's risk tolerance;

c. describe the return objectives of capital preservation, capital appreciation, current income, and total return and describe the investment constraints of liquidity, time horizon, tax concerns, legal and regulatory factors, and unique needs and preferences;

d. describe the importance of asset allocation, in terms of the percentage of a portfolio's return that can be explained by the target asset allocation and list reasons for the differences in the average asset allocation among citizens of different countries.

Reading 53: An Introduction to Portfolio Management
The candidate should be able to:

a. define risk aversion and discuss evidence that suggests that individuals are generally risk averse;

b. list the basic assumptions behind the Markowitz Portfolio Theory;

c. compute the expected return for an individual investment and for a portfolio;

d. compute the variance and standard deviation for an individual investment;

e. compute the covariance of rates of return, and show how it is related to the correlation coefficient;

f. list the components of the portfolio standard deviation formula, and explain which component is most important to consider when adding an investment to a portfolio;

g. describe the efficient frontier and explain the implications for incremental returns as an investor assumes more risk;

h. define optimal portfolio and show how each investor may have a different optimal portfolio.

Reading 54: An Introduction to Asset Pricing Models
The candidate should be able to:

a. list the assumptions of the capital market theory;

b. explain what happens to the expected return, the standard deviation of returns, and possible risk-return combinations when a risk-free asset is combined with a portfolio of risky assets;

c. identify the market portfolio, and describe the role of the market portfolio in the formation of the capital market line (CML);

d. define systematic and unsystematic risk and explain why an investor should not expect to receive additional return for assuming unsystematic risk;

e. describe the capital asset pricing model, diagram the security market line (SML), and define beta;

f. calculate and interpret using the SML, the expected return on a security, and evaluate whether the security is undervalued, overvalued, or properly valued;

g. describe the effect on the SML of relaxing each of its main underlying assumptions line.

THE ASSET ALLOCATION DECISION*
by Frank K. Reilly and Keith C. Brown

LEARNING OUTCOMES

Reading 52: The Asset Allocation Decision

The candidate should be able to:

a. describe the steps in the portfolio management process and explain the reasons for a policy statement;

b. explain why investment objectives should be expressed in terms of both risk and return and list the factors that may affect an investor's risk tolerance;

c. describe the return objectives of capital preservation, capital appreciation, current income, and total return and describe the investment constraints of liquidity, time horizon, tax concerns, legal and regulatory factors, and unique needs and preferences;

d. describe the importance of asset allocation, in terms of the percentage of a portfolio's return that can be explained by the target asset allocation and list reasons for the differences in the average asset allocation among citizens of different countries.

Note:
Although this reading addresses the taxation of individual investors from the viewpoint of a U.S. investor, candidates are not expected to know the U.S. tax code.

INTRODUCTION   1

Investors know that *risk drives return*. Therefore, the practice of investing funds and managing portfolios should focus primarily on managing risk rather than on managing returns.

This reading examines some of the practical implications of risk management in the context of asset allocation. **Asset allocation** is the process of deciding how to distribute an investor's wealth among different countries and asset classes for investment purposes. An **asset class** is comprised of securities that have similar

---

* The authors acknowledge the collaboration of Professor Edgar Norton of Illinois State University on this reading.

Investment Analysis and Portfolio Management, Eighth Edition, by Frank K. Reilly and Keith C. Brown, Copyright © 2005. Reprinted with permission of South-Western, a division of Thomson Learning.

characteristics, attributes, and risk/return relationships. A broad asset class, such as "bonds," can be divided into smaller asset classes, such as Treasury bonds, corporate bonds, and high-yield bonds. We will see that, in the long run, the highest compounded returns will most likely accrue to those investors with larger exposures to risky assets. We will also see that although there are no shortcuts or guarantees to investment success, maintaining a reasonable and disciplined approach to investing will increase the likelihood of investment success over time.

The asset allocation decision is not an isolated choice; rather, it is a component of a structured four-step portfolio management process that we present in this reading. As we will see, the first step in the process is to develop an investment policy statement, or plan, that will guide all future decisions. Much of an asset allocation strategy depends on the investor's policy statement, which includes the investor's goals or objectives, constraints, and investment guidelines.

What we mean by an "investor" can range from an individual to trustees overseeing a corporation's multibillion-dollar pension fund, a university endowment, or invested premiums for an insurance company. Regardless of who the investor is or how simple or complex the investment needs, he or she should develop a policy statement before making long-term investment decisions. Although most of our examples will be in the context of an individual investor, the concepts we introduce here—investment objectives, constraints, benchmarks, and so on—apply to any investor, individual or institutional. We'll review historical data to show the importance of the asset allocation decision and discuss the need for investor education, an important issue for individuals or companies who offer retirement or savings plans to their employees. The reading concludes by examining asset allocation strategies across national borders to show the effect of market environment and culture on investing patterns; what is appropriate for a U.S.-based investor is not necessarily appropriate for a non-U.S.-based investor.

2 INDIVIDUAL INVESTOR LIFE CYCLE

Financial plans and investment needs are as different as each individual. Investment needs change over a person's life cycle. How individuals structure their financial plan should be related to their age, financial status, future plans, risk aversion characteristics, and needs.

The Preliminaries

Before embarking on an investment program, we need to make sure other needs are satisfied. No serious investment plan should be started until a potential investor has adequate income to cover living expenses and has a safety net should the unexpected occur.

Insurance   Life insurance should be a component of any financial plan. Life insurance protects loved ones against financial hardship should death occur before our financial goals are met. The death benefit paid by the insurance company can help pay medical bills and funeral expenses and provide cash that family members can use to maintain their lifestyle, retire debt, or invest for future needs (for example, children's education, spouse retirement). Therefore, one of the first steps in developing a financial plan is to purchase adequate life insurance coverage.

Insurance can also serve more immediate purposes, including being a means to meet long-term goals, such as retirement planning. On reaching retirement age, you can receive the cash or surrender value of your life insurance policy and use the proceeds to supplement your retirement lifestyle or for estate planning purposes.

Insurance coverage also provides protection against other uncertainties. *Health* insurance helps to pay medical bills. *Disability* insurance provides continuing income should you become unable to work. *Automobile and home* (or rental) insurances provide protection against accidents and damage to cars or residences.

Although nobody ever expects to use his or her insurance coverage, a first step in a sound financial plan is to have adequate coverage "just in case." Lack of insurance coverage can ruin the best-planned investment program.

Cash Reserve   Emergencies, job layoffs, and unforeseen expenses happen, and good investment opportunities emerge. It is important to have a cash reserve to help meet these occasions. In addition to providing a safety cushion, a cash reserve reduces the likelihood of being forced to sell investments at inopportune times to cover unexpected expenses. Most experts recommend a cash reserve equal to about six months' living expenses. Calling it a "cash" reserve does not mean the funds should be in cash; rather, the funds should be in investments you can easily convert to cash with little chance of a loss in value. Money market or short-term bond mutual funds and bank accounts are appropriate vehicles for the cash reserve.

Similar to the financial plan, an investor's insurance and cash reserve needs will change over his or her life. The need for disability insurance declines when a person retires. In contrast, other insurance, such as supplemental Medicare coverage or long-term care insurance, may become more important.

Life Cycle Net Worth and Investment Strategies

Assuming the basic insurance and cash reserve needs are met, individuals can start a serious investment program with their savings. Because of changes in their net worth and risk tolerance, individuals' investment strategies will change over their lifetime. In the following sections, we review various phases in the investment life cycle. Although each individual's needs and preferences are different, some general traits affect most investors over the life cycle. The four life cycle phases are shown in Exhibit 52-1 (the third and fourth phases—spending and gifting—are shown as concurrent) and described here.

Accumulation Phase   Individuals in the early-to-middle years of their working careers are in the **accumulation phase**. As the name implies, these individuals are attempting to accumulate assets to satisfy fairly immediate needs (for example, a down payment for a house) or longer-term goals (children's college education, retirement). Typically, their net worth is small, and debt from car loans or their own past college loans may be heavy. As a result of their typically long investment time horizon and their future earning ability, individuals in the accumulation phase are willing to make relatively high-risk investments in the hopes of making above-average nominal returns over time.

EXHIBIT 52-1	Rise and Fall of Personal Net Worth over a Lifetime

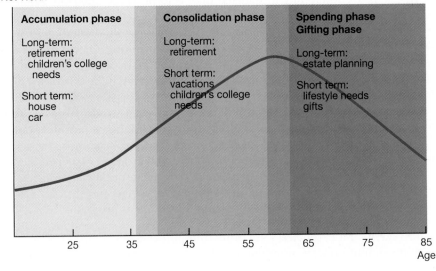

Here we must emphasize the wisdom of investing early and regularly in one's life. Funds invested in early life-cycle phases, with returns compounding over time, will reap financial benefits during later phases. Exhibit 52-2 shows growth from an initial $10,000 investment over 20, 30, and 40 years at assumed annual returns of 7 and 8 percent. The middle-aged person who invests $10,000 "when he or she can afford it" will only reap the benefits of compounding for 20 years or so before retirement. The younger person who saves will reap the much higher benefits of funds invested for 30 or 40 years. Regularly investing $2,000 a year

EXHIBIT 52-2	Benefits of Investing Early

		The Future Value of an Initial $10,000 Investment	The Future Value of Investing $2,000 Annually	The Future Value of the Initial Investment Plus the Annual Investment
Interest rate	7.0%			
20 years		$38,696.84	$81,990.98	$120,687.83
30 years		$76,122.55	$188,921.57	$265,044.12
40 years		$149,744.58	$399,270.22	$549,014.80
Interest rate	8.0%			
20 years		$46,609.57	$91,523.93	$138,133.50
30 years		$100,626.57	$226,566.42	$327,192.99
40 years		$217,245.21	$518,113.04	$735,358.25

Source: Calculations by authors.

reaps large benefits over time, as well. A person who has invested a total of $90,000—an initial $10,000 investment followed by $2,000 annual investments over 40 years—will have over half a million dollars accumulated from the 7 percent return. If the funds are invested more aggressively and earn the 8 percent return, the accumulation will be nearly three-quarters of a million dollars.

Consolidation Phase   Individuals in the **consolidation phase** are typically past the midpoint of their careers, have paid off much or all of their outstanding debts, and perhaps have paid, or have the assets to pay, their children's college bills. Earnings exceed expenses, so the excess can be invested to provide for future retirement or estate planning needs. The typical investment horizon for this phase is still long (20 to 30 years), so moderately high risk investments are attractive. At the same time, because individuals in this phase are concerned about capital preservation, they do not want to take very large risks that may put their current nest egg in jeopardy.

Spending Phase   The **spending phase** typically begins when individuals retire. Living expenses are covered by social security income and income from prior investments, including employer pension plans. Because their earning years have concluded (although some retirees take part-time positions or do consulting work), they seek greater protection of their capital. At the same time, they must balance their desire to preserve the nominal value of their savings with the need to protect themselves against a decline in the *real* value of their savings due to inflation. The average 65-year-old person in the United States has a life expectancy of about 20 years. Thus, although their overall portfolio may be less risky than in the consolidation phase, they still need some risky growth investments, such as common stocks, for inflation (purchasing power) protection.

The transition into the spending phase requires a sometimes difficult change in mindset; throughout our working life we are trying to save; suddenly we can spend. We tend to think that if we spend less, say 4 percent of our accumulated funds annually instead of 5, 6, or 7 percent, our wealth will last far longer. But a bear market early in our retirement can greatly reduce our accumulated funds. Fortunately, there are planning tools that can give a realistic view of what can happen to our retirement funds should markets fall early in our retirement years; this insight can assist in budgeting and planning to minimize the chance of spending (or losing) all the saved retirement funds. Annuities, which transfer risk from the individual to the annuity firm (most likely an insurance company), are another possibility. With an annuity, the recipient receives a guaranteed, lifelong stream of income. Options can allow for the annuity to continue until both a husband and wife die.

Gifting Phase   The **gifting phase** is similar to, and may be concurrent with, the spending phase. In this stage, individuals believe they have sufficient income and assets to cover their current and future expenses while maintaining a reserve for uncertainties. Excess assets can be used to provide financial assistance to relatives or friends, to establish charitable trusts, or to fund trusts as an estate planning tool to minimize estate taxes.

Life Cycle Investment Goals

During the investment life cycle, individuals have a variety of financial goals. **Near-term, high-priority goals** are shorter-term financial objectives that individuals set to fund purchases that are personally important to them, such as accumulating funds to make a house down payment, buy a new car, or take a trip. Parents with teenage children may have a near-term, high-priority goal to accumulate funds to help pay college expenses. Because of the emotional importance of these goals and their short time horizon, high-risk investments are not usually considered suitable for achieving them.

Long-term, high-priority goals typically include some form of financial independence, such as the ability to retire at a certain age. Because of their long-term nature, higher-risk investments can be used to help meet these objectives.

Lower-priority goals are just that—it might be nice to meet these objectives, but it is not critical. Examples include the ability to purchase a new car every few years, redecorate the home with expensive furnishings, or take a long, luxurious vacation. A well-developed policy statement considers these diverse goals over an investor's lifetime. The following sections detail the process for constructing an investment policy, creating a portfolio that is consistent with the policy and the environment, managing the portfolio, and monitoring its performance relative to its goals and objectives over time.

3   THE PORTFOLIO MANAGEMENT PROCESS

The process of managing an investment portfolio never stops. Once the funds are initially invested according to the plan, the real work begins in monitoring and updating the status of the portfolio and the investor's needs.

The first step in the portfolio management process, as seen in Exhibit 52-3, is for the investor, either alone or with the assistance of an investment advisor, to construct a **policy statement**. The policy statement is a road map; in it, investors specify the types of risks they are willing to take and their investment goals and constraints. All investment decisions are based on the policy statement to ensure they are appropriate for the investor. We examine the process of constructing a policy statement in the following section. Because investor needs change over time, the policy statement must be periodically reviewed and updated.

EXHIBIT 52-3	**The Portfolio Management Process**

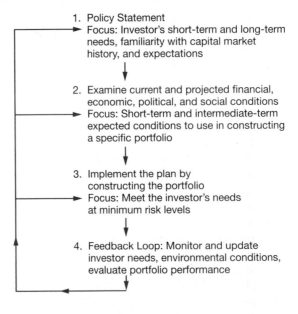

1. Policy Statement
   Focus: Investor's short-term and long-term needs, familiarity with capital market history, and expectations

2. Examine current and projected financial, economic, political, and social conditions
   Focus: Short-term and intermediate-term expected conditions to use in constructing a specific portfolio

3. Implement the plan by constructing the portfolio
   Focus: Meet the investor's needs at minimum risk levels

4. Feedback Loop: Monitor and update investor needs, environmental conditions, evaluate portfolio performance

The process of investing seeks to peer into the future and determine strategies that offer the best possibility of meeting the policy statement guidelines. In the second step of the portfolio management process, the manager should study current financial and economic conditions and forecast future trends. The investor's needs, as reflected in the policy statement, and financial market expectations will jointly determine **investment strategy**. Economies are dynamic; they are affected by numerous industry struggles, politics, and changing demographics and social attitudes. Thus, the portfolio will require constant monitoring and updating to reflect changes in financial market expectations.

The third step of the portfolio management process is to **construct the portfolio**. With the investor's policy statement and financial market forecasts as input, the advisors implement the investment strategy and determine how to allocate available funds across different countries, asset classes, and securities. This involves constructing a portfolio that will minimize the investor's risks while meeting the needs specified in the policy statement.

The fourth step in the portfolio management process is the **continual monitoring** of the investor's needs and capital market conditions and, when necessary, updating the policy statement. Based upon all of this, the investment strategy is modified accordingly. A component of the monitoring process is to evaluate a portfolio's performance and compare the relative results to the expectations and the requirements listed in the policy statement. Once you have completed the four steps, it is important to recognize that this is continuous—it is essential to revisit all the steps to ensure that the policy statement is still valid, that the economic outlook has not changed, etc.

THE NEED FOR A POLICY STATEMENT   4

As noted in the previous section, a policy statement is a road map that guides the investment process. Constructing a policy statement is an invaluable planning tool that will help the investor understand his or her needs better as well as assist an advisor or portfolio manager in managing a client's funds. While it does not guarantee investment success, a policy statement will provide discipline for the investment process and reduce the possibility of making hasty, inappropriate decisions. There are two important reasons for constructing a policy statement: First, it helps the investor decide on realistic investment goals after learning about the financial markets and the risks of investing. Second, it creates a standard by which to judge the performance of the portfolio manager.

Understand and Articulate Realistic Investor Goals

When asked about their investment goal, people often say, "to make a lot of money," or some similar response. Such a goal has two drawbacks: First, it may not be appropriate for the investor, and second, it is too open-ended to provide guidance for specific investments and time frames. Such an objective is well suited for someone going to the racetrack or buying lottery tickets, but it is inappropriate for someone investing funds in financial and real assets for the long term.

An important purpose of writing a policy statement is to help investors understand their own needs, objectives, and investment constraints. As part of this, investors need to learn about financial markets and the risks of investing. This background will help prevent them from making inappropriate investment decisions in the future and will increase the possibility that they will satisfy their specific, measurable financial goals.

Thus, the policy statement helps the investor to specify realistic goals and become more informed about the risks and costs of investing. Market values of assets, whether they be stocks, bonds, or real estate, can fluctuate dramatically. For example, during the October 1987 crash, the Dow Jones Industrial Average (DJIA) fell more than 20 percent in one day; in October 1997, the Dow fell "only" 7 percent. A review of market history shows that it is not unusual for asset prices to decline by 10 percent to 20 percent over several months—for example, the months following the market peak in March 2000, and the major decline when the market reopened after September 11, 2001. Investors will typically focus on a single statistic, such as an 11 percent average annual rate of return on stocks, and expect the market to rise 11 percent every year. Such thinking ignores the risk of stock investing. Part of the process of developing a policy statement is for the investor to become familiar with the risks of investing, because we know that a strong positive relationship exists between risk and return.

One expert in the field recommends that investors should think about the following set of questions and explain their answers as part of the process of constructing a policy statement:

1. What are the real risks of an adverse financial outcome, especially in the short run?

2. What probable emotional reactions will I have to an adverse financial outcome?

3. How knowledgeable am I about investments and markets?

4. What other capital or income sources do I have? How important is this particular portfolio to my overall financial position?

5. What, if any, legal restrictions may affect my investment needs?

6. What, if any, unanticipated consequences of interim fluctuations in portfolio value might affect my investment policy?

Adapted from Charles D. Ellis, *Investment Policy: How to Win the Loser's Game* (Homewood, IL: Dow Jones-Irwin, 1985), 25–26. Reproduced with permission of the McGraw-Hill Companies.

In summary, constructing a policy statement is mainly the investor's responsibility. It is a process whereby investors articulate their realistic needs and goals and become familiar with financial markets and investing risks. Without this information, investors cannot adequately communicate their needs to the portfolio manager. Without this input from investors, the portfolio manager cannot construct a portfolio that will satisfy clients' needs; the result of bypassing this step will most likely be future aggravation, dissatisfaction, and disappointment.

Standards for Evaluating Portfolio Performance

The policy statement also assists in judging the performance of the portfolio manager. Performance cannot be judged without an objective standard; the policy statement provides that objective standard. The portfolio's performance should be compared to guidelines specified in the policy statement, not on the portfolio's overall return. For example, if an investor has a low tolerance for risky investments, the portfolio manager should not be fired simply because the portfolio does not perform as well as the risky S&P 500 stock index. Because risk drives returns, the investor's lower-risk investments, as specified in the investor's policy statement, will probably earn lower returns than if all the investor's funds were placed in the stock market.

The policy statement will typically include a **benchmark portfolio**, or comparison standard. The risk of the benchmark, and the assets included in the benchmark, should agree with the client's risk preferences and investment needs. Notably, both the client and the portfolio manager must agree that the benchmark portfolio reflects the risk preferences and appropriate return requirements of the client. In turn, the investment performance of the portfolio manager should be compared to this benchmark portfolio. For example, an investor who specifies low-risk investments in the policy statement should compare the portfolio manager's performance against a low-risk benchmark portfolio. Likewise, an investor seeking high-risk, high-return investments should compare the portfolio's performance against a high-risk benchmark portfolio.

Because it sets an objective performance standard, the policy statement acts as a starting point for periodic portfolio review and client communication with managers. Questions concerning portfolio performance or the manager's faithfulness to the policy can be addressed in the context of the written policy guidelines. Managers should mainly be judged by whether they consistently followed the client's policy guidelines. The portfolio manager who makes unilateral deviations from policy is not working in the best interests of the client. Therefore, even significant deviations that result in higher portfolio returns can and should be grounds for the manager's dismissal.

Thus, we see the importance of the client constructing the policy statement: The client must first understand his or her own needs before communicating them to the portfolio manager. In turn, the portfolio manager must implement the client's desires by following the investment guidelines. As long as policy is followed, shortfalls in performance should not be a major concern. Remember that the policy statement is designed to impose an investment discipline on the client and portfolio manager. The less knowledgeable they are, the more likely clients are to inappropriately judge the performance of the portfolio manager.

Other Benefits

A sound policy statement helps to protect the client against a portfolio manager's inappropriate investments or unethical behavior. Without clear, written guidance, some managers may consider investing in high-risk investments, hoping to earn a quick return. Such actions are probably counter to the investor's specified needs and risk preferences. Though legal recourse is a possibility against such action, writing a clear and unambiguous policy statement should reduce the possibility of such inappropriate manager behavior.

Just because one specific manager currently manages your account does not mean that person will always manage your funds. As with other positions, your portfolio manager may be promoted or dismissed or take a better job. Therefore, after a while, your funds may come under the management of an individual you do not know and who does not know you. To prevent costly delays during this transition, you can ensure that the new manager "hits the ground running" with a clearly written policy statement. A policy statement should prevent delays in monitoring and rebalancing your portfolio and will help create a seamless transition from one money manager to another.

To sum up, a clearly written policy statement helps avoid future potential problems. When the client clearly specifies his or her needs and desires, the portfolio manager can more effectively construct an appropriate portfolio. The policy statement provides an objective measure for evaluating portfolio performance, helps guard against ethical lapses by the portfolio manager, and aids in the transition between money managers. Therefore, the first step before beginning any investment program, whether it is for an individual or a multibillion-dollar pension fund, is to construct a policy statement.

An appropriate policy statement should satisfactorily answer the following questions:

1. Is the policy carefully designed to meet the specific needs and objectives of this particular investor? (Cookie-cutter or one-size-fits-all policy statements are generally inappropriate.)

2. Is the policy written so clearly and explicitly that a competent stranger could use it to manage the portfolio in conformance with the client's needs? In case of a manager transition, could the new manager use this policy statement to handle your portfolio in accordance with your needs?

3. Would the client have been able to remain committed to the policies during the capital market experiences of the past 60 to 70 years? That is, does the client fully understand investment risks and the need for a disciplined approach to the investment process?

4. Would the portfolio manager have been able to maintain the policies specified over the same period? (Discipline is a two-way street; we do not want the portfolio manager to change strategies because of a disappointing market.)

5. Would the policy, if implemented, have achieved the client's objectives? (Bottom line: Would the policy have worked to meet the client's needs?)

Adapted from Charles D. Ellis, *Investment Policy: How to Win the Loser's Game* (Homewood, IL: Dow Jones-Irwin, 1985), 62. Reproduced with permission of the McGraw-Hill Companies.

---

5   INPUT TO THE POLICY STATEMENT

Before an investor and advisor can construct a policy statement, they need to have an open and frank exchange of information, ideas, fears, and goals. To build a framework for this information-gathering process, the client and advisor need to discuss the client's investment objectives and constraints. To illustrate this framework, we discuss the investment objectives and constraints that may confront "typical" 25-year-old and 65-year-old investors.

Investment Objectives

The investor's **objectives** are his or her investment goals expressed in terms of both risk and returns. The relationship between risk and returns requires that goals not be expressed only in terms of returns. Expressing goals only in terms of returns can lead to inappropriate investment practices by the portfolio manager, such as the use of high-risk investment strategies or account "churning," which involves moving quickly in and out of investments in an attempt to buy low and sell high.

For example, a person may have a stated return goal such as "double my investment in five years." Before such a statement becomes part of the policy statement, the client must become fully informed of investment risks associated with such a goal, including the possibility of loss. *A careful analysis of the client's risk tolerance should precede any discussion of return objectives.* It makes little sense for a person who is risk averse to invest funds in high-risk assets. Investment firms survey clients to gauge their risk tolerance. Sometimes investment magazines or books contain tests that individuals can take to help them evaluate their risk tolerance (see Exhibit 52-4). Subsequently, an advisor will use the results of this evaluation to categorize a client's risk tolerance and suggest an initial asset allocation such as those contained in Exhibit 52-5.

Risk tolerance is more than a function of an individual's psychological makeup; it is affected by other factors, including a person's current insurance coverage and cash reserves. Risk tolerance is also affected by an individual's family situation (for example, marital status and the number and ages of children) and by his or her age. We know that older persons generally have shorter investment time frames within which to make up any losses; they also have years of experience, including living through various market gyrations and "corrections" (a euphemism for downtrends or crashes) that younger people have not experienced or whose effect they do not fully appreciate. Risk tolerance is also influenced by one's current net worth and income expectations. All else being equal, individuals with higher incomes have a greater propensity to undertake risk because their incomes can help cover any shortfall. Likewise, individuals with larger net worths can afford to place some assets in risky investments while the remaining assets provide a cushion against losses.

A person's return objective may be stated in terms of an absolute or a relative percentage return, but it may also be stated in terms of a general goal, such as **capital preservation**, current income, capital appreciation, or total return.

Capital preservation means that investors want to minimize their risk of loss, usually in real terms: They seek to maintain the purchasing power of their investment. In other words, the return needs to be no less than the rate of inflation. Generally, this is a strategy for strongly risk-averse investors or for funds needed in the short-run, such as for next year's tuition payment or a down payment on a house.

Capital appreciation is an appropriate objective when the investors want the portfolio to grow in real terms over time to meet some future need. Under this strategy, growth mainly occurs through capital gains. This is an aggressive strategy for investors willing to take on risk to meet their objective. Generally, longer-term investors seeking to build a retirement or college education fund may have this goal.

When **current income** is the return objective, the investors want the portfolio to concentrate on generating income rather than capital gains. This strategy sometimes suits investors who want to supplement their earnings with income generated by their portfolio to meet their living expenses. Retirees may favor this objective for part of their portfolio to help generate spendable funds.

The objective for the **total return** strategy is similar to that of capital appreciation; namely, the investors want the portfolio to grow over time to meet a future need. Whereas the capital appreciation strategy seeks to do this primarily through capital gains, the total return strategy seeks to increase portfolio value by both capital gains and reinvesting current income. Because the total return strategy has both income and capital gains components, its risk exposure lies between that of the current income and capital appreciation strategies.

Investment Objective: 25-Year-Old What is an appropriate investment objective for our typical 25-year-old investor? Assume he holds a steady job, is a valued employee, has adequate insurance coverage, and has enough money in the bank to provide a cash reserve. Let's also assume that his current long-term, high-priority investment goal is to build a retirement fund. Depending on his risk

EXHIBIT 52-4	How Much Risk Is Right for You?

You've heard the expression "no pain, no gain"? In the investment world, the comparable phrase would be "no risk, no reward."

How you feel about risking your money will drive many of your investment decisions. The risk-comfort scale extends from very conservative (you don't want to risk losing a penny regardless of how little your money earns) to very aggressive (you're willing to risk much of your money for the possibility that it will grow tremendously). As you might guess, most investors' tolerance for risk falls somewhere in between.

If you're unsure of what your level of risk tolerance is, this quiz should help.

1. You win $300 in an office football pool. You: (a) spend it on groceries, (b) purchase lottery tickets, (c) put it in a money market account, (d) buy some stock.

2. Two weeks after buying 100 shares of a $20 stock, the price jumps to over $30. You decide to: (a) buy more stock; it's obviously a winner, (b) sell it and take your profits, (c) sell half to recoup some costs and hold the rest, (d) sit tight and wait for it to advance even more.

3. On days when the stock market jumps way up, you: (a) wish you had invested more, (b) call your financial advisor and ask for recommendations, (c) feel glad you're not in the market because it fluctuates too much, (d) pay little attention.

4. You're planning a vacation trip and can either lock in a fixed room-and-meals rate of $150 per day or book standby and pay anywhere from $100 to $300 per day. You: (a) take the fixed-rate deal, (b) talk to people who have been there about the availability of last-minute accommodations, (c) book standby and also arrange vacation insurance because you're leery of the tour operator, (d) take your chances with standby.

5. The owner of your apartment building is converting the units to condominiums. You can buy your unit for $75,000 or an option on a unit for $15,000. (Units have recently sold for close to $100,000, and prices seem to be going up.) For financing, you'll have to borrow the down payment and pay mortgage and condo fees higher than your present rent. You: (a) buy your unit, (b) buy your unit and look for another to buy, (c) sell the option and arrange to rent the unit yourself, (d) sell the option and move out because you think the conversion will attract couples with small children.

6. You have been working three years for a rapidly growing company. As an executive, you are offered the option of buying up to 2% of company stock: 2,000 shares at $10 a share. Although the company is privately owned (its stock does not trade on the open market), its majority owner has made handsome profits selling three other businesses and intends to sell this one eventually. You: (a) purchase all the shares you can and tell the owner you would invest more if allowed, (b) purchase all the shares, (c) purchase half the shares, (d) purchase a small amount of shares.

7. You go to a casino for the first time. You choose to play: (a) quarter slot machines, (b) $5 minimum-bet roulette, (c) dollar slot machines, (d) $25 minimum-bet blackjack.

8. You want to take someone out for a special dinner in a city that's new to you. How do you pick a place? (a) read restaurant reviews in the local newspaper, (b) ask coworkers if they know of a suitable place, (c) call the only other person you know in this city, who eats out a lot but only recently moved there, (d) visit the city sometime before your dinner to check out the restaurants yourself.

9. The expression that best describes your lifestyle is: (a) no guts, no glory, (b) just do it!, (c) look before you leap, (d) all good things come to those who wait.

10. Your attitude toward money is best described as: (a) a dollar saved is a dollar earned, (b) you've got to spend money to make money, (c) cash and carry only, (d) whenever possible, use other people's money.

SCORING SYSTEM: Score your answers this way: (1) a-1, b-4, c-2, d-3 (2) a-4, b-1, c-3, d-2 (3) a-3, b-4, c-2, d-1 (4) a-2, b-3, c-1, d-4 (5) a-3, b-4, c-2, d-1 (6) a-4, b-3, c-2, d-1 (7) a-1, b-3, c-2, d-4 (8) a-2, b-3, c-4, d-1 (9) a-4, b-3, c-2, d-1 (10) a-2, b-3, c-1, d-4.

What your total score indicates:

▶ 10–17: You're not willing to take chances with your money, even though it means you can't make big gains.

▶ 18–25: You're semi-conservative, willing to take a small chance with enough information.

▶ 26–32: You're semi-aggressive, willing to take chances if you think the odds of earning more are in your favor.

▶ 33–40: You're aggressive, looking for every opportunity to make your money grow, even though in some cases the odds may be quite long. You view money as a tool to make more money.

Source: Adapted from *Feathering Your Nest: The Retirement Planner.* Copyright © 1993 by Lisa Berger. Used by permission of Workman Publishing Company, Inc., New York. All Rights Reserved.

EXHIBIT 52-5	Initial Risk and Investment Goal Categories and Asset Allocations Suggested by Investment Firms

Fidelity Investments Suggested Asset Allocations:

	Cash/ Short-Term	Bonds	Domestic Equities	Foreign Equities
Short-term	100%	0%	0%	0%
Conservative	30	50	20	0
Balanced	10	40	45	5
Growth	5	25	60	10
Aggressive growth	0	15	70	15
Most aggressive	0	0	80	20

Vanguard Investments Suggested Asset Allocations:

	Cash/Short-Term	Bonds	Stocks
Income-oriented	0%	100%	0%
	0	80%	20%
	0	70%	30%
Balanced	0%	60%	40%
	0	50%	50%
	0	40%	60%
Growth	0%	30%	70%
	0	20%	80%
	0	0%	100%

T. Rowe Price Matrix

Non-retirement-goals Matrix

Your Time Horizon

		3–5 years	6–10 years	11+ years
Your Risk Tolerance	Higher	**Strategy 2** 20% cash 40% bonds 40% stocks	**Strategy 3** 10% cash 30% bonds 60% stocks	**Strategy 5** 100% stocks
	Moderate	**Strategy 1** 30% cash 50% bonds 20% stocks	**Strategy 2** 20% cash 40% bonds 40% stocks	**Strategy 4** 20% bonds 80% stocks
	Lower	**All Cash** 100% cash	**Strategy 1** 30% cash 50% bonds 20% stocks	**Strategy 3** 10% cash 30% bonds 60% stocks

Source: Based on data sampled from Personal.Fidelity.com, Vanguard.com, and TRowePrice.com.

preferences, he can select a strategy carrying moderate to high amounts of risk because the income stream from his job will probably grow over time. Further, given his young age and income growth potential, a low-risk strategy, such as capital preservation or current income, is inappropriate for his retirement fund goal; a total return or capital appreciation objective would be most appropriate. Here's a possible objective statement:

> Invest funds in a variety of moderate- to higher-risk investments. The average risk of the equity portfolio should exceed that of a broad stock market index, such as the NYSE stock index. Foreign and domestic equity exposure should range from 80 percent to 95 percent of the total portfolio. Remaining funds should be invested in short- and intermediate-term notes and bonds.

Investment Objective: 65-Year-Old   Assume our typical 65-year-old investor likewise has adequate insurance coverage and a cash reserve. Let's also assume she is retiring this year. This individual will want less risk exposure than the 25-year-old investor, because her earning power from employment will soon be ending; she will not be able to recover any investment losses by saving more out of her paycheck. Depending on her income from social security and a pension plan, she may need some current income from her retirement portfolio to meet living expenses. Given that she can be expected to live an average of another 20 years, she will need protection against inflation. A risk-averse investor will choose a combination of current income and capital preservation strategy; a more risk-tolerant investor will choose a combination of current income and total return in an attempt to have principal growth outpace inflation. Here's an example of such an objective statement:

> Invest in stock and bond investments to meet income needs (from bond income and stock dividends) and to provide for real growth (from equities). Fixed-income securities should comprise 55–65 percent of the total portfolio; of this, 5–15 percent should be invested in short-term securities for extra liquidity and safety. The remaining 35–45 percent of the portfolio should be invested in high-quality stocks whose risk is similar to the S&P 500 index.

More detailed analyses for our 25-year-old and our 65-year-old would make more specific assumptions about the risk tolerance of each, as well as clearly enumerate their investment goals, return objectives, the funds they have to invest at the present, the funds they expect to invest over time, and the benchmark portfolio that will be used to evaluate performance.

Investment Constraints

In addition to the investment objective that sets limits on risk and return, certain other constraints also affect the investment plan. Investment constraints include liquidity needs, an investment time horizon, tax factors, legal and regulatory constraints, and unique needs and preferences.

Liquidity Needs   An asset is **liquid** if it can be quickly converted to cash at a price close to fair market value. Generally, assets are more liquid if many traders are interested in a fairly standardized product. Treasury bills are a highly liquid security; real estate and venture capital are not.

Investors may have liquidity needs that the investment plan must consider. For example, although an investor may have a primary long-term goal, several near-term goals may require available funds. Wealthy individuals with sizable tax obligations need adequate liquidity to pay their taxes without upsetting their investment plan. Some retirement plans may need funds for shorter-term purposes, such as buying a car or a house or making college tuition payments.

Our typical 25-year-old investor probably has little need for liquidity as he focuses on his long-term retirement fund goal. This constraint may change, however, should he face a period of unemployment or should near-term goals, such as honeymoon expenses or a house down payment, enter the picture. Should any changes occur, the investor needs to revise his policy statement and financial plans accordingly.

Our soon-to-be-retired 65-year-old investor has a greater need for liquidity. Although she may receive regular checks from her pension plan and social security, it is not likely that they will equal her working paycheck. She will want some of her portfolio in liquid securities to meet unexpected expenses or bills.

Time Horizon   Time horizon as an investment constraint briefly entered our earlier discussion of near-term and long-term high-priority goals. A close (but not perfect) relationship exists between an investor's time horizon, liquidity needs, and ability to handle risk. Investors with long investment horizons generally require less liquidity and can tolerate greater portfolio risk: less liquidity because the funds are not usually needed for many years; greater risk tolerance because any shortfalls or losses can be overcome by returns earned in subsequent years.

Investors with shorter time horizons generally favor more liquid and less risky investments because losses are harder to overcome during a short time frame.

Because of life expectancies, our 25-year-old investor has a longer investment time horizon than our 65-year-old investor. But, as discussed earlier, this does not mean the 65-year-old should place all her money in short-term CDs; she needs the inflation protection that long-term investments such as common stock can provide. Still, because of the time horizon constraint, the 25-year-old will probably have a greater proportion of his portfolio in equities—including stocks in small firms and international firms—than the 65-year-old.

Tax Concerns   Investment planning is complicated by the tax code; taxes complicate the situation even more if international investments are part of the portfolio. Taxable income from interest, dividends, or rents is taxable at the investor's marginal tax rate. The marginal tax rate is the proportion of the next one dollar in income paid as taxes. Exhibit 52-6 shows the marginal tax rates for different levels of taxable income. As of 2004, the top federal marginal tax rate was 35 percent.

Capital gains or losses arise from asset price changes. They are taxed differently than income. Income is taxed when it is received; capital gains or losses are taxed only when an asset is sold and the gain or loss, relative to its initial cost or **basis**, is realized. **Unrealized capital gains** (or *losses*) reflect the price change in currently held assets that have *not* been sold; the tax liability on unrealized capital gains can be deferred indefinitely. If appreciated assets are passed on to an heir upon the investor's death, the basis of the assets is considered to be their value on the date of the holder's death. The heirs can then sell the assets and pay lower capital gains taxes if they wish. **Realized capital gains** occur when an appreciated asset has been sold; taxes are due on the realized capital gains only. As of 2004, the maximum tax rate on stock dividends and long-term capital gains is 15 percent.

Some find the difference between average and marginal income tax rates confusing. The **marginal tax rate** is the part of each additional dollar in income that is paid as tax. Thus, a married person, filing jointly, with an income of $50,000 will have a marginal tax rate of 15 percent. The 15 percent marginal tax rate should be used to determine after-tax returns on investments.

EXHIBIT 52-6	Individual Marginal Tax Rates, 2004

For updates, go to the IRS Web site, www.irs.gov.

	If Taxable Income		The Tax Is		
		Then			
	Is Over	**But Not Over**	**This Amount**	**Plus This %**	**Of the Excess Over**
Single	$0	$7,150	$0	10%	$0
	$7,150	$29,050	$715	15%	$7,150
	$29,050	$70,350	$4,000	25%	$29,050
	$70,350	$146,750	$14,325	28%	$70,350
	$146,750	$319,100	$35,717	33%	$146,750
	$319,100	—	$92,592	35%	$319,100
Married Filing Jointly	$0	$14,300	$0	10%	$0
	$14,300	$58,100	$1,430	15%	$14,300
	$58,100	$117,250	$8,000	25%	$58,600
	$117,250	$178,650	$22,787	28%	$117,250
	$178,650	$319,100	$39,979	33%	$178,650
	$319,100	—	$86,328	35%	$319,100

The **average tax rate** is simply a person's total tax payment divided by their total income. It represents the average tax paid on each dollar the person earned. From Exhibit 52-6, a married person, filing jointly, will pay $6,785 in tax on a $50,000 income [$1,430 + 0.15($50,000 − $14,300)]. This average tax rate is $6,785/$50,000 or 13.6 percent. Note that the average tax rate is a weighted average of the person's marginal tax rates paid on each dollar of income. The first $14,000 of income has a 10 percent marginal tax rate; the next $36,000 has a 15 percent marginal tax rate:

$$\frac{\$14,000}{\$50,000} \times 0.10 + \frac{\$36,000}{\$50,000} \times 0.15 = 0.136, \text{ or the average tax rate of 13.6 percent}$$

Another tax factor is that some sources of investment income are exempt from federal and state taxes. For example, interest on federal securities, such as Treasury bills, notes, and bonds, is exempt from state taxes. Interest on municipal bonds (bonds issued by a state or other local governing body) is exempt from federal taxes. Further, if investors purchase municipal bonds issued by a local governing body of the state in which they live, the interest is exempt from both state and federal income tax. Thus, high-income individuals have an incentive to purchase municipal bonds to reduce their tax liabilities.

The after-tax return on taxable investment income is

After-Tax Income Return = Pre-Tax Income Return × (1 − Marginal Tax Rate)

Thus, the after-tax return on a taxable bond investment should be compared to that of municipals before deciding which a tax-paying investor should purchase.[1] Alternatively, we could compute a municipal's equivalent taxable yield, which is what a taxable bond investment would have to offer to produce the same after-tax return as the municipal. It is given by

$$\text{Equivalent Taxable Yield} = \frac{\text{Municipal Yield}}{(1 - \text{Marginal Tax Rate})}$$

To illustrate, if an investor is in the 28 percent marginal tax bracket, a taxable investment yield of 8 percent has an after-tax yield of 8 percent $\times$ (1 − 0.28) or 5.76 percent; an equivalent-risk municipal security offering a yield greater than 5.76 percent offers the investor greater after-tax returns. On the other hand, a municipal bond yielding 6 percent has an equivalent taxable yield of 6 percent/(1 − 0.28) = 8.33 percent; to earn more money after taxes, an equivalent-risk taxable investment has to offer a return greater than 8.33 percent.

There are other means of reducing investment tax liabilities. Contributions to an IRA (individual retirement account) may qualify as a tax deduction if certain income limits are met. Even without that deduction, taxes on any investment returns of an IRA, including any income, are deferred until the funds are withdrawn from the account. Any funds withdrawn from an IRA are taxable as current income, regardless of whether growth in the IRA occurs as a result of capital gains, income, or both. For this reason, to minimize taxes advisors recommend investing in stocks in taxable accounts and bonds in tax-deferred accounts such as IRAs. When funds are withdrawn from a tax-deferred account such as a regular IRA, assets are taxed (at most) at a 35 percent income tax rate (Exhibit 52-6)—even if the source of the stock return is primarily capital gains. In a taxable account, capital gains are taxed at the maximum 15 percent capital gains rate.

The benefits of deferring taxes can dramatically compound over time. For example, $1000 invested in an IRA at a tax-deferred rate of 8 percent grows to $10,062.66 over thirty years; in a taxable account (assuming a 28 percent marginal (federal + state) tax rate), the funds would grow to only $5,365.91. After thirty years, the value of the tax-deferred investment has grown to be nearly twice as large as the taxable investment.

With various stipulations, as of 2005, tax-deductible contributions of up to $4,000 (to be raised to $5,000 by 2008) can be made to a traditional IRA. A Roth IRA contribution is *not* tax deductible and contribution limits mirror those of the traditional IRA. The returns in a Roth IRA will grow on a tax-deferred basis and can be withdrawn, tax-free, if the funds are invested for at least five years and are withdrawn after the investor reaches age $59\frac{1}{2}$.[2]

For money you intend to invest in some type of IRA, the advantage of the Roth IRA's tax-free withdrawals will outweigh the tax-deduction benefit from the regular IRA—unless you expect your tax rate when the funds are withdrawn to be substantially less than when you initially invest the funds. Let's illustrate this with a hypothetical example.

Suppose you are considering investing $2,000 in either a regular or Roth IRA. Let's assume for simplicity that your combined federal and state marginal tax rate is 28 percent and that, over your 20-year time horizon, your $2,000

---

[1] Realized capital gains on municipal securities are taxed, as are all other capital gains; similarly for capital losses. Only the income from municipals is exempt from federal income tax.

[2] Earlier tax-free withdrawals are possible if the funds are to be used for educational purposes or first-time home purchases.

investment will grow to $20,000, tax-deferred in either account; this represents an average annual return of 12.2 percent.

In a Roth IRA, no tax is deducted when the $2,000 is invested; in a regular IRA, the $2,000 investment is tax-deductible and will lower your tax bill by $560 (0.28 × $2,000).

Thus, in a Roth IRA, only $2,000 is assumed to be invested; for a regular IRA, both the $2,000 and the $560 tax savings are assumed to be invested. We will assume the $560 is invested at an after-tax rate of 12.2% × (1 − 0.28) = 8.8 percent. After 20 years, this amount will grow to $3,025. The calculations in Exhibit 52-7 show that at the end of the 20-year time horizon the Roth IRA will give you more after-tax dollars unless you believe your tax bracket will be lower then *and you invest the regular IRA tax savings*.

Another tax-deferred investment is the cash value of life insurance contracts; these accumulate tax-free until the funds are withdrawn. Also, employers may offer 401(k) or 403(b) plans, which allow the employee to reduce taxable income by making tax-deferred investments. Many times employee contributions are matched by employer donations (up to a specified limit), thus allowing the employees to double their investment with little risk.

At times investors face a trade-off between taxes and diversification needs. If entrepreneurs concentrate much of their wealth in equity holdings of their firm, or if employees purchase substantial amounts of their employer's stock through payroll deduction plans during their working life, their portfolios may contain a large amount of unrealized capital gains. In addition, the risk position of such a portfolio may be quite high because it is concentrated in a single company. The decision to sell some of the company stock in order to diversify the portfolio's risk by reinvesting the proceeds in other assets must be balanced against the resulting tax liability.

EXHIBIT 52-7	Comparing the Regular versus Roth IRA Returns	
	Regular IRA	**Roth IRA**
Invested funds:	$2,000 + $560 tax savings on the tax-deductible IRA investment	$2,000 (no tax deduction)
Time horizon:	20 years	20 years
Rate of return assumption:	12.2 percent tax-deferred on the IRA investment; 8.8 percent on invested tax savings (represents the after-tax return on 12.2 percent)	12.2 percent tax-deferred on the IRA investment
Funds available after 20 years (taxes ignored)	$20,000 (pre-tax) from IRA investment; $3,025 (after-tax) from invested tax savings	$20,000 from IRA investment
Funds available after 20 years, 15 percent marginal tax rate at retirement	$20,000 less tax (0.15 × $20,000) plus $3,025 from invested tax savings equals $20,025	$20,000
Funds available after 20 years, 28 percent marginal tax rate at retirement	$20,000 less tax (0.28 × $20,000) plus $3,025 from invested tax savings equals $17,425	$20,000
Funds available after 20 years, 40 percent marginal tax rate at retirement	$20,000 less tax (0.40 × $20,000) plus $3,025 from invested tax savings equals $15,025	$20,000

Our typical 25-year-old investor probably is in a fairly low tax bracket, so detailed tax planning and tax-exempt income, such as that available from municipals, will not be major concerns. Nonetheless, he should still invest as much as possible into such tax-deferred plans as IRAs or 401(k)s for the retirement portion of his portfolio. If other funds are available for investment, they should be allocated based on his shorter- and longer-term investment goals.

Our 65-year-old investor may face a different situation. If she had been in a high tax bracket prior to retiring—and therefore has sought tax-exempt income and tax-deferred investments—her situation may change shortly after retirement. After her retirement, without large regular paychecks, the need for tax-deferred investments or tax-exempt income becomes less. Taxable income may then offer higher after-tax yields than tax-exempt municipals if her tax bracket is lower. If her employer's stock is a large component of her retirement account, she must make careful decisions regarding the need to diversify versus the cost of realizing large capital gains (in her lower tax bracket).

Legal and Regulatory Factors   Both the investment process and the financial markets are highly regulated and subject to numerous laws. At times, these legal and regulatory factors constrain the investment strategies of individuals and institutions.

For example, funds removed from a regular IRA, Roth IRA, or 401(k) plan before age $59\frac{1}{2}$ are taxable and subject to an additional 10 percent withdrawal penalty. You may also be familiar with the tag line in many bank CD advertisements—"substantial interest penalty upon early withdrawal." Regulations and rules such as these may make such investments unattractive for investors with substantial liquidity needs in their portfolios.

Regulations can also constrain the investment choices available to someone in a fiduciary role. A *fiduciary*, or trustee, supervises an investment portfolio of a third party, such as a trust account or discretionary account.[3] The fiduciary must make investment decisions in accordance with the owner's wishes; a properly written policy statement assists this process. In addition, trustees of a trust account must meet the prudent-man standard, which means that they must invest and manage the funds as a prudent person would manage his or her own affairs. Notably, the prudent-man standard is based on the composition of the entire portfolio, not each individual asset.[4]

All investors must respect certain laws, such as insider trading prohibitions against the purchase and sale of securities on the basis of important information that is not publicly known. Typically, the people possessing such private, or insider, information are the firm's managers, who have a fiduciary duty to their shareholders. Security transactions based on access to insider information violates the fiduciary trust the shareholders have placed with management because the managers seek personal financial gain from their privileged position as agents for the shareholders.

For our typical 25-year-old investor, legal and regulatory matters will be of little concern, with the possible exception of insider trading laws and the penalties associated with early withdrawal of funds from tax-deferred retirement accounts. Should he seek a financial advisor to assist him in constructing a financial plan, that advisor would have to obey the regulations pertinent to a client-advisor relationship. Similar concerns confront our 65-year-old investor. In addition, as a

---

[3] A discretionary account is one in which the fiduciary, many times a financial planner or stockbroker, has the authority to purchase and sell assets in the owner's portfolio without first receiving the owner's approval.

[4] As we will discuss in Reading 53, it is sometimes wise to hold assets that are individually risky in the context of a well-diversified portfolio, even if the investor is strongly risk averse.

retiree, if she wants to do estate planning and set up trust accounts, she should seek legal and tax advice to ensure her plans are properly implemented.

Unique Needs and Preferences   This category covers the individual and sometimes idiosyncratic concerns of each investor. Some investors may want to exclude certain investments from their portfolio solely on the basis of personal preference or for social consciousness reasons. For example, they may request that no firms that manufacture or sell tobacco, alcohol, pornography, or environmentally harmful products be included in their portfolio. Some mutual funds screen according to this type of social responsibility criterion.

Another example of a personal constraint is the time and expertise a person has for managing his or her portfolio. Busy executives may prefer to relax during nonworking hours and let a trusted advisor manage their investments. Retirees, on the other hand, may have the time but believe they lack the expertise to choose and monitor investments, so they also may seek professional advice.

In addition, a business owner with a large portion of her wealth—and emotion—tied up in her firm's stock may be reluctant to sell even when it may be financially prudent to do so and then reinvest the proceeds for diversification purposes. Further, if the stock holdings are in a private company, it may be difficult to find a buyer unless shares are sold at a discount from their fair market value. Because each investor is unique, the implications of this final constraint differ for each person; there is no "typical" 25-year-old or 65-year-old investor. Each individual will have to decide—and then communicate specific goals in a well-constructed policy statement.

6   CONSTRUCTING THE POLICY STATEMENT

As we have seen, the policy statement allows the investor to communicate his or her objectives (risk and return) and constraints (liquidity, time horizon, tax, legal and regulatory, and unique needs and preferences). This communication gives the advisor a better chance of implementing an investment strategy that will satisfy the investor. Even if an advisor is not used, each investor needs to take this first important step of the investment process and develop a financial plan to guide the investment strategy. To do without a plan or to plan poorly is to place the success of the financial plan in jeopardy.

General Guidelines

Constructing a policy statement is the investor's responsibility, but investment advisors often assist in the process. The following lists of recommendations for both the investor and the advisor provide guidelines for good policy statement construction.

In the process of constructing a policy statement, investors should think about the following set of questions and be able to explain their answers:

1. What are the real risks of an adverse financial outcome, especially in the short run?

2. What probable emotional reactions will I have to an adverse financial outcome?

3. How knowledgeable am I about investments and markets?

4. What other capital or income sources do I have? How important is this particular portfolio to my overall financial position?

5. What, if any, legal restrictions may affect my investment needs?

6. What, if any, unanticipated consequences of interim fluctuations in portfolio value might affect my investment policy?

Adapted from Charles D. Ellis, *Investment Policy: How to Win the Loser's Game.* Homewood IL: Dow Jones-Irwin, 1985, pp. 25–26.

In assisting an investor in the policy statement process, an advisor should ensure that the policy statement satisfactorily answers the following questions:

1. Is the policy carefully designed to meet the specific needs and objectives of this particular investor? (Cookie-cutter or one-size-fits-all policy statements are generally inappropriate.)

2. Is the policy written so clearly and explicitly that a competent stranger could manage the portfolio in conformance with the client's needs? In case of a manager transition, could the new manager use this policy to handle the portfolio in accordance with the client's needs?

3. Would the client have been able to remain committed to the policies during the capital market experiences of the past 60 to 70 years? That is, does the client fully understand investment risks and the need for a disciplined approach to the investment process?

4. Would the portfolio manager have been able to maintain fidelity to the policy over the same period? (Discipline is a two-way street; we do not want the portfolio manager to change strategies because of a disappointing market.)

5. Would the policy, if implemented, achieve the client's objectives? (Bottom line: would the policy have worked to meet the client's needs?)

Adapted from Charles D. Ellis, *Investment Policy: How to Win the Loser's Game.* Homewood IL: Dow Jones-Irwin, 1985, p. 62.

Some Common Mistakes

When constructing their policy statements, participants in employer-sponsored retirement plans need to realize that through such plans 30–40 percent of their retirement funds may be invested in their employer's stock. Having so much money invested in one asset violates diversification principles and could be costly. To put this in context, most mutual funds are limited by law to having no more than 5 percent of their assets in any one company's stock; a firm's pension plan can invest no more than 10 percent of their funds in its own stock. As noted by Schulz (1996), individuals are unfortunately doing what government regulations prevent many institutional investors from doing. In addition, some studies point out that the average stock allocation in retirement plans is lower than it should be to allow for growth of principal over time.

Another consideration is the issue of stock trading. A number of studies by Barber and Odean (1999, 2000, 2001) and Odean (1998, 1999) have shown that many individual investors trade stocks too often (driving up commissions), sell stocks with gains too early (prior to further price increases), and hold onto losers too long (as the price continues to fall). These results are especially true for men and online traders.

Investors, in general, seem to neglect that important first step to achieve financial success: they do not plan for the future. Studies of retirement plans discussed by Ruffenach (2001) and Clements (1997a, b, c) show that Americans are not saving enough to finance their retirement years and they are not planning sufficiently for what will happen to their savings after they retire. Around 25 percent of workers have saved less than $50,000 for their retirement and 60 percent of workers surveyed confessed they were "behind schedule" in planning and saving for retirement.

7   THE IMPORTANCE OF ASSET ALLOCATION

A major reason why investors develop policy statements is to determine an overall investment strategy. Though a policy statement does not indicate which specific securities to purchase and when they should be sold, it should provide guidelines as to the asset classes to include and the relative proportions of the investor's funds to invest in each class. How the investor divides funds into different asset classes is the process of asset allocation. Rather than present strict percentages, asset allocation is usually expressed in ranges. This allows the investment manager some freedom, based on his or her reading of capital market trends, to invest toward the upper or lower end of the ranges. For example, suppose a policy statement requires that common stocks be 60 percent to 80 percent of the value of the portfolio and that bonds should be 20 percent to 40 percent of the portfolio's value. If a manager is particularly bullish about stocks, she will increase the allocation of stocks toward the 80 percent upper end of the equity range and decrease bonds toward the 20 percent lower end of the bond range. Should she be more optimistic about bonds, that manager may shift the allocation closer to 40 percent of the funds invested in bonds with the remainder in equities.

A review of historical data and empirical studies provides strong support for the contention that the asset allocation decision is a critical component of the portfolio management process. In general, there are four decisions involved in constructing an investment strategy:

▶ What asset classes should be considered for investment?

▶ What policy weights should be assigned to each eligible asset class?

▶ What are the allowable allocation ranges based on policy weights?

▶ What specific securities or funds should be purchased for the portfolio?

The asset allocation decision comprises the first two points. How important is the asset allocation decision to an investor? In a word, *very*. Several studies by Ibbotson and Kaplan (2000); Brinson, Hood, and Beebower (1986); and Brinson, Singer, and Beebower (1991) have examined the effect of the normal policy weights on investment performance, using data from both pension funds and mutual funds, from periods of time extending from the early 1970s to the late 1990s. The studies all found similar results: About 90 percent of a fund's returns over time can be explained by its target asset allocation policy. Exhibit 52-8 shows

EXHIBIT 52-8	Time-Series Regression of Monthly Fund Return versus Fund Policy Return: One Mutual Fund, April 1988–March 1998

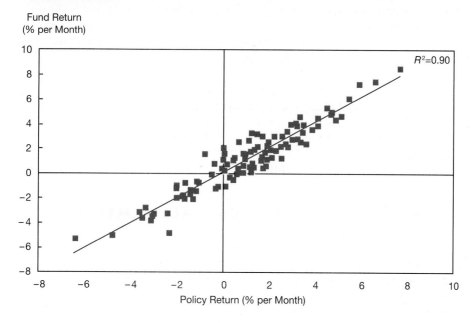

Fund Return (% per Month)

$R^2 = 0.90$

Policy Return (% per Month)

Note: The sample fund's policy allocations among the general asset classes were 52.4 percent U.S. large-cap stocks, 9.8 percent U.S. small-cap stocks, 3.2 percent non-U.S. stocks, 20.9 percent U.S. bonds, and 13.7 percent cash.

Source: Copyright 2000, Association for Investment Management and Research. Reproduced and republished from "Does Asset Allocation Policy Explain 40, 90 or 100 Percent of Performance?" in the *Financial Analysts Journal,* January/February 2000, with permission from the CFA Institute. All Rights Reserved.

the relationship between returns on the target or policy portfolio allocation and actual returns on a sample mutual fund.

Rather than looking at just one fund and how the target asset allocation determines its returns, some studies have looked at how much the asset allocation policy affects returns on a variety of funds with different target weights. For example, Ibbotson and Kaplan (2000) found that, across a sample of funds, about 40 percent of the difference in fund returns is explained by differences in asset allocation policy. And what does asset allocation tell us about the *level* of a particular fund's returns? The studies by Brinson and colleagues (1986, 1991) and Ibbotson and Kaplan (2000) answered that question as well. They divided the policy return (what the fund return would have been had it been invested in indexes at the policy weights) by the actual fund return (which includes the effects of varying from the policy weights and security selection). Thus, a fund that was passively invested at the target weights would have a ratio value of 1.0, or 100 percent. A fund managed by someone with skill in market timing (for moving in and out of asset classes) and security selection would have a ratio less than 1.0 (or less than 100 percent); the manager's skill would result in a policy return less than the actual fund return. The studies showed the opposite: The policy return/actual return ratio averaged over 1.0, showing that asset allocation explains slightly more than 100 percent of the level of a fund's returns. Because of market efficiency, fund managers practicing market timing and security selection, on average, have difficulty surpassing passively invested index returns, after taking into account the expenses and fees of investing.

Thus, asset allocation is a very important decision. Across all funds, the asset allocation decision explains an average of 40 percent of the variation in fund returns. For a single fund, asset allocation explains 90 percent of the fund's variation in returns over time and slightly more than 100 percent of the average fund's level of return.

Good investment managers may add some value to portfolio performance, but the major source of investment return—and risk—over time is the asset allocation decision (Brown, 2000).

Real Investment Returns after Taxes and Costs

Exhibit 52-9 provides additional historical perspectives on returns. It indicates how an investment of $1 would have grown over the 1981–2004 period and, using fairly conservative assumptions, examines how investment returns are affected by taxes and inflation.

Focusing first on stocks, funds invested in 1981 in the Dow Jones Wilshire 5000 stocks would have averaged a 12.36 percent annual return by the end of

EXHIBIT 52-9	The Effect of Taxes and Inflation on Investment Returns: 1981–2004

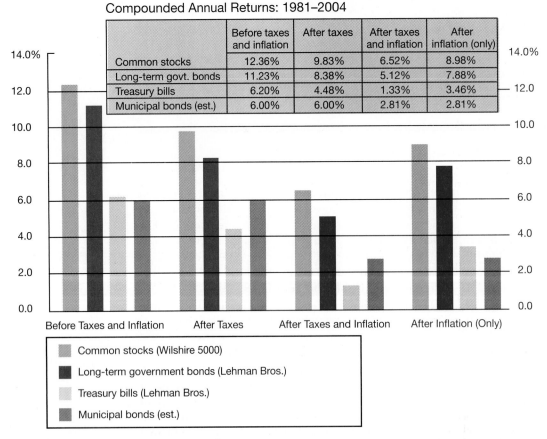

Compounded Annual Returns: 1981–2004

	Before taxes and inflation	After taxes	After taxes and inflation	After inflation (only)
Common stocks	12.36%	9.83%	6.52%	8.98%
Long-term govt. bonds	11.23%	8.38%	5.12%	7.88%
Treasury bills	6.20%	4.48%	1.33%	3.46%
Municipal bonds (est.)	6.00%	6.00%	2.81%	2.81%

Common stocks (Wilshire 5000)
Long-term government bonds (Lehman Bros.)
Treasury bills (Lehman Bros.)
Municipal bonds (est.)

Assumptions: 28 percent tax rate on income; 20 percent on price change. Compound inflation rate was 3.1 percent for full period.
Source: Computations by authors, using data indicated.

2004. Unfortunately, this return is unrealistic because if the funds were invested over time, taxes would have to be paid and inflation would erode the real purchasing power of the invested funds.

Except for tax-exempt investors and tax-deferred accounts, annual tax payments reduce investment returns. Incorporating taxes into the analysis lowers the after-tax average annual return of a stock investment to 9.83 percent.

But the major reduction in the value of our investment is caused by inflation. The real after-tax average annual return on a stock over this time frame was only 6.52 percent, which is quite a bit less than our initial unadjusted 12.36 percent return!

This example shows the long-run impact of taxes and inflation on the real value of a stock portfolio. For bonds and bills, however, the results in Exhibit 52-9 show something even more surprising. After adjusting for taxes, long-term bonds maintained their purchasing power; T-bills barely provided value in real terms. One dollar invested in long-term government bonds in 1981 gave the investor an annual average after-tax real return of 5.12 percent. An investment in Treasury bills earned an average rate of only 1.33 percent after taxes and inflation. Municipal bonds, because of the protection they offer from taxes, earned an average annual real return of almost 3.00 percent during this time.

This historical analysis demonstrates that, for taxable investments, a reasonable way to maintain purchasing power over time when investing in financial assets is to invest in common stocks. Put another way, an asset allocation decision for a taxable portfolio that does not include a substantial commitment to common stocks makes it difficult for the portfolio to maintain real value over time.[5]

Notably, the fourth column, labeled "After inflation (only)," is more encouraging since it refers to results for a tax-free retirement account that is only impacted by inflation. These results should encourage investors to take advantage of such opportunities.

Returns and Risks of Different Asset Classes

By focusing on returns, we have ignored its partner—risk. Assets with higher long-term returns have these returns to compensate for their risk. Exhibit 52-10 illustrates returns (unadjusted for costs and taxes) for several asset classes over time. As expected, the higher returns available from equities (both large cap and small cap) come at the cost of higher risk. This is precisely why investors need a policy statement and why the investor and manager must understand the capital markets and have a disciplined approach to investing. Safe Treasury bills will sometimes outperform equities, and, because of their higher risk, common stocks sometimes lose significant value. These are times when undisciplined and uneducated investors become frustrated, sell their stocks at a loss, and vow never to invest in equities again. In contrast, these are times when disciplined investors stick to their investment plan and position their portfolios for the next bull market.[6] By holding

---

[5] Of course other equity-oriented investments, such as venture capital or real estate, may also provide inflation protection after adjusting for portfolio costs and taxes. Future studies of the performance of Treasury inflation-protected securities (TIPs) will likely show their usefulness in protecting investors from inflation as well.

[6] Newton's law of gravity seems to work two ways in financial markets. What goes up must come down; it also appears over time that what goes down may came back up. Contrarian investors and some "value" investors use this concept of reversion to the mean to try to outperform the indexes over time.

EXHIBIT 52-10	Summary Statistics of Annual Returns, 1984–2003, U.S. Securities		
	Geometric Mean (%)	Arithmetic Mean (%)	Standard Deviation (%)
Large company stocks (S&P 500)	13.33	14.74	17.92
Small company stocks (S&P SmallCap 600)	10.82	12.86	21.21
Government bonds (Lehman Brothers)	9.07	9.20	5.33
Corporate bonds (Lehman Brothers)	10.07	10.24	5.99
Intermediate-term corporate bonds (Lehman Brothers)	9.25	9.34	4.37
Intermediate-term government bonds (Lehman Brothers)	8.43	8.50	3.84
30-day Treasury bill	5.23	5.23	0.64
U.S. inflation	3.01	3.01	0.81

Source: Calculations by authors, using data noted.

on to their stocks and perhaps purchasing more at depressed prices, the equity portion of the portfolio will experience a substantial increase in the future.

The asset allocation decision determines to a great extent both the returns and the volatility of the portfolio. Exhibit 52-10 indicates that stocks are riskier than bonds or T-bills. Exhibit 52-11 shows that stocks have sometimes earned returns lower than those of T-bills for extended periods of time. Sticking with an investment policy and riding out the difficult times can earn attractive long-term rates of return.[7]

EXHIBIT 52-11	Higher Returns Offered by Equities over Long Time Periods Time Frame: 1934–2003
Length of Holding Period (calendar years)	Percentage of Periods That Stock Returns Trailed T-Bill Returns*
1	35.7%
5	18.2
10	11.5
20	0.0
30	0.0

*Price change plus reinvested income
Source: Author calculations.

---

[7] The added benefits of diversification—combining different asset classes in the portfolio—may reduce overall portfolio risk without harming potential return. The topic of diversification is discussed in Reading 53.

One popular way to measure risk is to examine the variability of returns over time by computing a standard deviation or variance of annual rates of return for an asset class. This measure, which is contained in Exhibit 52-10, indicates that stocks are risky and T-bills are relatively safe. Another intriguing measure of risk is the probability of *not* meeting your investment return objective. From this perspective, the results in Exhibit 52-11 show that if the investor has a long time horizon (i.e., approaching 20 years), the risk of equities is small and that of T-bills is large because of their differences in long-term expected returns.

Asset Allocation Summary

A carefully constructed policy statement determines the types of assets that should be included in a portfolio. The asset allocation decision, not the selection of specific stocks and bonds, determines most of the portfolio's returns over time. Although seemingly risky, investors seeking capital appreciation, income, or even capital preservation over long time periods will do well to include a sizable allocation to the equity portion in their portfolio. As noted in this section, a strategy's risk may depend on the investor's goals and time horizon. As demonstrated, investing in T-bills may be a riskier strategy than investing in common stocks due to reinvestment risks and the risk of not meeting long-term investment return goals after considering inflation and taxes.

Asset Allocation and Cultural Differences   Thus far, our analysis has focused on U.S. investors. Non-U.S. investors make their asset allocation decisions in much the same manner; but because they face different social, economic, political, and tax environments, their allocation decisions differ from those of U.S. investors. Exhibit 52-12 shows the equity allocations of pension funds in several countries. As shown, the equity allocations vary dramatically from 79 percent in Hong Kong to 37 percent in Japan and only 8 percent in Germany.

National differences can explain much of the divergent portfolio strategies. Of these six nations, the average age of the population is highest in Germany and Japan and lowest in the United States and the United Kingdom, which helps explain the greater use of equities in the latter countries. Government privatization programs during the 1980s in the United Kingdom encouraged equity ownership among individual and institutional investors. In Germany, regulations

EXHIBIT 52-12	Equity Allocations in Pension Fund Portfolios
Country	**Percentage in Equities**
Hong Kong	79
United Kingdom	78
Ireland	68
United States	58
Japan	37
Germany	8

Source: Copyright 1998, Association for Investment Management and Research. Reproduced and republished from "Client Expectations and the Demand to Minimize Downside Risk" from the seminar proceedings *Asset Allocation in a Changing World,* 1998, with permission from the CFA Institute. All Rights Reserved.

prevent insurance firms from having more than 20 percent of their assets in equities. Both Germany and Japan have banking sectors that invest privately in firms and whose officers sit on corporate boards. Since 1980, the cost of living in the United Kingdom has increased at a rate about two times that of Germany; this inflationary bias in the U.K. economy favors equities in U.K. asset allocations. Exhibit 52-13 shows the positive relationship between the level of inflation in a country and its pension fund allocation to equity. These results indicate that the general economic environment, as well as demographics, has an effect on the asset allocation in a country.

The need to invest in equities for portfolio growth is less in Germany, where workers receive generous state pensions. Germans tend to show a cultural aversion to the stock market: Many Germans are risk averse and consider stock investing a form of gambling. Although this attitude is changing, the German stock market is rather illiquid, and Gumbel (1995) noted that only a handful of stocks account for 50 percent of total stock trading volume. New legislation that encourages 401(k)-like plans in Germany may encourage citizens to invest more in equities.

Other Organization for Economic Cooperation and Development (OECD) countries place regulatory restrictions on institutional investors. As noted by Witschi (1998) and Chernoff (1996), pension funds in Austria must have at least 50 percent of their assets in bank deposits or schilling-denominated bonds. Belgium limits pension funds to a minimum 15 percent investment in government bonds. Finland places a 5 percent limit on investments outside its borders by pension funds, and French pension funds must invest a minimum of 34 percent in public debt instruments.

Asset allocation policy and strategy are determined in the context of an investor's objectives and constraints. Among the factors that explain differences in investor behavior across countries, however, are their political and economic environments.

EXHIBIT 52-13	Asset Allocation and Inflation for Different Countries' Equity Allocation as of December 1997; Average Inflation Measured Over 1980–1997

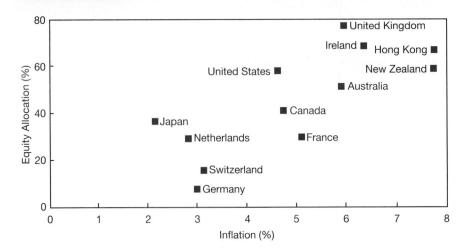

THE INTERNET

Investments Online

Many inputs go into an investment policy statement as an investor maps out his or her objectives and constraints. Some inputs and helpful information are available in the following Web sites. Many of the sites mentioned contain important information and insights about asset allocation decisions, as well.

www.ssa.gov Information on a person's expected retirement funds from Social Security can be obtained by using the Social Security Administration's Web site.

www.ibbotson.com Ibbotson is the source of much data and analysis that is helpful to the investor education and asset allocation process. Many professional financial planners make use of Ibbotson's data and education resources.

www.mfea.com/InvestmentStrategies/Calculators/default.asp contains links to calculators on Web sites of mutual fund families.

Sites with information and sample Monte Carlo simulations for spending plans in retirement include: www.financialengines.com, www.troweprice.com (after getting to the individual investor page, click on investment planning and tools, then tools, and calculators, investment planning tools, then investment strategy planner); www3.troweprice.com/ric/RIC/ (for a retirement income calculator), and www.decisioneering.com.

Many professional organizations have Web sites for use by their members, those interested in seeking professional finance designations, and those interested in seeking advice from a professional financial adviser. These sites include:

www.cfainstitute.org CFA Institute awards the CFA (Chartered Financial Analyst) designation. This site provides information about the CFA designation, CFA Institute publications, investor education, and various Internet resources.

www.theamericancollege.edu This is the Web site for The American College, which is the training arm of the insurance industry. The American College offers the CLU and ChFC designations, which are typically earned by insurance professionals.

www.cfp.net The Certified Financial Planner Board of Standards home page. Contains links to find a CFP™ mark holder and other information about the financial planning profession.

www.napfa.org This is the home page for the National Association of Personal Financial Advisors. This is the trade group for fee-only financial planners. Fee-only planners do not sell products on commission, or, should they recommend a commission-generating product, they pass the commission on to the investor. This site features press releases, finding a fee-only planner in your area, a list of financial resources on the Web, and position openings in the financial planning field.

www.fpanet.org The Financial Planning Association's Web site. The site offers features and topics of interest to financial planners including information on earning the CFP designation and receiving the *Journal of Financial Planning*.

www.aset.org The home page of the American Saving Education Council.

SUMMARY

▶ In this reading, we saw that investors need to prudently manage risk within the context of their investment goals and preferences. Income, spending, and investing behavior will change over a person's lifetime.

▶ We reviewed the importance of developing an investment policy statement before implementing a serious investment plan. By forcing investors to examine their needs, risk tolerance, and familiarity with the capital markets, policy statements help investors correctly identify appropriate objectives and constraints. In addition, the policy statement becomes a standard by which to judge the performance of the portfolio manager.

▶ We also reviewed the importance of the asset allocation decision in determining long-run portfolio investment returns and risks. Because the asset allocation decision follows setting the objectives and constraints, it is clear that the success of the investment program depends on the first step, the construction of the policy statement.

AN INTRODUCTION TO PORTFOLIO MANAGEMENT

by Frank K. Reilly and Keith C. Brown

LEARNING OUTCOMES

The candidate should be able to:

a. define risk aversion and discuss evidence that suggests that individuals are generally risk averse;

b. list the basic assumptions behind the Markowitz Portfolio Theory;

c. compute the expected return for an individual investment and for a portfolio;

d. compute the variance and standard deviation for an individual investment;

e. compute the covariance of rates of return, and show how it is related to the correlation coefficient;

f. list the components of the portfolio standard deviation formula, and explain which component is most important to consider when adding an investment to a portfolio;

g. describe the efficient frontier and explain the implications for incremental returns as an investor assumes more risk;

h. define optimal portfolio and show how each investor may have a different optimal portfolio.

INTRODUCTION 1

One of the major advances in the investment field during the past few decades has been the recognition that the creation of an optimum investment portfolio is not simply a matter of combining numerous unique individual securities that have desirable risk-return characteristics. Specifically, it has been shown that an investor must consider the relationship *among* the investments to build an optimum portfolio that will meet investment objectives. The recognition of what is important in creating a portfolio was demonstrated in the derivation of portfolio theory.

In this reading we explain portfolio theory step by step. We introduce the basic portfolio risk formula for combining different assets. Once you understand this formula and its implications, you will understand not only *why* you should diversify your portfolio but also *how* you should diversify.

2   SOME BACKGROUND ASSUMPTIONS

Before presenting portfolio theory, we need to clarify some general assumptions of the theory. This includes not only what we mean by an *optimum portfolio* but also what we mean by the terms *risk aversion* and *risk*.

One basic assumption of portfolio theory is that as an investor you want to maximize the returns from your total set of investments for a given level of risk. To adequately deal with such an assumption, certain ground rules must be laid. First, your portfolio should *include all of your assets and liabilities,* not only your stocks or even your marketable securities but also such items as your car, house, and less marketable investments such as coins, stamps, art, antiques, and furniture. The full spectrum of investments must be considered because the returns from all these investments interact, and *this relationship among the returns for assets in the portfolio is important.* Hence, a good portfolio is not simply a collection of individually good investments.

Risk Aversion

Portfolio theory also assumes that investors are basically **risk averse**, meaning that, given a choice between two assets with equal rates of return, they will select the asset with the lower level of risk. Evidence that most investors are risk averse is that they purchase various types of insurance, including life insurance, car insurance, and health insurance. Buying insurance basically involves an outlay of a given known amount to guard against an uncertain, possibly larger, outlay in the future. Further evidence of risk aversion is the difference in promised yield (the required rate of return) for different grades of bonds that supposedly have different degrees of credit risk. Specifically, the promised yield on corporate bonds increases from AAA (the lowest risk class) to AA to A, and so on, indicating that investors require a higher rate of return to accept higher risk.

This does not imply that everybody is risk averse, or that investors are completely risk averse regarding all financial commitments. The fact is, not everybody buys insurance for everything. Some people have no insurance against anything, either by choice or because they cannot afford it. In addition, some individuals buy insurance related to some risks such as auto accidents or illness, but they also buy lottery tickets and gamble at race tracks or in casinos, where it is known that the expected returns are negative (which means that participants are willing to pay for the excitement of the risk involved). This combination of risk preference and risk aversion can be explained by an attitude toward risk that depends on the amount of money involved. Researchers such as Friedman and Savage (1948) speculate that this is the case for people who like to gamble for small amounts (in lotteries or slot machines) but buy insurance to protect themselves against large losses such as fire or accidents.

While recognizing such attitudes, our basic assumption is that most investors committing large sums of money to developing an investment portfolio are risk averse. Therefore, we expect a positive relationship between expected return and expected risk. Notably, this is also what we generally find in terms of historical results—that is, most studies find a positive relationship between the rates of return on various assets and their measures of risk.

Definition of Risk

Although there is a difference in the specific definitions of *risk* and *uncertainty,* for our purposes and in most financial literature the two terms are used interchangeably. For most investors, *risk* means *the uncertainty of future outcomes.* An alternative definition might be *the probability of an adverse outcome.* In our subsequent discussion of portfolio theory, we will consider several measures of risk that are used when developing and applying the theory.

MARKOWITZ PORTFOLIO THEORY   3

In the early 1960s, the investment community talked about risk, but there was no specific measure for the term. To build a portfolio model, however, investors had to quantify their risk variable. The basic portfolio model was developed by Harry Markowitz (1952, 1959), who derived the expected rate of return for a portfolio of assets and an expected risk measure. Markowitz showed that the variance of the rate of return was a meaningful measure of portfolio risk under a reasonable set of assumptions, and he derived the formula for computing the variance of a portfolio. This portfolio variance formula not only indicated the importance of diversifying investments to reduce the total risk of a portfolio but also showed *how* to effectively diversify. The Markowitz model is based on several assumptions regarding investor behavior.

1. Investors consider each investment alternative as being represented by a probability distribution of expected returns over some holding period.
2. Investors maximize one-period **expected utility**, and their utility curves demonstrate **diminishing marginal utility** of wealth.
3. Investors estimate the risk of the portfolio on the basis of the variability of expected returns.
4. Investors base decisions solely on expected return and risk, so their utility curves are a function of expected return and the expected variance (or standard deviation) of returns only.
5. For a given risk level, investors prefer higher returns to lower returns. Similarly, for a given level of expected return, investors prefer less risk to more risk.

Under these assumptions, *a single asset or portfolio of assets is considered to be efficient if no other asset or portfolio of assets offers higher expected return with the same (or lower) risk or lower risk with the same (or higher) expected return.*

Alternative Measures of Risk

One of the best-known measures of risk is the *variance,* or *standard deviation of expected returns.*[1] It is a statistical measure of the dispersion of returns around the

---

[1] We consider the variance and standard deviation as one measure of risk because the standard deviation is the square root of the variance.

expected value whereby a larger variance or standard deviation indicates greater dispersion. The idea is that the more disperse the expected returns, the greater the uncertainty of future returns.

Another measure of risk is the *range of returns*. It is assumed that a larger range of expected returns, from the lowest to the highest expected return, means greater uncertainty and risk regarding future expected returns.

Instead of using measures that analyze all deviations from expectations, some observers believe that investors should be concerned only with returns below expectations, which means only deviations below the mean value. A measure that only considers deviations below the mean is the *semivariance*. An extension of the semivariance measure only computes expected returns *below zero* (that is, negative returns), or returns below the returns of some specific asset such as T-bills, the rate of inflation, or a benchmark. These measures of risk implicitly assume that investors want to *minimize the damage* (regret) from returns less than some target rate. Assuming that investors would welcome returns above some target rate, the returns above such a target rate are not considered when measuring risk.

Although there are numerous potential measures of risk, we will use the variance or standard deviation of returns because (1) this measure is somewhat intuitive, (2) it is a correct and widely recognized risk measure, and (3) it has been used in most of the theoretical asset pricing models.

Expected Rates of Return

We compute the expected rate of return for an *individual investment* as shown in Exhibit 53-1. The expected return for an individual risky asset with the set of potential returns and an assumption of the different probabilities used in the example would be 10.3 percent.

The expected rate of return for a *portfolio* of investments is simply the weighted average of the expected rates of return for the individual investments in the portfolio. The weights are the proportion of total value for the individual investment.

The expected rate of return for a hypothetical portfolio with four risky assets is shown in Exhibit 53-2. The expected return for this portfolio of investments would be 11.5 percent. The effect of adding or dropping any investment from the portfolio would be easy to determine; we would use the new weights

EXHIBIT 53-1	Computation of the Expected Return for an Individual Asset	
Probability	**Possible Rate of Return (percent)**	**Expected Return (percent)**
0.35	0.08	0.0280
0.30	0.10	0.0300
0.20	0.12	0.0240
0.15	0.14	0.0210
		E(R) = 0.1030

EXHIBIT 53-2	Computation of the Expected Return for a Portfolio of Risky Assets	
Weight (w_i) **(percent of portfolio)**	**Expected Security** **Return (R_i)**	**Expected Portfolio** **Return ($w_i \times R_i$)**
0.20	0.10	0.0200
0.30	0.11	0.0330
0.30	0.12	0.0360
0.20	0.13	0.0260
		$E(R_{port}) = 0.1150$

based on value and the expected returns for each of the investments. We can generalize this computation of the expected return for the portfolio $E(R_{port})$ as follows:

$$E(R_{port}) = \sum_{i=1}^{n} w_i R_i$$

(53-1)

where:

w_i = the weight of an individual asset in the portfolio, or the percent of the portfolio in Asset i

R_i = the expected rate of return for Asset i

Variance (Standard Deviation) of Returns for an Individual Investment

As noted, we will be using the variance or the standard deviation of returns as the measure of risk. Therefore, at this point we demonstrate how to compute the standard deviation of returns for an individual investment. Subsequently, after discussing some other statistical concepts, we will consider the determination of the standard deviation for a *portfolio* of investments.

The variance, or standard deviation, is a measure of the variation of possible rates of return R_i from the expected rate of return $E(R_i)$ as follows:

$$\text{Variance} = \sigma^2 = \sum_{i=1}^{n} \left[R_i - E(R_i) \right]^2 P_i$$

(53-2)

where:

P_i = probability of the possible rate of return R_i

$$\text{Standard Deviation} = \sigma = \sqrt{\sum_{i=1}^{n} \left[R_i - E(R_i) \right]^2 P_i}$$

(53-3)

The computation of the variance and standard deviation of returns for the individual risky asset in Exhibit 53-1 is set forth in Exhibit 53-3.

EXHIBIT 53-3	Computation of the Variance for an Individual Risky Asset				
Possible Rate of Return (R_i)	**Expected Return $E(R_i)$**	**$R_i - E(R_i)$**	**$[R_i - E(R_i)]^2$**	**P_i**	**$[R_i - E(R_i)]^2P_i$**
0.08	0.103	−0.023	0.0005	0.35	0.000185
0.10	0.103	−0.003	0.0000	0.30	0.000003
0.12	0.103	0.017	0.0003	0.20	0.000058
0.14	0.103	0.037	0.0014	0.15	0.000205
					0.000451

Variance = σ^2 = 0.000451

Standard Deviation = σ = 0.021237

Variance (Standard Deviation) of Returns for a Portfolio

Two basic concepts in statistics, covariance and correlation, must be understood before we discuss the formula for the variance of the rate of return for a portfolio.

Covariance of Returns   In this subsection we discuss what the covariance of returns is intended to measure, give the formula for computing it, and present an example of its computation. **Covariance** is a measure of the degree to which two variables move together relative to their individual mean values over time. In portfolio analysis, we usually are concerned with the covariance of *rates of return* rather than prices or some other variable.[2] A positive covariance means that the rates of return for two investments tend to move in the same direction relative to their individual means during the same time period. In contrast, a negative covariance indicates that the rates of return for two investments tend to move in different directions relative to their means during specified time intervals over time. The *magnitude* of the covariance depends on the variances of the individual return series, as well as on the relationship between the series.

Exhibit 53-4 contains the monthly closing index values for U.S. stocks (measured by the Wilshire 5000 index) and bonds (measured by the Lehman Brothers Treasury Bond Index). Both indexes are total return indexes—that is, the stock index includes dividends paid and the bond index includes accrued interest, as discussed in Reading 56. We can use these data to compute monthly rates of return for these two assets during 2004. Exhibits 53-5 and 53-6 contain a time-series plot of the monthly rates of return for the two assets during 2004. Although the rates of return for the two assets moved together during some months, in other months they moved in opposite directions. The covariance statistic provides an *absolute* measure of how they moved together over time.

---

[2] Returns, of course, can be measured in a variety of ways, depending on the type of asset. We defined returns (R_i) as:

$$R_i = \frac{EV - BV + CF}{BV}$$

where EV is ending value, BV is beginning value, and CF is the cash flow during the period.

EXHIBIT 53-4	Computation of Monthly Rates of Return for U.S. Stocks and Bonds	

	Wilshire 5000 Index	**Lehman Brothers Treasury Bonds**
Date	**Monthly Rate of Return (%)**	**Monthly Rate of Return (%)**
Jan-04	2.23	1.77
Feb-04	1.46	2.00
Mar-04	−1.07	1.50
Apr-04	−2.13	−5.59
May-04	1.38	−0.54
Jun-04	2.08	0.95
Jul-04	−3.82	1.73
Aug-04	0.33	3.74
Sep-04	1.78	0.84
Oct-04	1.71	1.51
Nov-04	4.68	−2.19
Dec-04	3.63	2.31
	Mean = 1.02	Mean = 0.67

Sources: Wilshire Associates and Lehman Brothers.

EXHIBIT 53-5	Time-Series Plot of Monthly Returns for Wilshire 5000 Index, 2004

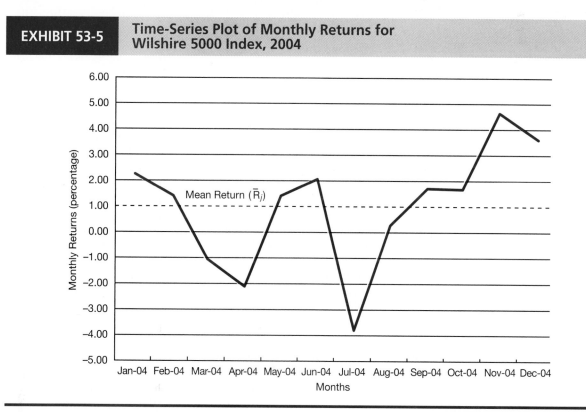

| EXHIBIT 53-6 | Time-Series Plot of Monthly Returns for Lehman Brothers Treasury Bond Index, 2004 |

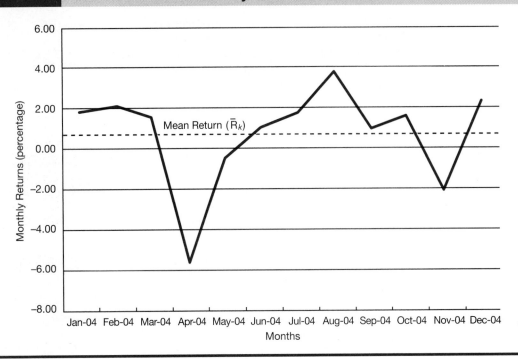

For two assets, *i* and *j*, we define the covariance of rates of return as

$$\text{Cov}_{ij} = E\{[R_i - E(R_i)][R_j - E(R_j)]\}$$

(53-4)

When we apply this formula to the monthly rates of return for the Wilshire 5000 and the Treasury bond indexes during 2004, it becomes

$$\frac{1}{11} \sum_{i=1}^{12} [R_i - \overline{R}_i][R_j - \overline{R}_j]$$

Note that when we apply formula 53-4 to actual sample data, we use the sample mean ($\overline{R}$) as an estimate of the expected return and divide the values by ($n - 1$) rather than by *n* to avoid statistical bias.

As can be seen, if the rates of return for one asset are above (below) its mean rate of return ($\overline{R}$) during a given period and the returns for the other asset are likewise above (below) its mean rate of return during this same period, then the *product* of these deviations from the mean is positive. If this happens consistently, the covariance of returns between these two assets will be some large positive value. If, however, the rate of return for one of the securities is above its mean return while the return on the other security is below its mean return, the product will be negative. If this contrary movement happens consistently, the covariance between the rates of return for the two assets will be a large negative value.

Exhibit 53-7 contains the monthly rates of return during 2004 for the Wilshire 5000 index and the Lehman Brothers Treasury Bond Index as computed in Exhibit 53-4. One might expect the returns for the two asset indexes to

EXHIBIT 53-7	Computation of Covariance of Returns for Wilshire 5000 Index and Lehman Brothers Treasury Bond Index, 2004

Date	Wilshire 5000 (R_i)	Lehman Treasury Bond Index (R_j)	Wilshire 5000 $R_i - \bar{R}_i$	Lehman Treasury Bond Index $R_j - \bar{R}_j$	Wilshire 5000 $R_i - \bar{R}_i$ $\times$ Lehman Treasury Bond Index $R_j - \bar{R}_j$
Jan-04	2.23	1.77	1.21	1.10	1.33
Feb-04	1.46	2.00	0.44	1.34	0.59
Mar-04	−1.07	1.50	−2.09	0.83	−1.74
Apr-04	−2.13	−5.59	−3.15	−6.26	19.73
May-04	1.38	−0.54	0.36	−1.21	−0.43
Jun-04	2.08	0.95	1.06	0.28	0.30
Jul-04	−3.82	1.73	−4.84	1.06	−5.16
Aug-04	0.33	3.74	−0.69	3.07	−2.12
Sep-04	1.78	0.84	0.76	0.17	0.13
Oct-04	1.71	1.51	0.69	0.84	0.58
Nov-04	4.68	−2.19	3.66	−2.86	−10.46
Dec-04	3.63	2.31	2.61	1.64	4.28
Mean =	1.02	0.67			Sum = 7.00

$$\text{Cov}_{ij} = 7.00/11 = 0.637$$

have reasonably low covariance because of the differences in the nature of these assets. The arithmetic mean of the monthly returns were

$$(\bar{R}_i) = \frac{1}{11}\sum_{i=1}^{12} R_{it} = 1.02$$

and

$$(\bar{R}_j) = \frac{1}{11}\sum_{j=1}^{12} R_{jt} = 0.67$$

We rounded all figures to the nearest hundredth of 1 percent, so there may be small rounding errors. The average monthly return was 1.02 percent for the Wilshire 5000 and 0.67 percent for the Treasury bonds. The results in Exhibit 53-7 show that the covariance between the rates of return for these two assets was

$$\text{Cov}_{ij} = \frac{1}{11} \times 7.00$$
$$= 0.637$$

Interpretation of a number such as 0.637 is difficult; is it high or low for covariance? We know the relationship between the two assets is generally positive, but it is not possible to be more specific. Exhibit 53-8 contains a scatterplot with paired values of R_{it} and R_{jt} plotted against each other. This plot demonstrates the linear nature and strength of the relationship. It is not surprising that the relationship

EXHIBIT 53-8	Scatterplot of Monthly Returns for Wilshire 5000 and Lehman Brothers Treasury Bond Index, 2004

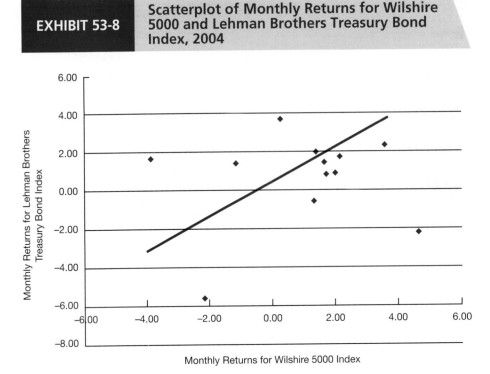

Monthly Returns for Wilshire 5000 Index

during 2004 was not very strong, since during five months the two assets moved counter to each other. As a result, the overall covariance was a small positive value.

Covariance and Correlation   Covariance is affected by the variability of the two individual return indexes. Therefore, a number such as the 0.637 in our example might indicate a weak positive relationship if the two individual indexes were volatile, but would reflect a strong positive relationship if the two indexes were stable. Obviously, we want to standardize this covariance measure. We do so by taking into consideration the variability of the two individual return indexes, as follows:

$$r_{ij} = \frac{Cov_{ij}}{\sigma_i \sigma_j} \qquad\qquad \textbf{(53-5)}$$

where:

r_{ij} = the correlation coefficient of returns
σ_i = the standard deviation of R_{it}
σ_j = the standard deviation of R_{jt}

Standardizing the covariance by the product of the individual standard deviations yields the **correlation coefficient** r_{ij}, which can vary only in the range −1 to +1. A value of +1 indicates a perfect positive linear relationship between R_i and R_j, meaning the returns for the two-assets move together in a completely linear manner. A value of −1 indicates a perfect negative relationship between the two return indexes, so that when one asset's rate of return is above its mean, the other asset's rate of return will be below its mean by a comparable amount.

To calculate this standardized measure of the relationship, we need to compute the standard deviation for the two individual return indexes. We already have the values for $(R_{it} - \overline{R}_i)$ and $(R_{jt} - \overline{R}_j)$ in Exhibit 53-7. We can square each

EXHIBIT 53-9	Computation of Standard Deviation of Returns for the Wilshire 5000 Index and Lehman Brothers Treasury Bond Index, 2004			
	Wilshire 5000 Index		**Lehman Brothers Treasury Bonds**	
Date	$R_i - \bar{R}_i$	$(R_i - \bar{R}_i)^2$	$R_j - \bar{R}_j$	$(R_j - \bar{R}_j)^2$
Jan-04	1.21	1.46	1.10	1.21
Feb-04	0.44	0.19	1.34	1.79
Mar-04	−2.09	4.38	0.83	0.69
Apr-04	−3.15	9.93	−6.26	39.17
May-04	0.36	0.13	−1.21	1.47
Jun-04	1.06	1.12	0.28	0.08
Jul-04	−4.84	23.44	1.06	1.13
Aug-04	−0.69	0.48	3.07	9.42
Sep-04	0.76	0.58	0.17	0.03
Oct-04	0.69	0.47	0.84	0.70
Nov-04	3.66	13.38	−2.86	8.18
Dec-04	2.61	6.80	1.64	2.69
		Sum = 62.36		Sum = 66.56

$$\text{Variance}_i = 62.36/11 = 5.67$$
$$\text{Standard Deviation}_i = (5.67)^{1/2} = 2.38$$

$$\text{Variance}_j = 66.56/11 = 6.05$$
$$\text{Standard Deviation}_j = (6.05)^{1/2} = 2.46$$

of these values and sum them as shown in Exhibit 53-9 to calculate the variance of each return series; again, we divide by $(n - 1)$ to avoid statistical bias.

$$\sigma_i^2 = \frac{1}{11} 62.36 = 5.67$$

and

$$\sigma_j^2 = \frac{1}{11} 66.56 = 6.05$$

The standard deviation for each index is the square root of the variance for each, as follows:

$$\sigma_i = \sqrt{5.67} = 2.38$$
$$\sigma_j = \sqrt{6.05} = 2.46$$

Thus, based on the covariance between the two indexes and the individual standard deviations, we can calculate the correlation coefficient between returns for common stocks and Treasury bonds during 2004:

$$r_{ij} = \frac{\text{Cov}_{ij}}{\sigma_i \sigma_j} = \frac{0.637}{(2.38)(2.46)} = \frac{0.637}{5.8548} = 0.109$$

Obviously, this formula also implies that

$$\text{Cov}_{ij} = r_{ij}\sigma_i\sigma_j = (0.109)(2.38)(2.46) = 0.638$$

Standard Deviation of a Portfolio

As noted, a correlation of $+1.0$ indicates perfect positive correlation, and a value of -1.0 means that the returns moved in completely opposite directions. A value of zero means that the returns had no linear relationship, that is, they were uncorrelated statistically. That does *not* mean that they are independent. The value of $r_{ij} = 0.109$ is not significantly different from zero. This insignificant positive correlation is not unusual for stocks versus bonds during short time intervals such as one year.

Portfolio Standard Deviation Formula   Now that we have discussed the concepts of covariance and correlation, we can consider the formula for computing the standard deviation of returns for a *portfolio* of assets, our measure of risk for a portfolio. In Exhibit 53-2, we showed that the expected rate of return of the portfolio was the weighted average of the expected returns for the individual assets in the portfolio; the weights were the percentage of value of the portfolio. One might assume it is possible to derive the standard deviation of the portfolio in the same manner, that is, by computing the weighted average of the standard deviations for the individual assets. This would be a mistake. Markowitz (1959) derived the general formula for the standard deviation of a portfolio as follows:

$$\sigma_{\text{port}} = \sqrt{\sum_{i=1}^{n} w_i^2 \sigma_i^2 + \sum_{i=1}^{n}\sum_{\substack{j=1 \\ i \neq j}}^{n} w_i w_j \text{Cov}_{ij}} \tag{53-6}$$

where

σ_{port} = the standard deviation of the portfolio

w_i = the weights of an individual asset in the portfolio, where weights are determined by the proportion of value in the portfolio

σ_i^2 = the variance of rates of return for asset i

Cov_{ij} = the covariance between the rates of return for assets i and j, where $\text{Cov}_{ij} = r_{ij} \sigma_i \sigma_j$

This formula indicates that the standard deviation for a portfolio of assets is a function of the weighted average of the individual variances (where the weights are squared), *plus* the weighted covariances between all the assets in the portfolio. The very important point is that the standard deviation for a portfolio of assets encompasses not only the variances of the individual assets but *also* includes the covariances between all the pairs of individual assets in the portfolio. Further, it can be shown that, in a portfolio with a large number of securities, this formula reduces to the sum of the weighted covariances.

Impact of a New Security in a Portfolio   Although in most of the following discussion we will consider portfolios with only two assets (because it is possible to show the effect in two dimensions), we will also demonstrate the computations for a three-asset portfolio. Still, it is important at this point to consider what happens in a large portfolio with many assets. Specifically, what happens to the portfolio's standard deviation when we add a new security to such a portfolio? As shown by the formula, we see two effects. The first is the asset's own variance of returns, and the second is the covariance between the returns of this new asset and the returns of *every other asset that is already in the portfolio*. The relative weight of these numerous covariances is substantially greater than the asset's unique variance; the more assets in the portfolio, the more this is true. This means that the important factor to consider when adding an investment to a portfolio that contains a number of other investments is *not* the new security's own variance but *its average covariance with all the other investments in the portfolio.*

Portfolio Standard Deviation Calculation   Because of the assumptions used in developing the Markowitz portfolio model, any asset or portfolio of assets can be described by two characteristics: the expected rate of return and the expected standard deviation of returns. Therefore, the following demonstrations can be applied to two *individual* assets, two *portfolios* of assets, or two *asset classes* with the indicated return—standard deviation characteristics and correlation coefficients.

Equal Risk and Return—Changing Correlations   Consider first the case in which both assets have the same expected return and expected standard deviation of return. As an example, let's assume

$$E(R_1) = 0.20, \qquad E(\sigma_1) = 0.10$$
$$E(R_2) = 0.20, \qquad E(\sigma_2) = 0.10$$

To show the effect of different covariances, we assume different levels of correlation between the two assets. We also assume that the two assets have equal weights in the portfolio ($w_1 = 0.50$; $w_2 = 0.50$). Therefore, the only value that changes in each example is the correlation between the returns for the two assets.

Now consider the following five correlation coefficients and the covariances they yield. Since $Cov_{ij} = r_{ij}\sigma_i\sigma_j$, the covariance will be equal to $r_{1,2}$ (0.10)(0.10) because the standard deviation of both assets is 0.10.

a. For $r_{1,2} = 1.00$, $Cov_{1,2} = (1.00)(0.10)(0.10) = 0.01$
b. For $r_{1,2} = 0.50$, $Cov_{1,2} = (0.50)(0.10)(0.10) = 0.005$
c. For $r_{1,2} = 0.00$, $Cov_{1,2} = (0.00)(0.10)(0.10) = 0.000$
d. For $r_{1,2} = -0.50$, $Cov_{1,2} = (-0.50)(0.10)(0.10) = -0.005$
e. For $r_{1,2} = -1.00$, $Cov_{1,2} = (-1.00)(0.10)(0.10) = -0.01$

Now let's see what happens to the standard deviation of the portfolio under these five conditions.

When we apply the general portfolio formula from Equation 53-6 to a two-asset portfolio, it is

$$\sigma_{port} = \sqrt{w_1^2\sigma_1^2 + w_2^2\sigma_2^2 + 2w_1w_2r_{1,2}\sigma_1\sigma_2} \qquad \textbf{(53-7)}$$

or

$$\sigma_{port} = \sqrt{w_1^2\sigma_1^2 + w_2^2\sigma_2^2 + 2w_1w_2Cov_{1,2}}$$

Thus, in Case a:

$$\sigma_{port(a)} = \sqrt{(0.5)^2(0.10)^2 + (0.5)^2(0.10)^2 + 2(0.5)(0.5)(0.01)}$$
$$= \sqrt{(0.25)(0.01) + (0.25)(0.01) + 2(0.25)(0.01)}$$
$$= \sqrt{0.01}$$
$$= 0.10$$

In this case, where the returns for the two assets are perfectly positively correlated, the standard deviation for the portfolio is, in fact, the weighted average of the individual standard deviations. The important point is that we get no real benefit from combining two assets that are perfectly correlated; they are like one asset already because their returns move together.

Now consider Case b, where $r_{1,2}$ equals 0.50.

$$\sigma_{\text{port(b)}} = \sqrt{(0.5)^2(0.10)^2 + (0.5)^2(0.10)^2 + 2(0.5)(0.5)(0.005)}$$
$$= \sqrt{(0.0025) + (0.0025) + 2(0.25)(0.005)}$$
$$= \sqrt{0.0075}$$
$$= 0.0866$$

The only term that changed from Case a is the last term, $Cov_{1,2}$, which changed from 0.01 to 0.005. As a result, the standard deviation of the portfolio declined by about 13 percent, from 0.10 to 0.0866. Note that *the expected return of the portfolio did not change* because it is simply the weighted average of the individual expected returns; it is equal to 0.20 in both cases.

You should be able to confirm through your own calculations that the standard deviations for Portfolios c and d are as follows:

c. 0.0707
d. 0.05

The final case, where the correlation between the two assets is −1.00, indicates the ultimate benefits of diversification.

$$\sigma_{\text{port(e)}} = \sqrt{(0.5)^2(0.10)^2 + (0.5)^2(0.10)^2 + 2(0.5)(0.5)(-0.01)}$$
$$= \sqrt{(0.0050) + (-0.0050)}$$
$$= \sqrt{0}$$
$$= 0$$

Here, the negative covariance term exactly offsets the individual variance terms, leaving an overall standard deviation of the portfolio of zero. *This would be a risk-free portfolio.*

Exhibit 53-10 illustrates a graph of such a pattern. Perfect negative correlation gives a mean combined return for the two securities over time equal to the mean for each of them, so the returns for the portfolio show no variability. Any returns above and below the mean for each of the assets are *completely offset* by the

EXHIBIT 53-10	Time Patterns of Returns for Two Assets with Perfect Negative Correlation

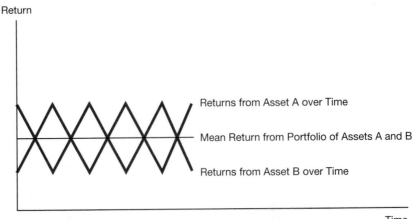

EXHIBIT 53-11	Risk-Return Plot for Portfolios with Equal Returns and Standard Deviations but Different Correlations

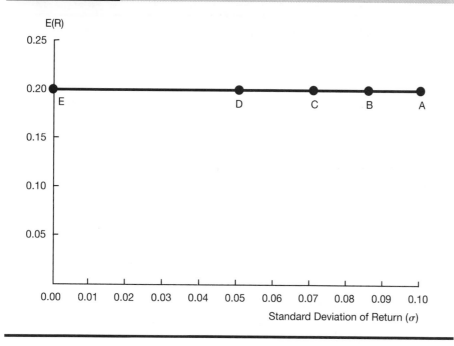

return for the other asset, so there is *no variability* in total returns—that is, *no risk*—for the portfolio. Thus, a pair of completely negatively correlated assets provides the maximum benefits of diversification by completely eliminating risk.

The graph in Exhibit 53-11 shows the difference in the risk-return posture for our five cases. As noted, the only effect of the change in correlation is the change in the standard deviation of this two-asset portfolio. Combining assets that are not perfectly correlated does *not* affect the expected return of the portfolio, but it *does* reduce the risk of the portfolio (as measured by its standard deviation). When we eventually reach the ultimate combination of perfect negative correlation, risk is eliminated.

Combining Stocks with Different Returns and Risk   We have seen what happens when only the correlation coefficient (covariance) differs between the assets. We now consider two assets (or portfolios) with different expected rates of return and individual standard deviations.[3] We will show what happens when we vary the correlations between them. We will assume two assets with the following characteristics.

Asset	E(R)	w	σ^2	σ_1
1	0.10	0.50	0.0049	0.07
2	0.20	0.50	0.0100	0.10

---

[3] As noted, these could be two asset classes. For example, Asset 1 could be low risk-low return bonds and Asset 2 could be higher return-higher risk stocks.

We will use the previous set of correlation coefficients, but we must recalculate the covariances because this time the standard deviations of the assets are different. The results are shown in the following table.

Case	Correlation Coefficient ($r_{1,2}$)	Covariance ($r_{1,2}\sigma_1\sigma_2$)
a	+1.00	0.0070
b	+0.50	0.0035
c	0.00	0.0000
d	−0.50	−0.0035
e	−1.00	−0.0070

Because we are assuming the same weights in all cases $(0.50 - 0.50)$, the expected return in every instance will be

$$E(R_{port}) = 0.50(0.10) + 0.50(0.20)$$
$$= 0.15$$

The portfolio standard deviation for Case a will be

$$\sigma_{port(a)} = \sqrt{(0.5)^2(0.07)^2 + (0.5)^2(0.10)^2 + 2(0.5)(0.5)(0.0070)}$$
$$= \sqrt{0.007225}$$
$$= 0.085$$

Again, with perfect positive correlation, the portfolio standard deviation is the weighted average of the standard deviations of the individual assets:

$$(0.5)(0.07) + (0.5)(0.10) = 0.085$$

As you might envision, changing the weights with perfect positive correlation causes the portfolio standard deviation to change in a linear fashion. This will be an important point to remember when we discuss the capital asset pricing model (CAPM).

For Cases b, c, d, and e, the portfolio standard deviations are as follows:[4]

$$\sigma_{port(b)} = \sqrt{(0.001225) + (0.0025) + (0.5)(0.0035)}$$
$$= \sqrt{0.005475}$$
$$= 0.07399$$

$$\sigma_{port(c)} = \sqrt{(0.001225) + (0.0025) + (0.5)(0.00)}$$
$$= 0.0610$$

$$\sigma_{port(d)} = \sqrt{(0.001225) + (0.0025) + (0.5)(-0.0035)}$$
$$= 0.0444$$

$$\sigma_{port(e)} = \sqrt{(0.003725) + (0.5)(-0.0070)}$$
$$= 0.015$$

---

[4] In all the following examples, we will skip some steps because you are now aware that only the last term changes. You are encouraged to work out the individual steps to ensure that you understand the computational procedure.

EXHIBIT 53-12	Risk-Return Plot for Portfolios with Different Returns, Standard Deviations, and Correlations

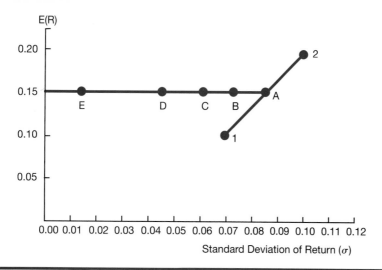

Note that, in this example, with perfect negative correlation the portfolio standard deviation is not zero. This is because the different examples have equal weights, but the asset standard deviations are not equal.

Exhibit 53-12 shows the results for the two individual assets and the portfolio of the two assets assuming the correlation coefficients vary as set forth in Cases a through e. As before, the expected return does not change because the proportions are always set at 0.50–0.50, so all the portfolios lie along the horizontal line at the return, R = 0.15.

Constant Correlation with Changing Weights   If we changed the weights of the two assets while holding the correlation coefficient constant, we would derive a set of combinations that trace an ellipse starting at Asset 2, going through the 0.50–0.50 point, and ending at Asset 1. We can demonstrate this with Case c, in which the correlation coefficient of zero eases the computations. We begin with 100 percent in Asset 2 (Case f) and change the weights as follows, ending with 100 percent in Asset 1 (Case 1):

Case	w_1	w_2	$E(R_i)$
f	0.00	1.00	0.20
g	0.20	0.80	0.18
h	0.40	0.60	0.16
i	0.50	0.50	0.15
j	0.60	0.40	0.14
k	0.80	0.20	0.12
l	1.00	0.00	0.10

We already know the standard deviation (σ) for portfolio (i). In Cases f, g, h, j, k, and l, the standard deviations are[5]

$$\begin{aligned}
\sigma_{\text{port}(g)} &= \sqrt{(0.20)^2(0.07)^2 + (0.80)^2(0.10)^2 + 2(0.20)(0.80)(0.00)} \\
&= \sqrt{(0.04)(0.0049) + (0.64)(0.01) + (0)} \\
&= \sqrt{0.006596} \\
&= 0.0812
\end{aligned}$$

$$\begin{aligned}
\sigma_{\text{port}(h)} &= \sqrt{(0.40)^2(0.07)^2 + (0.60)^2(0.10)^2 + 2(0.40)(0.60)(0.00)} \\
&= \sqrt{0.004384} \\
&= 0.0662
\end{aligned}$$

$$\begin{aligned}
\sigma_{\text{port}(j)} &= \sqrt{(0.60)^2(0.07)^2 + (0.40)^2(0.10)^2 + 2(0.60)(0.40)(0.00)} \\
&= \sqrt{0.003364} \\
&= 0.0580
\end{aligned}$$

$$\begin{aligned}
\sigma_{\text{port}(k)} &= \sqrt{(0.80)^2(0.07)^2 + (0.20)^2(0.10)^2 + 2(0.80)(0.20)(0.00)} \\
&= \sqrt{0.003536} \\
&= 0.0595
\end{aligned}$$

The various weights with a constant correlation yield the following risk-return combinations.

Case	w_1	w_2	$E(R_i)$	$E(\sigma_{\text{port}})$
f	0.00	1.00	0.20	0.1000
g	0.20	0.80	0.18	0.0812
h	0.40	0.60	0.16	0.0662
i	0.50	0.50	0.15	0.0610
j	0.60	0.40	0.14	0.0580
k	0.80	0.20	0.12	0.0595
l	1.00	0.00	0.10	0.0700

A graph of these combinations appears in Exhibit 53-13. We could derive a complete curve by simply varying the weighting by smaller increments.

A notable result is that with low, zero, or negative correlations, it is possible to derive portfolios that have *lower risk than either single asset*. In our set of examples where $r_{ij} = 0.00$, this occurs in Cases h, i, j, and k. This ability to reduce risk is the essence of diversification.

As shown in Exhibit 53-13, assuming the normal risk-return relationship where assets with higher risk (larger standard deviation of returns) provide high rates of return, it is possible for a conservative investor to experience *both* lower risk *and* higher return by diversifying into a higher risk-higher return asset, assuming that the correlation between the two assets is fairly low. Exhibit 53-13

---

[5] Again, you are encouraged to fill in the steps we skipped in the computations.

| EXHIBIT 53-13 | Portfolio Risk-Return Plots for Different Weights When $r_{i,j} = +1.00; +0.50; 0.00;$ $-0.50; -1.00$ |

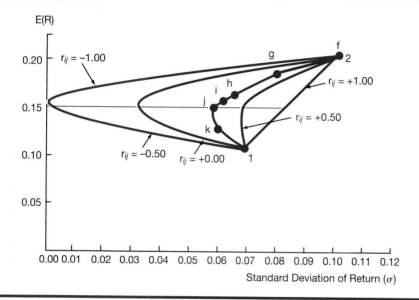

shows that, in the case where we used the correlation of zero (0.00), the low-risk investor at Point 1—who would receive a return of 10 percent and risk of 7 percent—could *increase* the return to 14 percent *and* experience a *decline* in risk to 5.8 percent by investing (diversifying) 40 percent of the portfolio in riskier Asset 2. As noted, the benefits of diversification are critically dependent on the correlation between assets. The exhibit shows that there is even some benefit when the correlation is 0.50 rather than zero.

Exhibit 53-13 also shows that the curvature in the graph depends on the correlation between the two assets or portfolios. With $r_{ij} = +1.00$, the combinations lie along a straight line between the two assets. When $r_{ij} = 0.50$, the curve is to the right of the $r_{ij} = 0.00$ curve; when $r_{ij} = -0.50$, it is to the left. Finally, when $r_{ij} = -1.00$, the graph would be two straight lines that would touch at the vertical line (zero risk) with some combination. It is possible to solve for the specified set of weights that would give a portfolio with zero risk. In this case, it is $w_1 = 0.412$ and $w_2 = 0.588$.

A Three-Asset Portfolio

A demonstration of what occurs with a three-asset portfolio is useful because it shows the dynamics of the portfolio process when assets are added. It also shows the rapid growth in the computations required, which is why we will stop at three! We will assume the following characteristics for the next example:

Asset Classes	E(R)	E(σ)	w
Stocks (S)	0.12	0.20	0.60
Bonds (B)	0.08	0.10	0.30
Cash equivalent (C)	0.04	0.03	0.10

In this example, we will combine three asset classes we have been discussing: stocks, bonds, and cash equivalents.[6] The correlations are

$$r_{S,B} = 0.25; \; r_{S,C} = -0.08; \; r_{B,C} = 0.15$$

Given the weights specified, the $E(R_{port})$ is

$$E(R_{port}) = (0.60)(0.12) + (0.30)(0.08) + (0.10)(0.04)$$
$$= (0.072 + 0.024 + 0.004) = 0.100 = 10.00\%$$

When we apply the generalized formula from Equation 53-6 to the expected standard deviation of a three-asset portfolio, it is

$$\sigma_{port}^2 = (w_S^2 \sigma_S^2 + w_B^2 \sigma_B^2 + w_C^2 \sigma_C^2) \qquad \textbf{(53-8)}$$
$$+ (2w_S w_B \sigma_S \sigma_B r_{S,B} + 2w_S w_C \sigma_S \sigma_C r_{S,C} + 2w_B w_C \sigma_B \sigma_C r_{B,C})$$

From the characteristics specified, the standard deviation of this three-asset-class portfolio (σ_{port}) would be

$$\sigma_{port}^2 = [(0.6)^2 (0.20)^2 + (0.3)^2 (0.10)^2 + (0.1)^2 (0.03)^2]$$
$$+ \{[2(0.6)(0.3)(0.20)(0.10)(0.25)] + [2(0.6)(0.1)(0.20)(0.03)(-0.08)]$$
$$+ [2(0.3)(0.1)(0.10)(0.03)(0.15)]\}$$
$$= [0.015309 + (0.0018) + (-0.0000576) + (0.000027)]$$
$$= 0.0170784$$
$$\sigma_{port} = (0.0170784)^{1/2} = 0.1306 = 13.06\%$$

Estimation Issues

It is important to keep in mind that the results of this portfolio asset allocation depend on the accuracy of the statistical inputs. In the current instance, this means that for every asset (or asset class) being considered for inclusion in the portfolio, we must estimate its expected returns and standard deviation. We must also estimate the correlation coefficient among the entire set of assets. The number of correlation estimates can be significant—for example, for a portfolio of 100 securities, the number is 4,950 (that is, $99 + 98 + 97 + \ldots$). The potential source of error that arises from these approximations is referred to as *estimation risk*.

We can reduce the number of correlation coefficients that must be estimated by assuming that stock returns can be described by the relationship of each stock to a market index—that is, a single index market model, as follows:

$$R_i = a_i + b_i R_m + \varepsilon_i \qquad \textbf{(53-9)}$$

where:

b_i = the slope coefficient that relates the returns for Security i to the returns for the aggregate stock market

R_m = the returns for the aggregate stock market

---

[6] The asset allocation articles regularly contained in the *Wall Street Journal* generally refer to these three asset classes.

If all the securities are similarly related to the market and a slope coefficient b_i is derived for each one, it can be shown that the correlation coefficient between two Securities i and j is

$$r_{ij} = b_i b_j \frac{\sigma_m^2}{\sigma_i \sigma_j}$$

(53-10)

where:

σ_m^2 = the variance of returns for the aggregate stock market

This reduces the number of estimates from 4,950 to 100—that is, once we have derived a slope estimate b_i for each security, we can compute the correlation estimates. Keep in mind that this assumes that the single index market model provides a good estimate of security returns.

The Efficient Frontier

If we examined different two-asset combinations and derived the curves assuming all the possible weights, we would have a graph like that in Exhibit 53-14. The envelope curve that contains the best of all these possible combinations is referred to as the **efficient frontier**. Specifically, the efficient frontier represents that set of portfolios that has the maximum rate of return for every given level of risk or the minimum risk for every level of return. An example of such a frontier is shown in Exhibit 53-15. Every portfolio that lies on the efficient frontier has either a higher rate of return for equal risk or lower risk for an equal rate of return than some portfolio beneath the frontier. Thus, we would say that Portfolio A in Exhibit 53-15 *dominates* Portfolio C because it has an equal rate of return but substantially less risk. Similarly, Portfolio B dominates Portfolio C because it has equal risk but a higher expected rate of return. Because of the benefits of diversification among imperfectly correlated assets, we would expect the efficient frontier to be

EXHIBIT 53-14	**Numerous Portfolio Combinations of Available Assets**

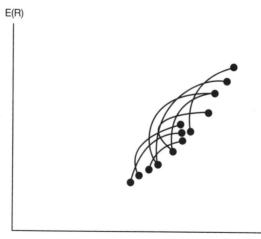

Standard Deviation of Return (σ)

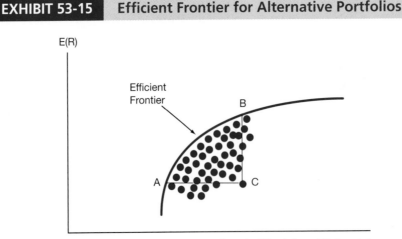

EXHIBIT 53-15   **Efficient Frontier for Alternative Portfolios**

made up of *portfolios* of investments rather than individual securities. Two possible exceptions arise at the end points, which represent the asset with the highest return and the asset with the lowest risk.

As an investor, you will target a point along the efficient frontier based on your *utility function,* which reflects your attitude toward risk. No portfolio on the efficient frontier can dominate any other portfolio on the efficient frontier. All of these portfolios have different return and risk measures, with expected rates of return that increase with higher risk.

The Efficient Frontier and Investor Utility

The curve in Exhibit 53-15 shows that the slope of the efficient frontier curve decreases steadily as we move upward. This implies that adding equal increments of risk as we move up the efficient frontier gives diminishing increments of expected return. To evaluate this situation, we calculate the slope of the efficient frontier as follows:

$$\frac{\Delta E(R_{port})}{\Delta E(\sigma_{port})} \qquad\qquad \textbf{(53-11)}$$

An individual investor's utility curves specify the trade-offs he or she is willing to make between expected return and risk. In conjunction with the efficient frontier, these utility curves determine which *particular* portfolio on the efficient frontier best suits an individual investor. Two investors will choose the same portfolio from the efficient set only if their utility curves are identical.

Exhibit 53-16 shows two sets of utility curves along with an efficient frontier of investments. The curves labeled U_1, U_2, and U_3 are for a strongly risk-averse investor. These utility curves are quite steep, indicating that the investor will not tolerate much additional risk to obtain additional returns. The investor is equally disposed toward any $E(R)$, $E(\sigma)$ combinations along the specific utility curve U_1.

The curves labeled $(U_{3'}, U_{2'}, U_{1'})$ characterize a less risk-averse investor. Such an investor is willing to tolerate a bit more risk to get a higher expected return.

The optimal portfolio is the efficient portfolio that has the highest utility for a given investor. It lies at the point of tangency between the efficient frontier and the U_1 curve with the highest possible utility. A conservative investor's highest

EXHIBIT 53-16 Selecting an Optimal Risky Portfolio

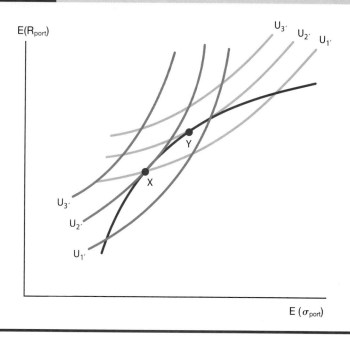

utility is at Point X in Exhibit 53-16, where the U_2 curve just touches the efficient frontier. A less risk-averse investor's highest utility occurs at Point Y, which represents a portfolio on the efficient frontier with higher expected returns and higher risk than the portfolio at X.

THE INTERNET

Investments Online

By seeking to operate on the efficient frontier, portfolio managers try to minimize risk for a certain level of return, or maximize return for a given level of risk. Software programs, called optimizers, are used by portfolio managers to determine the shape of the efficient frontier as well as to determine some of the portfolios which lie on it. Financial planners use information on past returns and manager performance, in addition to optimizers, to make recommendations to their clients. Some interesting Web sites for money managers include:

www.pionline.com This is the home page for *Pensions and Investments,* a newspaper for money managers. Items on the home page include links to news of interest to managers, and ePIPER performance data on a number of equity, fixed income, real estate, and global portfolios from money manager and pension funds. Contains many links to organizations such as central banks, consultants, and sellers of investment-related products.

www.investmentnews.com *Investment News* is a sister publication to *Pensions and Investments,* with a focus toward the financial advisor. This site includes information on financial planning, the mutual fund industry, regulation, equity performance, and industry trends.

Software for creating efficient frontiers is available from firms such as Ibbotson Associates (www.ibbotson.com), Zephyr Associates (www.styleadvisor.com), Wagner Associates (www.wagner.com), and Efficient Solutions, Inc. (www.effisols.com).

William J. Bernstein's Web site,www.efficientfrontier.com, offers articles from his web-zine, *Efficient Frontier,* an online journal of practical asset allocation.

SUMMARY

▶ The basic Markowitz portfolio model derives the expected rate of return for a portfolio of assets and a measure of expected risk, which is the standard deviation of expected rate of return. Markowitz showed that the expected rate of return of a portfolio is the weighted average of the expected return for the individual investments in the portfolio. The standard deviation of a portfolio is a function not only of the standard deviations for the individual investments but *also* of the covariance between the rates of return for all the pairs of assets in the portfolio. In a large portfolio, these covariances are the important factors.

▶ Different weights or amounts of a portfolio held in various assets yield a curve of potential combinations. Correlation coefficients among assets are the critical factor to consider when selecting investments. Investors can maintain their rate of return while reducing the risk level of their portfolio by combining assets or portfolios that have low-positive or negative correlation.

▶ Assuming numerous assets and a multitude of combination curves, the efficient frontier is the envelope curve that encompasses all of the best combinations. It defines the set of portfolios that has the highest expected return for each given level of risk or the minimum risk for each given level of return. From this set of dominant portfolios, investors select the one that lies at the point of tangency between the efficient frontier and their highest utility curve. Because risk-return utility functions differ, the point of tangency and, therefore, the portfolio choice will differ among investors.

At this point, you understand that an optimum portfolio is a combination of investments, each having desirable individual risk-return characteristics that also fit together based on their correlations. Because many foreign stock and bond investments provide superior rates of return compared with U.S. securities *and* have low correlations with portfolios of U.S. stocks and bonds, including these foreign securities in your portfolio will help you to reduce the overall risk of your portfolio while possibly increasing your rate of return.

PROBLEMS FOR READING 53

1. The following are the monthly rates of return for Madison Corp. and for Sophie Electric during a six-month period.

Month	Madison Corp.	Sophie Electric
1	−0.04	0.07
2	0.06	−0.02
3	−0.07	−0.10
4	0.12	0.15
5	−0.02	−0.06
6	0.05	0.02

Compute the following.

A. Average monthly rate of return $\bar{R}_i$ for each stock

B. Standard deviation of returns for each stock

C. Covariance between the rates of return

D. The correlation coefficient between the rates of return

What level of correlation did you expect? How did your expectations compare with the computed correlation? Would these two stocks offer a good chance for diversification? Why or why not?

2. You are considering two assets with the following characteristics.

$$E(R_1) = 0.15 \quad E(\sigma_1) = 0.10 \quad w_1 = 0.5$$

$$E(R_2) = 0.20 \quad E(\sigma_2) = 0.20 \quad w_2 = 0.5$$

Compute the mean and standard deviation of two portfolios if $r_{1,2} = 0.40$ and $−0.60$, respectively. Plot the two portfolios on a risk-return graph and briefly explain the results.

3. Given: $E(R_1) = 0.10$

$E(R_2) = 0.15$

$E(\sigma_1) = 0.03$

$E(\sigma_2) = 0.05$

Calculate the expected returns and expected standard deviations of a two-stock portfolio in which Stock 1 has a weight of 60 percent under the following conditions.

A. $r_{1,2} = 1.00$

B. $r_{1,2} = 0.75$

C. $r_{1,2} = 0.25$

D. $r_{1,2} = 0.00$

E. $r_{1,2} = −0.25$

F. $r_{1,2} = −0.75$

G. $r_{1,2} = −1.00$

$4\frac{5}{8}$ $4\frac{11}{16}$ $-\frac{9}{8}$

$5\frac{1}{2}$ $5\frac{1}{2}$ $-$ $\frac{9}{8}$

$5\frac{1}{2}$ $21\frac{3}{16}$ $-\frac{1}{16}$

$20\frac{5}{8}$ $21\frac{3}{16}$ $-$ $\frac{7}{8}$

$17\frac{3}{8}$ $18\frac{1}{8}$ $+$

$15\frac{1}{2}$ $6\frac{1}{2}$ $-$ $\frac{1}{2}$

$6\frac{1}{2}$ $6\frac{1}{2}$ $-$

$7\frac{1}{4}$ $31\frac{1}{32}$ $-$ $\frac{1}{8}$

$15\frac{1}{16}$

1 $\frac{9}{8}$

$9\frac{1}{16}$

$19\frac{1}{32}$

$7\frac{15}{16}$ $7\frac{13}{16}$ $7\frac{15}{16}$

$7\frac{15}{16}$ $2\frac{11}{32}$ $2\frac{1}{2}$ $+$

$2\frac{5}{8}$ $2\frac{1}{4}$ $2\frac{1}{4}$

$2\frac{3}{4}$ $11\frac{3}{8}$ $11\frac{3}{4}$ $+$

$6\frac{1}{16}$ $12\frac{1}{16}$ $11\frac{3}{8}$ $11\frac{3}{4}$ $+$

87 $33\frac{3}{4}$ 33 $33\frac{1}{8}$ $-$

902 $25\frac{5}{8}$ $24\frac{9}{16}$ $25\frac{5}{8}$ $+$

$11\frac{5}{8}$ $11\frac{7}{8}$ $+$

833 12 $11\frac{5}{8}$

16 $10\frac{1}{2}$ $10\frac{1}{2}$ $10\frac{7}{8}$ $-$

78 $15\frac{7}{8}$ $15\frac{13}{16}$ $15\frac{7}{8}$ $-$

4508 $9\frac{1}{16}$ $8\frac{1}{4}$ $8\frac{7}{8}$

430 $11\frac{1}{4}$ $10\frac{1}{8}$ $10\frac{5}{8}$

$4\frac{1}{8}$

AN INTRODUCTION TO ASSET PRICING MODELS

by Frank K. Reilly and Keith C. Brown

READING

54

LEARNING OUTCOMES

The candidate should be able to:

a. list the assumptions of the capital market theory;

b. explain what happens to the expected return, the standard deviation of returns, and possible risk-return combinations when a risk-free asset is combined with a portfolio of risky assets;

c. identify the market portfolio, and describe the role of the market portfolio in the formation of the capital market line (CML);

d. define systematic and unsystematic risk and explain why an investor should not expect to receive additional return for assuming unsystematic risk;

e. describe the capital asset pricing model, diagram the security market line (SML), and define beta;

f. calculate and interpret using the SML, the expected return on a security, and evaluate whether the security is undervalued, overvalued, or properly valued;

g. describe the effect on the SML of relaxing each of its main underlying assumptions line.

INTRODUCTION **1**

Following the development of portfolio theory by Markowitz, two major theories have been put forth that derive a model for the valuation of risky assets. In this reading, we introduce one of these two models—that is, the capital asset pricing model (CAPM). The background on the CAPM is important at this point in the book because the risk measure implied by this model is a necessary input for our subsequent discussion on the valuation of risky assets. The presentation concerns capital market theory and the capital asset pricing model that was developed almost concurrently by three individuals. Subsequently, an alternative

Investment Analysis and Portfolio Management, Eighth Edition, by Frank K. Reilly and Keith C. Brown, Copyright © 2005. Reprinted with permission of South-Western, a division of Thomson Learning.

multifactor asset valuation model was proposed, the arbitrage pricing theory (APT). This has led to the development of numerous other multifactor models that are the subject of the following reading.

2   CAPITAL MARKET THEORY: AN OVERVIEW

Because capital market theory builds on portfolio theory, this reading begins where the discussion of the Markowitz efficient frontier ended. We assume that you have examined the set of risky assets and derived the aggregate efficient frontier. Further, we assume that you and all other investors want to maximize your utility in terms of risk and return, so you will choose portfolios of risky assets on the efficient frontier at points where your utility maps are tangent to the frontier as shown in Exhibit 53-16. When you make your investment decision in this manner, you are referred to as a *Markowitz efficient investor.*

Capital market theory extends portfolio theory and develops a model for pricing all risky assets. The final product, the **capital asset pricing model (CAPM)**, will allow you to determine the required rate of return for any risky asset.

We begin with a discussion of the underlying assumptions of the capital market theory and the factors that led to its development following the Markowitz portfolio theory. This includes an analysis of the effect of assuming the existence of a risk-free asset.

Notably, assuming the existence of a risk-free rate has significant implications for the potential return and risk and alternative risk-return combinations. This discussion implies the existence of a portfolio of risky assets on the efficient frontier, which we call the market portfolio. We discuss the market portfolio in the third section and what it implies regarding different types of risk.

The fourth section considers which types of risk are relevant to an investor who believes in capital market theory. Having defined a measure of risk, we consider how you determine your required rate of return on an investment. A final step in the investment process is when you compare this required rate of return to your estimate of the asset's expected rate of return during your investment horizon to determine whether the asset is undervalued or overvalued. The section ends with a demonstration of how to calculate the risk measure implied by capital market theory.

Background for Capital Market Theory

When dealing with any theory in science, economics, or finance, it is necessary to articulate a set of assumptions that specify how the world is expected to act. This allows the theoretician to concentrate on developing a theory that explains how some facet of the world will respond to changes in the environment. In this section, we consider the main assumptions that underlie the development of capital market theory.

Assumptions of Capital Market Theory   Because capital market theory builds on the Markowitz portfolio model, it requires the same assumptions, along with some additional ones:

1. All investors are Markowitz efficient investors who want to target points on the efficient frontier. The exact location on the efficient frontier and, therefore, the specific portfolio selected will depend on the individual investor's risk-return utility function.

2. Investors can borrow or lend any amount of money at the risk-free rate of return (*RFR*). Clearly, it is always possible to lend money at the nominal risk-free rate by buying risk-free securities such as government T-bills. It is not always possible to borrow at this risk-free rate, but we will see that assuming a higher borrowing rate does not change the general results.

3. All investors have homogeneous expectations; that is, they estimate identical probability distributions for future rates of return. Again, this assumption can be relaxed. As long as the differences in expectations are not vast, their effects are minor.

4. All investors have the same one-period time horizon such as one month, six months, or one year. The model will be developed for a single hypothetical period, and its results could be affected by a different assumption. A difference in the time horizon would require investors to derive risk measures and risk-free assets that are consistent with their investment horizons.

5. All investments are infinitely divisible, which means that it is possible to buy or sell fractional shares of any asset or portfolio. This assumption allows us to discuss investment alternatives as continuous curves. Changing it would have little impact on the theory.

6. There are no taxes or transaction costs involved in buying or selling assets. This is a reasonable assumption in many instances. Neither pension funds nor religious groups have to pay taxes, and the transaction costs for most financial institutions are less than 1 percent on most financial instruments. Again, relaxing this assumption modifies the results, but it does not change the basic thrust.

7. There is no inflation or any change in interest rates, or inflation is fully anticipated. This is a reasonable initial assumption, and it can be modified.

8. Capital markets are in equilibrium. This means that we begin with all investments properly priced in line with their risk levels.

You may consider some of these assumptions unrealistic and wonder how useful a theory we can derive with these assumptions. In this regard, two points are important. First, as mentioned, relaxing many of these assumptions would have only a minor effect on the model and would not change its main implications or conclusions. Second, a theory should never be judged on the basis of its assumptions but rather on how well it explains and helps us predict behavior in the real world. If this theory and the model it implies help us explain the rates of return on a wide variety of risky assets, it is useful, even if some of its assumptions are unrealistic. Such success implies that the questionable assumptions must be unimportant to the ultimate objective of the model, which is to explain asset pricing and rates of return on assets.

Development of Capital Market Theory   The major factor that allowed portfolio theory to develop into capital market theory is the concept of a risk-free asset. Following the development of the Markowitz portfolio model, several authors considered the implications of assuming the existence of a **risk-free asset**, that is, an asset with *zero variance*. As we will show, such an asset would have zero correlation with all other risky assets and would provide the *risk-free rate of return (RFR)*. It would lie on the vertical axis of a portfolio graph.

This assumption of a risk-free asset allows us to derive a generalized theory of capital asset pricing under conditions of uncertainty from the Markowitz portfolio theory. This achievement is generally attributed to William Sharpe (1964), who received a Nobel Prize for it, but Lintner (1965) and Mossin (1966) derived similar theories independently. Consequently, you may see references to the Sharpe-Lintner-Mossin (SLM) capital asset pricing model.

Risk-Free Asset

As noted, the assumption of a risk-free asset in the economy is critical to asset pricing theory. Therefore, this section explains the meaning of a risk-free asset and shows the effect on the risk and return measures when this risk-free asset is combined with a portfolio on the Markowitz efficient frontier.

We have defined a **risky asset** as one from which future returns are uncertain, and we have measured this uncertainty by the variance, or standard deviation, of expected returns. Because the expected return on a risk-free asset is entirely certain, the standard deviation of its expected return is zero ($\sigma_{RF} = 0$). The rate of return earned on such an asset should be the risk-free rate of return *(RFR)*, which should equal the expected long-run growth rate of the economy with an adjustment for short-run liquidity. The next subsections show what happens when we introduce this risk-free asset into the risky world of the Markowitz portfolio model.

Covariance with a Risk-Free Asset   Recall that the covariance between two sets of returns is

$$\text{Cov}_{ij} = \sum_{i=1}^{n}[R_i - E(R_i)][R_j - E(R_j)]/n \qquad \textbf{(54-1)}$$

Because the returns for the risk-free asset are certain, $\sigma_{RF} = 0$, which means that $R_i = E(R_i)$ during all periods. Thus, $R_i - E(R_i)$ will equal zero, and the product of this expression with any other expression will equal zero. Consequently, the covariance of the risk-free asset with any risky asset or portfolio of assets will always equal zero. Similarly, the correlation between any risky asset i, and the risk-free asset, RF, would be zero because it is equal to

$$r_{RF,i} = \text{Cov}_{RF,i}/\sigma_{RF}\sigma_j$$

Combining a Risk-Free Asset with a Risky Portfolio   What happens to the average rate of return and the standard deviation of returns when you combine a risk-free asset with a portfolio of risky assets such as those that exist on the Markowitz efficient frontier?

Expected Return   Like the expected return for a portfolio of two risky assets, the expected rate of return for a portfolio that includes a risk-free asset is the weighted average of the two returns:

$$E(R_{\text{port}}) = w_{RF}(RFR) + (1 - w_{RF})E(R_i)$$

where:

w_{RF} = the proportion of the portfolio invested in the risk-free asset
$E(R_i)$ = the expected rate of return on risky Portfolio i

Standard Deviation   Recall from Reading 53 (Equation 53-7) that the expected variance for a two-asset portfolio is

$$\sigma_{\text{port}}^2 = w_1^2\sigma_1^2 + w_2^2\sigma_2^2 + 2w_1w_2r_{1,2}\sigma_1\sigma_2$$

Substituting the risk-free asset for Security 1, and the risky asset portfolio for Security 2, this formula would become

$$\sigma_{\text{port}}^2 = w_{RF}^2\sigma_{RF}^2 + (1 - w_{RF})^2\sigma_i^2 + 2w_{RF}(1 - w_{RF})r_{RFi}\sigma_{RF}\sigma_i$$

We know that the variance of the risk-free asset is zero, that is, $\sigma_{\text{RF}}^2 = 0$. Because the correlation between the risk-free asset and any risky asset, i, is also zero, the factor $r_{\text{RF},i}$ in the preceding equation also equals zero. Therefore, any component of the variance formula that has either of these terms will equal zero. When you make these adjustments, the formula becomes

$$\sigma_{\text{port}}^2 = (1 - w_{\text{RF}})^2 \sigma_i^2$$

The standard deviation is

$$\sigma_{\text{port}} = \sqrt{(1 - w_{\text{RF}})^2 \sigma_i^2}$$
$$= (1 - w_{\text{RF}}) \sigma_i$$

Therefore, the standard deviation of a portfolio that combines the risk-free asset with risky assets is *the linear proportion of the standard deviation of the risky asset portfolio.*

The Risk-Return Combination   Because both the expected return *and* the standard deviation of return for such a portfolio are linear combinations, a graph of possible portfolio returns and risks looks like a straight line between the two assets. Exhibit 54-1 shows a graph depicting portfolio possibilities when a risk-free asset is combined with alternative risky portfolios on the Markowitz efficient frontier.

You can attain any point along the straight line *RFR*-A by investing some portion of your portfolio in the risk-free asset w_{RF} and the remainder $(1 - w_{\text{RF}})$ in the risky asset portfolio at Point A on the efficient frontier. This set of portfolio possibilities dominates all the risky asset portfolios on the efficient frontier below Point A because some portfolio along Line *RFR*-A has equal variance with a higher rate of return than the portfolio on the original efficient frontier. Likewise, you can attain any point along the Line *RFR*-B by investing in some combination of the risk-free asset and the risky asset portfolio at Point B. Again, these

EXHIBIT 54-1	**Portfolio Possibilities Combining the Risk-Free Asset and Risky Portfolios on the Efficient Frontier**

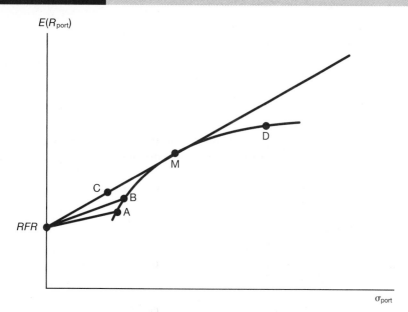

potential combinations dominate all portfolio possibilities on the original efficient frontier below Point B (including Line *RFR*-A).

You can draw further lines from the *RFR* to the efficient frontier at higher and higher points until you reach the point where the line is tangent to the frontier, which occurs in Exhibit 54-1 at Point M. The set of portfolio possibilities along Line *RFR*-M dominates *all* portfolios below Point M. For example, you could attain a risk and return combination between the *RFR* and Point M (Point C) by investing one-half of your portfolio in the risk-free asset (that is, lending money at the *RFR*) and the other half in the risky portfolio at Point M.

Risk-Return Possibilities with Leverage   An investor may want to attain a higher expected return than is available at Point M in exchange for accepting higher risk. One alternative would be to invest in one of the risky asset portfolios on the efficient frontier beyond Point M such as the portfolio at Point D. A second alternative is to add *leverage* to the portfolio by *borrowing* money at the risk-free rate and investing the proceeds in the risky asset portfolio at Point M. What effect would this have on the return and risk for your portfolio?

If you borrow an amount equal to 50 percent of your original wealth at the risk-free rate, w_{RF} will not be a positive fraction but, rather, a negative 50 percent ($w_{RF} = -0.50$). The effect on the expected return for your portfolio is:

$$E(R_{port}) = w_{RF}(RFR) + (1 - w_{RF})E(R_M)$$
$$= -0.50(RFR) + [1 - (-0.50)]E(R_M)$$
$$= -0.50(RFR) + 1.50E(R_M)$$

The return will increase in a *linear* fashion along the Line *RFR*-M because the gross return increases by 50 percent, but you must pay interest at the *RFR* on the money borrowed. For example, assume that $E(RFR) = .06$ and $E(R_M) = .12$. The return on your leveraged portfolio would be:

$$E(R_{port}) = -0.50(0.06) + 1.5(0.12)$$
$$= -0.03 + 0.18$$
$$= 0.15$$

The effect on the standard deviation of the leveraged portfolio is similar.

$$\sigma_{port} = (1 - w_{RF})\sigma_M$$
$$= [1 - (-0.50)]\sigma_M = 1.50\sigma_M$$

where:
σ_M = the standard deviation of the M portfolio

Therefore, *both return and risk increase in a linear fashion along the original Line RFR-M,* and this extension dominates everything below the line on the original efficient frontier. Thus, you have a new efficient frontier: the straight line from the *RFR* tangent to Point M. This line is referred to as the **capital market line (CML)** and is shown in Exhibit 54-2.

Our discussion of portfolio theory stated that, when two assets are perfectly correlated, the set of portfolio possibilities falls along a straight line. Therefore, because the CML is a straight line, it implies that all the portfolios on the CML are perfectly positively correlated. This positive correlation appeals to our intuition because all these portfolios on the CML combine the risky asset Portfolio M and the risk-free asset. You either invest part of your portfolio in the risk-free asset (i.e., you *lend* at the *RFR*) and the rest in the risky asset Portfolio M, or you *borrow* at the risk-free rate and invest these funds in the risky asset portfolio. In either case, all the variability comes from the risky asset M portfolio. The only difference between

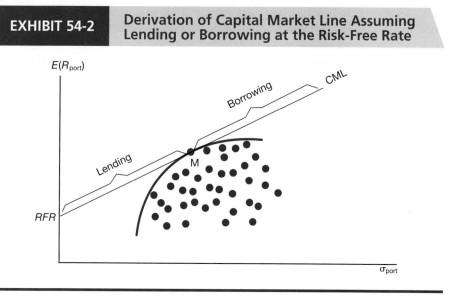

EXHIBIT 54-2 — Derivation of Capital Market Line Assuming Lending or Borrowing at the Risk-Free Rate

the alternative portfolios on the CML is the magnitude of the variability, which is caused by the proportion of the risky asset portfolio in the total portfolio.

The Market Portfolio

Because Portfolio M lies at the point of tangency, it has the highest portfolio possibility line, and everybody will want to invest in Portfolio M and borrow or lend to be somewhere on the CML. This portfolio must, therefore, include *all risky assets*. If a risky asset were not in this portfolio in which everyone wants to invest, there would be no demand for it and therefore it would have no value.

Because the market is in equilibrium, it is also necessary that all assets are included in this portfolio *in proportion to their market value*. If, for example, an asset accounts for a higher proportion of the M portfolio than its market value justifies, excess demand for this asset will increase its price until its relative market value becomes consistent with its proportion in the M portfolio.

This portfolio that includes all risky assets is referred to as the **market portfolio**. It includes not only U.S. common stocks but *all* risky assets, such as non-U.S. stocks, U.S. and non-U.S. bonds, options, real estate, coins, stamps, art, or antiques. Because the market portfolio contains all risky assets, it is a **completely diversified portfolio**, which means that all the risk unique to individual assets in the portfolio is diversified away. Specifically, the unique risk of any single asset is offset by the unique variability of all the other assets in the portfolio.

This unique (diversifiable) risk is also referred to as **unsystematic risk**. This implies that only **systematic risk**, which is defined as the variability in all risky assets caused by macro-economic variables, remains in the market portfolio. This systematic risk, measured by the standard deviation of returns of the market portfolio, can change over time if and when there are changes in the macroeconomic variables that affect the valuation of all risky assets.[1] Examples of such macro-economic variables would be variability of growth in the money supply, interest rate volatility, and variability in such factors as industrial production, corporate earnings, and corporate cash flow.

---

[1] For an analysis of changes in the standard deviation (volatility) of returns for stocks and bonds in the United States, see Schwert (1989); Spiro (1990); Officer (1973); and Reilly, Wright, and Chan (2000).

How to Measure Diversification   As noted earlier, all portfolios on the CML are perfectly positively correlated, which means that all portfolios on the CML are perfectly correlated with the completely diversified market Portfolio M. As noted by Lorie (1975), this implies a measure of complete diversification. Specifically, a completely diversified portfolio would have a correlation with the market portfolio of +1.00. This is logical because complete diversification means the elimination of all the unsystematic or unique risk. Once you have eliminated all unsystematic risk, only systematic risk is left, which cannot be diversified away. Therefore, completely diversified portfolios would correlate perfectly with the market portfolio because it has only systematic risk.

Diversification and the Elimination of Unsystematic Risk   As discussed in Reading 53, the purpose of diversification is to reduce the standard deviation of the total portfolio. This assumes imperfect correlations among securities.[2] Ideally, as you add securities, the average covariance for the portfolio declines. An important question is, about how many securities must be included to arrive at a completely diversified portfolio? To discover the answer, you must observe what happens as you increase the sample size of the portfolio by adding securities that have some positive correlation. The typical correlation between U.S. securities is about 0.5 to 0.6.

One set of studies examined the average standard deviation for numerous portfolios of randomly selected stocks of different sample sizes. Specifically, Evans and Archer (1968) and Tole (1982) computed the standard deviation for portfolios of increasing numbers up to 20 stocks. The results indicated a large initial impact wherein the major benefits of diversification were achieved rather quickly. Specifically, about 90 percent of the maximum benefit of diversification was derived from portfolios of 12 to 18 stocks. Exhibit 54-3 shows a graph of the effect.

A subsequent study by Statman (1987) compared the benefits of lower risk from diversification to the added transaction costs with more securities. It

EXHIBIT 54-3	Number of Stocks in a Portfolio and the Standard Deviation of Portfolio Return

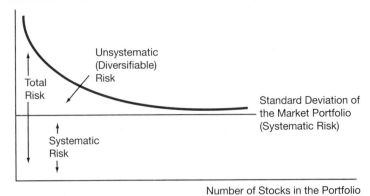

---

[2] The discussion in Reading 53 leads one to conclude that securities with negative correlation would be ideal. Although this is true in theory, it is difficult to find such assets in the real world

concluded that a well-diversified stock portfolio must include at least 30 stocks for a borrowing investor and 40 stocks for a lending investor.

An important point to remember is that, by adding stocks to the portfolio that are not perfectly correlated with stocks in the portfolio, you can reduce the overall standard deviation of the portfolio but you *cannot eliminate variability.* The standard deviation of your portfolio will eventually reach the level of the market portfolio, where you will have diversified away all unsystematic risk, but you still have market or systematic risk. You cannot eliminate the variability and uncertainty of macroeconomic factors that affect all risky assets. At the same time, you can attain a lower level of systematic risk by diversifying globally versus only diversifying within the United States because some of the systematic risk factors in the U.S. market (such as U.S. monetary policy) are not correlated with systematic risk variables in other countries such as Germany and Japan. As a result, if you diversify globally, you eventually get down to a world systematic risk level.

The CML and the Separation Theorem   The CML leads all investors to invest in the same risky asset portfolio, the M portfolio. Individual investors should only differ regarding their position on the CML, which depends on their risk preferences.

In turn, how they get to a point on the CML is based on their *financing decisions.* If you are relatively risk averse, you will lend some part of your portfolio at the *RFR* by buying some risk-free securities and investing the remainder in the market portfolio of risky assets. For example, you might invest in the portfolio combination at Point A in Exhibit 54-4. In contrast, if you prefer more risk, you might borrow funds at the *RFR* and invest everything (all of your capital plus what you borrowed) in the market portfolio, building the portfolio at Point B. This financing decision provides more risk but greater returns than the market portfolio. As discussed earlier, because portfolios on the CML dominate other portfolio possibilities, the CML becomes the efficient frontier of portfolios, and investors decide where they want to be along this efficient frontier. Tobin (1958)

EXHIBIT 54-4	Choice of Optimal Portfolio Combinations on the CML

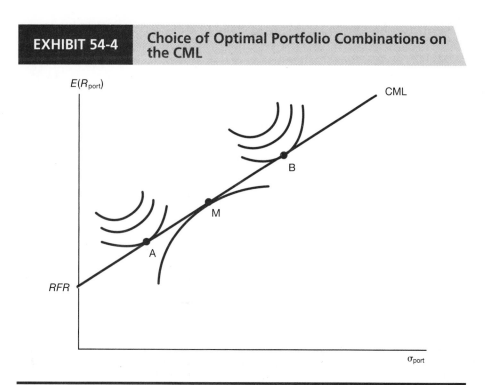

called this division of the investment decision from the financing decision the **separation theorem**. Specifically, to be somewhere on the CML efficient frontier, you initially decide to invest in the market Portfolio M, which means that you will be on the CML. This is your *investment* decision. Subsequently, based on your risk preferences, you make a separate *financing* decision either to borrow or to lend to attain your preferred risk position on the CML.

A Risk Measure for the CML In this section, we show that the relevant risk measure for risky assets is *their covariance with the M portfolio,* which is referred to as their systematic risk. The importance of this covariance is apparent from two points of view.

First, in discussing the Markowitz portfolio model, we noted that the relevant risk to consider when adding a security to a portfolio is *its average covariance with all other assets in the portfolio.* In this reading, we have shown that *the only relevant portfolio is the M portfolio.* Together, these two findings mean that the only important consideration for any individual risky asset is its average covariance with all the risky assets in the M portfolio or, simply, *the asset's covariance with the market portfolio.* This covariance, then, is the relevant risk measure for an individual risky asset.

Second, because all individual risky assets are a part of the M portfolio, one can describe their rates of return in relation to the returns for the M portfolio using the following linear model:

$$R_{it} = a_i + b_i R_{Mt} + \varepsilon \tag{54-2}$$

where:

$$
\begin{aligned}
R_{i,t} &= \text{return for asset } i \text{ during period } t \\
a_i &= \text{constant term for asset } i \\
b_i &= \text{slope coefficient for asset } i \\
R_{Mt} &= \text{return for the M portfolio during period } t \\
\varepsilon &= \text{random error term}
\end{aligned}
$$

The variance of returns for a risky asset could be described as

$$
\begin{aligned}
\text{Var}(R_{it}) &= \text{Var}(a_i + b_i R_{Mt} + \varepsilon) \\
&= \text{Var}(a_i) + \text{Var}(b_i R_{Mt}) + \text{Var}(\varepsilon) \\
&= 0 + \text{Var}(b_i R_{Mt}) + \text{Var}(\varepsilon)
\end{aligned}
\tag{54-3}
$$

Note that $\text{Var}(b_i R_{Mt})$ is the variance of return for an asset related to the variance of the market return, or the *systematic variance or risk.* Also, $\text{Var}(\varepsilon)$ is the residual variance of return for the individual asset that is not related to the market portfolio. This residual variance is the variability that we have referred to as the unsystematic or *unique risk* or unsystematic or unique *variance* because it arises from the unique features of the asset. Therefore:

$$\text{Var}(R_{i,t}) = \text{Systematic Variance} + \text{Unsystematic Variance} \tag{54-4}$$

We know that a completely diversified portfolio such as the market portfolio has had all the unsystematic variance eliminated. Therefore, the unsystematic variance of an asset is not relevant to investors, because they can and do eliminate it when making an asset part of the market portfolio. Therefore, investors should not expect to receive added returns for assuming this unsystematic (unique) risk. Only the systematic variance is relevant because it *cannot* be diversified away, because it is caused by macroeconomic factors that affect all risky assets.

THE CAPITAL ASSET PRICING MODEL: EXPECTED RETURN AND RISK

Up to this point, we have considered how investors make their portfolio decisions, including the significant effects of a risk-free asset. The existence of this risk-free asset resulted in the derivation of a capital market line (CML) that became the relevant efficient frontier. Because all investors want to be on the CML, an asset's covariance with the market portfolio of risky assets emerged as the relevant risk measure.

Now that we understand this relevant measure of risk, we can proceed to use it to determine an appropriate expected rate of return on a risky asset. This step takes us into the **capital asset pricing model (CAPM)**, which is a model that indicates what should be the expected or required rates of return on risky assets. This transition is important because it helps you to value an asset by providing an appropriate discount rate to use in any valuation model. Alternatively, if you have already estimated the rate of return that you think you will earn on an investment, you can compare this *estimated* **rate of return** to the *required* rate of return implied by the CAPM and determine whether the asset is undervalued, overvalued, or properly valued.

To accomplish the foregoing, we demonstrate the creation of a security market line (SML) that visually represents the relationship between risk and the expected or the required rate of return on an asset. The equation of this SML, together with estimates for the return on a risk-free asset and on the market portfolio, can generate expected or required rates of return for any asset based on its systematic risk. You compare this required rate of return to the rate of return that you estimate that you will earn on the investment to determine if the investment is undervalued or overvalued. After demonstrating this procedure, we finish the section with a demonstration of how to calculate the systematic risk variable for a risky asset.

The Security Market Line (SML)

We know that the relevant risk measure for an individual risky asset is its covariance with the market portfolio ($\text{Cov}_{i,M}$). Therefore, we can draw the risk-return relationship as shown in Exhibit 54-5 with the systematic covariance variable ($\text{Cov}_{i,M}$) as the risk measure.

The return for the market portfolio (R_M) should be consistent with its own risk, which is the covariance of the market with itself. If you recall the formula for covariance, you will see that the covariance of any asset with itself is its variance, $\text{Cov}_{i,i} = \sigma_i^2$. In turn, the covariance of the market with itself is the variance of the market rate of return $\text{Cov}_{M,M} = \sigma_M^2$. Therefore, the equation for the risk-return line in Exhibit 54-5 is:

$$
\begin{aligned}
E(R_i) &= RFR + \frac{R_M - RFR}{\sigma_M^2}(\text{Cov}_{i,M}) \\
&= RFR + \frac{\text{Cov}_{i,M}}{\sigma_M^2}(R_M - RFR)
\end{aligned}
$$

(54-5)

Defining $\text{Cov}_{i,M}/\sigma_M^2$ as beta, (β_i), this equation can be stated:

$$
E(R_i) = RFR + \beta_i(R_M - RFR)
$$

(54-6)

Beta can be viewed as a *standardized* measure of systematic risk. Specifically, we already know that the covariance of any asset i with the market portfolio (Cov_{iM})

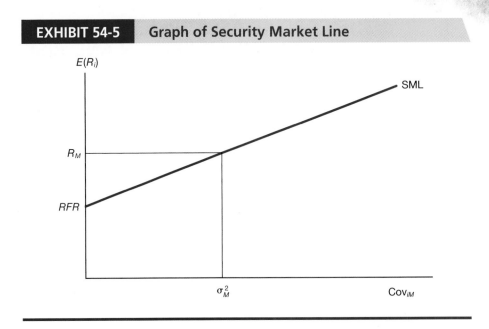

EXHIBIT 54-5   **Graph of Security Market Line**

is the relevant risk measure. Beta is a standardized measure of risk because it relates this covariance to the variance of the market portfolio. As a result, the market portfolio has a beta of 1. Therefore, if the β_i for an asset is above 1.0, the asset has higher normalized systematic risk than the market, which means that it is more volatile than the overall market portfolio.

Given this standardized measure of systematic risk, the SML graph can be expressed as shown in Exhibit 54-6. This is the same graph as in Exhibit 54-5, except there is a different measure of risk. Specifically, the graph in Exhibit 54-6 replaces the covariance of an asset's returns with the market portfolio as the risk measure with the standardized measure of systematic risk (beta), which is the covariance of an asset with the market portfolio divided by the variance of the market portfolio.

Determining the Expected Rate of Return for a Risky Asset   Equation 54-6 and the graph in Exhibit 54-6 tell us that the expected (required) rate of return for a

EXHIBIT 54-6   **Graph of SML with Normalized Systematic Risk**

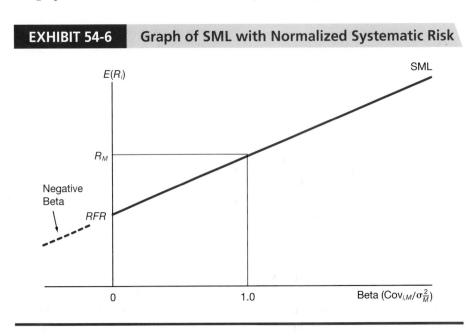

risky asset is determined by the *RFR* plus a risk premium for the individual asset. In turn, the risk premium is determined by the systematic risk of the asset (β_i), and the prevailing **market risk premium** ($R_M - RFR$). To demonstrate how you would compute the expected or required rates of return, consider the following example stocks assuming you have already computed betas:

Stock	Beta
A	0.70
B	1.00
C	1.15
D	1.40
E	−0.30

Assume that we expect the economy's *RFR* to be 5 percent (0.05) and the return on the market portfolio (R_M) to be 9 percent (0.09). This implies a market risk premium of 4 percent (0.04). With these inputs, the SML equation would yield the following expected (required) rates of return for these five stocks:

$$E(R_i) = RFR + \beta_i(R_M - RFR)$$
$$E(R_A) = 0.05 + 0.70\,(0.09 - 0.05)$$
$$= 0.078 = 7.80\%$$
$$E(R_B) = 0.05 + 1.00\,(0.09 - 0.05)$$
$$= 0.09 = 9.00\%$$
$$E(R_C) = 0.05 + 1.15\,(0.09 - 0.05)$$
$$= 0.096 = 9.60\%$$
$$E(R_D) = 0.05 + 1.40\,(0.09 - 0.05)$$
$$= 0.106 = 10.60\%$$
$$E(R_E) = 0.05 + (-0.30)\,(0.09 - 0.05)$$
$$= 0.05 - 0.012$$
$$= 0.038 = 3.8\%$$

As stated, these are the expected (required) rates of return that these stocks should provide based on their systematic risks and the prevailing SML.

Stock A has lower risk than the aggregate market, so you should not expect (require) its return to be as high as the return on the market portfolio of risky assets. You should expect (require) Stock A to return 7.80 percent. Stock B has systematic risk equal to the market's (beta = 1.00), so its required rate of return should likewise be equal to the expected market return (9 percent). Stocks C and D have systematic risk greater than the market's, so they should provide returns consistent with their risk. Finally, Stock E has a *negative* beta (which is quite rare in practice), so its required rate of return, if such a stock could be found, would be below the *RFR* of 5 percent.

In equilibrium, *all* assets and *all* portfolios of assets should plot on the SML. That is, all assets should be priced so that their **estimated rates of return**, which are the actual holding period rates of return that you anticipate, are consistent with their levels of systematic risk. Any security with an estimated rate of return that plots above the SML would be considered underpriced because it implies that you *estimated* you would receive a rate of return on the security that is above its *required* rate of return based on its systematic risk. In contrast, assets with estimated rates of return that plot below the SML would be considered overpriced. This

| EXHIBIT 54-7 | Price, Dividend, and Rate of Return Estimates | | | |

Stock	Current Price (P_t)	Expected Price (P_{t+1})	Expected Dividend (D_{t+1})	Estimated Future Rate of Return (Percent)
A	25	26	1.00	8.00%
B	40	42	0.50	6.20
C	33	37	1.00	15.15
D	64	66	1.10	5.16
E	50	53	—	6.00

position relative to the SML implies that your estimated rate of return is below what you should require based on the asset's systematic risk.

In a completely efficient market in equilibrium, you would not expect any assets to plot off the SML because, in equilibrium, all stocks should provide holding period returns that are equal to their required rates of return. Alternatively, a market that is fairly efficient but not completely efficient may misprice certain assets because not everyone will be aware of all the relevant information for an asset.

A superior investor has the ability to derive value estimates for assets that are consistently superior to the consensus market evaluation. As a result, such an investor will earn better rates of return than the average investor on a risk-adjusted basis.

Identifying Undervalued and Overvalued Assets Now that we understand how to compute the rate of return one should expect or require for a specific risky asset using the SML, we can compare this *required* rate of return to the asset's *estimated* rate of return over a specific investment horizon to determine whether it would be an appropriate investment. To make this comparison, you need an independent estimate of the return outlook for the security based on either fundamental or technical analysis techniques, which will be discussed in subsequent readings. Let us continue the example for the five assets discussed in the previous subsection.

Assume that analysts in a major trust department have been following these five stocks. Based on extensive fundamental analysis, the analysts provide the expected price and dividend estimates contained in Exhibit 54-7. Given these projections, you can compute the estimated rates of return the analysts would anticipate during this holding period.

| EXHIBIT 54-8 | Comparison of Required Rate of Return to Estimated Rate of Return | | | | |

Stock	Beta	Required Return $E(R_i)$	Estimated Return	Estimated Return Minus $E(R_i)$	Evaluation
A	0.70	7.80	8.00	0.20	Properly valued
B	1.00	9.00	6.20	−2.80	Overvalued
C	1.15	9.60	15.15	5.55	Undervalued
D	1.40	10.60	5.16	−5.44	Overvalued
E	−0.30	3.80	6.00	2.20	Undervalued

| EXHIBIT 54-9 | Plot of Estimated Returns on SML Graph |

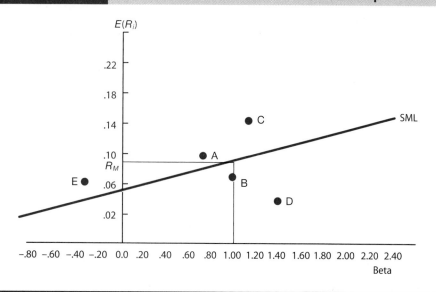

Exhibit 54-8 summarizes the relationship between the required rate of return for each stock based on its systematic risk as computed earlier, and its estimated rate of return (from Exhibit 54-7) based on the current and future prices, and its dividend outlook. This difference between estimated return and expected (required) return is sometimes referred to as a stock's *alpha* or its excess return. This alpha can be positive (the stock is undervalued) or negative (the stock is overvalued). If the alpha is zero, the stock is on the SML and is properly valued in line with its systematic risk.

Plotting these estimated rates of return and stock betas on the SML we specified earlier gives the graph shown in Exhibit 54-9. Stock A is almost exactly on the line, so it is considered properly valued because its estimated rate of return is almost equal to its required rate of return. Stocks B and D are considered overvalued because their estimated rates of return during the coming period are less than what an investor should expect (require) for the risk involved. As a result, they plot below the SML. In contrast, Stocks C and E are expected to provide rates of return greater than we would require based on their systematic risk. Therefore, both stocks plot above the SML, indicating that they are undervalued stocks.

Assuming that you trusted your analyst to forecast estimated returns, you would take no action regarding Stock A, but you would buy Stocks C and E and sell Stocks B and D. You might even sell Stocks B and D short if you favored such aggressive tactics.

Calculating Systematic Risk: The Characteristic Line   The systematic risk input for an individual asset is derived from a regression model, referred to as the asset's **characteristic line** with the market portfolio:

$$R_{i,t} = \alpha_i + \beta_i R_{M,t} + \varepsilon \tag{54-7}$$

where:
$R_{i,t}$ = the rate of return for Asset i during Period t
$R_{M,t}$ = the rate of return for the market portfolio M during Period t
α_i = the constant term, or intercept, of the regression, which equals $\overline{R}_i - \beta_i \overline{R}_M$
β_i = the systematic risk (beta) of Asset i equal to $\text{Cov}_{i,M}/\sigma_M^2$
ε = the random error term

EXHIBIT 54-10   Scatterplot of Rates of Return

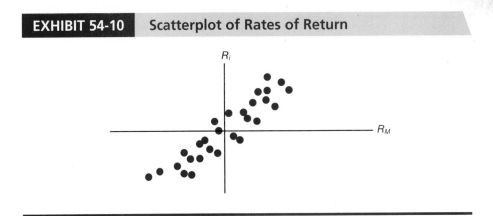

The characteristic line (Equation 54-7) is the regression line of best fit through a scatterplot of rates of return for the individual risky asset and for the market portfolio of risky assets over some designated past period, as shown in Exhibit 54-10.

The Impact of the Time Interval   In practice, the number of observations and the time interval used in the regression vary. Value Line Investment Services derives characteristic lines for common stocks using weekly rates of return for the most recent five years (260 weekly observations). Merrill Lynch, Pierce, Fenner & Smith uses monthly rates of return for the most recent five years (60 monthly observations). Because there is no theoretically correct time interval for analysis, we must make a trade-off between enough observations to eliminate the impact of random rates of return and an excessive length of time, such as 15 or 20 years, over which the subject company may have changed dramatically. Remember that what you really want is the *expected* systematic risk for the potential investment. In this analysis, you are analyzing historical data to help you derive a reasonable estimate of the asset's expected systematic risk.

A couple of studies have considered the effect of the time interval used to compute betas (weekly versus monthly). Statman (1981) examined the relationship between Value Line (VL) betas and Merrill Lynch (ML) betas and found a relatively weak relationship. Reilly and Wright (1988) analyzed the differential effects of return computation, market index, and the time interval and showed that the major cause of the differences in beta was the use of monthly versus weekly return intervals. Also, the interval effect depended on the sizes of the firms. The shorter weekly interval caused a larger beta for large firms and a smaller beta for small firms. For example, the average beta for the smallest decile of firms using monthly data was 1.682, but the average beta for these small firms using weekly data was only 1.080. The authors concluded that the return time interval makes a difference, and its impact increases as the firm size declines.

The Effect of the Market Proxy   Another significant decision when computing an asset's characteristic line is which indicator series to use as a proxy for the market portfolio of all risky assets. Most investigators use the Standard & Poor's 500 Composite Index as a proxy for the market portfolio, because the stocks in this index encompass a large proportion of the total market value of U.S. stocks and it is a value-weighted series, which is consistent with the theoretical market series. Still, this series contains only large-cap U.S. stocks, most of them listed on the NYSE. Previously, it was noted that the market portfolio of all risky assets should include U.S. stocks and bonds, non-U.S. stocks and bonds, real estate, coins, stamps, art, antiques, and any other marketable risky asset from around the world.[3]

Example Computations of a Characteristic Line   The following examples show how you would compute characteristic lines for General Electric (GE) based on the monthly rates of return during 2004.[4] Twelve monthly rates are not enough observations for statistical purposes, but they provide a good example. We demonstrate the computations using two different proxies for the market portfolio. First, we use the standard S&P 500 as the market proxy. Second, we use the Morgan Stanley (M-S) World Equity Index as the market proxy. This analysis demonstrates the effect of using a global portfolio of stocks as the market proxy.

The monthly price changes are computed using the closing prices for the last day of each month. These data for GE, the S&P 500, and the M-S World Index are contained in Exhibit 54-11. Exhibit 54-12 contains the scatterplot of the percentage price changes for GE and the S&P 500. During this 12-month period, there were only 2 months when GE had returns that were not consistent with the S&P 500. As a result, the covariance between GE and the S&P 500 series was a reasonable positive value (3.57). The covariance divided by the variance of the S&P 500 market portfolio (4.38) indicates that GE's beta relative to the S&P 500 was equal to 0.82. This analysis indicates that, during this limited time period, GE was less risky than the aggregate market proxied by the S&P 500. When we draw the computed characteristic line on Exhibit 54-12, the scatterplots are reasonably close to the characteristic line except for two observations, which is consistent with the correlation coefficient of 0.43.

The computation of the characteristic line for GE using the M-S World Index as the proxy for the market is contained in Exhibit 54-11, and the scatterplots are in Exhibit 54-13. At this point, it is important to consider what one might expect to be the relationship between the beta relative to the S&P 500 versus the betas with the M-S World Index. This requires a consideration of the two components that go into the computation of beta: (1) the covariance between the stock and the benchmark and (2) the variance of returns for the benchmark series. Notably, there is no obvious answer regarding what will happen to the beta for either series because one would expect both components to change. Specifically, the covariance of GE with the S&P 500 will probably be higher than the covariance with the global series because you are matching a U.S. stock with a U.S. market index rather than a world index. Thus, one would expect the covariance with the global index to be smaller. At the same time, the variance of returns for the world stock index should also be smaller than the variance for the S&P 500 because the world index is a more diversified stock portfolio.

Therefore, the direction of change for the beta will depend on the relative change in the two components. Empirically, as demonstrated by Reilly and Akhtar (1995), the beta is typically smaller with the world stock index because the covariance is definitely lower, but the variance is only slightly smaller. The results of this example were consistent with these expectations. The beta of GE with the world stock index was definitely smaller (0.59 vs. 0.82) because the covariance of GE with the global index was smaller as expected (3.30 vs. 3.57), but the variance of the global market proxy was not smaller as hypothesized (it was 5.59 vs. 4.38). The fact that the betas with the alternative market proxies differed is significant

---

[3] Substantial discussion surrounds the market index used and its impact on the empirical results and usefulness of the CAPM. This concern is discussed further and demonstrated in the subsequent section on computing an asset's characteristic line.

[4] These betas are computed using only monthly price changes for GE, the S&P 500, and the M-S World Index (dividends are not included). This is done for simplicity but it is also based on a study by Sharpe and Cooper (1972a) that indicated that betas derived with and without dividends have a correlation coefficient of 0.99.

EXHIBIT 54-11   Computation of Beta for General Electric with Selected Indexes

Date	Index			Return			S&P 500 (1) $R(S\&P) - \bar{R}(S\&P)$	MSCI World (2) $R(MSCI) - \bar{R}(MSCI)$	GE (3) $R(GE) - \bar{R}(GE)$	(4)[a]	(5)[b]
	S&P 500	MSCI World	GE	S&P 500	MSCI World	GE					
Dec-03	1111.92	1,036.32	30.98	—	—	—					
Jan-04	1131.13	1,052.29	33.63	1.73	1.54	8.55	0.99	0.50	7.11	7.02	3.58
Feb-04	1144.94	1,068.65	32.52	1.22	1.55	(3.30)	0.48	0.52	(4.75)	(2.28)	(2.46)
Mar-04	1126.21	1,059.16	30.52	(1.64)	(0.89)	(6.15)	(2.38)	(1.93)	(7.60)	18.05	14.63
Apr-04	1107.3	1,035.66	29.95	(1.68)	(2.22)	(1.87)	(2.42)	(3.26)	(3.32)	8.02	10.79
May-04	1120.68	1,042.63	31.12	1.21	0.67	3.91	0.47	(0.36)	2.46	1.15	(0.90)
Jun-04	1140.84	1,062.51	32.40	1.80	1.91	4.11	1.06	0.87	2.67	2.82	2.32
Jul-04	1101.72	1,026.99	33.25	(3.43)	(3.34)	2.62	(4.17)	(4.38)	1.18	(4.90)	(5.15)
Aug-04	1104.24	1,029.63	32.79	0.23	0.26	(1.38)	(0.51)	(0.78)	(2.83)	1.45	2.21
Sep-04	1114.58	1,047.86	33.58	0.94	1.77	2.41	0.20	0.73	0.96	0.19	0.71
Oct-04	1130.2	1,072.70	34.12	1.40	2.37	1.61	0.66	1.33	0.16	0.11	0.21
Nov-04	1173.82	1,127.34	35.36	3.86	5.09	3.63	3.12	4.06	2.19	6.82	8.87
Dec-04	1211.92	1,169.34	36.50	3.25	3.73	3.22	2.51	2.69	1.78	4.45	4.78
									Total =	42.89	39.59
Average (R)				0.74	1.04	1.45					
Standard Deviation				2.09	2.36	3.97					

Cov(GE, S&P) = 42.89/12 = 3.57
Cov(GE, MSCI) = 39.59/12 = 3.30
Correlation Coef.(GE, S&P) = 3.57/(2.09 × 3.97) = 0.430

Var(S&P) = St. Dev.(S&P)^2 = 2.09^2 = 4.38
Var(MSCI) = St. Dev.(MSCI)^2 = 2.36^2 = 5.59

Beta(GE, S&P) = 3.57/4.38 = 0.82
Beta(GE, MSCI) = 3.30/5.59 = 0.59

Alpha(GE, S&P) = 1.45 − (0.82 × 0.74) = 0.843
Alpha(GE, MSCI) = 1.45 − (0.59 × 1.04) = 0.836
Correlation Coef.(GE, MSCI) = 3.30/(2.36 × 3.97) = 0.352

[a] Column 4 is equal to Column 1 multiplied by Column 3.
[b] Column 5 is equal to Column 2 multiplied by Column 3.

| EXHIBIT 54-12 | Scatterplot of General Electric (GE) and the S&P 500 with Characteristic Line for GE: 2004 |

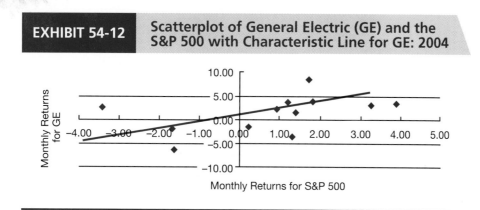

Monthly Returns for S&P 500

and reflects the potential problem in a global investment environment. Specifically, it means that selecting the appropriate proxy for the market portfolio is an important decision when measuring risk.

RELAXING THE ASSUMPTIONS   4

Earlier in the reading, several assumptions were set forth related to the CAPM. In this section, we discuss the impact on the capital market line (CML) and the security market line (SML) when we relax several of these assumptions.

Differential Borrowing and Lending Rates

One of the first assumptions of the CAPM was that investors could borrow and lend any amount of money at the risk-free rate. It is reasonable to assume that investors can *lend* unlimited amounts at the risk-free rate by buying government securities (e.g., T-bills). In contrast, one may question the ability of investors to borrow unlimited amounts at the T-bill rate because most investors must pay a premium relative to the prime rate when borrowing money. For example, when T-bills are yielding 4 percent, the prime rate will probably be about 6 percent, and most individuals would have to pay about 7 percent to borrow at the bank.

| EXHIBIT 54-13 | Scatterplot of General Electric (GE) and the MSCI World Index with Characteristic Line for GE: 2004 |

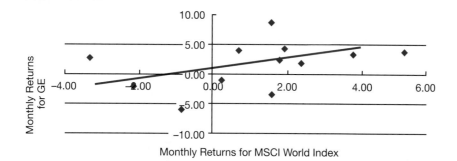

Monthly Returns for MSCI World Index

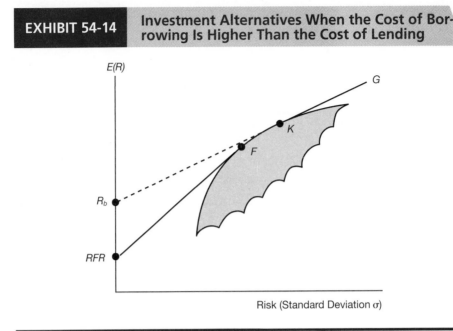

| EXHIBIT 54-14 | Investment Alternatives When the Cost of Borrowing Is Higher Than the Cost of Lending |

Because of this differential, there will be two different lines going to the Markowitz efficient frontier, as shown in Exhibit 54-14. The segment *RFR-F* indicates the investment opportunities available when an investor combines risk-free assets (i.e., lending at the *RFR*) and Portfolio F on the Markowitz efficient frontier. It is not possible to extend this line any farther if it is assumed that you cannot borrow at this risk-free rate to acquire further units of Portfolio F. If it is assumed that you can borrow at R_b, the point of tangency from this rate would be on the curve at Point K. This indicates that you could borrow at R_b and use the proceeds to invest in Portfolio K to extend the CML along the line segment *K-G*. Therefore, the CML is made up of *RFR-F-K-G;* that is, a line segment (*RFR-F*), a curve segment (*F-K*), and another line segment (*K-G*). As noted by Brennan (1969), this implies that you can either lend or borrow, but the borrowing portfolios are not as profitable as when it was assumed that you could borrow at the *RFR*. In this instance, because you must pay a borrowing rate that is higher than the *RFR*, your net return is less—that is, the slope of the borrowing line (*K-G*) is below that for *RFR-F*.

Zero-Beta Model

If the market portfolio (M) is mean-variance efficient (i.e., it has the lowest risk for a given level of return among the attainable set of portfolios), an alternative model, derived by Black (1972), does not require a risk-free asset. Specifically, within the set of feasible alternative portfolios, several portfolios exist where the returns are completely uncorrelated with the market portfolio; the beta of these portfolios with the market portfolio is zero. From among the several zero-beta portfolios, you would select the one with minimum variance. Although this portfolio does not have any systematic risk, it does have some unsystematic risk. The availability of this zero-beta portfolio will not affect the CML, but it will allow construction of a linear SML, as shown in Exhibit 54-15. In the model, the intercept is the expected return for the zero-beta portfolio. Similar to the earlier proof in this reading, the combinations of this zero-beta portfolio and the market

EXHIBIT 54-15   Security Market Line with a Zero-Beta Portfolio

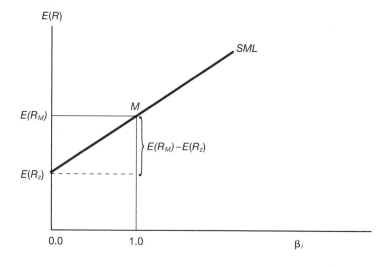

portfolio will be a linear relationship in return and risk because the covariance between the zero-beta portfolio (R_z) and the market portfolio is similar to what it was with the risk-free asset. Assuming the return for the zero-beta portfolio is greater than that for a risk-free asset, the slope of the line through the market portfolio would not be as steep; that is, the market risk premium would be smaller. The equation for this zero-beta CAPM line would be:

$$E(R_i) = E(R_z) + B_i[E(R_M) - E(R_z)] \tag{54-8}$$

Obviously, the risk premiums for individual assets would be a function of the beta for the individual security and the market risk premium:

$$[E(R_M) - E(R_z)]$$

Some of the empirical results discussed in the next section support this model with its higher intercept and flatter slope. Alternatively, several studies have specifically tested this model and had conflicting results. Specifically, studies by Gibbons (1982) and Shanken (1985b) rejected the model, while a study by Stambaugh (1982) supported the zero-beta CAPM.

Transaction Costs

The basic assumption is that there are no transaction costs, so investors will buy or sell mispriced securities until they again plot on the SML. For example, if a stock plots above the SML, it is underpriced so investors should buy it and bid up its price until its estimated return is in line with its risk—that is, until it plots on the SML. Assuming there are transaction costs, investors will not correct all mispricing because in some instances the cost of buying and selling the mispriced security will offset any potential excess return. Therefore, securities will plot very close to the SML—but not exactly on it. Thus, the SML will be a band of securities, as shown in Exhibit 54-16, rather than a single line. Obviously, the width of

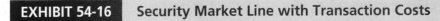

| EXHIBIT 54-16 | Security Market Line with Transaction Costs |

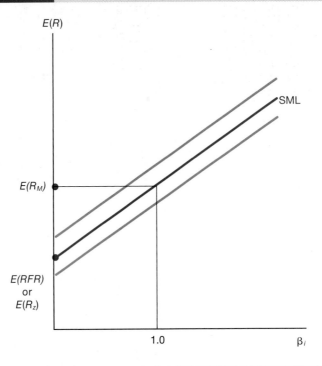

the band is a function of the amount of the transaction costs. In a world with a large proportion of trading by institutions at pennies per share and with discount brokers available for individual investors, the band should be quite narrow.

Dimson (1979) considered the existence of transaction costs and how they affect the extent of diversification by investors. Earlier in the reading, we discussed the relationship between the number of stocks in a portfolio and the variance of the portfolio (see Exhibit 54-3). Initially, the variance declined rapidly, approaching about 90 percent of complete diversification with about 15 to 18 securities. An important question is, How many securities must be added to derive the last 10 percent? Because of transaction costs, Brennan and Subramanyam (1996) show that at some point the additional cost of diversification would exceed its benefit, especially when considering the costs of monitoring and analyzing the added securities.

Heterogeneous Expectations and Planning Periods

If all investors had different expectations about risk and return, each would have a unique CML and/or SML, and the composite graph would be a set (band) of lines with a breadth determined by the divergence of expectations. If all investors had similar information and background, the band would be reasonably narrow.

The impact of *planning periods* is similar. Recall that the CAPM is a one-period model, corresponding to the planning period for the individual investor. Thus, if you are using a one-year planning period, your CML and SML could differ from mine, if I assume a one-month planning period.

Taxes

The rates of return that we normally record and that were used throughout the model were pretax returns. In fact, the actual returns for most investors are affected as follows:

$$E(R_i)(AT) = \frac{(P_e - P_b) \times (1 - T_{cg}) + (Div) \times (1 - T_i)}{P_b}$$

(54-9)

where:

$R_i(AT)$ = after-tax rate of return
P_e = ending price
P_b = beginning price
T_{cg} = tax on capital gain or loss
Div = dividend paid during period
T_i = tax on ordinary income

Clearly, tax rates differ between individuals and institutions. For institutions that do not pay taxes, the original pretax model is correctly specified—that is, T_{cg} and T_i take on values of zero. As noted by Black and Scholes (1979) and Litzenberger and Ramaswamy (1979), because investors have heavy tax burdens, this could cause major differences in the CML and SML among investors. Studies by Elton, Gruber, and Rentzler (1983); Miller and Scholes (1982); and Christie (1990) have examined the effect of the differential taxes on dividends versus capital gains but the evidence is not unanimous.

EMPIRICAL TESTS OF THE CAPM

5

When we discussed the assumptions of capital market theory, we pointed out that a theory should not be judged on the basis of its assumptions, but on *how well it explains the relationships that exist in the real world*. When testing the CAPM, there are two major questions. First, *How stable is the measure of systematic risk (beta)?* Because beta is our principal risk measure, it is important to know whether past betas can be used as estimates of future betas. Also, how do the alternative published estimates of beta compare? Second, *Is there a positive linear relationship as hypothesized between beta and the rate of return on risky assets?* More specifically, how well do returns conform to the following SML equation, discussed earlier as Equation 54-6.

$$E(R_i) = RFR + \beta_i(R_M - RFR)$$

Some specific questions might include:

▶ Does the intercept approximate the prevailing *RFR*?

▶ Was the slope of the line positive and was it consistent with the slope implied by the prevailing risk premium $(R_M - RFR)$?

We consider these two major questions in the following section.

Stability of Beta

Numerous studies have examined the stability of beta and generally concluded that the risk measure was *not* stable for individual stocks, but the stability of the beta for *portfolios* of stocks increased dramatically. Further, the larger the port-folio of stocks (e.g., over 50 stocks) and the longer the period (over 26 weeks), the more stable the beta of the portfolio. Also, the betas tended to regress toward the mean. Specifically, high-beta portfolios tended to decline over time toward unity (1.00), whereas low-beta portfolios tended to increase over time toward unity.

Carpenter and Upton (1981) considered the influence of the trading vol-ume on beta stability and contended that the predictions of betas were slightly better using the volume-adjusted betas. A **small-firm effect** wherein the beta for low-volume securities was biased downward was documented by Ibbotson, Kaplan, and Peterson (1997).

Comparability of Published Estimates of Beta

In contrast to deriving your own estimate of beta for a stock, you may want to use a published source for speed or convenience, such as Merrill Lynch's *Security Risk Evaluation Report* (published monthly) and the weekly *Value Line Investment Survey*. Both services use the following market model equation:

$$(R_{i,t}) = RFR + \beta_i R_{M,t} + E_t$$

Notably, they differ in the data used. Specifically, Merrill Lynch uses *60 monthly observations* and the S&P 500 as the market proxy, whereas the *Value Line* estimates beta using *260 weekly observations* and the NYSE composite series as the market proxy. They both use an adjustment process because of the regression tendencies.

As noted earlier, Statman (1981) documented a difference between the betas for the two services. Subsequently, Reilly and Wright (1988) showed that the reason for the difference was due to the return interval used (weekly vs. monthly) by the two services and demonstrated that market value also made a difference. Handa, Kothari, and Wasley (1989) concurred with the differences in betas and showed that the specific reason the return interval was the cause was that an asset's covari-ance with the market and the market's variance did not change proportionally with the returns interval. They also confirmed that size impacted the effect.

6   RELATIONSHIP BETWEEN SYSTEMATIC RISK AND RETURN

The ultimate question regarding the CAPM is whether it is useful in explaining the return on risky assets. Specifically, is there a positive linear relationship between the systematic risk and the rates of return on these risky assets? Sharpe and Cooper (1972b) found a positive relationship between return and risk, although it was not completely linear.

Because of the statistical problems with individual stocks, Black, Jensen, and Scholes (1972) examined the risk and return for portfolios of stocks and found a positive linear relationship between monthly excess return and portfolio beta, although the intercept was higher than the zero value expected. Exhibit 54-17 contains charts from this study, which show that (1) most of the measured SMLs had a positive slope, (2) the slopes change between periods, (3) the intercepts are not zero, and (4) the intercepts likewise change between periods.

EXHIBIT 54-17	Average Excess Monthly Rates of Return Compared to Systematic Risk During Alternative Time Periods

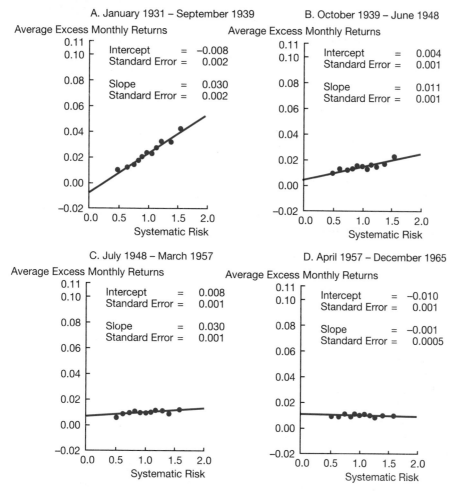

Source: Michael C. Jensen, ed., *Studies in the Theory of Capital Markets* (New York: Praeger Publishers, 1972): 96–97. Reprinted with permission.

Effect of Skewness on the Relationship

Beyond the analysis of return and beta, several authors also have considered the impact of skewness on expected returns. You will recall from your statistics course that skewness reflects the presence of too many large positive or negative observations in a distribution. A normal distribution is symmetric, which means that balance exists between positive and negative observations. In contrast, positive skewness indicates an abnormal number of large positive price changes.

Investigators contended that skewness helped explain the prior results wherein the model appeared to underprice low-beta stocks (so investors received returns above expectations) and overprice high-beta stocks (so investors received returns lower than expected). Some early results confirmed these expectations, but also found that high-beta stocks had high-positive skewness, which implied that investors prefer stocks with high-positive skewness that provide an opportunity for very large returns.

Kraus and Litzenberger (1976) tested a CAPM with a skewness term and confirmed that investors are willing to pay for positive skewness. The importance of skewness was supported in studies by Sears and Wei (1988) and subsequently by Lim (1989).

Effect of Size, P/E, and Leverage

In the efficient markets hypothesis (EMH) reading, we discussed the size effect (the small-firm anomaly) and the P/E effect and showed that these variables have an inverse impact on returns after considering the CAPM. These results imply that size and P/E are additional risk factors that need to be considered along with beta. Specifically, expected returns are a positive function of beta, but investors also require higher returns from relatively small firms and for stocks with relatively low P/E ratios.

Bhandari (1988) found that financial leverage also helps explain the cross section of average returns after both beta and size are considered. This implies a multivariate CAPM with three risk variables: beta, size, and financial leverage.

Effect of Book-to-Market Value: The Fama-French Study

A study by Fama and French (1992) attempted to evaluate the joint roles of market beta, size, E/P, financial leverage, and the book-to-market equity ratio in the cross section of average returns on the NYSE, AMEX, and Nasdaq stocks. While some earlier studies found a significant positive relationship between returns and beta, this study finds that the relationship between beta and the average rate of return disappears during the recent period 1963 to 1990, even when beta is used alone to explain average returns. In contrast, univariate tests between average returns and size, leverage, E/P, and book-to-market equity (BE/ME) indicate that all of these variables are significant and have the expected sign.

In the multivariate tests, the results contained in Exhibit 54-18 show that the negative relationship between size [In (ME)] and average returns is robust to the inclusion of other variables. Further, the positive relation between BE/ME and average returns also persists when the other variables are included. Interestingly, when both of these variables are included, the book-to-market value ratio (BE/ME) has the consistently stronger role in explaining average returns. The joint effect of size and BE/ME is shown in Exhibit 54-18. The seventh regression that includes both of these variables indicates that both coefficients are significant. Further, they are still significant when the two P/E ratio variables are included in the tenth regression.

Fama and French conclude that between 1963 and 1990, size and book-to-market equity capture the cross-sectional variation in average stock returns associated with size, E/P, book-to-market equity, and leverage. Moreover, of the two variables, the book-to-market equity ratio appears to subsume E/P and leverage. Following these results, Fama and French (1993) suggested the use of a three-factor CAPM model. This model was used by Fama and French (1996) to explain a number of the anomalies from prior studies.

Summary of CAPM Risk-Return Empirical Results

Most of the early evidence regarding the relationship between rates of return and systematic risk of portfolios supported the CAPM; there was evidence that the intercepts were generally higher than implied by the *RFR* that prevailed, which is either consistent with a zero-beta model or the existence of higher borrowing

EXHIBIT 54-18	Average Slopes (*t*-Statistics) from Month-by-Month Regressions of Stock Returns on *β*, Size, Book-to-Market Equity, Leverage, and E/P: July 1963 to December 1990

Stocks are assigned the post-ranking β of the size-β portfolio they are in at the end of June of year t. BE is the book value of common equity plus balance-sheet deferred taxes, A is total book assets, and E is earnings (income before extraordinary items, plus income-statement deferred taxes, minus preferred dividends). BE, A, and E are for each firm's latest fiscal year ending in calendar year $t - 1$. The accounting ratios are measured using market equity ME in December of year $t - 1$. Firm size $\ln$(ME) is measured in June of year t. In the regressions, these values of the explanatory variables for individual stocks are matched with returns for the CRSP tapes from the University of Chicago for the months from July of year t to June of year $t + 1$. The gap between the accounting data and the returns ensures that the accounting data are available prior to the returns. If earnings are positive, $E(+)/P$ is the ratio of total earnings to market equity and E/P dummy is 0. If earnings are negative, $E(+)/P$ is 0 and E/P dummy is 1.

The average slope is the time-series average of the monthly regression slopes for July 1963 to December 1990, and the *t*-statistic is the average slope divided by its time-series standard error.

On average, there are 2,267 stocks in the monthly regressions. To avoid giving extreme observations heavy weight in the regressions, the smallest and largest 0.5% of the observations of $E(+)/P$, BE/ME, A/ME, and A/BE are set equal to the next largest or smallest values of the ratios (the 0.005 and 0.995 fractiles). This has no effect on inferences.

β	ln(ME)	ln(BE/ME)	ln(A/ME)	ln(A/BE)	E/P Dummy	E(−)/P
0.15						
(0.46)						
	−0.15					
	(−2.58)					
−0.37	−0.17					
(−1.21)	(−3.41)					
		0.50				
		(5.71)				
			0.50	−0.57		
			(5.69)	(−5.34)		
					0.57	4.72
					(2.28)	(4.57)
	−0.11	0.35				
	(−1.99)	(4.44)				
	−0.11		0.35	−0.50		
	(−2.06)		(4.32)	(−4.56)		
	−0.16				0.06	2.99
	(−3.06)				(0.38)	(3.04)
	−0.13	0.33			−0.14	0.87
	(−2.47)	(4.46)			(−0.90)	(1.23)
	−0.13		0.32	−0.46	−0.08	1.15
	(−2.47)		(4.28)	(−4.45)	(−0.56)	(1.57)

Source: Eugene F. Fama and Kenneth French, "The Cross Section of Expected Stock Returns," *Journal of Finance* 47, no. 2 (June 1992): 439. Reprinted with permission of Blackwell Publishing.

rates. In a search for other variables that could explain these unusual returns, additional variables were considered including the third moment of the distribution (skewness). The results indicated that positive skewness and high betas were correlated.

The efficient markets literature provided extensive evidence that size, the P/E ratio, financial leverage, and the book-to-market value ratio have explanatory power regarding returns beyond beta.

The Fama-French study considered most of the variables suggested and concluded that the two dominant variables were size and the book value to market value ratio.

In contrast to Fama and French, who measure beta with monthly returns, Kothari, Shanken, and Sloan (1995) measured beta with annual returns to avoid trading problems and found substantial compensation for beta risk. They suggested that the results obtained by Fama and French may have been periodic to this time frame and might not be significant over a longer period. Pettengill, Dundaram, and Matthur (1995) noted that empirical studies typically use realized returns to test the CAPM model when theory specifies expected returns. When they adjusted for negative market excess returns, they found a consistent and significant relationship between beta and rates of return. When Jagannathan and Wang (1996) employed a conditional CAPM that allows for changes in betas and in the market risk premium, this model performed well in explaining the cross section of returns. Grundy and Malkiel (1996) also contend that beta is a very useful measure of risk during declining markets, which is when it is important. Finally, when Reilly and Wright (2004) examined the risk-adjusted performance for 31 different asset classes utilizing betas computed using a very broad proxy for the market portfolio, the risk-return relationship was significant and as expected in theory.

7 THE MARKET PORTFOLIO: THEORY VERSUS PRACTICE

Throughout our presentation of the CAPM, we noted that the market portfolio included *all* the risky assets in the economy. Further, in equilibrium, the various assets would be included in the portfolio in proportion to their market value. Therefore, this market portfolio should contain not only U.S. stocks and bonds but also real estate, options, art, stamps, coins, foreign stocks and bonds, and so on, with weights equal to their relative market value.

Although this concept of a market portfolio of all risky assets is reasonable in theory, it is difficult to implement when testing or using the CAPM. The easy part is getting a stock series for U.S. and foreign stocks. As noted in Reading 56, there also are some well-regarded U.S. and global bond series available. Because of the difficulty in deriving series that are available monthly in a timely fashion for numerous other assets, most studies have been limited to using a stock or bond series alone. In fact, the vast majority of studies have chosen the S&P 500 series or some other broad stock series that is obviously limited to only U.S. stocks, which constitutes *less than 20 percent* of a truly global risky asset portfolio. At best, it was assumed that the particular series used as a proxy for the market portfolio was highly correlated with the true market portfolio.

Most academicians recognize this potential problem but assume that the deficiency is not serious. Several articles by Roll (1977a, 1978, 1980, 1981), however, concluded that, on the contrary, the use of these indexes as a proxy for the market portfolio had very serious implications for tests of the model and especially for using the model when evaluating portfolio performance. Roll referred to this problem as a **benchmark error** because the practice is to compare the performance of a portfolio manager to the return of an unmanaged portfolio of equal risk—that is, the market portfolio adjusted for risk would be the benchmark. Roll's point is that, if the benchmark is mistakenly specified, you cannot measure the performance of a portfolio manager properly. A mistakenly specified market portfolio can have two effects. First, the beta computed for alternative portfolios would be wrong because the market portfolio used to compute the portfolio's systematic risk is inappropriate. Second, the SML derived would be wrong because it goes from the *RFR* through the improperly specified M portfolio. Exhibit 54-19 shows an example where the true portfolio risk (β_T) is underestimated (β_e), possibly because of the proxy market portfolio used in computing the estimated beta. As shown, the portfolio being evaluated may appear to be above the SML using β_e, which would imply superior management. If, in fact, the true risk (β_T) is greater, the portfolio being evaluated will shift to the right and be below the SML, which would indicate inferior performance.

Exhibit 54-20 indicates that the intercept and slope will differ if (1) there is an error in selecting a proper risk-free asset and (2) if the market portfolio selected is not the correct mean-variance efficient portfolio. Obviously, it is very possible that under these conditions, a portfolio judged to be superior relative to the first SML (i.e., the portfolio plotted above the measured SML) could be inferior relative to the true SML (i.e., the portfolio would plot below the true SML).

Roll contends that a test of the CAPM requires an analysis of whether the proxy used to represent the market portfolio is mean-variance efficient (on the Markowitz efficient frontier) and whether it is the true optimum market portfolio. Roll showed that if the proxy market portfolio (e.g., the S&P 500 index) is mean-variance efficient, it is mathematically possible to show a linear relationship between returns and betas derived with this portfolio. Unfortunately, this is not a true test of the CAPM because you are not working with the true SML (see Exhibit 54-21).

A demonstration of the impact of the benchmark problem is provided in a study by Reilly and Akhtar (1995). Exhibit 54-22 shows the substantial difference in average beta for the 30 stocks in the DJIA during three alternative periods using two

| **EXHIBIT 54-19** | **Differential Performance Based on an Error in Estimating Systematic Risk** |

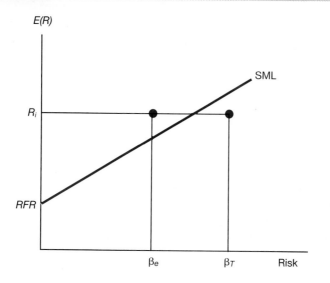

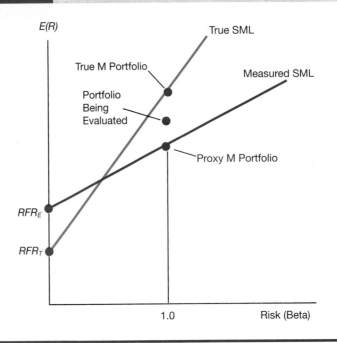

EXHIBIT 54-20   Differential SML Based on Measured Risk-Free Asset and Proxy Market Portfolio

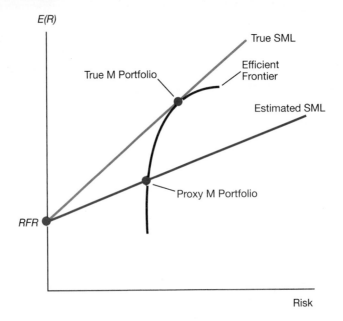

EXHIBIT 54-21   Differential SML Using Market Proxy That Is Mean-Variance Efficient

different proxies for the market portfolio: (1) the S&P 500 Index, and (2) the Brinson Partners Global Security Market Index (GSMI). The GSMI includes not only U.S. and international stocks but also U.S. and international bonds. The results in Exhibit 54.22 are as one would expect because, as we know from earlier discussions in this reading (Equations 54-5 and 54-6), beta is equal to:

$$\text{Beta} = \frac{\text{Cov}_{i,\text{M}}}{\sigma_{\text{M}}^2}$$

where:

$\text{Cov}_{i,\text{M}}$ = the covariance between asset i and the M portfolio
σ_{M}^2 = the variance of the M portfolio

As we change from an all-U.S. stock index to a world stock and bond index (GSMI), we would expect the covariance with U.S. stocks to decline. The other component of beta is the variance for the market portfolio. As shown in Exhibit 54-22, although the covariance between the U.S. stocks and the GSMI is lower, the variance of the GSMI market portfolio, which is highly diversified with stocks *and* bonds from around the world, is substantially lower (about 25 to 33 percent). As a result, the beta is substantially larger (about 27 to 48 percent larger) when the Brinson GSMI is used rather than the S&P 500 Index. Notably, the Brinson GSMI has a composition of assets that is substantially closer to the true M portfolio than the S&P 500 proxy that contains only U.S. stocks. Notably, the results for the recent period were completely consistent with the original results from 1983-1994.

EXHIBIT 54-22	The Average Beta for the 30 Stocks in the Dow Jones Industrial Average during Alternative Time Periods Using Different Proxies for the Market Portfolio

	Alternative Market Proxies	
Time Period	**S&P 500**	**Brinson GSMI**
2000–2004		
Average beta	0.961	1.305
Mean index return	−0.006	0.001
Standard deviation of index returns	0.048	0.031
1989–1994		
Average beta	0.991	1.264
Mean index return	0.010	0.008
Standard deviation of index returns	0.036	0.026
1983–1988		
Average beta	0.820	1.215
Mean index return	0.014	0.014
Standard deviation of index returns	0.049	0.031

Source: Adapted from Frank K. Reilly and Rashid A. Akhtar, "The Benchmark Error Problem with Global Capital Markets," *Journal of Portfolio Management* 22, no. 1 (Fall 1995): 33–52. The updated results were provided by Frank K. Reilly. This copyrighted material is reprinted with permission from *Journal of Portfolio Management*, a publication of Institutional Investor, Inc.

EXHIBIT 54-23	Components of Security Market Lines Using Alternative Market Proxies								
	2000–2004			**1989–1994**			**1983–1988**		
	R_M	RFR	$(R_M - RFR)$	R_M	RFR	$(R_M - RFR)$	R_M	RFR	$(R_M - RFR)$
S&P 500	−2.01	3.05	−5.06	13.07	5.71	7.36	18.20	8.31	9.90
Brinson GSMI	3.02	3.05	−0.03	10.18	5.71	4.48	18.53	8.31	10.22

Source: Adapted from Frank K. Reilly and Rashid A. Akhtar, "The Benchmark Error Problem with Global Capital Markets," *Journal of Portfolio Management* 22, no. 1 (Fall 1995): 33–52. The updated results were provided by Frank K. Reilly. This copyrighted material is reprinted with permission from *Journal of Portfolio Management,* a publication of Institutional Investor, Inc.

There also was a difference in the SMLs implied by each of the market proxies. Exhibit 54-23 contains the average *RFR*, the market returns, and the slope of the SML during three time periods for the two indexes. Clearly, the slopes differ dramatically among the alternative indexes and over time. Needless to say, the benchmark used does make a difference.

In summary, an incorrect market proxy will affect both the beta risk measures and the position and slope of the SML that is used to evaluate portfolio performance. In general, the errors will tend to overestimate the performance of portfolio managers because the proxy used for the market portfolio is probably not as efficient as the true market portfolio, so the slope of the SML will be underestimated. Also, the beta measure generally will be underestimated because the true market portfolio will have a lower variance than the typical market proxy because the true market portfolio is more diversified.

Roll's benchmark problems, however, do not invalidate the value of the CAPM as *a normative model of asset pricing;* they only indicate a problem in *measurement* when attempting to test the theory and when using this model for evaluating portfolio performance. Therefore, it is necessary to develop a better market portfolio proxy similar to the Brinson GSMI.

8 WHAT IS NEXT?

At this point, we have discussed the basic theory of the CAPM, the impact of changing some of its major assumptions, the empirical evidence that does and does not support the theory, and its dependence on a market portfolio of all risky assets. In addition, the model assumes that investors have quadratic utility functions and that the distribution of security prices is normal (symmetrically distributed), with a variance term that can be estimated.

The tests of the CAPM indicated that the beta coefficients for individual securities were not stable, but the portfolio betas generally were stable assuming long enough sample periods and adequate trading volume. There was mixed support for a positive linear relationship between rates of return and systematic risk for portfolios of stock, with some recent evidence indicating the need to consider additional risk variables. In addition, several papers have criticized the tests of the model and the usefulness of the model in portfolio evaluation because of its dependence on a market portfolio of risky assets that is not currently available.

Consequently, the academic community has considered alternative asset pricing models.

THE INTERNET

Investments Online

Asset pricing models show how risk measures or underlying return-generating factors will affect asset returns. Estimates from such models are usually proprietary and are available from providers only by buying their research. Of course, users can always purchase their raw data elsewhere (see some of our earlier Internet discussions) and develop their own estimates of beta and factor sensitivities.

www.valueline.com The Value Line Investment Survey has been a long-time favorite of investors and many local and college/university libraries subscribe to it. It is a popular source of finding a stock's beta. Value Line Publishing, Inc.'s Web site contains useful information for the on-line researcher and student of investments. Its site features investment-related articles, sample pages from the Value Line Investment Survey, and a product directory, which lists the venerable investment survey as well as Value Line's mutual fund, options, and convertibles survey, and others.

www.wsharpe.com William F. Sharpe, the 1990 winner of the Nobel prize in Economics because of his development of the Capital Asset Pricing Model, has a home page on the Internet. Among other items, Web surfers can read drafts of a sophisticated textbook in progress, some of his published papers, and case studies he has written. Sharpe's site offers monthly returns data on a number of mutual funds, stock indices, and bond indices, and links to other finance sites.

gsb.uchicago.edu/fac/eugene.fama/ The home page of Eugena Fama, whose empirical work first found support...and then lack of support...for beta as a risk measure.

www.moneychimp.com This is an informative education site on investments and includes CAPM calculators for estimating a stock's return and a "market simulator" to show the effect of randomness on a portfolio's return over time.

OPTIONAL SEGMENT
ENDS

SUMMARY

▶ The assumptions of capital market theory expand on those of the Markowitz portfolio model and include consideration of the risk-free rate of return. The correlation and covariance of any asset with a risk-free asset are zero, so that any combination of an asset or portfolio with the risk-free asset generates a linear return and risk function. Therefore, when you combine the risk-free asset with any risky asset on the Markowitz efficient frontier, you derive a set of straight-line portfolio possibilities.

▶ The dominant line is the one that is tangent to the efficient frontier. This dominant line is referred to as the *capital market line (CML)*, and all investors should target points along this line depending on their risk preferences.

▶ Because all investors want to invest in the risky portfolio at the point of tangency, this portfolio—referred to as the market portfolio—must contain all risky assets in proportion to their relative market values. Moreover, the investment decision and the financing decision can be separated because, although everyone will want to invest in the market portfolio, investors will make different financing decisions about whether to lend or borrow based on their individual risk preferences.

▶ Given the CML and the dominance of the market portfolio, the relevant risk measure for an individual risky asset is its covariance with the market portfolio, that is, its *systematic risk*. When this covariance is standardized by the covariance for the market portfolio, we derive the well-known beta measure of systematic risk and a security market line (SML) that relates the expected or required rate of return for an asset to its beta. Because all individual securities and portfolios should plot on this SML, you can determine the expected (required) return on a security based on its systematic risk (its beta).

▶ Alternatively, assuming security markets are not always completely efficient, you can identify undervalued and overvalued securities by comparing your estimate of the rate of return to be earned on an investment to its expected (required) rate of return. The systematic risk variable (beta) for an individual risky asset is computed using a regression model that generates an equation referred to as the asset's *characteristic line*.

▶ When we relax several of the major assumptions of the CAPM, the required modifications are reasonably minor and do not change the overall concept of the model. Empirical studies have indicated stable portfolio betas, especially when enough observations were used to derive the betas and there was adequate volume. Although the early tests confirmed the expected relationship between returns and systematic risk (with allowance for the zero-beta model), several subsequent studies indicated that the univariate beta model needed to be supplemented with additional variables that considered skewness, size, P/E, leverage, and the book value/market value ratio. A study by Fama and French contended that during the period 1963 to 1990, beta was not relevant. In their study, the most significant variables were book-to-market value (BE/ME) and size. Subsequent studies both supported their findings and differed with them because some more recent authors have found a significant relationship between beta and rates of return on stocks.

▶ Another problem has been raised by Roll, who contends that it is not possible to empirically derive a true market portfolio, so it is not possible to test the CAPM model properly or to use the model to evaluate portfolio performance. A study by Reilly and Akhtar provided empirical support for this contention by demonstrating significant differences in betas, SMLs, and expected returns with alternative benchmarks.

PROBLEMS FOR READING 54

1. You expect an *RFR* of 10 percent and the market return (R_M) of 14 percent. Compute the expected (required) return for the following stocks, and plot them on an SML graph.

Stock	Beta	E(R)
U	0.85	
N	1.25	
D	−0.20	

2. *CFA Examination Level II*
An analyst expects a risk-free return of 4.5 percent, a market return of 14.5 percent, and the returns for Stocks A and B that are shown in the following table.

	Stock Information	
Stock	Beta	Analyst's Estimated Return
A	1.2	16%
B	0.8	14%

A. Show on the graph provided in the answer book:
   (1) Where Stocks A and B would plot on the security market line (SML) if they were fairly valued using the capital asset pricing model (CAPM)
   (2) Where Stocks A and B actually plot on the same graph according to the returns estimated by the analyst and shown in the table
   [6 minutes]
B. State whether Stocks A and B are undervalued or overvalued if the analyst uses the SML for strategic investment decisions. [4 minutes]

4⅝ 4¹¹/₁₆
5½ — ⅜
5½ 5½ — ⅜
5½ 21³/₁₆ — ¹/₁₆
20⅝ 21³/₁₆
17³/₈ 18⅛ + ⅞
6½ 6½ — ½
7¼ 6½ 31/₃₂ — ⅛
15/₁₆ 9/₁₆
9/₁₆ 9/₁₆
1⁹/₃₂ 7¹⁵/₁₆
7¹⁵/₁₆ 7¹³/₁₆ 7¹⁵/₁₆
2⅝ 2¹¹/₃₂ 2½ +
2¾ 2¼ 2¼
6⅛ 12¹/₁₆ 11³/₈ 11¾ +
87 33¾ 33 33¼ —
502 25⅝ 24⁹/₁₆ 25⅝ +
833 12 11⅝ 11⁷/₈ +
11⅝
16 10½ 10½ 10⅞ —
78 15⅞ 15¹³/₁₆ 15⅞ —
4508 9¹/₁₆ 8¼ 8⅞ +
430 11¼ 10⅛

APPENDIX

Appendix A Solutions to End-of-Reading Problems

SOLUTIONS FOR READING 47

1. C

$$NPV = -50{,}000 + \frac{15{,}000}{1.08} + \frac{15{,}000}{1.08^2} + \frac{20{,}000}{1.08^3} + \frac{10{,}000}{1.08^4} + \frac{5{,}000}{1.08^5}$$

$$NPV = -50{,}000 + 13{,}888.89 + 12{,}860.08 + 15{,}876.64 + 7{,}350.30$$
$$+ \ 3{,}402.92$$

$$NPV = -50{,}000 + 53{,}378.83 = 3{,}378.83$$

The IRR, found with a financial calculator, is 10.88 percent.

2. C

Year	Cash Flow	Cumulative Cash Flow	Discounted Cash Flow	Cumulative DCF
0	−50,000	−50,000	−50,000	−50,000
1	15,000	−35,000	13,888.89	−36,111.11
2	15,000	−20,000	12,860.08	−23,251.03
3	20,000	0	15,876.64	−7,374.38
4	10,000	10,000	7,350.30	−24.09
5	5,000	15,000	3,402.92	3,378.83

As the table shows, the cumulative cash flow offsets the initial investment in exactly three years. The payback period is 3.00 years. The discounted payback period is between four and five years. The discounted payback period is 4 years plus $24.09/3{,}402.92 = 0.007$ of the fifth year cash flow, or $4.007 = 4.01$ years. The discounted payback period is $4.01 - 3.00 = 1.01$ years longer than the payback period.

3. B

$$NPV = \sum_{t=0}^{3} \frac{CF_t}{(1+r)^t} = -100 + \frac{40}{1.20} + \frac{80}{1.20^2} + \frac{120}{1.20^3} = \$58.33$$

4. D

The IRR can be found using a financial calculator or with trial and error. Using trial and error, the total PV is equal to zero if the discount rate is 28.79 percent.

		Present Value			
Year	Cash Flow	28.19%	28.39%	28.59%	28.79%
0	−150,000	−150,000	−150,000	−150,000	−150,000
1	100,000	78,009	77,888	77,767	77,646
2	120,000	73,025	72,798	72,572	72,346
Total		1,034	686	338	−8

A more precise IRR of 28.7854 percent has a total PV closer to zero.

5. A

$$\text{The NPV} = -750 + \sum_{t=1}^{7} \frac{175}{1.10^t} = -750 + 851.97 = 101.97 \text{ million won.}$$

The IRR, found with a financial calculator, is 14.02 percent. (The PV is -750, N = 7, and PMT = 175.)

6. B

Year	Cash Flow	Cumulative Cash Flow
0	−750	−750
1	175	−575
2	175	−400
3	175	−225
4	175	−50
5	175	125
6	175	300
7	175	475

The payback period is between four and five years. The payback period is four years plus $50/175 = 0.29$ of the fifth year cash flow, or 4.29 years.

Year	Cash Flow	Discounted Cash Flow	Cumulative DCF
0	−750	−750	−750
1	175	159.09	−590.91
2	175	144.63	−446.28
3	175	131.48	−314.80
4	175	119.53	−195.27
5	175	108.66	−86.61
6	175	98.78	12.17
7	175	89.80	101.97

The discounted payback period is between five and six years. The discounted payback period is five years plus $86.61/98.78 = 0.88$ of the sixth year cash flow, or 5.88 years.

7. D

$$\text{The present value of future cash flows is PV} = \frac{2,000}{0.08} = 25,000.$$

$$\text{The profitability index is PI} = \frac{\text{PV}}{\text{Investment}} = \frac{25,000}{20,000} = 1.25.$$

8. C

$$\text{PV} = \sum_{t=1}^{7} \frac{115}{1.10^t} + \frac{50}{1.10^7} = 585.53 \text{ million euros}$$

$$\text{PI} = \frac{585.53}{375} = 1.56$$

9. C

The IRR would stay the same because both the initial outlay and the after-tax cash flows double, so that the return on each dollar invested remains the same. All of the cash flows and their present values double. The difference between total present value of the future cash flows and the initial outlay (the NPV) also doubles.

10. A

If the cumulative cash flow in one year equals the outlay and additional cash flows are not very large, this scenario is possible. For example, assume the outlay is 100, the cash flow in Year 1 is 100 and the cash flow in Year 2 is 5. The required return is 10 percent. This project would have a payback of 1.0 years, an NPV of −4.96, and an IRR of 4.77 percent.

11. A

The vertical intercept changes from 60 to 65, and the horizontal intercept changes from 21.86 percent to 20.68 percent.

12. B

When valuing mutually exclusive projects, the decision should be made with the NPV method because this method uses the most realistic discount rate, namely the opportunity cost of funds. In this example, the reinvestment rate for the NPV method (here 10 percent) is more realistic than the reinvestment rate for the IRR method (here 21.86 percent or 18.92 percent).

13. B

For these projects, a discount rate of 13.16 percent would yield the same NPV for both (an NPV of 6.73).

14. C

Discount rates of 0 percent and approximately 61.8 percent both give a zero NPV.

Rate	NPV
0%	0.00
20%	4.40
40%	3.21
60%	0.29
61.8%	0.00
80%	−3.02
100%	−6.25

SOLUTIONS FOR READING 48

1. B

The cost of equity is defined as the rate of return required by stockholders.

2. B

Wrong answers:

A. The appropriate rate of tax to use is the marginal tax rate, not the average tax rate.

C. The investment opportunity schedule is downward sloping.

D. The target capital structure is that capital structure for which the company has as an objective, which may or may not be represented by its current capital structure.

3. D

First calculate the growth rate using the sustainable growth calculation, and then calculate the cost of equity using the rearranged dividend discount model:

$g = (1 - \text{dividend payout ratio})(\text{return on equity}) = (1 - 0.30)(15\%) = 10.5\%$

$r_e = (D_1 / P_0) + g = (\$2.30 / \$45) + 10.50\% = 15.61\%$

4. C

$FV = \$1,000; PMT = \$40; N = 10; PV = \$900$

Solve for i. The six-month yield, i, is 5.3149%

$YTM = 5.3149\% \times 2 = 10.62985\%$

$r_d(1 - t) = 10.62985\%(1 - 0.38) = 6.5905\%$

5. C

The bond rating approach depends on knowledge of the company's rating and can be compared with yields on bonds in the public market.

6. B

The company can issue preferred stock at 6.5%.

$P_p = \$1.75/0.065 = \$26.92$

Note: Dividends are not tax deductible so there is no adjustment for taxes.

7. B

Cost of equity $= D_1/P_0 + g = \$1.50 / \$30 + 7\% = 5\% + 7\% = 12\%$

$WACC = [(0.445)(0.08)(1 - 0.4)] + [(0.555)(0.12)] = 8.8\%$

8. B

The weighted average cost of capital, using weights derived from the current capital structure, is the best estimate of the cost of capital for the average-risk project of a company.

9. C

$w_d = \$63/(\$220 + 63) = 0.223$

$w_e = \$220/(\$220 + 63) = 0.777$

SOLUTIONS FOR READING 49

1. D

Operating risk is the sensitivity of operating earnings to changes in the number of units produced and sold. *Sales risk* refers to the uncertainty of the number of units produced and sold and the price at which units are sold. *Business risk* is the joint effect of sales risk and operating risk. *Total leverage* is the joint effect of operating leverage and financial leverage.

2. D

Operating leverage is the sensitivity of earnings before interest and taxes to changes in the number of units produced and sold. The *degree* of operating leverage is the elasticity of operating earnings with respect to the number of units produced and sold.

3. C

Calculations:

$$DOL = \frac{40 \text{ million}(\$100 - \$65)}{\left[40 \text{ million}(\$100 - \$65)\right] - \$1.05 \text{ billion}}$$

$$= \frac{\$1.400 \text{ billion}}{\$1.400 \text{ billion} - \$1.05 \text{ billion}}$$

$$= \frac{\$1.4}{\$0.35}$$

$$= 4$$

$$\text{Operating breakeven} = \frac{\$1.05 \text{ billion}}{35} = 30 \text{ million units}$$

▶ Fulcrum produces positive operating income if it produces more than *30* million units. If it produces and sells fewer than 30 million, it will generate a loss.

▶ The DOL is 4.

▶ If unit sales increase by 5 percent, Fulcrum's operating earnings are expected to increase by $4 \times 5\% = 20\%$.

▶ Increasing fixed production costs will *increase* the sensitivity of Fulcrum's operating earnings to changes in sales.

4. C

Business risk results from economic factors and operating leverage.

5. C

The degree of total leverage of the Grundlegend Company exceeds that of the Basic Company, but the extent of the difference depends on the amount of interest expense, not the amount of debt. In the case of financial leverage, it is the interest that acts as a fulcrum.

6. B

$$\text{Operating breakeven units} = \frac{\text{¥}1290 \text{ million}}{(\text{¥}3529 - \text{¥}1500)} = 635{,}781.173 \text{ units}$$

$$\text{Operating breakeven sales} = \text{¥}3529 \times 635{,}781.173 \text{ units} = \text{¥}2{,}243{,}671{,}760$$

or

$$\text{Operating breakeven sales} = \frac{\text{¥}1290 \text{ million}}{1 - \left(\text{¥}1500 / \text{¥}3529\right)} = \text{¥}2{,}243{,}671{,}760$$

$$\text{Total breakeven} = \frac{¥1290 \text{ million} + ¥410 \text{ million}}{(¥3529 - ¥1500)} = \frac{¥1700 \text{ million}}{¥2029}$$

$$= 837{,}851.1582 \text{ units}$$

Breakeven sales $= ¥3529 \times 837{,}851.1582 \text{ units} = ¥2{,}956{,}776{,}737$

or

$$\text{Breakeven sales} = \frac{¥1700 \text{ million}}{1 - \left(\frac{¥1500}{¥3529}\right)} = ¥2{,}956{,}776{,}737$$

7. A

$$\text{Total breakeven}_{\text{Gearing}} = \frac{(\$40{,}000{,}000 + \$20{,}000{,}000)}{(\$200 - \$120)} = 750{,}000 \text{ units}$$

$$\text{Total breakeven}_{\text{Hebelkraft}} = \frac{(\$90{,}000{,}000 + \$20{,}000{,}000)}{(\$200 - \$100)} = 1{,}100{,}000 \text{ units}$$

8. B

Proposition I, or the capital structure irrelevance theory, states that the level of debt versus equity has no effect on company value in the absence of taxes and imperfect markets.

9. D

The cost of equity rises with the level of debt because equity capital providers demand more potential return for the added financial risk.

10. C

$r_e = r_a + (r_a - r_d)(D/E)$
Note: If $D/(D + E) = 0.50$, then $D/E = 1.0$
$r_e = 0.10 + (0.10 - 0.05)(1.0)(1 - 0.2)$
$r_e = 0.10 + \left[0.05(0.90)\right] = 0.10 + 0.04 = 0.14, \text{ or } 14\%$

SOLUTIONS FOR READING 50

1. C

A cash dividend would decrease stockholders' equity, increasing the debt/equity ratio. A cash dividend would reduce cash, resulting in a lower current ratio. A stock dividend would leave both of these ratios unchanged.

2. D

A stock dividend will decrease the price per share, all other things being equal. A stock split will reduce the price and earnings per share proportionately, leaving the price-to-earnings ratio the same.

3. B

If the P/E is 32x, the earnings/price ratio is $1/32 = 3.125\%$. When the cost of capital is greater than the earnings yield (E/P), earnings dilution will result from the buyback.

4. Dividend chronology

Friday, 10 June	B
Thursday, 23 June	F
Friday, 24 June	E
Sunday, 26 June	D
Tues, 28 June	A
Sunday, 10 July	C

  ▶ B. The declaration date is the day that the corporation issues a statement declaring a dividend.

  ▶ E. The ex-date is the first day that the stock trades "ex" (i.e. without) the dividend. If the stock is bought on the ex-date, the seller (not the buyer) will receive the dividend.

  ▶ A. The holder-of-record date is the date that the company uses to document which shareholders will receive the dividend.

  ▶ C. The payment date is the date that the company sends out its dividend checks.

5. C

6. A

To receive the dividend, one must purchase before the ex-date.

7. C

For each dollar of WL pretax income: [$1.00 × 0.40 = $0.40 in corporate taxes] plus $0.60 in net income paid in dividends × 0.30 = $0.18 in personal income taxes. Total tax = $0.40 + $0.18 = $0.58.

8. C

9. D

10. C

Decreases send negative signals regarding future prospects.

11. A

Last year's DPS = \$0.60

Expected increase in EPS = \$4 − \$3 = \$1

Target payout ratio = 0.25

5-year adjustment factor = 1/5 = 0.2

Expected DPS = last year's DPS + (increase in EPS) × target payout × adjustment factor

= \$0.60 + (\$1.00 × 0.25 × 0.2)

= \$0.65

12. B

13. D

The ex-dividend stock price declines to €40 − €1.50 = €38.50. She will purchase €150,000/€38.50 = 3,896 additional shares. This increases her total shares owned to 103,896.

14. A

To receive the dividend, one must purchase before the ex-date.

SOLUTIONS FOR READING 53

1.

Month	Madison(R_i)	General Electric(R_j)	$R_i - E(R_i)$	$R_j - E(R_j)$	$[R_i - E(R_i)] \times [R_i - E(R_i)]$
1	−.04	.07	−.057	.06	−.0034
2	.06	−.02	.043	−.03	−.0013
3	−.07	−.10	−.087	−.11	.0096
4	.12	.15	.103	.14	.0144
5	−.02	−.06	−.037	−.07	.0026
6	.05	.02	.033	.01	.0003
Sum	.10	.06			.0222

1A.

$$E(R_{Madison}) = .10/6 = .0167 \qquad E(R_{GE}) = .06/6 = .01$$

1B.

$$\sigma_{Madison} = \sqrt{.0257/6} = \sqrt{.0043} = .06549$$

$$\sigma_{GE} = \sqrt{.04120/6} = \sqrt{.006867} = .08287$$

1C.

$$COV_{ij} = 1/6(.0222) = .0037$$

1D.

$$r_{ij} = \frac{.0037}{(.06549)(.08287)}$$

$$= \frac{.0037}{.005427}$$

$$= .682$$

One should have expected a positive correlation between the two stocks, since they tend to move in the same direction(s). Risk can be reduced by combining assets that have low positive or negative correlations, which is not the case for Madison and General Electric.

2.

$$E(R_1) = .15 \quad E(\sigma_1) = .10 \quad w_1 = .5$$

$$E(R_2) = .20 \quad E(\sigma_2) = .20 \quad w_2 = .5$$

$$E(R_{port}) = .5(.15) + .5(.20) = .175$$

If $r_{1,2} = .40$

$$\sigma_p = \sqrt{(.5)^2(.10)^2 + (.5)^2(.20)^2 + 2(.5)(.5)(.10)(.20)(.40)}$$
$$= \sqrt{.0025 + .01 + .004}$$
$$= \sqrt{.0165}$$
$$= 0.12845$$

If $r_{1,2} = -.60$

$$\sigma_p = \sqrt{(.5)^2(.10)^2 + (.5)^2(.20)^2 + 2(.5)(.5)(.10)(.20)(-.60)}$$
$$= \sqrt{.0025 + .01 + (-.006)}$$
$$= \sqrt{.0065}$$
$$= .08062$$

Expected
Return 17.5% |————X————————X————————

          0   8.06%   12.85%   Risk (Standard deviation)

The negative correlation coefficient reduces risk without sacrificing return.

3. For all values of $r_{1,2}$:

$$E(R_{port}) = (.6 \times .10) + (.4 \times .15) = .12$$
$$\sigma_{port} = \sqrt{(.6)^2(.03)^2 + (.4)^2(.05)^2 + 2(.6)(.4)(.03)(.05)(r_{1,2})}$$
$$= \sqrt{.000324 + .0004 + .00072(r_{1,2})}$$
$$= \sqrt{.000724 + .00072(r_{1,2})}$$

3A. $\sqrt{.000724 + .00072(1.0)} = \sqrt{.001444} = .0380$

3B. $\sqrt{.000724 + .00072(.75)} = \sqrt{.001264} = .0356$

3C. $\sqrt{.000724 + .00072(.25)} = \sqrt{.000904} = .0301$

3D. $\sqrt{.000724 + .00072(.00)} = \sqrt{.000724} = .0269$

3E. $\sqrt{.000724 + .00072(-.25)} = \sqrt{.000544} = .0233$

3F. $\sqrt{.000724 + .00072(-.75)} = \sqrt{.000184} = .0136$

3G. $\sqrt{.000724 + .00072(-1.0)} = \sqrt{.000004} = .0020$

SOLUTIONS FOR READING 54

1. $E(R_i) = RFR + \beta_i(R_M - RFR)$

$\qquad = .10 + \beta_i(.14 - .10)$

$\qquad = .10 + .04\beta_i$

Stock	Beta	(Required Return) $E(R_i) = .10 + .04\beta_i$
U	85	$.10 + .04(.85) = .10 + .034 = .134$
N	1.25	$.10 + .04(1.25) = .10 + .05 = .150$
D	−.20	$.10 + .04(−.20) = .10 + .008 = .092$

2. CFA Examination II (1998)

A. Security Market Line

i. *Fair-value plot.* The following template shows, using the CAPM, the expected return, ER, of Stock A and Stock B on the SML. The points are consistent with the following equations:

ER on stock = Risk-free rate + Beta × (Market return − Risk-free rate)

ER for A = 4.5% + 1.2(14.5% − 4.5%)
$\qquad$ = 16.5%

ER for B = 4.5% + 0.8(14.5% − 4.5%)
$\qquad$ = 12.5%

ii. *Analyst estimate plot.* Using the analyst's estimates, Stock A plots below the SML and Stock B, above the SML.

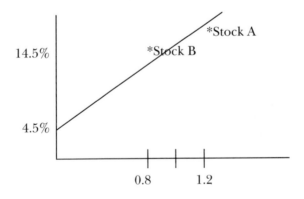

B. Over vs. Undervalue

Stock A is overvalued because it should provide a 16.5% return according to the CAPM whereas the analyst has estimated only a 16.0% return.

Stock B is undervalued because it should provide a 12.5% return according to the CAPM whereas the analyst has estimated a 14% return.

GLOSSARY

Abnormal rate of return The amount by which a security's actual return differs from its expected rate of return which is based on the market's rate of return and the security's relationship with the market.

Above full-employment equilibrium A macroeconomic equilibrium in which real GDP exceeds potential GDP.

Absolute dispersion The amount of variability present without comparison to any reference point or benchmark.

Absolute frequency The number of observations in a given interval (for grouped data).

Accelerated method A method of depreciation that allocates relatively large amounts of the depreciable cost of an asset to earlier years and reduced amounts to later years.

Accrual accounting The system of recording financial transactions as they come into existence as a legally enforceable claim, rather than when they settle.

Accrued interest (1) Interest earned but not yet due and payable. This is equal to the next coupon to be paid on a bond multiplied by the time elapsed since the last payment date and divided by the total coupon period. Exact conventions differ across bond markets. (2) Interest earned but not yet paid.

Additional information Information that is required or recommended under the GIPS standards and is not considered as "supplemental information" for the purposes of compliance.

Addition rule for probabilities A principle stating that the probability that A or B occurs (both occur) equals the probability that A occurs, plus the probability that B occurs, minus the probability that both A and B occur.

Additions Enlargements to the physical layout of a plant asset.

Add-on interest A procedure for determining the interest on a bond or loan in which the interest is added onto the face value of a contract.

Administrative fees All fees other than the trading expenses and the investment management fee. Administrative fees include custody fees, accounting fees, consulting fees, legal fees, performance measurement fees, or other related fees. These administrative fees are typically outside the control of the investment management firm and are not included in either the gross-of-fees return or the net-of-fees return. However, there are some markets and investment vehicles where administrative fees are controlled by the firm. (See the term "bundled fee.")

Aggregate demand The relationship between the quantity of real GDP demanded and the price level.

Aggregate hours The total number of hours worked by all the people employed, both full time and part time, during a year.

Aggregate production function The relationship between the quantity of real GDP supplied and the quantities of labor and capital and the state of technology.

Allocative efficiency A situation in which we cannot produce more of any good without giving up some of another good that we value more highly.

Alpha A term commonly used to describe a manager's abnormal rate of return, which is the difference between the return the portfolio actually produced and the expected return given its risk level.

Alternative hypothesis The hypothesis accepted when the null hypothesis is rejected.

American Depository Receipts (ADRs) Certificates of ownership issued by a U.S. bank that represent indirect ownership of a certain number of shares of a specific foreign firm. Shares are held on deposit in a bank in the firm's home country.

American option An option contract that can be exercised at any time until its expiration date. (1) An option contract that can be exercised at any time until its expiration date. (2) An option that can be exercised on any day through the expiration day. Also referred to as American-style exercise.

American terms With reference to U.S. dollar exchange rate quotations, the U.S. dollar price of a unit of another currency.

Amortization The periodic allocation of the cost of an intangible asset to the periods it benefits.

Amortizing and accreting swaps A swap in which the notional principal changes according to a formula related to changes in the underlying.

Analysis of variance (ANOVA) The analysis of the total variability of a dataset (such as observations on the dependent variable in a regression) into components representing different sources of variation; with reference to regression, ANOVA provides the inputs for an F-test of the significance of the regression as a whole.

Annual percentage rate The cost of borrowing expressed as a yearly rate.

Annuity A finite set of level sequential cash flows.

Annuity due   An annuity having a first cash flow that is paid immediately.

Anomalies   Security price relationships that appear to contradict a well-regarded hypothesis; in this case, the efficient market hypothesis.

A priori probability   A probability based on logical analysis rather than on observation or personal judgment.

Arbitrage   (1) The simultaneous purchase of an undervalued asset or portfolio and sale of an overvalued but equivalent asset or portfolio, in order to obtain a riskless profit on the price differential. Taking advantage of a market inefficiency in a risk-free manner. (2) A trading strategy designed to generate a guaranteed profit from a transaction that requires no capital commitment or risk bearing on the part of the trader. A simple example of an arbitrage trade would be the simultaneous purchase and sale of the same security in different markets at different prices. (3) The condition in a financial market in which equivalent assets or combinations of assets sell for two different prices, creating an opportunity to profit at no risk with no commitment of money. In a well-functioning financial market, few arbitrage opportunities are possible. Equivalent to the law of one price. (4) A risk-free operation that earns an expected positive net profit but requires no net investment of money.

Arbitrage pricing theory (APT)   A theory that posits that the expected return to a financial asset can be described by its relationship with several common risk factors. The multifactor APT can be contrasted with the single-factor CAPM.

Arithmetic mean (AM)   The sum of the observations divided by the number of observations.

Arrears swap   A type of interest rate swap in which the floating payment is set at the end of the period and the interest is paid at that same time.

Asian call option   A European-style option with a value at maturity equal to the difference between the stock price at maturity and the average stock price during the life of the option, or $0, whichever is greater.

Asset allocation   The process of deciding how to distribute an investor's wealth among different asset classes for investment purposes.

Asset class   Securities that have similar characteristics, attributes, and risk/return relationships.

Asset impairment   Loss of revenue-generating potential of a long-lived asset before the end of its useful life; the difference between an asset's carrying value and its fair value, as measured by the present value of the expected cash flows.

Assets under management (AUM)   The total market value of the assets managed by an investment firm.

At-the-money option   An option for which the strike (or exercise) price is close to (at) the current market price of the underlying asset.

Automatic fiscal policy   A change in fiscal policy that is triggered by the state of the economy.

Automatic stabilizers   Mechanisms that stabilize real GDP without explicit action by the government.

Autonomous expenditure   The sum of those components of aggregate planned expenditure that are not influenced by real GDP. Autonomous expenditure equals investment, government purchases, exports, and the autonomous parts of consumption expenditure and imports.

Average cost pricing rule   A rule that sets price to cover cost including normal profit, which means setting the price equal to average total cost.

Average fixed cost   Total fixed cost per unit of output—total fixed cost divided by output.

Average product   The average product of a resource. It equals total product divided by the quantity of the resource employed.

Average tax rate   A person's total tax payment divided by his or her total income.

Average total cost   Total cost per unit of output.

Average variable cost   Total variable cost per unit of output.

Backwardation   A condition in the futures markets in which the benefits of holding an asset exceed the costs, leaving the futures price less than the spot price.

Balance of payments   (1) A summary of all economic transactions between a country and all other countries for a specific time period, usually a year. The balance-of-payments account reflects all payments and liabilities to foreigners (debits) and all payments and obligations received from foreigners (credits). (2) A record of all financial flows crossing the borders of a country during a given time period (a quarter or a year).

Balance of payments accounts   A country's record of international trading, borrowing, and lending.

Balance of trade   *See* Trade balance.

Balance sheet   A financial statement that shows what assets the firm controls at a fixed point in time and how it has financed these assets.

Balanced budget   A government budget in which tax revenues and expenditures are equal.

Balanced budget multiplier   The magnification on aggregate demand of a *simultaneous* change in government purchases and taxes that leaves the budget balance unchanged.

Balanced fund A mutual fund with, generally, a three-part investment objective: (1) to conserve the investor's principal, (2) to pay current income, and (3) to increase both principal and income. The fund aims to achieve this by owning a mixture of bonds, preferred stocks, and common stocks.

Bank discount basis A quoting convention that annualizes, on a 360-day year, the discount as a percentage of face value.

Barriers to entry Legal or natural constraints that protect a firm from potential competitors.

Barter The direct exchange of one good or service for other goods and services.

Basic earnings per share Total earnings divided by the weighted average number of shares actually outstanding during the period.

Basis The difference between the spot price of the underlying asset and the futures contract price at any point in time (e.g., the *initial* basis at the time of contract origination, the *cover* basis at the time of contract termination).

Basis swap (1) An interest rate swap involving two floating rates. (2) A swap in which both parties pay a floating rate.

Bayes' formula A method for updating probabilities based on new information.

Bear spread An option strategy that involves selling a put with a lower exercise price and buying a put with a higher exercise price. It can also be executed with calls.

Behavioral finance Involves the analysis of various psychological traits of individuals and how these traits affect how they act as investors, analysts, and portfolio managers.

Below full-employment equilibrium A macroeconomic equilibrium in which potential GDP exceeds real GDP.

Benchmark An independent rate of return (or hurdle rate) forming an objective test of the effective implementation of an investment strategy.

Benchmark bond A bond representative of current market conditions and used for performance comparison.

Benchmark error Situation where an inappropriate or incorrect benchmark is used to compare and assess portfolio returns and management.

Benchmark portfolio A comparison standard of risk and assets included in the policy statement and similar to the investor's risk preference and investment needs, which can be used to evaluate the investment performance of the portfolio manager.

Bernoulli random variable A random variable having the outcomes 0 and 1.

Bernoulli trial An experiment that can produce one of two outcomes.

Beta A standardized measure of systematic risk based upon an asset's covariance with the market portfolio.

Betterments Improvements that do not add to the physical layout of a plant asset.

Bid-ask spread The difference between the quoted ask and the bid prices.

Big tradeoff A tradeoff between equity and efficiency.

Bill-and-hold basis Sales on a bill-and-hold basis involve selling products but not delivering those products until a later date.

Binomial model A model for pricing options in which the underlying price can move to only one of two possible new prices.

Binomial option pricing model A valuation equation that assumes the price of the underlying asset changes through a series of discrete upward or downward movements.

Binomial random variable The number of successes in n Bernoulli trials for which the probability of success is constant for all trials and the trials are independent.

Binomial tree (1) A diagram representing price movements of the underlying in a binomial model. (2) The graphical representation of a model of asset price dynamics in which, at each period, the asset moves up with probability p or down with probability $(1 - p)$.

Black market An illegal trading arrangement in which the price exceeds the legally imposed price ceiling.

Black-Scholes option pricing model A valuation equation that assumes the price of the underlying asset changes continuously through the option's expiration date by a statistical process known as *geometric Brownian motion.*

Bond A long-term debt security with contractual obligations regarding interest payments and redemption.

Bond-equivalent basis A basis for stating an annual yield that annualizes a semiannual yield by doubling it.

Bond-equivalent yield The yield to maturity on a basis that ignores compounding.

Bond option An option in which the underlying is a bond; primarily traded in over-the-counter markets.

Bond price volatility The percentage changes in bond prices over time.

Book value of equity (or book value) (1) Shareholders' equity (total assets minus total liabilities) minus the value of preferred stock; common shareholders' equity. (2) The accounting value of a firm.

Book value per share   Book value of equity divided by the number of common shares outstanding.

Box spread   An option strategy that combines a bull spread and a bear spread having two different exercise prices, which produces a risk-free payoff of the difference in the exercise prices.

Brady bonds   Bonds issued by emerging countries under a debt-reduction plan named after Mr. Brady, former U.S. Secretary of the Treasury.

Brand name   A registered name that can be used only by its owner to identify a product or service.

Broker   (1) An agent who executes orders to buy or sell securities on behalf of a client in exchange for a commission. (2) *See* Futures commission merchants.

Budget deficit   A government's budget balance that is negative—expenditures exceed tax revenues.

Budget surplus   A government's budget balance that is positive—tax revenues exceed expenditures.

Bull spread   An option strategy that involves buying a call with a lower exercise price and selling a call with a higher exercise price. It can also be executed with puts.

Bundled fee   A fee that combines multiple fees into one "bundled" fee. Bundled fees can include any combination of management, transaction, custody, and other administrative fees. Two specific examples of bundled fees are the wrap fee and the all-in fee.

All-in fee   Due to the universal banking system in some countries, asset management, brokerage, and custody are often part of the same company. This allows banks to offer a variety of choices to customers regarding how the fee will be charged. Customers are offered numerous fee models in which fees may be bundled together or charged separately. All-in fees can include any combination of investment management, trading expenses, custody, and other administrative fees.

Wrap fee   Wrap fees are specific to a particular investment product. The U.S. Securities and Exchange Commission (SEC) defines a wrap fee account (now more commonly known as a separately managed account or SMA) as "any advisory program under which a specified fee or fees not based upon transactions in a client's account is charged for investment advisory services (which may include portfolio management or advice concerning the selection of other investment advisers) and execution of client transactions." A typical separately managed account has a contract or contracts (and fee) involving a sponsor (usually a broker or independent provider) acting as the investment advisor, an investment management firm typically as the subadvisor, other services (custody, consulting, reporting, performance, manager selection, monitoring, and execution of trades), distributor, and the client (brokerage customer). Wrap fees can be all-inclusive, asset-based fees (which may include any combination of management, transaction, custody, and other administrative fees).

Business cycle   The periodic but irregular up-and-down movement in production.

Business risk   The variability of operating income arising from the characteristics of the firm's industry. Two sources of business risk are sales variability and operating leverage.

Butterfly spread   An option strategy that combines two bull or bear spreads and has three exercise prices.

Buy-and-hold strategy   A passive portfolio management strategy in which securities (bonds or stocks) are bought and held to maturity.

Call   An option that gives the holder the right to buy an underlying asset from another party at a fixed price over a specific period of time.

Call market   A market in which trading for individual stocks only takes place at specified times. All the bids and asks available at the time are combined and the market administrators specify a single price that will possibly clear the market at that time.

Call option   Option to buy an asset within a certain period at a specified price called the *exercise price.*

Call premium   Amount above par that an issuer must pay to a bondholder for retiring the bond before its stated maturity.

Call provisions   Specifies when and how a firm can issue a call for bonds outstanding prior to their maturity.

Cap   (1) A contract on an interest rate, whereby at periodic payment dates, the writer of the cap pays the difference between the market interest rate and a specified cap rate if, and only if, this difference is positive. This is equivalent to a stream of call options on the interest rate. (2) A combination of interest rate call options designed to hedge a borrower against rate increases on a floating-rate loan.

Capital   The tools, equipment, buildings, and other constructions that businesses now use to produce goods and services.

Capital account   (1) The record of transactions with foreigners that involve either (a) the exchange of ownership rights to real or financial assets or (b) the extension of loans. (2) A component of the balance of payments that reflects unrequited (or unilateral) transfers corresponding to capital flows entailing no compensation (in the form of goods, services, or assets). Examples include investment capital given (without future repayment) in favor of poor countries, debt forgiveness, and expropriation losses.

Capital accumulation The growth of capital resources.

Capital appreciation A return objective in which the investor seeks to increase the portfolio value, primarily through capital gains, over time to meet a future need rather than dividend yield.

Capital asset pricing model (CAPM) A theory concerned with deriving the expected or required rates of return on risky assets based on the assets' systematic risk relative to a market portfolio.

Capital budgeting The process of planning expenditures on assets whose cash flows are expected to extend beyond one year.

Capital Employed (Real Estate) The denominator of the return expressions, defined as the "weighted-average equity" (weighted-average capital) during the measurement period. Capital employed should not include any income or capital return accrued during the measurement period. Beginning capital is adjusted by weighting the cash flows (contributions and distributions) that occurred during the period. Cash flows are typically weighted based on the actual days the flows are in or out of the portfolio. Other weighting methods are acceptable; however, once a methodology is chosen, it should be consistently applied.

Capital expenditure An expenditure for the purchase or expansion of a long-term asset, recorded in an asset account.

Capital market line (CML) The line from the intercept point that represents the risk-free rate tangent to the original efficient frontier; it becomes the new efficient frontier since investments on this line dominate all the portfolios on the original Markowitz efficient frontier.

Capital preservation A return objective in which the investor seeks to minimize the risk of loss; generally a goal of the risk-averse investor.

Capital return (real estate) The change in the market value of the real estate investments and cash/cash equivalent assets held throughout the measurement period (ending market value less beginning market value) adjusted for all capital expenditures (subtracted) and the net proceeds from sales (added). The return is computed as a percentage of the capital employed through the measurement period. Synonyms: capital appreciation return, appreciation return.

Capital stock The total quantity of plant, equipment, buildings, and inventories.

Capital structure A company's specific mixture of long-term financing.

Caplet Each component call option in a cap.

Capped swap A swap in which the floating payments have an upper limit.

Carried interest (private equity) The profits that general partners earn from the profits of the investments made by the fund (generally 20–25%). Also known as "carry."

Carrying value The unexpired part of an asset's cost. Also called *book value.*

Cartel A group of firms that has entered into a collusive agreement to restrict output and increase prices and profits.

Carve-Out A single or multiple asset class segment of a multiple asset class portfolio.

Cash For purposes of the statement of cash flows, both cash and cash equivalents.

Cash equivalents Short-term (90 days or less), highly liquid investments, including money market accounts, commercial paper, and U.S. Treasury bills.

Cash flow additivity principle The principle that dollar amounts indexed at the same point in time are additive.

Cash-generating efficiency A company's ability to generate cash from its current or continuing operations.

Cash price or spot price The price for immediate purchase of the underlying asset.

Cash settlement (1) A procedure for settling futures contracts in which the cash difference between the futures price and the spot price is paid instead of physical delivery. (2) A procedure used in certain derivative transactions that specifies that the long and short parties engage in the equivalent cash value of a delivery transaction.

CD equivalent yield *See* Money market yield.

Central bank A bank's bank and a public authority that regulates a nation's depository institutions and controls the quantity of money.

Central limit theorem A result in statistics that states that the sample mean computed from large samples of size n from a population with finite variance will follow an approximate normal distribution with a mean equal to the population mean and a variance equal to the population variance divided by n.

Certificates of deposit (CDs) Instruments issued by banks and S&Ls that require minimum deposits for specified terms and that pay higher rates of interest than deposit accounts.

Ceteris paribus Other things being equal—all other relevant things remaining the same.

Change in demand A change in buyers' plans that occurs when some influence on those plans other than the price of the good changes. It is illustrated by a shift of the demand curve.

Change in supply A change in sellers' plans that occurs when some influence on those plans other than the price of the good changes. It is illustrated by a shift of the supply curve.

Change in the quantity demanded A change in buyers' plans that occurs when the price of a good changes but all other influences on buyers' plans remain unchanged. It is illustrated by a movement along the demand curve.

Characteristic line Regression line that indicates the systematic risk (beta) of a risky asset.

Cheapest to deliver A bond in which the amount received for delivering the bond is largest compared with the amount paid in the market for the bond.

Classical A macroeconomist who believes that the economy is self-regulating and that it is always at full employment.

Clean price The price of a bond obtained as the total price of the bond minus accrued interest. Most bonds are traded on the basis of their clean price.

Closed-end fund (private equity) A type of investment fund where the number of investors and the total committed capital is fixed and not open for subscriptions and/or redemptions.

Closed-end investment company An investment company that issues only a limited number of shares, which it does not redeem (buy back). Instead, shares of a closed-end fund are traded in securities markets at prices determined by supply and demand.

Coefficient of variation (CV) The ratio of a set of observations' standard deviation to the observations' mean value.

Collar (1) A combination of a cap and a floor. (2) An option strategy involving the purchase of a put and sale of a call in which the holder of an asset gains protection below a certain level, the exercise price of the put, and pays for it by giving up gains above a certain level, the exercise price of the call. Collars also can be used to provide protection against rising interest rates on a floating-rate loan by giving up gains from lower interest rates.

Collateralized mortgage obligation (CMO) A debt security based on a pool of mortgage loans that provides a relatively stable stream of payments for a relatively predictable term.

Collateral trust bonds A mortgage bond wherein the assets backing the bond are financial assets like stocks and bonds.

Collusive agreement An agreement between two (or more) producers to restrict output, raise the price, and increase profits.

Combination A listing in which the order of the listed items does not matter.

Command system A method of organizing production that uses a managerial hierarchy.

Commercial bank A firm that is licensed by the Comptroller of the Currency in the U.S. Treasury or by a state agency to receive deposits and make loans.

Commercial paper Unsecured short-term corporate debt that is characterized by a single payment at maturity.

Commission brokers Employees of a member firm who buy or sell securities for the customers of the firm.

Committed capital (private equity) Pledges of capital to a venture capital fund. This money is typically not received at once but drawn down over three to five years, starting in the year the fund is formed. Also known as "commitments."

Common stock An equity investment that represents ownership of a firm, with full participation in its success or failure. The firm's directors must approve dividend payments.

Comparative advantage A person or country has a comparative advantage in an activity if that person or country can perform the activity at a lower opportunity cost than anyone else or any other country.

Competitive bid An underwriting alternative wherein an issuing entity (governmental body or a corporation) specifies the type of security to be offered (bonds or stocks) and the general characteristics of the issue, and the issuer solicits bids from competing investment banking firms with the understanding that the issuer will accept the highest bid from the bankers.

Competitive environment The level of intensity of competition among firms in an industry, determined by an examination of five competitive forces.

Competitive market A market that has many buyers and many sellers, so no single buyer or seller can influence the price.

Competitive strategy The search by a firm for a favorable competitive position within an industry within the known competitive environment.

Complement A good that is used in conjunction with another good.

Complement   With reference to an event S, the event that S does not occur.

Completely diversified portfolio   A portfolio in which all unsystematic risk has been eliminated by diversification.

Composite   Aggregation of individual portfolios representing a similar investment mandate, objective, or strategy.

Composite creation date   The date when the firm first groups the portfolios to create a composite. The composite creation date is not necessarily the earliest date for which performance is reported for the composite. (See composite inception date.)

Composite definition   Detailed criteria that determine the allocation of portfolios to composites. Composite definitions must be documented in the firm's policies and procedures.

Composite description   General information regarding the strategy of the composite. A description may be more abbreviated than the composite definition but includes all salient features of the composite.

Compounding   The process of accumulating interest on interest.

Computer-Assisted Execution System (CAES)   A service created by Nasdaq that automates order routing and execution for securities listed on domestic stock exchanges and involved on the Intermarket Trading System (ITS).

Conditional expected value   (1) Expected value of a variable conditional on some available information set. The expected value changes over time with changes in the information set. (2) The expected value of a stated event given that another event has occurred.

Conditional probability   The probability of an event given (conditioned on) another event.

Conditional variance   (1) Variance of a variable conditional on some available information set. (2) The variance of one variable, given the outcome of another.

Confidence interval   A range that has a given probability that it will contain the population parameter it is intended to estimate.

Consistency   A desirable property of estimators; a consistent estimator is one for which the probability of estimates close to the value of the population parameter increases as sample size increases.

Consistent   With reference to estimators, describes an estimator for which the probability of estimates close to the value of the population parameter increases as sample size increases.

Consolidated Quotation System (CQS)   An electronic quotation service for issues listed on the NYSE, the AMEX, or regional exchanges and traded on the Nasdaq InterMarket.

Constant maturity swap or CMT swap   A swap in which the floating rate is the rate on a security known as a constant maturity treasury or CMT security.

Constant maturity treasury or CMT   A hypothetical U.S. Treasury note with a constant maturity. A CMT exists for various years in the range of 2 to 10.

Constant returns to scale   Features of a firm's technology that leads to constant long-run average cost as output increases. When constant returns to scale are present, the LRAC curve is horizontal.

Consumer Price Index (CPI)   An index that measures the average of the prices paid by urban consumers for a fixed "basket" of the consumer goods and services.

Consumer surplus   The value of a good minus the price paid for it, summed over the quantity bought.

Consumption expenditure   The total payment for consumer goods and services.

Contango   A situation in a futures market where the current contract price is greater than the current spot price for the underlying asset.

Contestable market   A market in which firms can enter and leave so easily that firms in the market face competition from potential entrants.

Continuously compounded return   The natural logarithm of 1 plus the holding period return, or equivalently, the natural logarithm of the ending price over the beginning price.

Continuous market   A market where stocks are priced and traded continuously by an auction process or by dealers when the market is open.

Continuous random variable   A random variable for which the range of possible outcomes is the real line (all real numbers between – and +) or some subset of the real line.

Continuous time   Time thought of as advancing in extremely small increments.

Contract price   The transaction price specified in a forward or futures contract.

Convenience yield   (1) An adjustment made to the theoretical forward or futures contract delivery price to account for the preference that consumers have for holding spot positions in the underlying asset. (2) The nonmonetary return offered by an asset when the asset is in short supply, often associated with assets with seasonal production processes.

Conversion value   The value of the convertible security if converted into common stock at the stock's current market price.

Convertible bonds   A bond with the added feature that the bondholder has the option to turn the bond back to the firm in exchange for a specified number of common shares of the firm.

Convexity   (1) A measure of the change in duration with respect to changes in interest rates. (2) A measure of the degree to which a bond's price-yield curve departs from a straight line. This characteristic affects estimates of a bond's price volatility for a given change in yields.

Cooperative equilibrium The outcome of a game in which the players make and share the monopoly profit.

Copyright A government-sanctioned exclusive right granted to the inventor of a good, service, or productive process to produce, use, and sell the invention for a given number of years.

Correlation A number between –1 and +1 that measures the co-movement (linear association) between two random variables.

Correlation analysis The analysis of the strength of the linear relationship between two data series.

Correlation coefficient A standardized measure of the relationship between two variables that ranges from − 1.00 to + 1.00.

Cost averaging The periodic investment of a fixed amount of money.

Cost of carry (1) The cost associated with holding some asset, including financing, storage, and insurance costs. Any yield received on the asset is treated as a negative carrying cost. (2) The net amount that would be required to store a commodity or security for future delivery, usually calculated as physical storage costs plus financial capital costs less dividends paid to the underlying asset. (3) The costs of holding an asset.

Cost of carry model A model for pricing futures contracts in which the futures price is determined by adding the cost of carry to the spot price.

Cost-push inflation An inflation that results from an initial increase in costs.

Council of Economic Advisers The President's council whose main work is to monitor the economy and keep the President and the public well informed about the current state of the economy and the best available forecasts of where it is heading.

Counterparty A participant to a derivative transaction.

Country risk Uncertainty due to the possibility of major political or economic change in the country where an investment is located. Also called *political risk*.

Coupon Indicates the interest payment on a debt security. It is the coupon rate times the par value that indicates the interest payments on a debt security.

Covariance (1) A measure of the degree to which two variables, such as rates of return for investment assets, move together over time relative to their individual mean returns. (2) A measure of

the extent to which the returns on two assets move together. (3) A measure of the co-movement (linear association) between two random variables.

Covariance matrix A matrix or square array whose entries are covariances; also known as a variance–covariance matrix.

Covered call An option strategy involving the holding of an asset and sale of a call on the asset.

Credit analysis An active bond portfolio management strategy designed to identify bonds that are expected to experience changes in rating. This strategy is critical when investing in high-yield bonds.

Credit risk or default risk The risk of loss due to nonpayment by a counterparty.

Credit union A depository institution owned by a social or economic group such as firm's employees that accepts savings deposits and makes mostly consumer loans.

Creditor nation A country that during its entire history has invested more in the rest of the world than other countries have invested in it.

Cross elasticity of demand The responsiveness of the demand for a good to the price of a substitute or complement, other things remaining the same. It is calculated as the percentage change in the quantity demanded of the good divided by the percentage change in the price of the substitute or complement.

Cross-sectional analysis An examination of a firm's performance in comparison to other firms in the industry with similar characteristics to the firm being studied.

Cross-sectional data Observations over individual units at a point in time, as opposed to time-series data.

Crowding-out effect The tendency for a government budget deficit to decrease in investment.

Cumulative distribution function A function giving the probability that a random variable is less than or equal to a specified value.

Cumulative relative frequency For data grouped into intervals, the fraction of total observations that are less than the value of the upper limit of a stated interval.

Currency The bills and coins that we use today.

Currency appreciation The rise in the value of one currency in terms of another currency.

Currency depreciation The fall in the value of one currency in terms of another currency.

Currency drain An increase in currency held outside the banks.

Currency option An option that allows the holder to buy (if a call) or sell (if a put) an underlying currency at a fixed exercise rate, expressed as an exchange rate.

Current account A record of the payments for imports of goods and services, receipts from exports of goods and services, the interest income, and net transfers.

Current account (1) The record of all transactions with foreign nations that involve the exchange of merchandise goods and services, current income derived from investments, and unilateral gifts. (2) A component of the balance of payments covering all current transactions that take place in the normal business of the residents of a country, such as exports and imports, services, income, and current transfers.

Current credit risk The risk associated with the possibility that a payment currently due will not be made.

Current income A return objective in which the investor seeks to generate income rather than capital gains; generally a goal of an investor who wants to supplement earnings with income to meet living expenses.

Current P/E *See* Trailing P/E.

Current yield A bond's yield as measured by its current income (coupon) as a percentage of its market price.

Customer list A list of customers or subscribers.

Cyclical businesses Businesses with high sensitivity to business- or industry-cycle influences.

Cyclical company A firm whose earnings rise and fall with general economic activity.

Cyclical stock A stock with a high beta; its gains typically exceed those of a rising market and its losses typically exceed those of a falling market.

Cyclical surplus or deficit The actual surplus or deficit minus the structural surplus or deficit.

Cyclical unemployment The fluctuations in unemployment over the business cycle.

Daily settlement *See* Marking to market.

Data mining The practice of determining a model by extensive searching through a dataset for statistically significant patterns.

Day trader A trader holding a position open somewhat longer than a scalper but closing all positions at the end of the day.

Deadweight loss A measure of inefficiency. It is equal to the decrease in consumer surplus and producer surplus that results from an inefficient level of production.

Debentures Bonds that promise payments of interest and principal but pledge no specific assets. Holders have first claim on the issuer's income and unpledged assets. Also known as *unsecured bonds*.

Debtor nation A country that during its entire history has borrowed more from the rest of the world than it has lent to it.

Deciles Quantiles that divide a distribution into 10 equal parts.

Declining-balance method An accelerated method of depreciation in which depreciation is computed by applying a fixed rate to the carrying value (the declining balance) of a tangible long-lived asset.

Declining trend channel The range defined by security prices as they move progressively lower.

Deep in the money Options that are far in-the-money.

Deep out of the money Options that are far out-of-the-money.

Default risk The risk that an issuer will be unable to make interest and principal payments on time.

Default risk premium An extra return that compensates investors for the possibility that the borrower will fail to make a promised payment at the contracted time and in the contracted amount.

Defensive competitive strategy Positioning the firm so that its capabilities provide the best means to deflect the effect of the competitive forces in the industry.

Defensive stock A stock whose return is not expected to decline as much as that of the overall market during a bear market (a beta less than one).

Deflation A process in which the price level falls—a negative inflation.

Degree of confidence The probability that a confidence interval includes the unknown population parameter.

Degrees of freedom (df) The number of independent observations used.

Delivery A process used in a deliverable forward contract in which the long pays the agreed-upon price to the short, which in turn delivers the underlying asset to the long.

Delivery option The feature of a futures contract giving the short the right to make decisions about what, when, and where to deliver.

Delta The change in the price of the option with respect to a one dollar change in the price of the underlying asset; this is the option's *hedge ratio,* or the number of units of the underlying asset that can be hedged by a single option contract.

Delta hedge (1) A dynamic hedging strategy using options with continuous adjustment of the number of options used, as a function of the delta of the option. (2) An option strategy in which a position in an asset is converted to a risk-free position with a position in a specific number of options.

The number of options per unit of the underlying changes through time, and the position must be revised to maintain the hedge.

Demand   The relationship between the quantity of a good that consumers plan to buy and the price of the good when all other influences on buyers' plans remain the same. It is described by a demand schedule and illustrated by a demand curve.

Demand curve   A curve that shows the relationship between the quantity demanded of a good and its price when all other influences on consumers' planned purchases remain the same.

Demand for labor   The relationship between the quantity of labor demanded and the real wage rate when all other influences on firm's hiring plans remain the same.

Demand-pull inflation   An inflation that results from an initial increase in aggregate demand.

Dependent   With reference to events, the property that the probability of one event occurring depends on (is related to) the occurrence of another event.

Dependent variable   The variable whose variation about its mean is to be explained by the regression; the left-hand-side variable in a regression equation.

Depletion   The exhaustion of a natural resource through mining, cutting, pumping, or other extraction, and the way in which the cost is allocated.

Depository institution   A firm that takes deposits from households and firms and makes loans to other households and firms.

Depreciable cost   The cost of an asset less its residual value.

Depreciation   The decrease in the capital stock that results from wear and tear and obsolescence.
The periodic allocation of the cost of a tangible long-lived asset (other than land and natural resources) over its estimated useful life.

Derivatives   (1) Securities bearing a contractual relation to some underlying asset or rate. Options, futures, forward, and swap contracts, as well as many forms of bonds, are derivative securities. (2) A financial instrument that offers a return based on the return of some other underlying asset.

Derivatives dealers   The commercial and investment banks that make markets in derivatives. Also referred to as market makers.

Derivative security   An instrument whose market value ultimately depends upon, or derives from, the value of a more fundamental investment vehicle called the underlying asset or security.

Derived demand   The demand for a productive resource, which is derived from the demand for the goods and services produced by the resource.

Descriptive statistics   The study of how data can be summarized effectively.

Diff swaps   A swap in which the payments are based on the difference between interest rates in two countries but payments are made in only a single currency.

Diluted earnings per share   Total earnings divided by the number of shares that would be outstanding if holders of securities such as executive stock options and convertible bonds exercised their options to obtain common stock.

Diminishing marginal returns   The tendency for the marginal product of an additional unit of a factor of production is less than the marginal product of the previous unit of the factor.

Diminishing marginal utility   The decrease in marginal utility as the quantity consumed increases.

Direct method   The procedure for converting the income statement from an accrual basis to a cash basis by adjusting each item on the income statement.

Discount   (1) A bond selling at a price below par value due to capital market conditions. (2) To reduce the value of a future payment in allowance for how far away it is in time; to calculate the present value of some future amount. Also, the amount by which an instrument is priced below its face value.

Discounting   The conversion of a future amount of money to its present value.

Discount interest   A procedure for determining the interest on a loan or bond in which the interest is deducted from the face value in advance.

Discouraged workers   People who are available and willing to work but have not made specific efforts to find a job within the previous four weeks.

Discrete random variable   A random variable that can take on at most a countable number of possible values.

Discrete time   Time thought of as advancing in distinct finite increments.

Discretionary fiscal policy   A policy action that is initiated by an act of Congress.

Discretionary policy   A policy that responds to the state of the economy in a possibly unique way that uses all the information available, including perceived lessons from past "mistakes."

Diseconomies of scale   Features of a firm's technology that leads to rising long-run average cost as output increases.

Dispersion   (1) The variability around the central tendency. (2) A measure of the spread of the annual returns of individual portfolios within a composite. Measures may include, but are not limited to, high/low, inter-quartile range, and standard deviation (asset weighted or equal weighted).

Disposable income   Aggregate income minus taxes plus transfer payments.

Distinct business entity   A unit, division, department, or office that is organizationally and functionally segregated from other units, divisions, departments, or offices and retains discretion over the assets it manages and autonomy over the investment decision-making process. Possible criteria that can be used to determine this include: (a) being a legal entity; (b) having a distinct market or client type (e.g., institutional, retail, private client, etc.); (c) using a separate and distinct investment process

Dividend discount model (DDM)   A technique for estimating the value of a stock issue as the present value of all future dividends.

Dominant strategy equilibrium   A Nash equilibrium in which the best strategy of each player is to cheat (deny) regardless of the strategy of the other player.

Double-declining-balance method   An accelerated method of depreciation in which a fixed rate equal to twice the straight-line percentage is applied to the carrying value (the declining balance) of a tangible long-lived asset.

Down transition probability   The probability that an asset's value moves down in a model of asset price dynamics.

Dumping   The sale by a foreign firm of exports at a lower price that the cost of production.

Duopoly   A market structure in which two producers of a good or service compete.

DuPont system   A method of examining ROE by breaking it down into three component parts: (1) profit margin, (2) total asset turnover, and (3) financial leverage.

Duration   (1) A measure of an option-free bond's average maturity. Specifically, the weighted average maturity of all future cash flows paid by a security, in which the weights are the present value of these cash flows as a fraction of the bond's price. More importantly, a measure of a bond's price sensitivity to interest rate movements (*see* Modified duration). (2) A measure of the interest rate sensitivity of a bond's market price taking into consideration its coupon and term to maturity. (3) A measure of the size and timing of the cash flows paid by a bond. It quantifies these factors by summarizing them in the form of a single number. For bonds without option features attached, duration is interpreted as a weighted average maturity of the bond.

Dutch Book Theorem   A result in probability theory stating that inconsistent probabilities create profit opportunities.

Dynamic comparative advantage   A comparative advantage that a person or country possesses as a result of having specialized in a particular activity and then, as a result of learning-by-doing, having become the producer with the lowest opportunity cost.

Earnings momentum   A strategy in which portfolios are constructed of stocks of firms with rising earnings.

Earnings multiplier model   A technique for estimating the value of a stock issue as a multiple of its earnings per share.

Earnings surprise   A company announcement of earnings that differ from analysts' prevailing expectations.

Earnings yield   Earnings per share divided by price; the reciprocal of the P/E ratio.

EBITDA   Earnings before interest, taxes, depreciation, and amortization.

Economic depreciation   The change in the market value of capital over a given period.

Economic efficiency   A situation that occurs when the firm produces a given output at the least cost.

Economic growth   The expansion of production possibilities that results from capital accumulation and technological change.

Economic information   Data on prices, quantities, and qualities of goods and services and factors of production.

Economic model   A description of some aspect of the economic world that includes only those features of the world that are needed for the purpose at hand.

Economic profit   A firm's total revenue minus its opportunity cost.

Economic rent   The income received by the owner of a factor of production over and above the amount required to induce that owner to offer the factor for use.

Economics   The social science that studies the *choices* that individuals, businesses, governments, and entire societies make and how they cope with *scarcity* and the *incentives* that influence and reconcile those choices.

Economic theory   A generalization that summarizes what we think we understand about the economic choices that people make and the performance of industries and entire economies.

Economic value added (EVA)   Internal management performance measure that compares net operating profit to total cost of capital. Indicates how profitable company projects are as a sign of management performance.

Economies of scale   Features of a firm's technology that leads to a falling long-run average cost as output increases.

Economies of scope   Decreases in average total cost that occur when a firm uses specialized resources to produce a range of goods and services.

Effective annual rate   The amount by which a unit of currency will grow in a year with interest on interest included.

Effective annual yield (EAY)   An annualized return that accounts for the effect of interest on interest; EAY is computed by compounding 1 plus the holding period yield forward to one year, then subtracting 1.

Effective duration   Direct measure of the interest rate sensitivity of a bond (or any financial instrument) based upon price changes derived from a pricing model.

Efficiency   A desirable property of estimators; an efficient estimator is the unbiased estimator with the smallest variance among unbiased estimators of the same parameter.

Efficient capital market   A market in which security prices rapidly reflect all information about securities.

Efficient frontier   The set of portfolios that has the maximum rate of return for every given level of risk, or the minimum risk for every potential rate of return.

Efficient market   A market in which the actual price embodies all currently available relevant information. Resources are sent to their highest valued use.

Elastic demand   Demand with a price elasticity greater than 1; other things remaining the same, the percentage change in the quantity demanded exceeds the percentage change in price.

Elasticity of demand   The responsiveness of the quantity demanded of a good to a change in its price, other things remaining the same.

Elasticity of supply   The responsiveness of the quantity supplied of a good to a change in its price, other things remaining the same.

Empirical probability   The probability of an event estimated as a relative frequency of occurrence.

Employment Act of 1946   A landmark Congressional act that recognized a role for government actions to keep unemployment, keep the economy expanding, and keep inflation in check.

Employment-to-population ratio   The percentage of people of working age who have jobs.

Ending market value (private equity)   The remaining equity that a limited partner has in a fund. Also referred to as net asset value or residual value.

Entrepreneurship   The human resource that organizes labor, land, and capital. Entrepreneurs come up with new ideas about what and how to produce, make business decisions, and bear the risks that arise from their decisions.

Equation of exchange   An equation that states that the quantity of money multiplied by the velocity of circulation equals GDP.

Equilibrium price   The price at which the quantity demanded equals the quantity supplied.

Equilibrium quantity   The quantity bought and sold at the equilibrium price.

Equity forward   A contract calling for the purchase of an individual stock, a stock portfolio, or a stock index at a later date at an agreed-upon price.

Equity options   Options on individual stocks; also known as stock options.

Equity swap   A swap transaction in which one cash flow is tied to the return to an equity portfolio position, often an index such as the Standard and Poor's 500, while the other is based on a floating-rate index.

Error term   The portion of the dependent variable that is not explained by the independent variable(s) in the regression.

Estimate   The particular value calculated from sample observations using an estimator.

Estimated (or fitted) parameters   With reference to regression analysis, the estimated values of the population intercept and population slope coefficient(s) in a regression.

Estimated rate of return   The rate of return an investor anticipates earning from a specific investment over a particular future holding period.

Estimated useful life   The total number of service units expected from a long-term asset.

Estimation   With reference to statistical inference, the subdivision dealing with estimating the value of a population parameter.

Estimator   An estimation formula; the formula used to compute the sample mean and other sample statistics are examples of estimators.

Eurobonds   Bonds denominated in a currency not native to the country in which they are issued.

Eurodollar   A dollar deposited outside the United States.

European option   An option contract that can only be exercised on its expiration date.

European-style option or European option   An option exercisable only at maturity.

European terms With reference to U.S. dollar exchange rate quotations, the price of a U.S. dollar in terms of another currency.

European Union (EU) A formal association of European countries founded by the Treaty of Rome in 1957. Formerly known as the EEC.

Event study Research that examines the reaction of a security's price to a specific company, world event, or news announcement.

Ex-ante Before the fact.

Excess kurtosis Degree of peakedness (fatness of tails) in excess of the peakedness of the normal distribution.

Excess reserves A bank's actual reserves minus its required reserves.

Exchange for physicals (EEP) A permissible delivery procedure used by futures market participants, in which the long and short arrange a delivery procedure other than the normal procedures stipulated by the futures exchange.

Exchange rate risk Uncertainty due to the denomination of an investment in a currency other than that of the investor's own country.

Exchange-traded fund (ETF) A tradable depository receipt that gives investors a pro rata claim to the returns associated with a portfolio of securities (often designed to mimic an index, such as the Standard & Poor's 500) held in trust by a financial institution.

Exercise (or exercising the option) The process of using an option to buy or sell the underlying.

Exercise price The transaction price specified in an option contract; also known as the *strike price*.

Exercise price (or strike price or striking price, or strike) (1) The transaction price specified in an option contract. *See also* Strike price. (2) The fixed price at which an option holder can buy or sell the underlying.

Exercise rate or strike rate The fixed rate at which the holder of an interest rate option can buy or sell the underlying.

Exhaustive Covering or containing all possible outcomes.

Expansion A business cycle phase between a trough and a peak—phase in which real GDP increases.

Expected rate of return The return that analysts' calculations suggest a security should provide, based on the market's rate of return during the period and the security's relationship to the market.

Expected return The rate of return that an investor expects to get on an investment.

Expected utility The average utility arising from all possible outcomes.

Expected value The probability-weighted average of the possible outcomes of a random variable.

Expenditure A payment or obligation to make future payment for an asset or a service.

Expiration date The date on which a derivative contract expires.

Expiry The expiration date of a derivative security.

Exports The goods and services that we sell to people in other countries.

Extended DuPont System A method of examining *ROE* by breaking it down into five component parts.

External benefits Benefits that accrue to people other than the buyer of the good.

External cash flow Cash, securities, or assets that enter or exit a portfolio.

External costs Costs that are not borne by the producer of the good but borne by someone else.

External diseconomies Factors outside the control of a firm that raise the firm's costs as the industry produces a larger output.

External economies Factors beyond the control of a firm that lower the firm's costs as the industry produces a larger output.

Externality A cost or a benefit that arises from production and falls on someone other than the producer of or cost of a benefit that arises from consumption and falls on someone other than the consumer.

External valuation (real estate) An external valuation is an assessment of market value performed by a third party who is a qualified, professionally designated, certified, or licensed commercial property valuer/appraiser. External valuations must be completed following the valuation standards of the local governing appraisal body.

Extraordinary repairs Repairs that affect the estimated residual value or estimated useful life of an asset thereby increasing its carrying value.

Face value (1) The amount paid on a bond at redemption and traditionally printed on the bond certificate. This face value excludes the final coupon payment. Sometimes referred to as par value. (2) The promised payment at maturity separate from any coupon payment.

Factors of production The productive resources that businesses use to produce goods and services.

Federal budget The annual statement of the expenditures and tax revenues of the government of the United States together with the laws and regulations that approve and support those expenditures and taxes.

Federal funds rate The interest rate that banks charge each other on overnight loans of reserves.

Federal Open Market Committee The main policy-making organ of the Federal Reserve System.

Federal Reserve System The central bank of the United States.

Feedback-rule policy   A rule that specifies how policy actions respond to changes in the state of the economy.

Fee Schedule   The firm's current investment management fees or bundled fees for a particular presentation. This schedule is typically listed by asset level ranges and should be appropriate to the particular prospective client.

Fiduciary   A person who supervises or oversees the investment portfolio of a third party, such as in a trust account, and makes investment decisions in accordance with the owner's wishes.

Fiduciary call   A combination of a European call and a risk-free bond that matures on the option expiration day and has a face value equal to the exercise price of the call.

Financial account   A component of the balance of payments covering investments by residents abroad and investments by nonresidents in the home country. Examples include direct investment made by companies, portfolio investments in equity and bonds, and other investments and liabilities.

Financial innovation   The development of new financial products—new ways of borrowing and lending.

Financial risk   (1) The variability of future income arising from the firm's fixed financing costs, for example, interest payments. The effect of fixed financial costs is to magnify the effect of changes in operating profit on net income or earnings per share. (2) Risk relating to asset prices and other financial variables.

Financing activities   Business activities that involve obtaining resources from stockholders and creditors and providing the former with a return on their investments and the latter with repayment.

Firm   (1) For purposes of the GIPS standards, the term "firm" refers to the entity defined for compliance with the GIPS standards. See the term "distinct business entity." (2) An economic unit that hires factors of production and organizes those factors to produce and sell goods and services.

Fiscal imbalance   The present value of the government's commitments to pay benefits minus the present value of its tax revenues.

Fiscal policy   The government's attempt to achieve macroeconomic objectives such as full employment, sustained economic growth, and price level stability by setting and changing taxes, making transfer payments, and purchasing goods and services.

Fixed exchange rate   An exchange rate that is set at a determined amount by government policy.

Fixed exchange rate regime   A system in which the exchange rate between two currencies remains fixed at a preset level, known as official parity.

Fixed-income forward   A forward contract in which the underlying is a bond.

Fixed-income investments   Loans with contractually mandated payment schedules from firms or governments to investors.

Fixed-rule policy   A rule that specifies an action to be pursued independently of the state of the economy.

Flat trend channel   The range defined by security prices as they maintain a relatively steady level.

Flexible exchange rates   Exchange rates that are determined by the market forces of supply and demand. They are sometimes called floating exchange rates.

Flexible exchange rate system   A system in which exchange rates are determined by supply and demand.

Floating-rate loan   A loan in which the interest rate is reset at least once after the starting date.

Floor   (1) A contract on an interest rate, whereby the writer of the floor periodically pays the difference between a specified floor rate and the market interest rate if, and only if, this difference is positive. This is equivalent to a stream of put options on the interest rate. (2) A combination of interest rate put options designed to hedge a lender against lower rates on a floating-rate loan.

Floor brokers   Independent members of an exchange who act as brokers for other members.

Floored swap   A swap in which the floating payments have a lower limit.

Floorlet   Each component put option in a floor.

Flow   A quantity per unit of time.

Foreign bond   A bond issued by a foreign company on the local market and in the local currency (e.g., Yankee bonds in the United States, Bulldog bonds in the United Kingdom, or Samurai bonds in Japan).

Foreign exchange expectation   A relation that states that the forward exchange rate, quoted at time 0 for delivery at time 1, is equal to the expected value of the spot exchange rate at time 1. When stated relative to the current spot exchange rate, the relation states that the forward discount (premium) is equal to the expected exchange rate movement.

Foreign exchange market   The market in which the currency of one country is exchanged for the currency of another.

Foreign exchange rate   The price at which one currency exchanges for another.

Forward contract An agreement between two parties in which one party, the buyer, agrees to buy from the other party, the seller, an underlying asset at a later date for a price established at the start of the contract.

Forward discount A situation where, from the perspective of the domestic country, the spot exchange rate is smaller than the forward exchange rate with a foreign country.

Forward P/E *See* Leading P/E.

Forward premium A situation where, from the perspective of the domestic country, the spot exchange rate is larger than the forward exchange rate with a foreign country.

Forward price or forward rate The fixed price or rate at which the transaction scheduled to occur at the expiration of a forward contract will take place. This price is agreed on at the initiation date of the contract.

Forward rate A short-term yield for a future holding period implied by the spot rates of two securities with different maturities.

Forward rate agreement (FRA) A forward contract calling for one party to make a fixed interest payment and the other to make an interest payment at a rate to be determined at the contract expiration.

Four-firm concentration ratio A measure of market power that is calculated as the percentage of the value of sales accounted for by the four largest firms in an industry.

Franchise The right or license to an exclusive territory or market.

Franchise factor A firm's unique competitive advantage that makes it possible for a firm to earn excess returns (rates of return above a firm's cost of capital) on its capital projects. In turn, these excess returns and the franchise factor cause the firm's stock price to have a *P/E* ratio above its base *P/E* ratio that is equal to $1/k$.

Free cash flow to equity This cash flow measure equals cash flow from operations minus capital expenditures and debt payments.

Free-rider problem The absence of an incentive for people to pay for what they consume.

Frequency distribution A tabular display of data summarized into a relatively small number of intervals.

Frequency polygon A graph of a frequency distribution obtained by drawing straight lines joining successive points representing the class frequencies.

Frictional unemployment The unemployment that arises from normal labor turnover—from people entering and leaving the labor force and from the ongoing creation and destruction of jobs.

Full-costing A method of accounting for the costs of exploring and developing oil and gas resources in which all costs are recorded as assets and depleted over the estimated life of the producing resources.

Full-costing method A method of accounting for the costs of exploring and developing oil and gas resources in which all costs are recorded as assets and depleted over the estimated life of the producing resources.

Full employment A situation in which the quantity of labor demanded equal the quantity supplied. At full employment, there is no cyclical unemployment—all unemployment is frictional and structural.

Full price (or dirty price) (1) The total price of a bond, including accrued interest. (2) The price of a security with accrued interest.

Futures commission merchants (FCMs) Individuals or companies that execute futures transactions for other parties off the exchange.

Futures contract A variation of a forward contract that has essentially the same basic definition but with some additional features, such as a clearinghouse guarantee against credit losses, a daily settlement of gains and losses, and an organized electronic or floor trading facility.

Future value (FV) The amount to which a payment or series of payments will grow by a stated future date.

Game theory A tool that economists use to analyze strategic behavior—behavior that takes into account the expected behavior of others and the mutual recognition of independence.

Gamma A numerical measure of how sensitive an option's delta is to a change in the underlying.

GDP deflator One measure of the price level, which is the average of current-year prices as a percentage of base-year prices.

General Agreement on Tariffs and Trade An international agreement signed in 1947 to reduce tariffs on international trade.

Generally accepted accounting principles (GAAP) Accounting principles formulated by the Financial Accounting Standards Board and used to construct financial statements.

Generational accounting An accounting system that measures the lifetime tax burden and benefits of each generation.

Generational imbalance The division of the fiscal imbalance between the current and future generations, assuming that the current generation will enjoy the existing levels of taxes and benefits

Generic *See* Plain-vanilla.

Geometric mean (GM) A measure of central tendency computed by taking the nth root of the product of n non-negative values.

Goods and services The objects that people value and produce to satisfy their wants.

Goodwill The excess of the cost of a group of assets (usually a business) over the fair market value of the assets if purchased individually.

Government budget deficit The deficit that arises when federal government spends more than it collects in taxes.

Government budget surplus The surplus that arises when the federal government collects more in taxes than it spends.

Government debt The total amount of borrowing that the government has borrowed. It equals the sum of past budget deficits minus budget surpluses.

Government purchases Goods and services bought by the government.

Government purchases multiplier The magnification effect of a change in government purchases of goods and services on aggregate demand.

Government sector surplus or deficit An amount equal to net taxes minus government purchases of goods and services.

Great Depression A decade (1929–1939) of high unemployment and stagnant production throughout the world economy.

Gross domestic product (GDP) The market value of all the final goods and services produced within a country during a given time period—usually a year.

Gross-Of-Fees Return The return on assets reduced by any trading expenses incurred during the period.

Gross investment The total amount spent on purchases of new capital and on replacing depreciated capital.

Group depreciation The grouping of similar items to calculate depreciation.

Growth company A company that consistently has the opportunities and ability to invest in projects that provide rates of return that exceed the firm's cost of capital. Because of these investment opportunities, it retains a high proportion of earnings, and its earnings grow faster than those of average firms.

Growth stock A stock issue that generates a higher rate of return than other stocks in the market with similar risk characteristics.

Harmonic mean A type of weighted mean computed by averaging the reciprocals of the observations, then taking the reciprocal of that average.

Hedge A trading strategy in which derivative securities are used to reduce or completely offset a counterparty's risk exposure to an underlying asset.

Hedge fund An investment vehicle designed to manage a private, unregistered portfolio of assets according to any of several strategies. The investment strategy often employs arbitrage trading and significant financial leverage (e.g., short selling, borrowing, derivatives) while the compensation arrangement for the manager typically specifies considerable profit participation.

Hedge ratio The number of derivative contracts that must be transacted to offset the price volatility of an underlying commodity or security position.

Herfindahl-Hirschman Index A measure of market power that is calculated as the square of the market share of each firm (as a percentage) summed over the largest 50 firms (or over all firms if there are fewer than 50) in a market.

High-yield bond A bond rated below investment grade. Also referred to as *speculative-grade bonds* or *junk bonds*.

Histogram A bar chart of data that have been grouped into a frequency distribution.

Holding period return (HPR) The return that an investor earns during a specified holding period; a synonym for total return.

Holding period yield (HPY) (1) The total return from an investment for a given period of time stated as a percentage. (2) The return that an investor earns during a specified holding period; holding period return with reference to a fixed-income instrument.

Human capital The value of skills and knowledge possessed by the workforce.

Hurdle rate The discount rate (cost of capital) which the IRR must exceed if a project is to be accepted.

Hypothesis With reference to statistical inference, a statement about one or more populations.

Hypothesis testing With reference to statistical inference, the subdivision dealing with the testing of hypotheses about one or more populations.

Implicit rental rate The firm's opportunity cost of using its own capital.

Implied repo rate The rate of return from a cash-and-carry transaction implied by the futures price relative to the spot price.

Implied volatility The volatility that option traders use to price an option, implied by the price of the option and a particular option-pricing model.

Imports The goods and services that we buy from people in other countries.

Incentive A reward that encourages or a penalty that discourages an action.

Incentive system A method of organizing production that uses a market-like mechanism inside the firm.

Income effect The effect of a change in income on consumption, other things remaining the same.

Income elasticity of demand   The responsiveness of demand to a change in income, other things remaining the same. It is calculated as the percentage change in the quantity demanded divided by the percentage change in income.

Income statement   A financial statement that shows the flow of the firm's sales, expenses, and earnings over a period of time.

Incremental cash flows   The changes or increments to cash flows resulting from a decision or action.

Indenture   The legal agreement that lists the obligations of the issuer of a bond to the bondholder, including payment schedules, call provisions, and sinking funds.

Independent   With reference to events, the property that the occurrence of one event does not affect the probability of another event occurring.

Independent variable   A variable used to explain the dependent variable in a regression; a right-hand-side variable in a regression equation.

Index amortizing swap   An interest rate swap in which the notional principal is indexed to the level of interest rates and declines with the level of interest rates according to a predefined schedule. This type of swap is frequently used to hedge securities that are prepaid as interest rates decline, such as mortgage-backed securities.

Indexing   An investment strategy in which an investor constructs a portfolio to mirror the performance of a specified index.

Indirect method   The procedure for converting the income statement from an accrual basis to a cash basis by adjusting net income for items that do not affect cash flows, including depreciation, amortization, depletion, gains, losses, and changes in current assets and current liabilities.

Individual transferable quota (ITQ)   A production limit that is assigned to an individual who is free to transfer the quota to someone else.

Induced taxes   Taxes that vary with real GDP.

Industry life cycle analysis   An analysis that focuses on the industry's stage of development.

Inelastic demand   A demand with a price elasticity between 0 and 1; the percentage change in the quantity demanded is less than the percentage change in price.

Infant-industry argument   The argument that it is necessary to protect a new industry to enable it to grow into a mature industry that can compete in world markets.

Inferior good   A good for which demand decreases as income increases.

Inflation   A process in which the price level is rising and money is losing value.

Inflationary gap   The amount by which real GDP exceeds potential GDP.

Inflation rate   The percentage change in the price level from one year to the next.

Information   An attribute of a good market that includes providing buyers and sellers with timely, accurate information on the volume and prices of past transactions and on all currently outstanding bids and offers.

Informationally efficient market   A more technical term for an efficient capital market that emphasizes the role of information in setting the market price.

Information ratio   Statistic used to measure a portfolio's average return in excess of a comparison, benchmark portfolio divided by the standard deviation of this excess return.

Initial margin requirement   The margin requirement on the first day of a transaction as well as on any day in which additional margin funds must be deposited.

Initial public offering (IPO)   A new issue by a firm that has no existing public market.

Intangible assets   Long-term assets with no physical substance whose value is based on rights or advantages accruing to the owner.

Intellectual property rights   Property rights for discoveries owned by the creators of knowledge.

Interest   The income that capital earns.

Interest-on-interest   Bond income from reinvestment of coupon payments.

Interest rate   A rate of return that reflects the relationship between differently dated cash flows; a discount rate.

Interest rate call   An option in which the holder has the right to make a known interest payment and receive an unknown interest payment.

Interest rate cap or cap   A series of call options on an interest rate, with each option expiring at the date on which the floating loan rate will be reset, and with each option having the same exercise rate. A cap in general can have an underlying other than an interest rate.

Interest rate collar   A combination of a long cap and a short floor, or a short cap and a long floor. A collar in general can have an underlying other than an interest rate.

Interest rate floor or floor   A series of put options on an interest rate, with each option expiring at the date on which the floating loan rate will be reset, and with each option having the same exercise rate. A floor in general can have an underlying other than the interest rate.

Interest rate forward *See* Forward rate agreement.

Interest rate option An option in which the underlying is an interest rate.

Interest rate parity The relationship that must exist in an efficient market between the spot and forward foreign exchange rates between two countries and the interest rates in those countries.

Interest rate put An option in which the holder has the right to make an unknown interest payment and receive a known interest payment.

Interest rate risk The uncertainty of returns on an investment due to possible changes in interest rates over time.

Interest rate swap An agreement calling for the periodic exchange of cash flows, one based on an interest rate that remains fixed for the life of the contract and the other that is linked to a variable-rate index.

Intergenerational data mining A form of data mining that applies information developed by previous researchers using a dataset to guide current research using the same or a related dataset.

Intermarket Trading System (ITS) A computerized system that connects competing exchanges and dealers who trade stocks listed on an exchange. Its purpose is to help customers find the best market for these stocks at a point in time.

Internal liquidity (solvency) ratios Financial ratios that measure the ability of the firm to meet future short-term financial obligations.

Internal rate of return (IRR) The discount rate that makes net present value equal 0; the discount rate that makes the present value of an investment's costs (outflows) equal to the present value of the investment's benefits (inflows).

Internal Rate of Return (Private Equity) (IRR) IRR is the annualized implied discount rate (effective compounded rate) that equates the present value of all the appropriate cash inflows (paid-in capital, such as drawdowns for net investments) associated with an investment with the sum of the present value of all the appropriate cash outflows (such as distributions) accruing from it and the present value of the unrealized residual portfolio (unliquidated holdings). For an interim cumulative return measurement, any IRR depends on the valuation of the residual assets.

Internal Valuation (Real Estate) An internal valuation is an advisor's or underlying third-party manager's best estimate of market value based on the most current and accurate information available under the circumstances. An internal valuation could include industry practice techniques, such as discounted cash flow, sales comparison, replacement cost, or a review of all significant events (both general market and asset specific) that could have a material impact on the investment. Prudent assumptions and estimates must be used, and the process must be applied consistently from period to period, except where a change would result in better estimates of market value.

International Fisher relation The assertion that the interest rate differential between two countries should equal the expected inflation rate differential over the term of the interest rates.

Interval With reference to grouped data, a set of values within which an observation falls.

Interval scale A measurement scale that not only ranks data but also gives assurance that the differences between scale values are equal.

In the money An option that has positive intrinsic value.

In-the-money option (1) An option that has a positive value if exercised immediately. For example, a call when the strike price is below the current price of the underlying asset, or a put when the strike price is above the current price of the underlying asset. (2) An option that has positive intrinsic value. (3) Options that, if exercised, would result in the value received being worth more than the payment required to exercise.

Intrinsic value The portion of a call option's total value equal to the greater of either zero or the difference between the current value of the underlying asset and the exercise price; for a put option, intrinsic value is the greater of either zero or the exercise price less the underlying asset price. For a stock, it is the value derived from fundamental analysis of the stock's expected returns or cash flows.

Inverse floater A floating-rate note or bond in which the coupon is adjusted to move opposite to a benchmark interest rate.

Inverse relationship A relationship between variables that move in opposite directions.

Invested Capital (Private Equity) The amount of paid-in capital that has been invested in portfolio companies.

Investing activities Business activities that involve the acquisition and sale of marketable securities and long-term assets and the making and collecting of loans.

Investment The current commitment of dollars for a period of time in order to derive future payments that will compensate the investor for the time the funds are committed, the expected rate of inflation, and the uncertainty of future payments.

Investment The purchase of new plant, equipment, and buildings and additions to inventories.

Investment Advisor (Private Equity) Any individual or institution that supplies investment advice to clients on a per fee basis. The investment advisor inherently has no role in the management of the underlying portfolio companies of a partnership/fund.

Investment company A firm that sells shares of the company and uses the proceeds to buy portfolios of stock, bonds, or other financial instruments.

Investment decision process Estimation of intrinsic value for comparison with market price to determine whether or not to invest.

Investment demand The relationship between investment and real interest rate, other things remaining the same.

Investment horizon The time period used for planning and forecasting purposes or the future time at which the investor requires the invested funds.

Investment management company A company separate from the investment company that manages the portfolio and performs administrative functions.

Investment Management Fee The fee payable to the investment management firm for the on-going management of a portfolio. Investment management fees are typically asset based (percentage of assets), performance based (based on performance relative to a benchmark), or a combination of the two but may take different forms as well.

Investment Multiple (TVPI Multiple) (Private Equity) The ratio of total value to paid-in-capital. It represents the total return of the investment to the original investment not taking into consideration the time invested. Total value can be found by adding the residual value and distributed capital together.

Investment strategy A decision by a portfolio manager regarding how he or she will manage the portfolio to meet the goals and objectives of the client. This will include either active or passive management and, if active, what style in terms of top-down or buttom-up or fundamental versus technical.

IRR The discount rate which forces the PV of a project's inflows to equal the PV of its costs.

IRR rule An investment decision rule that accepts projects or investments for which the IRR is greater than the opportunity cost of capital.

January effect A frequent empirical anomaly where risk-adjusted stock returns in the month of January are significantly larger than those occurring in any other month of the year.

Job search The activity of looking for acceptable vacant jobs.

Joint probability The probability of the joint occurrence of stated events.

Keynesian An economist who believes that left alone, the economy would rarely operate at full employment and that to achieve full employment, active help from fiscal policy and monetary policy is required.

Kurtosis The statistical measure that indicates the peakedness of a distribution.

Labor The work time and work effort that people devote to producing goods and services.

Labor force The sum of the people who are employed and who are unemployed.

Labor force participation rate The percentage of the working-age population who are members of the labor force.

Labor productivity Real GDP per hour of work.

Labor union An organized group of workers whose purpose is to increase wages and to influence other job conditions.

Laffer curve The relationship between the tax rate and the amount of tax revenue collected.

Land The gifts of nature that we use to produce goods and services.

Law of demand Other things remaining the same, the higher the price of a good, the smaller is the quantity demanded of it.

Law of diminishing returns As a firm uses more of a variable input, with a given quantity of other inputs (fixed inputs), the marginal product of the variable input eventually diminishes.

Law of one price The condition in a financial market in which two financial instruments or combinations of financial instruments can sell for only one price. Equivalent to the principle that no arbitrage opportunities are possible.

Law of supply Other things remaining the same, the higher the price of a good, the greater is the quantity supplied of it.

Leading indicators A set of economic variables whose values reach peaks and troughs in advance of the aggregate economy.

Leading P/E (or forward P/E or prospective P/E) A stock's current price divided by next year's expected earnings.

Learning-by-doing People become more productive in an activity (learn) just by repeatedly producing a particular good or service (doing).

Leasehold A right to occupy land or buildings under a long-term rental contract.

Leasehold improvements Improvements to leased property that become the property of the lessor at the end of the lease.

Legal monopoly A market structure in which there is one firm and entry is restricted by the granting of a public franchise, government license, patent, or copyright.

Leptokurtic   Describes a distribution that is more peaked than a normal distribution.

License   The right to use a formula, technique, process, or design.

Likelihood   The probability of an observation, given a particular set of conditions.

Limit down   A limit move in the futures market in which the price at which a transaction would be made is at or below the lower limit.

Limited Partnership (Private Equity)   The legal structure used by most venture and private equity funds. Usually fixed life investment vehicles. The general partner or management firm manages the partnership using the policy laid down in a partnership agreement. The agreement also covers terms, fees, structures, and other items agreed between the limited partners and the general partner.

Limit move   A condition in the futures markets in which the price at which a transaction would be made is at or beyond the price limits.

Limit order   An order that lasts for a specified time to buy or sell a security when and if it trades at a specified price.

Limit pricing   The practice of setting the price at the highest level that inflicts a loss on an entrant.

Limit up   A limit move in the futures market in which the price at which a transaction would be made is at or above the upper limit.

Linear association   A straight-line relationship, as opposed to a relationship that cannot be graphed as a straight line.

Linear interpolation   The estimation of an unknown value on the basis of two known values that bracket it, using a straight line between the two known values.

Linear regression   Regression that models the straight-line relationship between the dependent and independent variable(s).

Linear relationship   A relationship between two variables that is illustrated by a straight line.

Liquid   Term used to describe an asset that can be quickly converted to cash at a price close to fair market value.

Liquidity premium   A premium added to the equilibrium interest rate on a security if that security cannot be converted to cash on short notice and at close to "fair market value."

Liquidity risk   Uncertainty due to the ability to buy or sell an investment in the secondary market.

Living wage   An hourly wage rate that enables a person who works a 40-hour week to rent adequate housing for not more than 30 percent of the amount earned.

Locked limit   A condition in the futures markets in which a transaction cannot take place because the price would be beyond the limits.

London InterBank Offer Rate (LIBOR)   (1) The rate at which international banks lend on the Eurocurrency market. This is the rate quoted to a top-quality borrower. The most common maturities are one month, three months, and six months. There is a LIBOR for the U.S. dollar and a few other major currencies. LIBOR is determined by the British Banking Association in London. *See* also Euribor. (2) The Eurodollar rate at which London banks lend dollars to other London banks; considered to be the best representative rate on a dollar borrowed by a private, high-quality borrower.

Long   The buyer of a derivative contract. Also refers to the position of owning a derivative.

Longitudinal data   Observations on characteristic(s) of the same observational unit through time.

Long position   The buyer of a commodity or security or, for a forward contract, the counterparty who will be the eventual buyer of the underlying asset.

Long run   A period of time in which the quantities of all resources can be varied.

Long-run aggregate supply curve   The relationship between the real GDP supplied and the price level in the long run when real GDP equals potential GDP.

Long-run average cost curve   The relationship between the lowest attainable average total cost and output when both capital and labor are varied.

Long-run industry supply curve   A curve that shows how the quantity supplied by an industry varies as the market price varies after all the possible adjustments have been made, including changes in plant size and the number of firms in the industry.

Long-run macroeconomic equilibrium   A situation that occurs when real GDP equals potential GDP—the economy is on its long-run aggregate supply curve.

Long-run Phillips curve   A curve that shows the relationship between inflation and unemployment when the actual inflation rate equals the expected inflation rate.

Long-term assets   Assets that have a useful life of more than one year, are used in the operation of a business, and are not intended for resale. Less commonly called *fixed assets*.

Long-term equity anticipatory securities (LEAPS)   Options originally created with expirations of several years.

Look-ahead bias   A bias caused by using information that was unavailable on the test date.

Lower bound   The lowest possible value of an option.

Lucas wedge The accumulated loss of output that results from a slowdown in the growth rate of real GDP per person.

M1 A measure of money that consists of currency and traveler's checks plus checking deposits owned by individuals and businesses.

M2 A measure of money that consists of M1 plus time deposits, savings deposits, and money market mutual funds and other deposits.

Macroeconomic long run. A time frame that is sufficiently long for real GDP to return to potential GDP so that full employment prevails.

Macaulay duration A measure of the time flow of cash from a bond where cash flows are weighted by present values discounted by the yield to maturity.

Macroeconomics The study of the performance of the national economy and the global economy.

Macroeconomic short run A period during which some money prices are sticky and real GDP might be below, above, or at potential GDP and unemployment might be above, below, or at the natural rate of unemployment.

Maintenance margin The required proportion that the investor's equity value must be to the total market value of the stock. If the proportion drops below this percent, the investor will receive a margin call.

Maintenance margin requirement The margin requirement on any day other than the first day of a transaction.

Management fee The compensation an investment company pays to the investment management company for its services. The average annual fee is about 0.5 percent of fund assets.

Margin (1) The percent of cost a buyer pays in cash for a security, borrowing the balance from the broker. This introduces leverage, which increases the risk of the transaction. (2) The amount of money that a trader deposits in a margin account. The term is derived from the stock market practice in which an investor borrows a portion of the money required to purchase a certain amount of stock. In futures markets, there is no borrowing so the margin is more of a down payment or performance bond.

Margin account The collateral posted with the futures exchange clearinghouse by an outside counterparty to insure its eventual performance; the *initial* margin is the deposit required at contract origination while the *maintenance* margin is the minimum collateral necessary at all times.

Marginal benefit The benefit that a person receives from consuming one more unit of a good or service. It is measured as the maximum amount that a person is willing to pay for one more unit of the good or service.

Marginal benefit curve A curve that shows the relationship between the marginal benefit of a good and the quantity of that good consumed.

Marginal cost The opportunity cost of producing one more unit of a good or service. It is the best alternative forgone. It is calculated as the increase in total cost divided by the increase in output.

Marginal cost pricing rule A rule that sets the price of a good or service equal to the marginal cost of producing it.

Marginal probability *See* Unconditional probability.

Marginal product The increase in total product that results from a one-unit increase in the variable input, with all other inputs remaining the same. It is calculated as the increase in total product divided by the increase in the variable input employed, when the quantities of all other inputs are constant.

Marginal product of labor The additional real GDP produced by an additional hour of labor when all other influences on production remain the same.

Marginal propensity to consume The fraction of a change in disposable income that is consumed. It is calculated as the change in consumption expenditure divided by the change in disposable income.

Marginal revenue The change in total revenue that results from a one-unit increase in the quantity sold. It is calculated as the change in total revenue divided by the change in quantity sold.

Marginal revenue product The change in total revenue that results from employing one more unit of a resource (labor) while the quantity of all other resources remains the same. It is calculated as the increase in total revenue divided by the increase in the quantity of the resource (labor).

Marginal social benefit The marginal benefit enjoyed by society—by the consumer of a good or service (marginal private benefit) plus the marginal benefit enjoyed by others (marginal external benefit).

Marginal social cost The marginal cost incurred by the entire society—by the producer and by everyone else on whom the cost falls—and is the sum of marginal private cost and the marginal external cost.

Marginal tax rate The part of each additional dollar in income that is paid as tax.

Margin call A request by an investor's broker for additional capital for a security bought on margin if the investor's equity value declines below the required maintenance margin.

Marked to market The settlement process used to adjust the margin account of a futures contract for daily changes in the price of the underlying asset.

Market demand   The relationship between the total quantity demanded of a good and its price. It is illustrated by the market demand curve.

Market failure   A state in which the market does not allocate resources efficiently.

Market order   An order to buy or sell a security immediately at the best price available.

Market portfolio   The portfolio that includes all risky assets with relative weights equal to their proportional market values.

Market power   The ability to influence the market, and in particular the market price, by influencing the total quantity offered for sale.

Market risk   The risk associated with interest rates, exchange rates, and equity prices.

Market risk premium   The amount of return above the risk-free rate that investors expect from the market in general as compensation for systematic risk.

Market Value   The current listed price at which investors buy or sell securities at a given time.

Market Value (Real Estate)   The most probable price that a property should bring in a competitive and open market under all conditions requisite to a fair sale, the buyer and seller each acting prudently and knowledgeably, and assuming the price is not affected by undue stimulus. Implicit in this definition is the consummation of a sale as of a specified date and the passing of title from seller to buyer under conditions whereby: (a) Buyer and seller are typically motivated. (b) Both parties are well informed or well advised and each acting in what they consider their own best interests. (c) A reasonable time is allowed for exposure in the open market. (d) Payment is made in terms of currency or in terms of financial arrangements comparable thereto. (e) The price represents the normal consideration for the property sold unaffected by special or creative financing or sales concessions granted by anyone associated with the sale.

Market value added (MVA)   External management performance measure to compare the market value of the company's debt and equity with the total capital invested in the firm.

Marking to market   (1) Procedure whereby potential profits and losses on a futures position are realized daily. The daily futures price variation is debited (credited) in cash to the loser (winner) at the end of the day. (2) A procedure used primarily in futures markets in which the parties to a contract settle the amount owed daily. Also known as the daily settlement.

McCallum rule   A rule that adjusts the growth rate of the monetary base to target the inflation rate but also to take into account changes in the trend productivity growth rate and fluctuations in aggregate demand.

Mean absolute deviation   With reference to a sample, the mean of the absolute values of deviations from the sample mean.

Mean excess return   The average rate of return in excess of the risk-free rate.

Means of payment   A method of settling a debt.

Mean–variance analysis   An approach to portfolio analysis using expected means, variances, and covariances of asset returns.

Measurement scales   A scheme of measuring differences. The four types of measurement scales are nominal, ordinal, interval, and ratio.

Measure of central tendency   A quantitative measure that specifies where data are centered.

Median   The value of the middle item of a set of items that has been sorted into ascending or descending order; the 50th percentile.

Mesokurtic   Describes a distribution with kurtosis identical to that of the normal distribution.

Microeconomics   The study of the choices that individuals and businesses make, the way those choices interact, and the influence governments exert on them.

Minimum efficient scale   The smallest quantity of output at which the long-run average cost curve reaches its lowest level.

Minimum wage   A regulation that makes the hiring of labor below a specified wage rate illegal.

Modal interval   With reference to grouped data, the most frequently occurring interval.

Mode   The most frequently occurring value in a set of observations.

Modified duration   (1) Measure of a bond's price sensitivity to interest rate movements. Equal to the duration of a bond divided by one plus its yield to maturity. (2) A measure of Macaulay duration divided by one plus the bond's periodic yield used to approximate the bond's price volatility. (3) An adjustment of the duration for the level of the yield. Contrast with Macaulay duration.

Monetarist   An economist who believes that the economy is self regulating and that it will normally operate at full employment, provided that monetary policy is not erratic and that the pace of money growth is kept steady.

Monetary base   The sum of the Federal Reserve notes, coins, and banks' deposits at the Fed.

Monetary policy   The Fed conducts the nation's monetary policy by changing in interest rates and adjusting the quantity of money.

Money   Any commodity or token that is generally acceptable as a means of payment.

Money market　The market for short-term debt securities with maturities of less than one year.

Money market fund　A fund that invests in short-term securities sold in the money market. (Large companies, banks, and other institutions also invest their surplus cash in the money market for short periods of time.) In the entire investment spectrum, these are generally the safest, most stable securities available. They include Treasury bills, certificates of deposit of large banks, and commercial paper (short-term IOUs of large corporations).

Money market mutual fund　A fund operated by a financial institution that sells shares in the fund and holds liquid assets such as U.S. Treasury bills and short-term commercial bills.

Money market yield (or CD equivalent yield)　A yield on a basis comparable to the quoted yield on an interest-bearing money market instrument that pays interest on a 360-day basis; the annualized holding period yield, assuming a 360-day year.

Money multiplier　The amount by which a change in the monetary base is multiplied to determine the resulting change in the quantity of money.

Moneyness　The relationship between the price of the underlying and an option's exercise price.

Money price　The number of dollars that must be given up in exchange for a good or service.

Money wage rate　The number of dollars that an hour of labor earns.

Monopolistic competition　A market structure in which a large number of firms compete by making similar but slightly different products.

Monopoly　A market structure in which there is one firm, which produces a good or service that has no close substitute and in which the firm is protected from competition by a barrier preventing the entry of new firms.

Monte Carlo simulation　A risk analysis technique in which probable future events are simulated on a computer, generating estimated rates of return and risk indexes.

Mortgage bonds　Bonds that pledge specific assets such as buildings and equipment. The proceeds from the sale of these assets are used to pay off bondholders in case of bankruptcy.

Moving average　The continually recalculating average of security prices for a period, often 200 days, to serve as an indication of the general trend of prices and also as a benchmark price.

Multifactor model　An empirical version of the APT where the investor chooses the exact number and identity of the common risk factors used to describe an asset's risk-return relationship. Risk factors are often designated as *macroeconomic* variables (e.g., inflation, changes in gross domestic product) or *microeconomic* variables (e.g., security-specific characteristics like firm size or book-to-market ratios).

Multiplication rule for probabilities　The rule that the joint probability of events A and B equals the probability of A given B times the probability of B.

Multiplier　The amount by which a change in autonomous expenditure is magnified or multiplied to determine the change in equilibrium expenditure and real GDP.

Multivariate distribution　A probability distribution that specifies the probabilities for a group of related random variables.

Multivariate normal distribution　A probability distribution for a group of random variables that is completely defined by the means and variances of the variables plus all the correlations between pairs of the variables.

Must　A required provision for claiming compliance with the GIPS standards.

Mutual fund　An investment company that pools money from shareholders and invests in a variety of securities, including stocks, bonds, and money market securities. A mutual fund ordinarily stands ready to buy back (redeem) its shares at their current net asset value, which depends on the market value of the fund's portfolio of securities at the time. Mutual funds generally continuously offer new shares to investors.

Mutually exclusive events　Events such that only one can occur at a time.

Nasdaq InterMarket　A trading system that includes Nasdaq market makers and ECNs that quote and trade stocks listed on the NYSE and the AMEX. It involves dealers from the Nasdaq market and the Intermarket Trading System (ITS). In many ways, this has become what had been labeled the third market.

Nash equilibrium　The outcome of a game that occurs when player A takes the best possible action given the action of player B and player B takes the best possible action given the action of player A.

National saving　The sum of private saving (saving by households and businesses) and government saving.

Natural monopoly　A monopoly that occurs when one firm can supply the entire market at a lower price than two or more firms can.

Natural rate of unemployment　The unemployment rate when the economy is at full employment. There is no cyclical unemployment; all unemployment is frictional and structural.

Natural resources　Long-term assets purchased for the economic value that can be taken from the land and used up.

Near-term, high-priority goal A short-term financial investment goal of personal importance, such as accumulating funds for making a house down payment or buying a car.

Needs-tested spending Government spending on programs that pay benefits to suitably qualified people and businesses.

Negative relationship A relationship between variables that move in opposite directions.

Negotiated sales An underwriting arrangement wherein the sale of a security issue by an issuing entity (governmental body or a corporation) is done using an investment banking firm that maintains an ongoing relationship with the issuer. The characteristics of the security issue are determined by the issuer in consultation with the investment banker.

Neoclassical growth theory A theory of economic growth that proposes that real GDP grows because technological change induces a level of saving and investment that makes capital per hour of labor grow.

Net asset value The market value of the assets owned by a fund.

Net borrower A country that is borrowing more from the rest of the world than it is lending to it.

Net exports The value of exports minus the value of imports.

Net investment Net increase in the capital stock—gross investment minus depreciation.

Net lender A country that is lending more to the rest of the world than it is borrowing from it.

Net-of-Fees Return The gross-of-fees return reduced by the investment management fee.

Net present value The present value of the future flow of marginal revenue product generated by capital minus the cost of the capital.

Net present value (NPV) A measure of the excess cash flows expected from an investment proposal. It is equal to the present value of the cash *inflows* from an investment proposal, discounted at the required rate of return for the investment, minus the present value of the cash *outflows* required by the investment, also discounted at the investment's required rate of return. If the derived net present value is a positive value (i.e., there is an excess net present value), the investment should be acquired since it will provide a rate of return above its required returns.

Net taxes Taxes paid to governments minus transfer payments received from governments.

Netting When parties agree to exchange only the net amount owed from one party to the other.

New issue Common stocks or bonds offered by companies for public sale.

New Keynesian A Keynesian who holds the view that not only is the money wage rate sticky but that prices of goods and services are also sticky.

Node Each value on a binomial tree from which successive moves or outcomes branch.

No-load fund A mutual fund that sells its shares at net asset value without adding sales charges.

Nominal GDP The value of the final goods and services produced in a given year valued at the prices that prevailed in that same year. It is a more precise name for GDP.

Nominal risk-free interest rate The sum of the real risk-free interest rate and the inflation premium.

Nominal scale A measurement scale that categorizes data but does not rank them.

Nominal yield A bond's yield as measured by its coupon rate.

Noncash investing and financing transactions Significant investing and financing transactions involving only long-term assets, long-term liabilities, or stockholders' equity that do not affect current cash inflows or outflows.

Nonlinear relation An association or relationship between variables that cannot be graphed as a straight line.

Nonparametric test A test that is not concerned with a parameter, or that makes minimal assumptions about the population from which a sample comes.

Nonrenewable natural resources Natural resources that can be used only once and that cannot be replaced once they have been used.

Nontariff barrier Any action other than a tariff that restricts international trade.

Normal backwardation The condition in futures markets in which futures prices are lower than expected spot prices.

Normal contango The condition in futures markets in which futures prices are higher than expected spot prices.

Normal good A good for which demand increases as income increases.

Normal profit The expected return for supplying entrepreneurial ability.

North American Free Trade Agreement An agreement, which became effective on January 1, 1994, to eliminate all barriers to international trade between the United States, Canada, and Mexico after a 15-year phasing in period.

Notes Intermediate-term debt securities with maturities longer than 1 year but less than 10 years.

Notional principal The principal value of a swap transaction, which is not exchanged but is used as a scale factor to translate interest rate differentials into cash settlement payments.

NPV rule An investment decision rule that states that an investment should be undertaken if its NPV is positive but not undertaken if its NPV is negative.

Null hypothesis The hypothesis to be tested.

Objective probabilities Probabilities that generally do not vary from person to person; includes a priori and objective probabilities.

Objectives The investor's goals expressed in terms of risk and return and included in the policy statement.

Obsolescence The process of becoming out of date, which is a factor in the limited useful life of tangible assets.

Offensive competitive strategy A strategy whereby a firm attempts to use its strengths to affect the competitive forces in the industry and, in so doing, improves the firm's relative position in the industry.

Official reserves The amount of reserves owned by the central bank of a government in the form of gold, Special Drawing Rights, and foreign cash or marketable securities.

Official settlements account A record of the change in a country's official reserves.

Off-market FRA A contract in which the initial value is intentionally set at a value other than zero and therefore requires a cash payment at the start from one party to the other.

Offsetting A transaction in exchange-listed derivative markets in which a party re-enters the market to close out a position.

Okun gap The gap between real GDP and potential GDP, and so is another name for the output gap.

Oligopoly A market structure in which a small number of firms compete.

One-sided hypothesis test (or one-tailed hypothesis test) A test in which the null hypothesis is rejected only if the evidence indicates that the population parameter is greater than (smaller than) θ_0. The alternative hypothesis also has one side.

Open-End Fund (Private Equity) A type of investment fund where the number of investors and the total committed capital is not fixed (i.e., open for subscriptions and/or redemptions).

Open market operation The purchase or sale of government securities—U.S. Treasury bills and bonds—by the Federal Reserve System in the open market.

Operating activities Business activities that involve the cash effects of transactions and other events that enter into the determination of net income.

Operating efficiency ratios Financial ratios intended to indicate how efficiently management is utilizing the firm's assets in terms of dollar sales generated per dollar of assets. Primary examples would be: total asset turnover, fixed asset turnover, or equity turnover.

Operating leverage The use of fixed-production costs in the firm's operating cost structure. The effect of fixed costs is to magnify the effect of a change in sales on operating profits.

Operating profitability ratios Financial ratios intended to indicate how profitable the firm is in terms of the percent of profit generated from sales. Alternative measures would include: operating profit (EBIT)/net sales; pretax profit (EBT)/net sales; and net profit/sales.

Opportunity cost The highest-valued alternative that we give up to something.

Optimal portfolio The portfolio on the efficient frontier that has the highest utility for a given investor. It lies at the point of tangency between the efficient frontier and the curve with the investor's highest possible utility.

Option A financial instrument that gives one party the right, but not the obligation, to buy or sell an underlying asset from or to another party at a fixed price over a specific period of time. Also referred to as contingent claims.

Option-adjusted spread A type of yield spread that considers changes in the term structure and alternative estimates of the volatility of interest rates.

Option contract An agreement that grants the owner the right, but not the obligation, to make a future transaction in an underlying commodity or security at a fixed price and within a predetermined time in the future.

Option premium The initial price that the option buyer must pay to the option seller to acquire the contract.

Option premium (or option price or premium) (1) The price of an option. (2) The initial price that the option buyer must pay to the option seller to acquire the contract. (3) The amount of money a buyer pays and seller receives to engage in an option transaction.

Ordinal scale A measurement scale that sorts data into categories that are ordered (ranked) with respect to some characteristic.

Ordinary annuity An annuity with a first cash flow that is paid one period from the present.

OTC Electronic Bulletin Board (OTCBB) A regulated quotation service that displays real-time quotes, last-sale prices, and volume information for a specified set of over-the-counter (OTC) securities that are not traded on the formal Nasdaq market.

Outcome A possible value of a random variable.

Out-of-sample test A test of a strategy or model using a sample outside the time period on which the strategy or model was developed.

Out-of-the-money option (1) An option that has no value if exercised immediately. For example, a call when the strike price is above the current price of the underlying asset, or a put when the strike price is below the current price of the underlying asset. (2) An option that has no intrinsic value. (3) Options that, if exercised, would require the payment of more money than the value received and therefore would not be currently exercised.

Overnight index swap (OIS) A swap in which the floating rate is the cumulative value of a single unit of currency invested at an overnight rate during the settlement period.

Overweighted A condition in which a portfolio, for whatever reason, includes more of a class of securities than the relative market value alone would justify.

Paid-In Capital (Private Equity) The amount of committed capital a limited partner has actually transferred to a venture fund. Also known as the cumulative drawdown amount.

Paired comparisons test A statistical test for differences based on paired observations drawn from samples that are dependent on each other.

Paired observations Observations that are dependent on each other.

Pairs arbitrage trade A trade in two closely related stocks involving the short sale of one and the purchase of the other.

Panel data Observations through time on a single characteristic of multiple observational units.

Parameter A descriptive measure computed from or used to describe a population of data, conventionally represented by Greek letters.

Parameter instability The problem or issue of population regression parameters that have changed over time.

Parametric test Any test (or procedure) concerned with parameters or whose validity depends on assumptions concerning the population generating the sample.

Par value *See* Principal. The principal amount repaid at maturity of a bond. Also called face value.

Patent A government-sanctioned exclusive right granted to the inventor of a good, service, or productive process to produce, use, and sell the invention for a given number of years.

Patent An exclusive right granted by the federal government for a period of 20 years to make a particular product or use a specific process.

Payback The time required for the added income from the convertible security relative to the stock to offset the conversion premium.

Payer swaption A swaption that allows the holder to enter into a swap as the fixed-rate payer and floating-rate receiver.

Payment date The date on which a firm actually mails dividend checks.

Payoff The value of an option at expiration.

Payoff matrix A table that shows the payoffs for every possible action by each player for every possible action by each other player.

Pegged exchange rate regime A system in which a country's exchange rate in relation to a major currency is set at a target value (the peg) but allowed to fluctuate within a small band around the target.

Percentiles Quantiles that divide a distribution into 100 equal parts.

Perfect competition A market in which there are many firms each selling an identical product; there are many buyers; there are no restrictions on entry into the industry; firms in the industry have no advantage over potential new entrants; and firms and buyers are well informed about the price of each firm's product.

Perfectly elastic demand Demand with an infinite price elasticity; the quantity demanded changes by an infinitely large percentage in response to a tiny price change.

Perfectly inelastic demand Demand with a price elasticity of zero; the quantity demanded remains constant when the price changes.

Perfect price discrimination Price discrimination that extracts the entire consumer surplus.

Performance appraisal (1) The assessment of an investment record for evidence of investment skill. (2) The evaluation of risk-adjusted performance; the evaluation of investment skill.

Performance measurement The calculation of returns in a logical and consistent manner.

Permutation An ordered listing.

Perpetuity (1) An investment without any maturity date. It provides returns to its owner indefinitely. (2) A perpetual annuity, or a set of never-ending level sequential cash flows, with the first cash flow occurring one period from now.

Personal trust An amount of money set aside by a grantor and often managed by a third party, the trustee. Often constructed so one party receives income from the trust's investments and another party receives the residual value of the trust after the income beneficiaries' death.

Phillips curve   A curve that shows a relationship between inflation and unemployment.

Physical deterioration   A decline in the useful life of a depreciable asset resulting from use and from exposure to the elements.

Plain-vanilla   Refers to a security, especially a bond or a swap, issued with standard features. Sometimes called generic.

Plain vanilla swap   An interest rate swap in which one party pays a fixed rate and the other pays a floating rate, with both sets of payments in the same currency.

Platykurtic   Describes a distribution that is less peaked than the normal distribution.

Point estimate   A single numerical estimate of an unknown quantity, such as a population parameter.

Policy statement   A statement in which the investor specifies investment goals, constraints, and risk preferences.

Pooled estimate   An estimate of a parameter that involves combining (pooling) observations from two or more samples.

Population   All members of a specified group.

Population mean   The arithmetic mean value of a population; the arithmetic mean of all the observations or values in the population.

Population standard deviation   A measure of dispersion relating to a population in the same unit of measurement as the observations, calculated as the positive square root of the population variance.

Population variance   A measure of dispersion relating to a population, calculated as the mean of the squared deviations around the population mean.

Portfolio   An individually managed pool of assets. A portfolio may be a subportfolio, account, or pooled fund.

Position trader   A trader who typically holds positions open overnight.

Positive relationship   A relationship between two variables that move in the same direction.

Potential GDP   The quantity of real GDP at full employment.

Posterior probability   An updated probability that reflects or comes after new information.

Potential credit risk   The risk associated with the possibility that a payment due at a later date will not be made.

Poverty   A situation in which a household's income is too low to be able to buy the quantities of food, shelter, and clothing that are deemed necessary.

Power of a test   The probability of correctly rejecting the null—that is, rejecting the null hypothesis when it is false.

Predatory pricing   Setting a low price to drive competitors out of business with the intention of setting a monopoly price when the competition has gone.

Preferences   A description of a person's likes and dislikes.

Preferred stock   An equity investment that stipulates the dividend payment either as a coupon or a stated dollar amount. The firm's directors may withhold payments.

Premium   A bond selling at a price above par value due to capital market conditions.

Present value   The amount of money that, if invested today, will grow to be as large as a given future amount when the interest that it will earn is taken into account.

Present value (PV)   (1) The current worth of future income after it is discounted to reflect the fact that revenues in the future are valued less highly than revenues now. (2) The current worth of a future cash flow. Obtained by discounting the future cash flow at the market-required rate of return. (3) The current (discounted) value of a future cash flow or flows.

Price ceiling   A regulation that makes it illegal to charge a price higher than a specified level.

Price continuity   A feature of a liquid market in which there are small price changes from one transaction to the next due to the depth of the market.

Price discovery   A feature of futures markets in which futures prices provide valuable information about the price of the underlying asset.

Price discrimination   The practice of selling different units of a good or service for different prices or of charging one customer different prices for different quantities bought.

Price/earnings (P/E) ratio   The number by which expected earnings per share is multiplied to estimate a stock's value; also called the *earnings multiplier.*

Price effect   The effect of a change in the price on the quantity of a good consumed, other things remaining the same.

Price elasticity of demand   A units-free measure of the responsiveness of the quantity demanded of a good to a change in its price, when all other influences on buyers' plans remain the same.

Price floor   A regulation that makes it illegal to charge a price lower than a specified level.

Price level   The average level of prices as measured by a price index.

Price limits   Limits imposed by a futures exchange on the price change that can occur from one day to the next.

Price momentum A portfolio strategy in which you acquire stocks that have enjoyed above-market stock price increases.

Price multiple The ratio of a stock's market price to some measure of value per share.

Price relative A ratio of an ending price over a beginning price; it is equal to 1 plus the holding period return on the asset.

Price risk The component of interest rate risk due to the uncertainty of the market price of a bond caused by changes in market interest rates.

Price taker A firm that cannot influence the price of the good or service it produces.

Price-weighted index An index calculated as an arithmetic mean of the current prices of the sampled securities.

Primary market The market in which newly issued securities are sold by their issuers, who receive the proceeds.

Principal-agent problem The problem of devising compensation rules that induce an agent to act in the best interest of a principal.

Prior probabilities Probabilities reflecting beliefs prior to the arrival of new information.

Private Equity Private equity includes, but is not limited to, organizations devoted to venture capital, leveraged buyouts, consolidations, mezzanine and distressed debt investments, and a variety of hybrids, such as venture leasing and venture factoring.

Private information Information that is available to one person but is too costly for anyone else to obtain.

Private placement A new issue sold directly to a small group of investors, usually institutions

Private sector surplus or deficit An amount equal to saving minus investment.

Probability A number between 0 and 1 describing the chance that a stated event will occur.

Probability density function A function with non-negative values such that probability can be described by areas under the curve graphing the function.

Probability distribution A distribution that specifies the probabilities of a random variable's possible outcomes.

Probability function A function that specifies the probability that the random variable takes on a specific value.

Producer surplus The price of a good minus the opportunity cost of producing it, summed over the quantity sold.

Product differentiation Making a product slightly different from the product of a competing firm.

Production efficiency A situation in which the economy cannot produce more of one good without producing less of some other good.

Production function The relationship between real GDP and the quantity of labor when all other influences on production remain the same.

Production method A method of depreciation that assumes depreciation is solely the result of use and that allocates depreciation based on the units of use or output during each period of an asset's useful life.

Production possibilities frontier The boundary between the combinations of goods and services that can be produced and the combinations that cannot.

Production quota An upper limit to the quantity of a good that may be produced in a specified period.

Productivity growth slowdown A slowdown in the growth rate of output per person.

Profit The income earned by entrepreneurship.

Property rights Social arrangements that govern the ownership, use, and disposal of resources or factors of production, goods, and services that are enforceable in the courts.

Prospective P/E *See* Leading P/E.

Protective put An option strategy in which a long position in an asset is combined with a long position in a put.

Public good A good or service that is both nonrival and nonexcludable—it can be consumed simultaneously by everyone and from which no one can be excluded.

Purchasing power parity The equal value of different monies.

Purchasing power parity (PPP) A theory stating that the exchange rate between two currencies will exactly reflect the purchasing power of the two currencies.

Pure discount instruments Instruments that pay interest as the difference between the amount borrowed and the amount paid back.

Put An option that gives the holder the right to sell an underlying asset to another party at a fixed price over a specific period of time.

Put option A contract giving the right to sell an asset at a specified price, on or before a specified date.

Put–call–forward parity The relationship among puts, calls, and forward contracts.

Put-call parity The relationship that must exist in an efficient market between the prices for put and call options having the same underlying asset, exercise price, and expiration date.

p-**Value**   The smallest level of significance at which the null hypothesis can be rejected; also called the marginal significance level.

Quality financial statements   Financial statements that most knowledgeable observers (analysts, portfolio managers) would consider conservatively prepared in terms of sales, expenses, earnings, and asset valuations. The results reported would reflect reasonable estimates and indicate what truly happened during the period and the legitimate value of assets and liabilities on the balance sheet.

Quantile (or fractile)   A value at or below which a stated fraction of the data lies.

Quantity demanded   The amount of a good or service that consumers plan to buy during a given time period at a particular price.

Quantity of labor demanded   The labor hours hired by the firms in the economy.

Quantity of labor supplied   The number of labor hours that all households in the economy plan to work.

Quantity supplied   The amount of a good or service that producers plan to sell during a given time period at a particular price.

Quantity theory of money   The proposition that in the long run, an increase in the quantity of money brings an equal percentage increase in the price level.

Quartiles   Quantiles that divide a distribution into four equal parts.

Quintiles   Quantiles that divide a distribution into five equal parts.

Quota   A quantitative restriction on the import of a particular good, which specifies the maximum amount that can be imported in a given time period.

Random number   An observation drawn from a uniform distribution.

Random number generator   An algorithm that produces uniformly distributed random numbers between 0 and 1.

Random variable   A quantity whose future outcomes are uncertain.

Random walk theory   (1) The theory that current stock prices already reflect known information about the future. Therefore, the future movement of stock prices will be determined by surprise occurrences. This will cause them to change in a random fashion. (2) A theory stating that all current information is reflected in current security prices and that future price movements are random because they are caused by unexpected news.

Range   The difference between the maximum and minimum values in a dataset.

Range forward   A trading strategy based on a variation of the put-call parity model where, for the same underlying asset but different exercise prices, a call option is purchased and a put option is sold (or vice versa).

Rational expectation   The most accurate forecast possible, a forecast that uses all the available information, including knowledge of the relevant economic forces that influence the variable being forecasted.

Ratio scales   A measurement scale that has all the characteristics of interval measurement scales as well as a true zero point as the origin.

Real business cycle theory   A theory that regards random fluctuations in productivity as the main source of economic fluctuations.

Real Estate   Real estate Investments include: (a) Wholly owned or partially owned properties, (b) Commingled funds, property unit trusts, and insurance company separate accounts, (c) Unlisted, private placement securities issued by private real estate investment trusts (REITs) and real estate operating companies (REOCs), and (d) Equity-oriented debt, such as participating mortgage loans or any private interest in a property where some portion of return to the investor at the time of investment is related to the performance of the underlying real estate.

Real estate investment trusts (REITs)   Investment funds that hold portfolios of real estate investments.

Real income   A household's income expressed as a quantity of goods that the household can afford to buy.

Real interest rate   The nominal interest rate adjusted for inflation; the nominal interest rate minus the inflation rate.

Realization Multiple (Private Equity)   The realization multiple (DPI) is calculated by dividing the cumulative distributions by the paid-in-capital.

Realized capital gains   Capital gains that result when an appreciated asset is sold; realized capital gains are taxable.

Real options   Options embedded in a firm's real assets that give managers valuable decision-making flexibility, such as the right to either undertake or abandon an investment project.

Real rate of interest   The money rate of interest minus the expected rate of inflation. The real rate of interest indicates the interest premium, in terms of real goods and services, that one must pay for earlier availability.

Real risk-free rate (RRFR)   The basic interest rate with no accommodation for inflation or uncertainty. The pure time value of money.

Real wage rate   The quantity of goods ands services that an hour's work can buy. It is equal to the money wage rate divided by the price level.

Receiver swaption   A swaption that allows the holder to enter into a swap as the fixed-rate receiver and floating-rate payer.

Recession   There are two common definitions of recession. They are (1) A business cycle phase in which real GDP decreases for at least two successive quarters. (2) A significant decline in activity spread across the economy, lasting for more than a few months, visible in industrial production, employment, real income, and wholesale-retail trade.

Recessionary gap   The amount by which potential GDP exceeds real GDP.

Reference base period   The period in which the CPI is defined to be 100.

Registered competitive market makers (RCMMs)   Members of an exchange who are allowed to use their memberships to buy or sell for their own account within the specific trading obligations set down by the exchange.

Registered traders   Members of the stock exchange who are allowed to use their memberships to buy and sell for their own account, which means they save commissions on their trading but they provide liquidity to the market, and they abide by exchange regulations on how they can trade.

Regression coefficients   The intercept and slope coefficient(s) of a regression.

Regulation   Rules administrated by a government agency to influence economic activity by determining prices, product standards and types, and conditions under which new firms may enter an industry.

Regulatory risk   The risk associated with the uncertainty of how derivative transactions will be regulated or with changes in regulations.

Relative dispersion   The amount of dispersion relative to a reference value or benchmark.

Relative frequency   With reference to an interval of grouped data, the number of observations in the interval divided by the total number of observations in the sample.

Relative price   The ratio of the price of one good or service to the price of another good or service. A relative price is an opportunity cost.

Renewable natural resources   Natural resources that can be used repeatedly without depleting what is available for future use.

Rent   The income that land earns.

Rent ceiling   A regulation that makes it illegal to charge a rent higher than a specified level.

Rent seeking   Any attempt to capture a consumer surplus, a producer surplus, or an economic profit.

Replacement value   The market value of a swap.

Required rate of return   The return that compensates investors for their time, the expected rate of inflation, and the uncertainty of the return.

Required reserve ratio   The ratio of reserves to deposits that banks are required, by regulation, to hold.

Reserve ratio   The fraction of a bank's total deposits that are held in reserves.

Reserves   Cash in a bank's vault plus the bank's deposits at Federal Reserve banks.

Ricardo-Barro effect   The equivalence of financing government purchases by taxes or by borrowing.

Residual value   The estimated net scrap, salvage, or trade-in value of a tangible asset at the estimated date of its disposal. Also called *salvage value* or *disposal value*.

Resistance level   A price at which a technician would expect a substantial increase in the supply of a stock to reverse a rising trend.

Return prediction studies   Studies wherein investigations attempt to predict the time series of future rates of return using public information. An example would be predicting above-average returns for the stock market based on the aggregate dividend yield—e.g., high dividend yield indicates above average future market returns.

Revenue bond   A bond that is serviced by the income generated from specific revenue-producing projects of the municipality.

Revenue expenditure   An expenditure for ordinary repairs and maintenance of a long-term asset, which is recorded by a debit to an expense account.

Rising trend channel   The range defined by security prices as they move progressively higher.

Risk averse   The assumption about investors that they will choose the least risky alternative, all else being equal.

Risk-free asset   An asset with returns that exhibit zero variance.

Risk management   The process of identifying the level of risk an entity wants, measuring the level of risk the entity currently has, taking actions that bring the actual level of risk to the desired level of risk, and monitoring the new actual level of risk so that it continues to be aligned with the desired level of risk.

Risk-neutral probabilities   Weights that are used to compute a binomial option price. They are the probabilities that would apply if a risk-neutral investor valued an option.

Risk-neutral valuation   The process by which options and other derivatives are priced by treating investors as though they were risk neutral.

Risk premium   (1) The difference between the expected return on an asset and the risk-free interest rate. (2) The increase over the nominal risk-free rate that investors demand as compensation for an investment's uncertainty. (3) The expected return on an investment minus the risk-free rate.

Risk premium (RP)   The increase over the nominal risk-free rate that investors demand as compensation for an investment's uncertainty.

Risky asset   An asset with uncertain future returns.

Rival   A good or services or a resource is rival if its use by one person decreases the quantity available for someone else.

Robust   The quality of being relatively unaffected by a violation of assumptions.

Runs test   A test of the weak-form efficient market hypothesis that checks for trends that persist longer in terms of positive or negative price changes than one would expect for a random series.

Safety-first rules   Rules for portfolio selection that focus on the risk that portfolio value will fall below some minimum acceptable level over some time horizon.

Sample   A subset of a population.

Sample excess kurtosis   A sample measure of the degree of a distribution's peakedness in excess of the normal distribution's peakedness.

Sample kurtosis   A sample measure of the degree of a distribution's peakedness.

Sample mean   The sum of the sample observations, divided by the sample size.

Sample selection bias   Bias introduced by systematically excluding some members of the population according to a particular attribute—for example, the bias introduced when data availability leads to certain observations being excluded from the analysis.

Sample skewness   A sample measure of degree of asymmetry of a distribution.

Sample standard deviation   The positive square root of the sample variance.

Sample statistic or statistic   A quantity computed from or used to describe a sample.

Sample variance   A sample measure of the degree of dispersion of a distribution, calculated by dividing the sum of the squared deviations from the sample mean by the sample size (n) minus 1.

Sampling   (1) A technique for constructing a passive index portfolio in which the portfolio manager buys a representative sample of stocks that comprise the benchmark index. (2) The process of obtaining a sample.

Sampling distribution   The distribution of all distinct possible values that a statistic can assume when computed from samples of the same size randomly drawn from the same population.

Sampling error   The difference between the observed value of a statistic and the quantity it is intended to estimate.

Sampling plan   The set of rules used to select a sample.

Sandwich spread   An option strategy that is equivalent to a short butterfly spread.

Saving   The amount of income that households have left after they have paid their taxes and bought their consumption goods and services.

Savings and loan association (S&L)   A depository institution that receives checking deposits and savings deposits and that makes personal, commercial, and home-purchase loans.

Savings bank   A depository institution, owned by its depositors, that accepts savings deposits and makes mortgage loans.

Saving supply   The relationship between saving and the real interest rate, other things remaining the same.

Scalper   A trader who offers to buy or sell futures contracts, holding the position for only a brief period of time. Scalpers attempt to profit by buying at the bid price and selling at the higher ask price.

Scarcity   Our inability to satisfy all our wants.

Scatter diagram   A diagram that plots the value of one economic variable against the value of another.

Scatter plot   A two-dimensional plot of pairs of observations on two data series.

Scenario analysis   A risk management technique involving the examination of the performance of a portfolio under specified situations. Closely related to stress testing.

Search activity   The time spent looking for someone with whom to do business.

Seasoned equity issues   New equity shares offered by firms that already have stock outstanding.

Seats   Memberships in a derivatives exchange.

Secondary market   The market in which outstanding securities are bought and sold by owners other than the issuers. Purpose is to provide liquidity for investors.

Sector rotation strategy   An active strategy that involves purchasing stocks in specific industries or stocks with specific characteristics (low *P/E*, growth, value) that are anticipated to rise in value more than the overall market.

Security market line (SML)   The line that reflects the combination of risk and return of alternative investments. In CAPM, risk is measured by systematic risk (beta).

SelectNet   An order-routing and trade-execution system for institutional investors (brokers and dealers) that allows communication through the Nasdaq system rather than by phone.

Self-interest   The choices that you think are the best for you.

Semideviation   The positive square root of semivariance (sometimes called semistandard deviation).

Semilogarithmic   Describes a scale constructed so that equal intervals on the vertical scale represent equal rates of change, and equal intervals on the horizontal scale represent equal amounts of change.

Semivariance   The average squared deviation below the mean.

Separation theorem   The proposition that the investment decision, which involves investing in the market portfolio on the capital market line, is separate from the financing decision, which targets a specific point on the CML based on the investor's risk preference.

Settlement date or payment date   The date on which the parties to a swap make payments.

Settlement period   The time between settlement dates.

Settlement price   The price determined by the exchange clearinghouse with which futures contract margin accounts are marked to market.

Settlement risk   When settling a contract, the risk that one party could be in the process of paying the counterparty while the counterparty is declaring bankruptcy.

Shareholders' equity   Total assets minus total liabilities.

Sharpe measure   A relative measure of a portfolio's benefit-to-risk ratio, calculated as its average return in excess of the risk-free rate divided by the standard deviation of portfolio returns.

Sharpe ratio   (1) The ratio of mean excess return (return minus the risk-free rate) to standard deviation of returns (or excess returns). (2) The average return in excess of the risk-free rate divided by the standard deviation of return; a measure of the average excess return earned per unit of standard deviation of return.

Shortfall risk   The risk that portfolio value will fall below some minimum acceptable level over some time horizon.

Short hedge   A short position in a forward or futures contract used to offset the price volatility of a long position in the underlying asset.

Short position   The seller of a commodity or security or, for a forward contract, the counterparty who will be the eventual seller of the underlying asset.

Short run   The short run in microeconomics has two meanings. For the firm, it is the period of time in which the quantity of at least one input is fixed and the quantities of the other inputs can be varied. The fixed input is usually capital—that is, the firm has a given plant size. For the industry, the short run is the period of time in which each firm has a given plant size and the number of firms in the industry is fixed.

Short-run aggregate supply curve   A curve that shows the relationship between the quantity of real GDP supplied and the price level in the short run when the money wage rate, other resource prices, and potential GDP remain constant.

Short-run industry supply curve   A curve that shows the quantity supplied by the industry at each price varies when the plant size of each firm and the number of firms in the industry remain the same.

Short-run macroeconomic equilibrium   A situation that occurs when the quantity of real GDP demanded equals quantity of real GDP supplied—at the point of intersection of the *AD* curve and the *SAS* curve.

Short-run Phillips curve   A curve that shows the tradeoff between inflation and unemployment, when the expected inflation rate and the natural rate of unemployment remain the same.

Short sale   The sale of borrowed securities with the intention of repurchasing them later at a lower price and earning the difference.

Should   Encouraged (recommended) to follow the recommendation of the GIPS standards but not required.

Shutdown point   The output and price at which the firm just covers its total variable cost. In the short run, the firm is indifferent between producing the profit-maximizing output and shutting down temporarily.

Signal   An action taken by an informed person (or firm) to send a message to uninformed people or an action taken outside a market that conveys information that can be used by that market.

Simple interest   The interest earned each period on the original investment; interest calculated on the principal only.

Simple random sample   A subset of a larger population created in such a way that each element of the population has an equal probability of being selected to the subset.

Simulation trial   A complete pass through the steps of a simulation.

Single-price monopoly   A monopoly that must sell each unit of its output for a same price to all its customers.

Sinking fund   (1) Bond provision that requires the bond to be paid off progressively rather than in full at maturity. (2) Bond provision that requires the issuer to redeem some or all of the bond systematically over the term of the bond rather than in full at maturity.

Skewed   Not symmetrical.

Skewness   A quantitative measure of skew (lack of symmetry); a synonym of skew.

Slope   The change in the value of the variable measured on the y-axis divided by the change in the value of the variable measured on the x-axis.

Small-firm effect   A frequent empirical anomaly where risk-adjusted stock returns for companies with low market capitalization (i.e., share price multiplied by number of outstanding shares) are significantly larger than those generated by high market capitalization (large cap) firms.

Small-Order Execution System (SOES)   A quotation and execution system for retail (nonprofessional) investors who place orders with brokers who must honor their prevailing bid-ask for automatic execution up to 1,000 shares.

Social interest   Choices that are the best for society as a whole.

Soft dollars   A form of compensation to a money manager generated when the manager commits the investor to paying higher brokerage fees in exchange for the manager receiving additional services (e.g., stock research) from the broker.

Software   Capitalized costs associated with computer programs developed for sale, lease, or internal use and amortized over the estimated economic life of the programs.

Sovereign risk   The risk that a government may default on its debt.

Spearman rank correlation coefficient   A measure of correlation applied to ranked data.

Specialist   The major market maker on U.S. stock exchanges who acts as a broker or dealer to ensure the liquidity and smooth functions of the secondary stock market.

Speculative company   A firm with a great degree of business and/or financial risk, with commensurate high earnings potential.

Speculative stock   A stock that appears to be highly overpriced compared to its intrinsic valuation.

Spending phase   Phase in the investment life cycle during which individuals' earning years end as they retire. They pay for expenses with income from social security and returns from prior investments and invest to protect against inflation.

Spot price   Current market price of an asset. Also called cash price.

Spot rate   The required yield for a cash flow to be received at some specific date in the future—for example, the spot rate for a flow to be received in one year, for a cash flow in two years, and so on.

Spread   An option strategy involving the purchase of one option and sale of another option that is identical to the first in all respects except either exercise price or expiration.

Spurious correlation   A correlation that misleadingly points towards associations between variables.

Stagflation   The combination of recession and inflation.

Standard deviation   A measure of variability equal to the square root of the variance.

Standardizing   A transformation that involves subtracting the mean and dividing the result by the standard deviation.

Standard normal distribution (or unit normal distribution)   The normal density with mean (μ) equal to 0 and standard deviation (σ) equal to 1.

Stated annual interest rate or quoted interest rate   A quoted interest rate that does not account for compounding within the year.

Statement of cash flows   A financial statement that shows how a company's operating, investing, and financing activities have affected cash during an accounting period.

Statistic   A quantity computed from or used to describe a sample of data.

Statistical inference   Making forecasts, estimates, or judgments about a larger group from a smaller group actually observed; using a sample statistic to infer the value of an unknown population parameter.

Statistically significant   A result indicating that the null hypothesis can be rejected; with reference to an estimated regression coefficient, frequently understood to mean a result indicating that the corresponding population regression coefficient is different from 0.

Statistics   The science of describing, analyzing, and drawing conclusions from data; also, a collection of numerical data.

Stock A quantity that exists at a point in time.

Stock dividend A dividend paid in the form of additional shares rather than in cash.

Stock split An action taken by a firm to increase the number of shares outstanding, such as doubling the number of shares outstanding by giving each stockholder two new shares for each one formerly held.

Storage costs or carrying costs The costs of holding an asset, generally a function of the physical characteristics of the underlying asset.

Straddle An option strategy involving the purchase of a put and a call with the same exercise price. A straddle is based on the expectation of high volatility of the underlying.

Straight-line method A method of depreciation that assumes depreciation depends only on the passage of time and that allocates an equal amount of depreciation to each accounting period in an asset's useful life.

Strangle A variation of a straddle in which the put and call have different exercise prices.

Strap An option strategy involving the purchase of two calls and one put.

Strategies All the possible actions of each player in a game.

Stratified random sampling A procedure by which a population is divided into subpopulations (strata) based on one or more classification criteria. Simple random samples are then drawn from each stratum in sizes proportional to the relative size of each stratum in the population. These samples are then pooled.

Stress testing A risk management technique in which the risk manager examines the performance of the portfolio under market conditions involving high risk and usually high correlations across markets. Closely related to scenario analysis.

Stress testing/scenario analysis A set of techniques for estimating losses in extremely unfavorable combinations of events or scenarios.

Strike price Price at which an option can be exercised (same as exercise price).

Strip An option strategy involving the purchase of two puts and one call.

Structural change Economic trend occurring when the economy is undergoing a major change in organization or in how it functions.

Structural surplus or deficit The budget balance that would occur if the economy were at full employment and real GDP were equal to potential GDP.

Structural unemployment The unemployment that arises when changes in technology or international competition change the skills needed to perform jobs or change the locations of jobs.

Structured note (1) A bond or note issued with some unusual, often option-like, clause. (2) A bond with an embedded derivative designed to create a payoff distribution that satisfies the needs of a specific investor clientele. (3) A variation of a floating-rate note that has some type of unusual characteristic such as a leverage factor or in which the rate moves opposite to interest rates.

Style analysis An attempt to explain the variability in the observed returns to a security portfolio in terms of the movements in the returns to a series of benchmark portfolios designed to capture the essence of a particular security characteristic such as size, value, and growth.

Subjective probability A probability drawing on personal or subjective judgment.

Subsidy A payment that the government makes to a producer.

Substitute A good that can be used in place of another good.

Substitution effect The effect of a change in price of a good or service on the quantity bought when the consumer (hypothetically) remains indifferent between the original and the new consumption situations—that is, the consumer remains on the same indifference curve.

Successful efforts accounting A method of accounting for the costs of exploring and developing oil and gas resources in which successful exploration is recorded as an asset and depleted over the estimated life of the resource and all unsuccessful efforts are immediately written off as losses.

Sunk cost The past cost of buying a plant that has no resale value.

Supplemental Information Any performance-related information included as part of a compliant performance presentation that supplements or enhances the required and/or recommended disclosure and presentation provisions of the GIPS standards.

Supply The relationship between the quantity of a good that producers plan to sell and the price of the good when all other influences on sellers' plans remain the same. It is described by a supply schedule and illustrated by a supply curve.

Supply curve A curve that shows the relationship between the quantity supplied and the price of a good when all other influences on producers' planned sales remain the same.

Supply of labor The relationship between the quantity of labor supplied and the real wage rate when all other influences on work plans remain the same.

Supply-side effects The effects of fiscal policy on employment, potential GDP, and aggregate supply.

Support level A price at which a technician would expect a substantial increase in price and volume for a stock to reverse a declining trend that was due to profit taking.

Survivorship bias The bias resulting from a test design that fails to account for companies that have gone bankrupt, merged, or are otherwise no longer reported in a database.

Sustainable growth rate A measure of how fast a firm can grow using internal equity and debt financing and a constant capital structure. Equal to retention rate _ ROE.

Swap (1) A contract whereby two parties agree to a periodic exchange of cash flows. In certain types of swaps, only the net difference between the amounts owed is exchanged on each payment date. (2) An agreement between two parties to exchange a series of future cash flows.

Swap spread The difference between the fixed rate on an interest rate swap and the rate on a Treasury note with equivalent maturity; it reflects the general level of credit risk in the market.

Swaption (1) An option to enter into a swap contract at a later date. (2) An option to enter into a swap.

SWOT analysis An examination of a firm's *S*trengths, *W*eaknesses, *O*pportunities, and *T*hreats. This analysis helps an analyst evaluate a firm's strategies to exploit its competitive advantages or defend against its weaknesses.

Symmetry principle A requirement that people in similar situations be treated similarly.

Synthetic call The combination of puts, the underlying, and risk-free bonds that replicates a call option.

Synthetic forward contract The combination of the underlying, puts, calls, and risk-free bonds that replicates a forward contract.

Synthetic put The combination of calls, the underlying, and risk-free bonds that replicates a put option.

Systematic risk The variability of returns that is due to macroeconomic factors that affect all risky assets. Because it affects all risky assets, it cannot be eliminated by diversification.

Systematic sampling A procedure of selecting every kth member until reaching a sample of the desired size. The sample that results from this procedure should be approximately random.

Tangible assets Long-term assets that have physical substance.

Tangible book value per share Common shareholders' equity minus intangible assets from the balance sheet, divided by the number of shares outstanding.

Tap Procedure by which a borrower can keep issuing additional amounts of an old bond at its current market value. This procedure is used for bond issues, notably by the British and French governments, as well as for some short-term debt instruments.

Target semideviation The positive square root of target semivariance.

Target semivariance The average squared deviation below a target value.

Tariff A tax that is imposed by the importing country when an imported good crosses its international boundary.

Tax incidence The division of the burden of a tax between the buyer and the seller.

Tax multiplier The magnification effect of a change in taxes on aggregate demand.

Tax wedge The gap between the before-tax and after-tax wage rates.

Taylor rule A rule that adjusts the federal funds rate to target the inflation rate and to take into account deviations of the inflation rate from its target and deviations of real GDP from potential GDP.

Technical analysis Estimation of future security price movements based on past price and volume movements.

Technological change The development of new goods and better ways of producing goods and services.

Technological efficiency A situation that occurs when the firm produces a given output by using the least amount of inputs.

Technology Any method of producing a good or service.

t-Distribution A symmetrical distribution defined by a single parameter, degrees of freedom, that is largely used to make inferences concerning the mean of a normal distribution whose variance is unknown.

Temporary New Account A tool that firms can use to remove the effect of significant cash flows on a portfolio. When a significant cash flow occurs in a portfolio, the firm may treat this cash flow as a "temporary new account," allowing the firm to implement the mandate of the portfolio without the impact of the cash flow on the performance of the portfolio.

Termination date The date of the final payment on a swap; also, the swap's expiration date.

Terms of trade The quantity of goods and services that a country exports to pay for its imports of goods and services.

Term structure of interest rates The relationship between term to maturity and yield to maturity for a sample of comparable bonds at a given time. Popularly known as the *yield curve.*

Term to maturity Specifies the date or the number of years before a bond matures or expires.

Test statistic A quantity, calculated based on a sample, whose value is the basis for deciding whether or not to reject the null hypothesis.

Theta The rate at which an option's time value decays.

Third market Over-the-counter trading of securities listed on an exchange.

Thrift institutions Thrift institutions include savings and loan associations, savings banks, and credit unions.

Tick The minimum price movement for the asset underlying a forward or futures contract; for Treasury bonds, one tick equals 1/32 of 1 percent of par value.

Time-period bias The possibility that when we use a time-series sample, our statistical conclusion may be sensitive to the starting and ending dates of the sample.

Time-series analysis An examination of a firm's performance data over a period of time.

Time-series data Observations of a variable over time.

Time-series graph A graph that measures time (for example, months or years) on the x-axis and the variable or variables in which we are interested on the y-axis.

Time to expiration The time remaining in the life of a derivative, typically expressed in years.

Time value decay The loss in the value of an option resulting from movement of the option price toward its payoff value as the expiration day approaches.

Time-weighted rate of return (1) The compound rate of growth of one unit of currency invested in a portfolio during a stated measurement period; a measure of investment performance that is not sensitive to the timing and amount of withdrawals or additions to the portfolio. (2) Calculation that computes period-by-period returns on an investment and removes the effects of external cash flows, which are generally client-driven, and best reflects the firm's ability to manage assets according to a specified strategy or objective.

Total cost The cost of all the productive resources that a firm uses.

Total Firm Assets Total firm assets are all assets for which a firm has investment management responsibility. Total firm assets include assets managed outside the firm (e.g., by subadvisors) for which the firm has asset allocation authority.

Total fixed cost The cost of the firm's fixed inputs.

Total probability rule for expected value A rule explaining the expected value of a random variable in terms of expected values of the random variable conditional on mutually exclusive and exhaustive scenarios.

Total product The total output produced by a firm in a given period of time.

Total return A return objective in which the investor wants to increase the portfolio value to meet a future need by both capital gains and current income reinvestment.

Total revenue The value of a firm's sales. It is calculated as the price of the good multiplied by the quantity sold.

Total revenue test A method of estimating the price elasticity of demand by observing the change in total revenue that results from a change in the price, when all other influences on the quantity sold remain the same.

Total variable cost The cost of all the firm's variable inputs.

Tracking error (1) The standard deviation of the difference in returns between an active investment portfolio and its benchmark portfolio; also called tracking error volatility. (2) The condition in which the performance of a portfolio does not match the performance of an index that serves as the portfolio's benchmark. (3) A synonym for tracking risk and active risk; also, the total return on a portfolio (gross of fees) minus the total return on a benchmark.

Tracking risk The standard deviation of the differences between a portfolio's returns and its benchmark's returns; a synonym of active risk.

Trade balance The balance of a country's exports and imports; part of the current account.

Trade Date Accounting The transaction is reflected in the portfolio on the date of the purchase or sale, and not on the settlement date. Recognizing the asset or liability within at least 3 days of the date the transaction is entered into (Trade Date, T + 1, T + 2 or T + 3) all satisfy the trade date accounting requirement for purposes of the GIPS standards. (See settlement date accounting.)

Trademark A registered symbol that can be used only by its owner to identify a product or service.

Tradeoff An exchange—giving up one thing to get something else.

Trading effect The difference in performance of a bond portfolio from that of a chosen index due to short-run changes in the composition of the portfolio.

Trading Expenses The costs of buying or selling a security. These costs typically take the form of brokerage commissions or spreads from either internal or external brokers. Custody fees charged per transaction should be considered custody fees and not direct transaction costs. Estimated trading expenses are not permitted.

Trading rule   A formula for deciding on current transactions based on historical data.

Trading turnover   The percentage of outstanding shares traded during a period of time.

Trailing P/E (or current P/E)   A stock's current market price divided by the most recent four quarters of earnings per share.

Tranche   Refers to a portion of an issue that is designed for a specific category of investors. French for "slice."

Transaction cost   The cost of executing a trade. Low costs characterize an operationally efficient market.

Transaction Expenses (Private Equity)   Include all legal, financial, advisory, and investment banking fees related to buying, selling, restructuring, and recapitalizing portfolio companies.

Transactions costs   The costs that arise from finding someone with whom to do business, of reaching an agreement about the price and other aspects of the exchange, and of ensuring that the terms of the agreement are fulfilled. The opportunity costs of conducting a transaction.

Treasury bill   A negotiable U.S. government security with a maturity of less than one year that pays no periodic interest but yields the difference between its par value and its discounted purchase price.

Treasury bond   A U.S. government security with a maturity of more than 10 years that pays interest periodically.

Treasury note   A U.S. government security with maturities of 1 to 10 years that pays interest periodically.

Tree diagram   A diagram with branches emanating from nodes representing either mutually exclusive chance events or mutually exclusive decisions.

Trend   The general tendency for a variable to move in one direction.

Trimmed mean   A mean computed after excluding a stated small percentage of the lowest and highest observations.

***t*-Test**   A hypothesis test using a statistic (*t*-statistic) that follows a *t*-distribution.

Two-sided hypothesis test (or two-tailed hypothesis test)   A test in which the null hypothesis is rejected in favor of the alternative hypothesis if the evidence indicates that the population parameter is either smaller or larger than a hypothesized value.

Type I error   The error of rejecting a true null hypothesis.

Type II error   The error of not rejecting a false null hypothesis.

Unbiasedness   Lack of bias. A desirable property of estimators, an unbiased estimator is one whose expected value (the mean of its sampling distribution) equals the parameter it is intended to estimate.

Uncertainty   A situation in which more than one event might occur but it is not known which one.

Unconditional probability (or marginal probability)   The probability of an event not conditioned on another event.

Uncovered interest rate parity   The assertion that expected currency depreciation should offset the interest differential between two countries over the term of the interest rate.

Underlying   (1) Refers to a security on which a derivative contract is written. (2) An asset that trades in a market in which buyers and sellers meet, decide on a price, and the seller then delivers the asset to the buyer and receives payment. The underlying is the asset or other derivative on which a particular derivative is based. The market for the underlying is also referred to as the spot market.

Underweighted   A condition in which a portfolio, for whatever reason, includes less of a class of securities than the relative market value alone would justify.

Unemployment rate   The percentage of the people in the labor force who are unemployed.

Unit elastic demand   Demand with a price elasticity of 1; the percentage change in the quantity demanded equals the percentage change in price.

Unit normal distribution   *See* Standard normal distribution.

Univariate distribution   A distribution that specifies the probabilities for a single random variable.

Unrealized capital gains   Capital gains that reflect the price appreciation of currently held unsold assets.

Unsystematic risk   Risk that is unique to an asset, derived from its particular characteristics. It can be eliminated in a diversified portfolio.

Unweighted index   An indicator series affected equally by the performance of each security in the sample regardless of price or market value. Also referred to as an *equal-weighted series*.

Unwind   The negotiated termination of a forward or futures position before contract maturity.

Up transition probability   The probability that an asset's value moves up.

U.S. interest rate differential   A gap equal to the U.S. interest rate minus the foreign interest rate.

U.S. Official reserves   The government's holdings of foreign currency.

Utilitarianism   A principle that states that we should strive to achieve "the greatest happiness for the greatest number of people."

Utility   The benefit or satisfaction that a person gets from the consumption of a good or service.

Utility of wealth   The amount of utility that a person attaches to a given amount of wealth.

Value   The maximum amount that a person is willing to pay for a good. The value of one more unit of the good or service is its marginal benefit.

Valuation   The process of determining the value of an asset or service.

Valuation analysis   An active bond portfolio management strategy designed to capitalize on expected price increases in temporarily undervalued issues.

Valuation process   Part of the investment decision process in which you estimate the value of a security.

Value at risk (VaR)   (1) A money measure of the minimum loss that is expected over a given period of time with a given probability. (2) A probability-based measure of loss potential for a company, a fund, a portfolio, a transaction, or a strategy over a specified period of time. (3) A money measure of the minimum value of losses expected during a specified time period at a given level of probability.

Value chain   The set of transformations to move from raw material to product or service delivery.

Value stocks   Stocks that appear to be undervalued for reasons besides earnings growth potential. These stocks are usually identified based on high dividend yields, low *P/E* ratios, or low price-to-book ratios.

Value-weighted index   An index calculated as the total market value of the securities in the sample. Market value is equal to the number of shares or bonds outstanding times the market price of the security.

Variance   The expected value (the probability-weighted average) of squared deviations from a random variable's expected value.

Variation margin   Profits or losses on open positions in futures and option contracts that are paid or collected daily.

Vega   The relationship between option price and volatility.

Velocity of circulation   The average number of times a dollar of money is used annually to buy the goods and services that make up GDP.

Venture Capital (Private Equity)   Risk capital in the form of equity and/or loan capital that is provided by an investment institution to back a business venture that is expected to grow in value.

Vintage Year (Private Equity)   The year that the venture capital or private equity fund or partnership first draws down or calls capital from its investors.

Volatility   (1) A measure of the uncertainty about the future price of an asset. Typically measured by the standard deviation of returns on the asset. (2) As used in option pricing, the standard deviation of the continuously compounded returns on the underlying asset.

Voluntary export restraint   An agreement between two governments in which the government of the exporting country agrees to restrain the volume of its own exports.

Wages   The income that labor earns.

Warrant   An instrument that allows the holder to purchase a specified number of shares of the firm's common stock from the firm at a specified price for a given period of time.

Weak-form efficient market hypothesis   The belief that security prices fully reflect all security market information.

Wealth   The market value of all the things that people own.

Weighted-average cost of capital   A weighted average of the after-tax required rates of return on a company's common stock, preferred stock, and long-term debt, where the weights are the fraction of each source of financing in the company's target capital structure.

Weighted mean   An average in which each observation is weighted by an index of its relative importance.

Winsorized mean   A mean computed after assigning a stated percent of the lowest values equal to one specified low value, and a stated percent of the highest values equal to one specified high value.

Working-age population   The total number of people aged 16 years and over who are not in jail, hospital, or some other form of institutional care.

Working capital management   The management of a company's short-term assets (such as inventory) and short-term liabilities (such as money owed to suppliers).

World Trade Organization   An international organization that places greater obligations on its member countries to observe the GATT rules.

Yankee bonds   Bonds sold in the United States and denominated in U.S. dollars but issued by a foreign firm or government.

Yield   The promised rate of return on an investment under certain assumptions.

Yield spread   The difference between the promised yields of alternative bond issues or market segments at a given time relative to yields on Treasury issues of equal maturity.

Yield to maturity   The total yield on a bond obtained by equating the bond's current market value to the discounted cash flows promised by the bond. Also called actuarial yield.

Yield to worst   Given a bond with multiple potential maturity dates and prices due to embedded call options, the practice is to calculate a yield to maturity for each of the call dates and prices and select the lowest yield (the most conservative possible yield) as yield to worst.

Zero-cost collar   A transaction in which a position in the underlying is protected by buying a put and selling a call with the premium from the sale of the call offsetting the premium from the purchase of the put. It can also be used to protect a floating-rate borrower against interest rate increases with the premium on a long cap offsetting the premium on a short floor.

INDEX